Anna Goppel
Killing Terrorists

Ideen & Argumente

Herausgegeben von
Wilfried Hinsch und Lutz Wingert

Anna Goppel
Killing Terrorists

___

A Moral and Legal Analysis

DE GRUYTER

ISBN: 978-3-11-048173-0
e-ISBN: 978-3-11-027727-2

Library of Congress Cataloging-in-Publication Data
A CIP catalog record for this book has been applied for at the Library of Congress

Bibliographic information published by the Deutsche Nationalbibliothek
The Deutsche Nationalbibliothek lists this publication in the Deutsche Nationalbibliografie;
detailed bibliographic data are available in the Internet at http://dnb.dnb.de.

© 2013 Walter de Gruyter GmbH, Berlin/Boston
Printing and Binding: Hubert & Co. GmbH & Co. KG, Göttingen
♾ Printed on acid-free paper
Printed in Germany

www.degruyter.com

Acknowledgments

Various people and institutions have helped me along the way as I completed this project. I am very grateful for their support. First and foremost, I would like to thank Stefan Gosepath who supervised my PhD thesis on which this book is based. His valuable personal and academic support was always forthcoming. I am particularly grateful for his confidence in me and my project right from the beginning which formed my academic path far beyond this book. I am indebted to Georg Mohr and Christian Walter for their examiners' reports. Specifically I would like to mention Christian Walter's comment regarding the territorial scope of non-international armed conflicts which I took into account in revising the book manuscript. I am thankful, too, to Martin Nettesheim for providing me with an institutional home. I profited significantly from several stays at the Centre for Applied Philosophy and Public Ethics at the University of Melbourne. I would like to thank all of my colleagues there for many extremely helpful discussions. I particularly would like to express my gratitude to Tony Coady and Igor Primoratz for their interest in my work and their cordial and encouraging way of engaging with me, and to Emma Larking and Jessica Wolfendale, who not only helped to advance this study during our many conversations, but also ensured that my stays in Melbourne will remain unforgettable experiences. I owe special thanks to the participants of various workshops and colloquia where I had the chance to discuss my ideas. Their feedback has been immeasurably helpful. I would particularly like to mention the summer courses at the Inter University Centre in Dubrovnik, for the regular invitations to which I would like to thank Bernd Ladwig and Georg Lohmann. For inspiring times in and beyond Dubrovnik I would also like to mention and specifically thank Corinna Mieth, Arnd Pollmann and Susanne Schmetkamp. I would like to thank Daniel Messelken, Henning Hahn, and Anne Schwenkenbecher for their constructive comments on parts of earlier versions of the manuscript. I am furthermore thankful to Peter Schaber for his continuous encouragement during the publication process. Particular gratitude I would like to express to Ludwig Siep, who over all the years in many inspiring, encouraging, and caring conversations was a priceless mentor and advisor to me. To Sarah Kelly, Chris Geissler, and Carina Fourie, I owe special thanks for their patient correcting of my English. I am grateful to several organizations for providing financial support for my research and the making of this book: the research programme Global challenges – transnational and transcultural solutions, at the University of Tuebingen; the German Academic Exchange Service (DAAD); and the University Research Priority Programme for Ethics (UFSPE) of the University of Zurich.

Writing a PhD thesis and revising it into a book manuscript comes with not only academic, but also emotional challenges. I am grateful to my sister and my brother, to Silja Neumann, Simone Jaeger and Claudia Schrag and to my friends in Berlin who with their great humour, their affection, and their positive outlook on life made my life colourful no matter how much I was struggling with writing. My final thanks go to my parents who taught me confidence in following my ideas and the faith that things do turn out well. I must thank my father in particular for his endless patience and encouragement in innumerable conversations.

Zuerich, August 2012

Contents

List of abbreviations

ACHPR   African Charter on Human and People's Rights, 27 June 1981
ACHR   American Convention on Human Rights, 22 November 1969
AI   Amnesty International
API   Protocol Additional to the Geneva Conventions of 12 August 1949, and relating to the
         Protection of Victims of International Armed Conflicts (Protocol I), 8 June 1977
APII   Protocol Additional to the Geneva Conventions of 12 August 1949, and relating to the
         Protection of Victims of Non-International Armed Conflicts (Protocol II), 8 June 1977
CAT   Convention against Torture and Other Cruel, Inhuman or Degrading Treatment or Pun-
         ishment, 10 December 1984
CCPR   International Covenant on Civil and Political Rights, 16 December 1966
CIA   Central Intelligence Agency
CPPCG   Convention on the Prevention and Punishment of the Crime of Genocide, 9 December
         1948
ECHR   European Convention for the Protection of Human Rights and Fundamental Freedoms,
         4 November 1950
ECtHR   European Court of Human Rights
ETA   Euskadi Ta Askatasuna
Fatah   Harakat al-Tahrir al-Watani al-Filastini
GA   General Assembly
GAL   Grupos Antiterroristas de Liberación
GCI   Geneva Convention for the Amelioration of the Condition of the Wounded and Sick in
         Armed Forces in the Field, 12 August 1949
GCII   Geneva Convention for the Amelioration of the Condition of Wounded, Sick and Ship-
         wrecked Members of Armed Forces at Sea, 12 August 1949
GCIII   Geneva Convention relative to the Treatment of Prisoners of War, 12 August 1949
GCIV   Geneva Convention relative to the Protection of Civilian Persons in Time of War, 12 Au-
         gust 1949
Hamas   Harakat al-Muqawama al-Islamyya
HCJ   Israeli High Court of Justice
HCIV   Hague Convention respecting the Laws and Customs of War on Land and its Annex:
         Regulations Concerning the Laws and Customs of War on Land, 18 October 1907
HRC   Human Rights Committee
ICC   International Criminal Court
ICJ   International Court of Justice
ICRC   International Committee of the Red Cross
ICTR   International Criminal Tribunal for Rwanda
ICTY   International Criminal Tribunal for the former Yugoslavia
IDF   Israel Defence Forces
ILC   International Law Commission
IRA   Irish Republican Army
KGB   Komitet Gosudarstvennoi Bezopasnosti
Mossad   HaMossad leModi'in uleTafkidim Meyuhadim
NATO   North Atlantic Treaty Organization
OAS   Organization of American States

PFLP Popular Front for the Liberation of Palestine
PLO   Palestine Liberation Organization
RAF   Rote Armee Fraktion
SECED Servicio Central de Documentación
SC   Security Council
UDHR Universal Declaration of Human Rights, 10 December 1948

Table of cases

International Court of Justice

UN Human Rights Committee

International Criminal Tribunal for the former Yugoslavia

International Criminal Tribunal for Rwanda

Eritrea Ethiopia Claim Commission

European Court of Human Rights

European Commission of Human Rights

National courts and commissions

Table of treaties

Table of UN documents

Security Council resolutions

SC Res. 237, 14 June 1967 —— 72

SC Res. 487, 19 June 1981 —— 184

SC Res. 787, 16 November 1992 —— 72

SC Res. 1041, 29 January 1996 —— 72

SC Res. 1059, 31 May 1996 —— 72

SC Res. 1083, 27 November 1996 —— 72

SC Res. 1368, 12 September 2001 —— 95f., 172f.

SC Res. 1373, 28 September 2001 —— 95f., 172f.

General Assembly resolutions

GA Res. 2443 (XXIII), Respect for and Implementation of Human Rights in Occupied Territories, 19 December 1968 —— 72

GA Res. 2444 (XXIII), Respect for Human Rights in Armed Conflicts, 19 December 1968 —— 72

GA Res. 2546 (XXIV), Respect for and Implementation of Human Rights in Occupied Territories, 11 December 1969 —— 72

GA Res. 2625 (XXV), Declaration on Principles of International Law Concerning Friendly Relations und Co-operation among States in Accordance with the Charter of the United Nations, 24 October 1970. [Quoted as Declaration on Friendly Relations] —— 179

GA Res. 2727 (XXV), Report of the Special Committee to Investigate Israeli Practices Affecting the Human Rights of the Population of the Occupied Territories, 15 December 1970 —— 72

Table of other materials

US documents

Executive Order No. 11905: United States Foreign Intelligence Activities, 18 February 1976, 41 Federal Register, 7703 —— 13

Executive Order No. 12036: United States Foreign Intelligence Activities, 24 January 1978, 3 C.F.R. 112, 129 (1978), 43 Federal Register, 1915 —— 13

Executive Order No. 12333: United States Intelligence Activities, 4 December 1981, 46 Federal Register, 59941 —— 13

US Department of State, Richard Boucher, Daily Press Briefing, 2 July 2001. Available at http://2001–2009.state.gov/r/pa/prs/dpb/2001/3933.htm, retrieved 13 June 2012 —— 239

US Department of State, Richard Boucher, Daily Press Briefing, 27 August 2001. Available at http://2001–2009.state.gov/r/pa/prs/dpb/2001/4656.htm, retrieved 13 June 2012 —— 241

Letter dated 20 June 1995 from the Acting Legal Adviser to the Department of State, together with Written Statement of the Government of the United States of America. Available at http://www.icj-cij.org/docket/files/95/8700.pdf, retrieved 14 March 2008 —— 71

National Security Strategy of the United States of America, March 2006. Available at http://georgewbush-whitehouse.archives.gov/nsc/nss/2006/, retrieved 13 June 2012 —— 97

US Department of Defense, News Transcript, DoD News Briefing – Secretary Rumsfeld and General Myers, 11 January 2002. Available at http://www.defense.gov/transcripts/transcript.aspx?transcriptid=2031, retrieved 13 June 2012 —— 123

White House, Ari Fleischer, Press Briefing, 3 August 2001. Available at http://www.presidency.ucsb.edu/ws/index.php?pid=47553#axzz1zrOEHoE1, retrieved 13 June 2012 —— 239

White House, Ari Fleischer, 58. White House Press Secretary Announcement of President Bush's Determination of the Legal Status of Taliban and Al Qaeda Detained, 7 February 2002. Available at http://www.state.gov/s/l/38727.htm, retrieved 8 April 2007 —— 133

White House, Fact Sheet: Status of Detainees at Guantanamo, 7 February 2002. Available at http://www.presidency.ucsb.edu/ws/?pid=79402#axzz1zrOEHoE1, retrieved 13 June 2012 —— 133

White House, Ari Fleischer, Press Gaggle, 5 November 2002. Available at http://www.presidency.ucsb.edu/ws/index.php?pid=47444#axzz1zrOEHoE1, retrieved 13 June 2012 —— 45, 228

Koh, Harold H. (2010), Legal Adviser, Department of State, The Obama Administration and International Law, Speech at the Annual Meeting of the American Association of International Law, 25 March 2010. Available at http://www.state.gov/s/l/releases/remarks/139119.htm, retrieved 22 March 2012 —— 42, 82f.

Brennan, John O. (2012), Assistant to the President for Homeland Security and Counterterrorism, The Ethics and Efficacy of the President's Counterterrorism Strategy", Speech at the Woodrow Wilson International Center for Scholars, 30 April 2012. Available at https://fas.org/irp/news/2012/04/brennan043012.html, retrieved March 2012 —— 82

Johnson, Jeh (2012), General Counsel of the Department of Defense, National Security Law, Lawyers and Lawyering in the Obama Administration, Speech at Yale Law School, 22 February 2012. Available at http://www.cfr.org/national-security-and-defense/jeh-johnsons-speech-national-security-law-lawyers-lawyering-obama-administration/p27448, retrieved 22 March 2012 —— 78

White House, Remarks by the President on Osama Bin Laden, 2 May 2011. Available at http://www.whitehouse.gov/the-press-office/2011/05/02/remarks-president-osama-bin-laden, retrieved 13 June 2012 —— 228

Other national documents

Germany, Aviation Security Act (*Gesetz zur Regelung von Luftsicherheitsaufgaben*, (LuftSiG), 11 January 2005; BGBl. P 78 —— 277

AI (2001c) Israel/Occupied Territories/Palestinian Authority, Broken Lives – A Year of Intifada, November 2001, AI Index: MDE 15/083/2001 —— 33

AI (2003), Israel and the Occupied Territories: Israel Must End its Policy of Assassinations, 4 July 2003, AI Index MDE 15/056/2003 —— 34, 237

AI (2004), Israel/Occupied Territories: Amnesty International Strongly Condemns the Assassination of Sheikh Yassin, 22 March 2004, AI Index MDE 15/029/2004 —— 33

AI (2005), United States of America, Guantanamo and Beyond: The Continuing Pursuit of Unchecked Executive Power, 13 May 2005, AI Index AMR 51/063/2005 —— 41

AI (1996 – 2002), Jahresberichte Spanien 1996 – 2002. All available at http://www2.amnesty.de/internet/deall.nsf/WNachLand?OpenView&Start=1&Count=200, retrieved 21 November 2007 —— 45

AI (2011), A Reflection on Justice, May 2011, AI Index AMR 51/038/2011 —— 44

Arbeitsgemeinschaft Kriegsursachenforschung (AKUF)/Forschungsstelle Kriege und Entwicklung (FKRE), Aktuelle Kriege und bewaffnete Konflikte. Available at http://www.sozialwiss.uni-hamburg.de/publish/Ipw/Akuf/kriege_aktuell.htm, retrieved 8 July 2008 —— 213

Centre for the Study of Civil War at the International Peace Research Institute, Oslo (PRIO)/Uppsala Conflict Data Program (UCDP), Armed Conflict Dataset Codebook, Version 4 – 2007. Available at http://www.pcr.uu.se/digitalAssets/55/55201_UCDP_PRIO_Codebook_v4 – 2007.pdf, retrieved 13 June 2012 —— 213

Human Rights Watch (2002), Background Paper on Geneva Conventions and Persons Held by U.S. Forces, 29 January 2002. Available at http://hrw.org/backgrounder/usa/pow-bck.htm, retrieved 18 April 2007 —— 123

ICRC Commentary on GCIII: Preux, Jean de, Geneva Convention relative to the Treatment of Prisoners of War: Commentary, (Volume III of the Commentary on the Geneva Conventions of 12 August 1949), (Geneva: ICRC, 1960) —— 85 f., 131 – 134

XXVIII — Table of other materials

ICRC Commentary on GCIV: Uhler, Oscar/Coursier, Henri, Geneva Convention relative to the Protection of Civilian Persons in Time of War: Commentary, (Volume IV of the Commentary on the Geneva Conventions of 12 August 1949), (Geneva: ICRC, 1958) —— 124–126, 153–155, 158, 162

ICRC Commentary on API: Sandoz, Yves/Winarski, Christoph/Zimmermann, Bruno, Commentary on the Additional Protocols of 8 June 1977 to the Geneva Convention of 12 August 1949, ICRC, (Geneva: Martinus Nijhoff Publishers, 1987), 2–1304 —— 110–112, 114, 136 f., 162

ICRC Commentary on APII: Sandoz, Yves/Winarski, Christoph/Zimmermann, Bruno, Commentary on the Additional Protocols of 8 June 1977 to the Geneva Convention of 12 August 1949, ICRC, (Geneva: Martinus Nijhoff Publishers, 1987), 1305–1489 —— 120, 145, 149 f.

Political Instability Task Force, Internal Wars and Failures of Governance, 1955–2006, PITF/Problem Set Codebook. Available at http://globalpolicy.gmu.edu/pitf/pitfcode.htm#21, retrieved 4 July 2008 —— 213

Introduction

The first country to publicly acknowledge the use of targeted killings and openly defend it was Israel, making headlines not least because of the decision on this matter by the Israeli High Court of Justice in December 2006.[1] Israel is joined by the United States of America; under the Barack Obama administration, the United States now publicly admits to the use of targeted killings in its global fight against Al Qaeda and other groups regarded as Al Qaeda affiliates, a strategy that had been implemented under the administration of George W. Bush. Since its most recent incorporation of the practice as a basic element of its counter-strategies, in the beginning of the second Intifada in 2000, until the end of 2011, Israel is reported to have killed more than 420 people (bystanders as well as targeted persons) in the course of targeted killings.[2] The United States of America is reported to have killed 2,486–3,188 individuals (bystanders as well as targeted persons) in Pakistan between 2004 and June 2012. Reportedly 317–921 people (bystanders as well as targeted persons) died of US targeted operations in Yemen in the period between 2002 and June 2012.[3]

Israel and the United States may be the only states that have publicly admitted to the use of targeted killings, but they are not the only states to make targeted killings part of their counter-terrorist strategies. Today, as in the past, these and other states have applied targeted killings in their fight against alleged terrorists. Provided the use of targeted killings has become public, states have been criticized for their conduct by politicians, in media statements, in the scholarly literature, and, though only in the case of Israel, in court. Targeted killings, however, have been defended equally forcefully. This lack of consensus as to whether states may resort to it is only one reason that demands a thorough assessment of the practice. It demands an analysis of the arguments with which the practice has been defended or attacked as well as of the principles and regulations governing state use of lethal force, on the grounds on which it may be accepted or condemned. The urgency of such an analysis is even more due to the nature of the practice itself, its disturbing consequences, which concern the existence of individual human beings as such, the personal integrity of those ordering, planning, and carrying out the killings, and the political credibility of states engaging in the practice. The analysis is all the more crucial because the public, without having comprehensively discussed and analysed the practice, appears to be increasingly comfortable with its

---

1 HCJ, *Public Committee against Torture v. Government of Israel.*
2 For the statistics, see fn. 26 in chapter 2.
3 http://www.thebureauinvestigates.com/category/projects/drones/, retrieved 20 June 2012. The website also includes figures on US drone strikes in Somalia.

application. Cases of targeted killings of alleged terrorists are reported in the press, but they generally do not trigger intense public discussion or criticism. And this is despite an absence of agreement on the justifiability of the practice.

In response to this need for discussion, this book seeks to provide a careful analysis of whether states are justified in targeting and killing terrorists and, if they are, under what circumstances. Drawing from the political reactions to the practice and the scholarly controversy surrounding it, it explores ongoing debates and addresses the central legal and moral questions in arguments about the justifiability of targeted killing of terrorists. As such, it discusses whether targeted killing of terrorists can be justified and concludes that both morality and international law limit justification of the practice to situations which typically do not occur in practice.

Both criticism and defence of the targeted killing of terrorists focus on law and morality, as separate categories or intertwined. This reflects the different lenses through which the practice can be reasonably analysed if the analysis seeks to formulate and enforce limits to state practices. It could of course be assessed from other perspectives, such as with a view to its economic consequences, which could very well impact a moral and legal assessment. Nevertheless, outside of the scope of law and morality these perspectives are a matter of political considerations and the question of prudence. These considerations should, under certain circumstances, prevent states from reverting to targeted killing, but would neither permit crossing boundaries set by international law nor exempt states from blame for morally wrong conduct. On this ground, additional perspectives outside the framework of law and philosophy will not be addressed in this book.

Targeted killing of terrorists can then be addressed from either a legal or a moral perspective. Furthermore, with regard to a legal assessment, the practice could be looked at from a national legal or an international legal perspective. All of these approaches are possible and theoretically defensible. This book chooses to address the issue from both a legal and a moral perspective, and with regard to the legal analysis, to focus on international law. The focus on international law makes sense in light of the fundamental role international law plays in state use of violence, its addressees, as well as the relevance of violence more generally in international relations to the practice of targeted killing.

The necessity and the use of an approach combining the international legal and moral perspective do not require much justification. For a book seeking to respond to actual debates about targeted killing of terrorists, the approach is required by the form of those debates themselves, which often draw on both areas. Moreover, a moral discussion alone ignores unequivocally accepted and fundamental regulations at the heart of international law, which, as such, have strong justifying power in public debates as well as in political decision-making. An international legal approach alone would fail in the face of (intuitively) powerful arguments formulated in legal as well as moral debates that identify characteristics of terrorism and the fight against it and demand new interpretations of existing legal regulations or altered international legal rules. Moreover, legal arguments alone lack the means to counter the claim that certain actions are justified in terms of morality despite being recognized as breaching legal rules. Nor can they meaningfully respond to claims that certain legal interpretations correspond to morality, seeking to ascribe a more comprehensive justification to these interpretations. These few arguments highlight some of the benefits of approaching the justifiability of targeted killing of terrorists from both a legal and a moral perspective. The need for this approach and the resulting benefits become more explicit as the book progresses, revealing the way in which the two lines of analysis intertwine, gain from, and support each other.

Discussing existing as well as additional, conceivable approaches to justify targeted killing of terrorists, I argue that certain forms and cases of the practice can theoretically be justified, both morally and legally. Both a moral and a legal justification, however, is limited to targeted killings in situations that can be considered wars, or in legal terms, armed conflicts. Even during warfare justification of targeted killing of terrorists is far more limited than often claimed by advocates of the practice. Moreover these justifications are restricted to rather theoretical circumstances not normally reflected in actual cases of targeted killing of terrorists. In peacetime, I argue, state use of lethal force is legally as well as morally only justified in light of imminent harm. This renders targeted killing, which by definition is not carried out in reaction to imminent harm, unjustifiable, both from an international legal and a moral perspective. This is particularly important in relation to my argument that conflicts with terrorists typically do not constitute either wars or armed conflicts, even if this is theoretically possible. This includes those conflicts that triggered the current use of, and discussions about, the targeted killing of terrorists. In practice, moral arguments could possibly provide an exception to the above conclusion if abstaining from an act of targeted killing would lead to horrendous consequences. On a theoretical level, however, such justification should not be formulated.

In terms of the structure of this book, the legal and philosophical arguments are developed separately. This is necessary in order to develop the international legal and moral assessments of targeted killing of terrorists and to do justice to the different approaches to legal and moral justification put forward in public and scholarly discussions. Together with additional steps necessary for the final analysis this requires the following tasks: first, laying the analytical groundwork, defining the terms involved, and grounding the issue in practice; second, addressing the international legal justifiability of the practice; and third, approaching the argument from a philosophical perspective. Final remarks relating the legal assessment to its moral counterpart will highlight the univocal judgment on targeted killing of terrorists and the unanimity with which this is expressed by international law and morality.

More specifically, in the *Groundwork*, I establish a working definition of targeted killing of terrorist for the purposes of this book. This frames the focus of discussion and allows a distinction between different forms and cases of the practice (chapter 1). Accounting for the literal meaning of the term 'targeted killing', as well as its current usage, and contrasting it to closely related forms of violence, I first develop an understanding of targeted killing that reflects the distinctive characteristics of the practice. A definition of the term 'terrorist', reflecting the core characteristics of the term and capturing incidents widely accepted as terrorism, makes it possible not only to provide the relevant regulations and principles governing targeted killing in general, but also to apply them to targeted killings *of terrorists* and draw conclusions regarding their justification. The distinction between different forms and cases of the practice, as intrinsic to its definition, allows for the classification of the findings of this book, and renders their consequences intelligible in relation to various practically imaginable forms and cases of targeted killing of terrorists.

A review of actual cases of targeted killings of alleged terrorists (chapter 2) then illustrates the current and past relevance of the issue under discussion, as well as the circumstances under which it is most passionately debated. This also reflects upon the practical relevance of the different forms and cases the practice takes, providing a useful background against which to assess the justifying relevance of the individual conclusions developed in the course of the book. Furthermore, the overview provides the basis for identifying those effects and implications of targeted killing of terrorists that are crucial for providing a practically relevant discussion of its justifiability.

Based on these distinctions I establish the moral and legal requirements for a justification of the practice, providing for a differentiated framework with regard to which the practice can be assessed. The structure of the legal and moral argument is, in this, inspired by existing justifications of targeted killing of terrorists, and thus allows for an adequate reply to the ongoing debate.

The assessment of the *international legal justification* starts with an analysis of the compatibility of targeted killing of terrorists with the right to life (chapter 3), which, owing to the structure of the right to life, requires distinguishing the right to life during peacetime from that during armed conflicts. The analysis of the latter explains the relevance of the right to life during times of armed conflicts and relates the human rights debate to the laws of war. As such, it elucidates the importance which the analysis of the compatibility of targeted killings of terrorists with the laws of war has in an assessment of the practice in terms of human rights.

Following the structure of the laws of war, the assessment of the compatibility of targeted killing of terrorists with this area of international law distinguishes between its compatibility with *jus in bello* (international humanitarian law) and *jus ad bellum*. This distinction is reflected in the questions of whether targeted killings of terrorists can be considered legal acts of warfare (chapter 4) and of whether they can be justified as acts of national self-defence (chapter 5).

Arguments that present the targeted killings of terrorists as legal acts of warfare often confuse different concepts within international humanitarian law. Even if they do not, they require a range of specific classifications and interpretations of the fight against terrorism, the terrorists themselves, and the applicable international legal regulations in order to reach the intended conclusion. A look at some prevailing arguments of this type reflects the practical relevance of the different arguments and allows for the identification of issues crucial to analysis. Following from this, it is appropriate to approach the justifiability of targeted killing of terrorists in a way that corresponds to the structure of international humanitarian law, or, in other words, to distinguish between acts of warfare in international armed conflicts, non-international armed conflicts, occupied territory, and the fight against terrorism as a 'new' type of armed conflict. The legal assessment of targeted killing of terrorists in terms of the right to life, as specified by international humanitarian law, plays a role, too, in analysing the argument of whether the practice can constitute an act of national self-defence, completing the legal assessment.

The discussion of the moral justification of targeted killing of terrorists mirrors the legal analysis, in that it distinguishes between peacetime and wartime reasoning. It explores different justifications of targeted killing of terrorists, yielding an explanation of the limits to state use of lethal force, which then provides the basis for assessing targeted killings of terrorists. The choice of approaches and the need for addressing them follow from the development of the argument itself, but they also reflect the defences of targeted killings put forth in public and scholarly statements.

In detail, the first chapter of this part of the book explores the justifying relevance of the wartime reasoning to targeted killing of terrorists (chapter 6). In peacetime, a philosophical assessment of the justifiability of targeted killing of terrorists requires a critical engagement with the argument that revenge or punishment justifies the practice (chapter 7), as well as an assessment of defences of the practice based on consequentialist moral theory (chapter 8) and, ultimately, an analysis of right-based accounts of justification. The concept of *Feindstrafrecht* (criminal law for enemies) accepts the existence of rights as a reference point for the justification of the use of lethal force, yet defends too radical an idea of full and absolute forfeiture of rights (chapter 9). Hence, like the first two approaches, it fails to offer a convincing justification for targeted killing of terrorists. Nevertheless, it puts forth an idea, that of forfeiture of the right to life, which, in a plausible, strictly regulated, and moderate formulation, helps to explain acceptable state uses of defensive lethal force, other-defence carried out by the state. Although individual self-defence or the corresponding concept of other-defence have not been used to justify targeted killings, a closer look at the concepts makes plausible the rights-based limits to state use of lethal force, seizing upon normative suggestions that evolved in the antecedent approaches to morally justify targeted killing of terrorists (chapter 10). As such, it also serves as a basis to approach conceivable arguments pointing beyond such a deontological account of justified killings. The last chapter addresses such arguments and allows for a final assessment of the moral justifiability of targeted killing of terrorists (chapter 11).

I will close with some *concluding remarks* that relate the legal assessment to its philosophical counterpart. They will highlight the congruity of the moral and legal assessments and the discrepancy between these assessments and the current use of targeted killings of terrorists.

Since March 2009, when I submitted my PhD thesis, which forms the basis of this book, there have been several political and scholarly developments that have had impact on the matters under discussion here. Foremost are the frequency with which the United States has resorted to targeted killing as well as its public acknowledgment of the practice. Another is the apparently growing public acceptance of the practice. Moreover, scholarly discussion about specific cases of targeted killing and the practice in general have, of course, continued to evolve. I have attempted to account for these developments, both practical developments and the progression of the scholarly debates, in revising and updating my doctoral thesis. Among those scholarly works published after I had finished my thesis for submission, I have considered and discussed, with regard to new developments as far as possible, those that appeared between 2009 and 2011. While I was unfortunately unable to include them, several articles and books were published in 2012 that would have merited attention, including the book edited by Claire Finkelstein, Jens David Ohlin and Andrew Altman *Targeted Killings. Law and Morality in an Asymmetrical World* (*Oxford: Oxford University Press*). I look forward, of course, to engaging with these works in future publications.

Part I: **Groundwork**

1 Defining 'targeted killing of terrorists'

Targeted killing is most often applied and discussed within the context of terrorism and counter-terrorism, but not exclusively so. The term describes a wider range of actions that also includes lethal force against persons not held to be terrorists. To specify what cases of force I will look at in this book, I will explain the concept of 'targeted killing', spell out the criteria for 'terrorist' in this book, combine the two concepts and differentiate between different forms of targeted killing of terrorists.

1.1 Defining 'targeted killing'

As for many terms that are regularly used to describe national or international politics, there exists no commonly accepted definition of 'targeted killing'. Its meaning evolved through actual usage, and the term cannot yet be found in any major encyclopaedia. The term has gained popularity in recent years. Primarily, this seems to be due to Israel's policy of targeted killing during the second Intifada, which started in September 2000, and the US administration's use of this practice in its fight against terrorism. But what actions does the term 'targeted killing' comprise?

The literal meaning of the term helps us to understand the nature of the practice described as targeted killing. It does not fully capture the meaning 'targeted killing' has gained in practice, however, particularly because the term as it is currently used only describes specific actor-victim-constellations. I will therefore, in a second step, describe the meaning 'targeted killing' has gained in practice. As applies to most terms that are used frequently but lack a commonly accepted definition, such a description does not correspond to all of the manners in which the term has been used. The majority of usages, however, share many features. This enables me to identify several characteristics that can be considered to be crucial to the current understanding of the term. Finally, in order to sharpen this understanding and explain why the term is used in this book, I will contrast targeted killing to similar forms of violence. Central to this comparison will be the terms 'assassination' and 'extrajudicial execution'. Both terms are often used by opponents of the practice to replace the term 'targeted killing' in order to express their legal or moral opposition.

The *literal meaning of 'targeted killing'* first implies that lethal force is actively directed against a specific target. In other words, the attacker deliberately chooses whom to attack and directs force against this target. Killing, secondly, obviously requires the target to be a living creature. The precise nature of this creature, however, is not specified by the term 'targeted killing' in its literal meaning. The literal meaning of 'targeted killing' finally implies that the killing is carried out intentionally. This can be understood in two ways. The first understanding concerns the intention to hit one specific target, as addressed in the point just made. The second possible understanding refers to the killing itself. An act of lethal force only qualifies as targeted killing if the killing itself was intended. If someone is targeted, that individual is not killed accidentally or in a reflex action. Direct force is actively directed against this individual, who is meant specifically to be killed.

No criteria beyond these three can be derived from the term itself. The term does not elucidate who acts or who is killed. Both attacker and victim could be state officials, prominent persons, or individuals fully unknown to the public. The victim does not even have to be human. The term furthermore does nothing to elucidate the motive which makes the actor carry out the killing or the ultimate aim he or she seeks to reach by applying lethal force. The attacker's motivation or aim could be the killing itself. It could be political in character or ideological, but it could be a number of other things, too. Finally, in its literal sense, the term 'targeted killing' is neutral regarding the legal or moral assessment of the act it describes. It describes a specific form of force, yet as a term it does not imply any judgement as to whether that practice is morally or legally right or wrong, justified or unjustified.

Current usage of the term 'targeted killing'[1] does not contradict its literal meaning. As the literal meaning suggests, a case of lethal violence can only be understood or described as targeted killing when it is carried out with the intention to kill the victim and when the target has been chosen deliberately.[2] Nevertheless, the meaning of 'targeted killing' as it has evolved through practical usage clarifies some of the aspects that the literal meaning leaves open.

First, 'targeted killing' only applies to violence carried out by state officials or by non-state actors acting on behalf of a state.[3] No reference could be found in which the term was applied to non-state violence not applied on behalf of a

---

1 When I speak of 'practical' or 'current usage' of the term 'targeted killing', I refer to how the term is used in practice – by state officials, court members, etc. – as well as to how it is used in scholarly literature. Both groups tend to apply the term without defining it explicitly. The manner in which they apply the term, however, suggests that they share a certain understanding of what acts of violence it comprises.

2 See, for example, David 2003a, 112. He defines targeted killing as 'the intentional slaying of a specific individual or group of individuals undertaken with explicit governmental approval'.

3 See, for example, David 2003a, 112.

state. Second, targeted killing only includes acts of lethal force that are directed against human beings. The term is used to describe the killing of non-state individuals and state officials.[4] Most frequently, however, it is used to describe lethal force used against non-state agents alleged to be involved in terrorism.[5] Third, targeted killing is planned lethal force. Most paradigmatically it describes the killing of an individual who, based on some decision-making process, has been selected to be killed. The killing of him or her is then planned and, once the situation allows, carried out.[6]

Not all authors, however, limit the practice to such cases. They also include the killing of individuals who are believed to be on their way to carry out an attack.[7] These cases can theoretically be based on a decision taken prior to the moment when the targeted person, due to carrying out an attack, was perceived as a concrete threat. More likely, however, the decision to use force is triggered by the concrete, though not yet imminent,[8] threat the individual is held to pose. In such a situation, I would argue, this sort of killing differs from targeted killing. Having said that, I will include these cases in the analysis. On the one hand, I do so because commentators refer to these situations to justify the practice of targeted killing. On the other hand, killing in these situations – different from killing carried out in light of a (suddenly) occurring imminent act of force that can no longer be described as a planned action – is not yet 'forced upon' the agent by the imminence of the otherwise occurring harm, but involves some extended decision-making process, and may be described as planned action to some extent. Killing carried out in light of imminent harm, however, can no longer be described as targeted killing, and will not be regarded as such in this book, irrespective of whether the threat suddenly occurred or developed over some time.[9]

---

4 See, for example, Thomas 2005.
5 See, for example, 2003; Moore, Molly 2003. David (2002a, 13) describes targeted killing as 'the Israeli policy of intentionally killing individuals who are on their way to commit a terrorist attack or those who are behind such attacks'.
6 See, for example, Gross, M. 2006, 324. He states that most accounts understand targeted killing as 'first, compiling lists of certain individuals who comprise specific threats and second, killing them when the opportunity presents itself during armed conflict'.
7 See David in fn. 5 in the current chapter. See also David 2002b, 5.
8 The term 'imminent' is used as describing the moment when the harmful act is about to be carried out. Its meaning will be addressed more specifically in chapter 10.
9 This also corresponds to the fact mentioned by Orna Ben-Naftali and Keren Michaeli (2003, 250) with regards to Israel that official confirmations of specific targeted killings do not provide any evidence as to the imminence of a harmful act for which the individual was targeted. Compare also chapter 2.1. For a contrary perspective, see Melzer 2008, 3–6, see also 239; Schmitz-Elvenich 2008, 12, see also 254.

Fourth, the term 'targeted killing' is used to describe lethal force that is carried out only against individuals who are not in state custody. And fifth, targeted killings are not based on court decisions, and hence they constitute extrajudicial use of lethal force.

Some commentators may want to add a sixth characteristic. In these cases, targeted killings are often presented as preventive, or, as I will call it, defensive[10] use of force.[11] The term is used here to describe acts of lethal force that are directed against persons held to be dangerous to other people.[12] It includes the use of lethal force to stop someone from carrying out a specific terrorist act. It also includes lethal force directed against a person held to be dangerous in a less concrete sense. This could be because he or she is held to pose a general threat, as has been stated with regard to certain state leaders, or because he or she is thought to be involved in terrorist activities and hence poses an abstract, though future, threat. As all of these cases seek to ward off future threats, they could all be described as a defensive use of force.

Not all of the forms that targeted killing can take, however, are limited to the defensive use of force. Descriptions show that not all cases are based on a thorough analysis of the actual threat the targeted individual poses. The prevention of future threats does not necessarily constitute the incentive for applying lethal force described as targeted killing. Motives of revenge and punishment for past deeds, in particular, often feature and sometimes are the only or predominant incentive.[13] Some of these killings, one may argue, involve the motive of deterrence. However, with a view to the targeted person as well as in light of the fact that they are responses to past deeds, these acts must be described as responsive. The characterization of targeted killings can thus not be limited to defensive.

Some commentators employ different terms to denote the practice otherwise described as targeted killing. Opponents of the practice tend to describe it as extrajudicial execution or assassination.[14] Both terms denote *forms of violence that*

---

10 See also chapter 1.3.

11 See, for example, Dudkevitch/O'Sullivan 2001; Gross, E. 2001; Kendall 2002, 1069/1078; Moore, Molly 2003.

12 David 2003a, 117.

13 See chapter 2.1.

14 There are other terms that are used instead of 'targeted killing', e. g. 'summary execution' (Anna Lindh, at the time foreign minister of Sweden, see Boot 2002), 'preventative strike' or 'the policy of targeted frustration' (see HCJ, *Public Committee against Torture v. Government of Israel*, para. 2), 'named killing' (Gross, M. 2006), 'pinpointed pre-emptive actions' (Ben-Naftali/Michaeli 2003, 250), or 'focused elimination' (Curtius, Mary (2001), 'Sharon Tells His Aides to Take PR Offensive', L.A. Times, 8 August 2001, Part A, Pg.1, quoted in Gross, E.

are closely related to the concept of targeted killing, adding certain aspects and implying judgements regarding its legality and morality.

Among the terms often used as substitutes for 'targeted killing', *'assassination'* is the most difficult to capture. The practice of assassination has long been subject to discussion.[15] Nevertheless, no commonly accepted definition of the term exists, and few legal documents refer to it explicitly. At the international level, only the Charter of the Organization of African Unity specifically addresses assassination. At the national level, it was most prominently referred to in bans on assassination issued by several presidents of the United States.[16] While these documents outlaw assassination, none of them defines the term.

Definitions which seem to best represent the current linguistic use of 'assassination' define it as '[t]he act of deliberately killing someone, [especially] a public figure, [usually] for hire or political reasons'[17] or 'any unlawful killing of particular individuals for political purposes'[18]. These definitions describe assassination as politically motivated and highlight the intention to kill as well as the fact that violence is directed against a specific target. Some authors further limit the concept to the killing of public figures or persons of public prominence.[19] In current legal discussions, scholars tend to differentiate between peacetime and war-

---

2005, 579). I will only address the terms 'extrajudicial execution' and 'assassination', since they seem to play the most prominent role among those terms that targeted killings are described with. Furthermore, they suffice to characterize the practice.

15 For a historical overview, see Schmitt 1992, 613–618.

16 First among US presidents, Gerald Ford banned assassination in 1976 (Executive Order No. 11905, at section 5 (g)). In 1978, Jimmy Carter issued a slightly changed version of the order (Executive Order No. 12036, at section 2–305). In 1981, Ronald Reagan issued Executive Order No. 12333, which is still in effect. It provides that 'no person employed by or acting on behalf of the United States Government shall engage in, or conspire to engage in, assassination' (at 2.11), and distinct from its predecessors, it also includes a section on indirect participation, which reads: 'No agency of the Intelligence Community shall participate in or request any person to undertake activities forbidden by this Order' (at 2.12). For the historical developments regarding the ban of assassination in the United States, see Schmitt 1992, 652–674.

17 Black's Law Dictionary 109 (7th ed. 1999), quoted in Godfrey 2003, 492.

18 Sofaer 1989, 117. Similar definitions can be found in other languages. In German 'assassination' may be translated as 'Attentat', which the Brockhaus (2006, Vol. 21, 659f.; translated from German by myself) defines as 'a politically, religiously or ideologically motivated attack against the lives of civilians or politicians as well as against individuals who hold high offices in the state, the economic or cultural field, and in the military, or against public figures. [...] With emerging global terrorism, assassination is no longer limited to attack on prominent political enemies but it is increasingly directed against individuals and groups of individuals in their roles as members of a party, state, race or religion.'

19 See, for example, David 2003a, 112.

time definitions of assassination. They define assassination in peacetime along the lines just mentioned.[20] For wartime situations they argue that killing constitutes assassination only when it is carried out by treacherous means.[21]

Given these different approaches, it is difficult to determine overlaps and differences between the two concepts of assassination and targeted killings. Nevertheless, most definitions and concepts of assassination seem to have certain aspects in common. These shared characteristics help to formulate a few general statements about the concept of assassination as such, and thus to highlight how it relates to targeted killing.

As with targeted killing, assassination implies the intention to kill as well as the intention to kill a specific person.[22] Furthermore, neither targeted killing nor assassination comprise lethal force triggered by an imminent threat posed to the life of others.

However, unlike the term 'targeted killing', the term 'assassination' does not reveal whether the act of lethal force has been carried out by state officials, by non-state agents on behalf of a state, or by non-state agents acting independently of any state involvement.[23] In this respect, targeted killing appears to be a more limited concept of lethal force than assassination.

Other than this rather technical difference, the second crucial distinction between targeted killing and assassination adds a moral and legal dimension and is, thus, of particular importance for the context addressed in this book. Assassination represents illegal conduct. The term is hardly ever employed to denote legal behaviour and most definitions explicitly distinguish assassination from legal homicide.[24] General definitions and peacetime definitions of assassination describe the practice for this purpose as unlawful killing or as murder.[25] In wartime definitions, commentators distinguish assassination from lawful killing in warfare by describing it as the killing of a specific person by treacherous means.[26] Thus defined, this understanding of assassination also reflects common linguistic usage of the term and corresponds to the way the term is used in legal documents.

The term 'targeted killing', in contrast, primarily serves a descriptive purpose and does not imply any legal or moral judgement. That said, current usage of the

---

20 See, for example, Harder 2002, 5.
21 Schmitt 1992, 632 f./641 f.; Wachtel 2005, 682 f.
22 Schmitt 1992, 632 f.
23 Schmitt 1992, 632 f.
24 For an exception, see Beres 1991, 231–249.
25 See, for example, Anderson, C. 1992, 294 f.; Wachtel 2005, 681.
26 See fn. 21 in the current chapter.

term often reveals the attempt to present the practice as legally or morally acceptable. Commentators often use it to distinguish the practice of targeted killing from practices that are generally held to be morally wrong and illegal. By using a different term they attempt to detach the practice from any such negative judgements. This explains why state officials or scholars who argue in favour of killing terrorists under certain conditions prefer describing such acts as targeted killings,[27] while opponents of such practices often utilize the term 'assassination'.[28] Nevertheless, the moral and legal assessment of targeted killing should not be confused with the descriptive character of the term. The term is furthermore also used by commentators who argue that specific targeted killings or the practice as such are illegal or immoral.[29]

To conclude, targeted killing and assassination are closely related. But when the actor's as well as the victim's identity is considered, the term 'targeted killing' describes a form of violence which is more limited than that denoted by 'assassination'. With regard to these aspects, assassination comprises all cases of targeted killing, yet the reverse is not true. With regards to their moral and legal implications, targeted killing, which as a term does not include any such assessment, does describe a concept that is wider than assassination, which only comprises illegal behaviour. This book will show whether targeted killings can be justified under certain circumstances or whether the practice always constitutes illegal behaviour. The term as such, however, does not express any such assessment.

Just as with the comparison between assassination and targeted killing, *extrajudicial execution*[30] and targeted killing have several aspects in common, differ on several points and, most importantly, include different assessments as to the legality of the forms of lethal force they describe. Firstly, an examination of extrajudicial execution highlights an important aspect of targeted killings, namely that the force applied is not based on a court decision. Extrajudicial execution moreover resembles targeted killing in that it does not comprise legal acts that are carried out by state agents to protect individuals from imminent danger to their lives. Furthermore, extrajudicial execution seems to comprise only acts car-

---

27 See, for example, David 2003a; Kendall 2002, in particular 2–5; Meisels 2004; Nolte 2004, 114.
28 See, for example, Gross, M. 2003.
29 See, for example, Downes 2004.
30 Extrajudicial execution is self-explanatory and its exact meaning is comparatively seldom addressed explicitly. For an analysis of its meaning and relationship to similar forms of violence, see Kaufman/Weiss Fagen 1981.

ried out, ordered or acquiesced to and tolerated by states.[31] 'Extrajudicial execution' also implies the intention to kill a person or a group of persons.[32] It, however, does not require the intention to target a *specific* person. Lethal force directed against individuals who have not been chosen specifically due to their identity can arguably be regarded as extrajudicial execution, but would not be described as targeted killing.

Most importantly – and in this respect it resembles assassination – 'extrajudicial execution' implies the illegality of the act it describes. By highlighting that the killing takes place without preceding due process of law,[33] the term 'extrajudicial execution' signifies that all killings it describes would have required a court decision ordering them in order to have been legal. Hence, it excludes all cases of lethal force that are legal despite the fact that no court authorized them, such as the killing of combatants in armed conflicts. It also excludes legal killings following due process of law.

To use the term 'extrajudicial execution' to describe cases of lethal force otherwise described as targeted killings thus reveals a negative legal and moral assessment of those cases. With regard to illegal acts, extrajudicial execution constitutes a wider concept of force than does targeted killing. All illegal targeted killings could be described as extrajudicial executions. However, not all extrajudicial executions could be described as illegal targeted killings. Due to the differences regarding the aspect of intention, extrajudicial execution comprises illegal targeted killings and additional cases of illegal lethal force applied by a state.

The comparison between the meaning of targeted killing and the forms of violence that 'assassination' and 'extrajudicial execution' describe has highlighted several aspects that these forms of violence share, and it has clarified important differences that exist between them. The differences are crucial to understanding not only what differentiates targeted killings from other forms of lethal force, but also why the term 'targeted killing' is preferred over 'assassination' and 'extrajudicial execution' in this book. The most important difference is to be found in the judgement the terms imply regarding the legal and moral justifiability of the practice they describe. While the term 'targeted killing' is legally neutral, 'assassination' and 'extrajudicial killing' imply that the acts they describe

---

31 See, for example, AI 1992. Edy Kaufman and Patricia Weiss Fagen (1981, 84) seem not to share this position.

32 This is already suggested by the term 'execution'. See also AI 1992; Kaufman/Weiss Fagen 1981, 81.

33 An act is extrajudicial if it is carried out without any process of law whatsoever, but also if it follows a court proceeding which did not adhere to minimal guarantees of due process of law. Kaufman/Weiss Fagen 1981, 81–83.

are illegal and immoral. Only a term that precludes both negative and positive preliminary judgements can serve the purpose of this book, namely to establish whether, or under what conditions, targeted killings can be justified.[34]

In addition, 'targeted killing' describes a specific practice that is not expressed as precisely by the terms 'assassination' or 'extrajudicial execution': the intentional use of lethal force against a specific person or group of persons outside state custody by state agents or non-state actors acting on behalf of a state, prior to the moment the harming act is about to be carried out.

1.2 Defining 'terrorist'

The definition of terrorist, the second term to be discussed in establishing what 'targeted killing of terrorists' means, can be elucidated in reference to the term 'terrorist act' or, more generally, in reference to the term 'terrorism'.[35] Terrorists are all those who themselves carry out or attempt to carry out terrorist acts. Terrorists are also those who participate as accomplices in a terrorist act, who intentionally participate in planning and organizing terrorist acts, or who direct or command others to commit terrorist acts.[36] Any person participating in terrorism in any of the manners thus addressed may be described as a terrorist.[37]

---

34 The contrary position is taken up by Georg Nolte (2004, 114), who argues that the usage of the term 'targeted killing' suggests that the practice is based on a legitimizing rational element.

35 'Terrorism' and 'terrorist act' will be understood identically. The term 'terrorist act' points to the action itself, but each act can also be described as terrorism. 'Terrorism' may be used to describe several acts but still does not exist independently of the act.

36 As far as they address different forms of involvement, the conventions and protocols that the international community has agreed upon regarding terrorism, and which address specific forms of violence often used in the context of terrorism, such as hijacking of aeroplanes, hostage taking, etc., differentiate between those forms of involvement and include them among the offences addressed. See in particular Convention on Offences and Certain Acts Committed on board Aircraft, Tokyo, 14 September 1963; Convention for the Suppression of Unlawful Seizure of Aircraft, The Hague, 16 December 1970 and the Protocol thereto of 10 September 2010, Beijing; Convention for the Suppression of Unlawful Acts against the Safety of Civil Aviation, Montreal, 23 September 1971; Convention on the Prevention and Punishment of Crimes Against International Protected Persons, New York, 14 December 1973; International Convention against the Taking of Hostages, New York, 17 December 1979; Protocol for the Suppression of Unlawful Acts of Violence at Airports Serving International Civil Aviation, Montreal, 24 February 1988; Convention for the Suppression of Unlawful Acts against the Safety of Maritime Navigation, Rome, 10 March 1988, and the Protocol thereto of 14 October 2005, London; Protocol for the Suppression of Unlawful Acts

Given that terrorists are defined with reference to terrorist acts, an understanding of what constitutes terrorism must precede an understanding of the meaning of 'terrorist'. There are several difficulties presented by this task. Scholars disagree on how terrorism is best defined. According to an estimate dating back several decades, the number of definitions offered in scholarly literature well exceeds one hundred.[38] Definitions used in practical contexts are similarly divergent. There is no internationally accepted definition of terrorism, nor do different organizations within one state always utilize the same definition of the term. Despite several attempts, starting in 1937, the international community has thus far failed to reach an agreement whenever it has addressed the question of how terrorism can be defined for legal purposes. Recent negotiations on a comprehensive convention on international terrorism demonstrate that states still disagree as to what should legally be considered terrorism.[39] As a result, the international community has also failed to agree on any legal instrument that deals with terrorism in general. The only instruments the international community has managed to agree upon are fourteen legal instruments (partly with

---

against the Safety of Fixed Platforms Located on the Continental Shelf, Rome, 10 March 1988; International Convention for the Suppression of Terrorist Bombing, New York, 15 December 1997; International Convention for the Suppression of the Financing of Terrorism, New York, 9 December 1999; International Convention for the Suppression of Acts of Nuclear Terrorism, New York, 13 April 2005; Convention on the Suppression of Unlawful Acts relating to International Civil Aviation, Beijing, 10 September 2010.

37 This, of course, does not mean that the question of whether these persons may be targeted and killed will be answered identically. I am not able to say yet whether the form of their involvement will influence my response to the question of whether it may be justified to target them. It has to be kept in mind, however, that the term 'terrorist' includes different forms of involvement and that the questions of whether targeted killing of terrorists can be justified may in fact involve several sub-questions which differ depending on the kind of terrorist considered.

38 Schmid 1983, 119–158.

39 The main points of disagreement are, as they were almost seventy years ago, whether and when state action can be considered terrorism, and whether and to what extent violent acts carried out during a struggle for national liberation, self-determination, and independence should be excluded from a definition of terrorism. The issues of disagreement have been the same since states began legally addressing terrorism in the international community. The degree of disagreement clearly decreased over time, yet recent negotiations about the Draft Comprehensive Convention on International Terrorism show that the same issues of disagreement come up again as soon as legal consequences are to be linked to the definition. For details, see, for example, UN Doc A/60/37 Annex II B; UN Doc A/C.6/60/L.6 Annex A; UN Doc A/C.6/58/L.10 Annex II; UN Doc A/57/37 Annex IV; UN Doc A/62/37 Annex; UN Doc A/66/37 Annex I B; UN Doc A/65/37 Annex I B.

amendments),[40] which address specific forms of violence, such as hijacking of aeroplanes, hostage taking, etc., which are often used in the context of terrorism or specific forms of terrorism. Due to the fact that these instruments only define the offence they deal with, no general definition of terrorism can be extracted from any of them. Hence, the international community at the moment exhibits a piecemeal approach towards terrorism, with no internationally agreed-upon definition of the phenomenon.

Given the different ways in which terrorism is understood in the scholarly literature and how the term has been used in practice, it makes little sense to attempt to settle upon a definition that would cover all of those understandings. Given the sometimes contradictory understandings, such a project is impossible. Moreover, in practice in particular, the term 'terrorism' has often been misused and applied to cases of violence which have nothing to do with terrorism. To base a definition on such usage of the term would inevitably lead to an imprecise and misleading understanding of terrorism. This would not advance the purpose of this book, to critically analyse the justifiability of targeted killing of terrorists in view of current developments. Still, the definition offered here seeks to define the term in a manner that captures the essence of what most commentators agree to be terrorism and, thus, to include the cases of terrorism that have confronted the international community in recent years and which were commonly considered terrorist acts. This necessarily involves a certain degree of stipulation.

What, then, will be understood as a terrorist act, and, thus, as a terrorist, within the parameters of this book? An act constitutes a terrorist act when it meets all of the following criteria: (1) it includes the use of violence or the threat of its use; (2) it is carried out intentionally; (3) it is directed against innocents; (4) it is carried out with the aim to influence the political or societal behaviour of an audience; (5) it may reasonably be argued that the act of violence by its nature or its context has the capacity to severely threaten or substantially shock people.

Ad (1) The first definitional aspect does not need any further explanation or defence against the accusation of describing terrorism unrealistically. It is widely accepted both in academic literature and in practical approaches.[41]

---

40 Convention on the Physical Protection of Nuclear Material, Vienna, 26 October 1979; Convention on the Making of Plastic Explosives for the Purpose of Detection, Montreal, 1 March 1991; for the other twelve conventions and protocols (and amendments), see fn. 36 in the current chapter.

41 For practical approaches, see, for example, EU Council Framework Decision on Combating Terrorism (2002); or Draft Comprehensive Convention on International Terrorism, see UN Doc. A/C.6/55/L.2; UN Doc. A/C.6/56/L.9; UN Doc. A/C.6/57/L.9; UN Doc. A/C.6/58/L.10. This consensus is only questioned by a handful of authors, such as Carl Wellman (1979, 251f.),

Ad (2) That terrorism is the *intentional* use or threat of violence is almost as widely agreed upon.[42] This also corresponds to common moral sentiments against terrorism. It is not incurred damage which makes people condemn terrorism, but the fact that it was caused deliberately, as part of a tactic.

Ad (3) To describe terrorism as violence against innocents reflects the principle that distinguishes terrorism from other forms of political violence. Terrorism uses innocent individuals to further its aims. Here, 'innocent' is not offered as a counterpart to 'guilty'. Rather, it is used in a 'technical sense'.[43] It describes all those people not engaged in the injustice that the terrorists fight against – or in other words, as Igor Primoratz puts it, 'those who are not responsible' for it 'in any plausible sense of the word'.[44] During warfare the term 'innocents' excludes all attacks on combatants as well as all attacks on civilians, during that time period in which they take a direct part in hostilities, from the scope of terrorism.[45] During peacetime the term, in principle, includes all civilians. Under specific circumstances, certain exceptions, however, are possible. The distinction drawn in warfare between combatants and non-combatants provides a plausible understanding of who may be regarded as sufficiently responsible for a certain situation, at least in one respect. Individuals cannot be regarded as being combatants during wartime based on their having voted for the government, their paying taxes, or their ideologically supporting the war effort. Likewise, individuals cannot be described as non-innocents in a particular situation during peacetime merely if they participate in the political or economic system as it is established. Individuals need to have an active role in a specific injustice to have the status of 'non-innocent' be legitimately ascribed to them in the relevant sense. This only applies, moreover, to individuals who are sufficiently responsible for a situation with regard to which it is possible to somehow make sense of the perpetrator's

---

who includes non-violent action in his definition of terrorism. Igor Primoratz replies to Wellman comprehensively in Primoratz 2004, 16 f.

42 For practical approaches, see, for example, EU Council Framework Decision on Combating Terrorism (2002); Draft Comprehensive Convention on Terrorism (see fn. 41 in the current chapter), or Canadian Bill C-36, Part II. 1. For definitions in the scholarly literature, see, for example, Coady 1985, 52; Primoratz 2004, 24; Walzer 2004, 130. David Rodin (2004) questions the claim that intention is necessary if one is to speak of terrorism and argues that acts of violence harming civilians out of recklessness have to be considered terrorism, too.

43 Coady 2004, 10.

44 Primoratz 2004, 18.

45 For definitions of terrorism that include this aspect, see Coady 1985, 51 f. Michael Walzer (2006a, 3) uses the term 'innocents'. His understanding of the term, however, parallels the meaning of non-combatant.

point of view, which is that the situation constitutes an injustice that may render resorting to violence defensible.[46]

I am, of course, not arguing that deciding whether a certain act of force constitutes terrorism depends on whether one shares the terrorist's view that the situation justifies the use of force. There are, however, limits in designating a certain situation as an injustice. To give an example, a limit is exceeded if terrorists argue that practising a religion or being a member of a certain religious group is itself an injustice which must be fought against. Moreover, it is important to note that I am not arguing that violence directed against those who can plausibly be held responsible for some injustice or evil is morally justified. I am merely arguing that such cases do not constitute terrorism, but rather some other form of violence.

This definition, by focusing on the specific target of a terrorist act, differs from definitions that do not address the target at all. It differs, too, from those definitions that do address the question of the target but leave it relatively unspecified, limiting the possible target to persons or to a combination of persons and property. In contrast to the definition I propose, these other definitions are often concerned to provide a definition of the term by listing all cases of violence that are or may be considered terrorism, such as an 'attack on a person's life which may cause death, [an] attack upon the physical integrity of a person, [or] kidnapping or hostage taking'[47].[48] This ignores the most distinguishing characteristic of terrorism. By focusing on innocents, as discussed above, the definition proposed here also differs from those which, while specifically addressing the category of the target,[49] regard violence directed against *civilians* as the factor

---

46 Tony Coady addressed this issue in a detailed and very convincing way in *Morality and Political Violence* (2008), 154–178.

47 Article 1 (a-c) EU Council Framework Decision on Combating Terrorism (2002).

48 Practical juridical approaches, in particular, often define terrorism in this way. Apart from the Council of Europe Framework Decision, see, for example, Draft Comprehensive Convention on Terrorism (see fn. 41 in the current chapter). Definitions that designate terrorism as the *unlawful* use of violence or the threat thereof (see also Draft Comprehensive Convention on Terrorism) imply statements about the target. For armed conflicts, they, for example, exclude actions that international humanitarian law allows for. According to this, attacks on civilians who do not take a direct part in hostilities always qualify as terrorism. As a result, these definitions often distinguish between terrorist and non-terrorist acts with reference to the target of the violence. Similar general statements may, however, only be made with regard to very few other groups. Hence, while the attribute 'unlawfully' may sometimes imply statements about the target, it does not allow one to generally identify terrorist acts with reference to the target.

49 A definition that includes specific cases and specifies the target was, for example, suggested in the report *A More Secure World: Our Shared Responsibility*, UN 2004, 52. The

crucial in distinguishing terrorism from other forms of violence.[50] This also applies to definitions that – with regard to the definitional aspect of the target – define terrorism as violence against innocents, but conceive of the category in a different manner than the one used here.[51] At the same time, the definition offered in this book is in agreement with many of these other definitions insofar as it highlights the terrorists' deliberate decision to *use* individuals or a group of people as a means to change a situation for which these individuals cannot be held responsible.[52]

There is an additional aspect to defining the target. Even without examining the issue in any great detail, there can be no doubt that violence targeting property can constitute terrorism. One can provide many examples, such as the use of force against closed public buildings during the night or against chemical factories or nuclear power stations. In terms of the definitional criterion of the target, for an act of violence against property to be considered a terrorist act, it is only necessary that it is directed against the property of innocents.

---

report suggests that the international community should agree on a definition of terrorism that explicitly includes all acts that are considered terrorism under the international anti-terrorism conventions. The report further mentions the definitions given in the International Convention for the Suppression of the Financing of Terrorism (see fn. 36 in the current chapter) and the Security Council resolution 1566 (2004) and includes a more general statement as to what acts have to be considered terrorism. It describes terrorism as 'any action, in addition to actions already specified by the existing conventions on aspects of terrorism, the Geneva Conventions and Security Council resolutions 1566 (2004), that is intended to cause death or serious bodily harm to civilians or non-combatants, when the purpose of such act, by its nature or context, is to intimidate a population, or to compel a Government or an international organisation to do or to abstain from doing any act'.

50 In addition to non-combatants, these terms appear in definitions that specifically refer to the target in order to distinguish terrorism from other forms of violence. Definitions which describe civilians as targets of terrorist acts are problematic in particular, for under certain circumstances they may not allow for differentiation between military personnel involved in warfare and military personnel in peacetime situations.

51 Not all commentators specify what they mean by 'innocent'. In addition to the way it is used in this book, the term can be understood in at least two ways. First, it is used in a way that parallels the use of 'non-combatant'; see e.g. Walzer 2006, 3. Second, the term could be understood as equivalent to 'not guilty'. It appears to me that scholars who elaborate upon the meaning of 'innocent' do not adhere to this moral conceptualization. Depending on the theory drawn upon regarding the moral guilt of combatants, it would apply to all combatants adhering to *jus in bello*, but certainly to those fighting a just war. Definitions that apply a moral understanding of 'innocent' determine attacks on these soldiers to be terrorism, provided that the other definitional requirements are fulfilled.

52 Coady 1985; Primoratz 2004.

Some authors further clarify that only attacks on certain properties can be considered terrorism.[53] Jenny Teichman, *inter alia*, claims that violence against property can only be considered terrorism 'if it [the property] is needed for life itself'.[54] It is true that differentiation is necessary in determining when violence against property can be considered terrorism. However, I believe that the nature of the property is irrelevant when violence is employed against the property of innocents: the difference does not hinge upon the property, but instead upon the kind of violence that is used and the intentional aim with which this violence is carried out. Examples can be given where the use of violence against an identical piece of property constitutes an act of terrorism in one case and not in another. Similarly, examples can be provided in which violence against innocents does constitute an act of terrorism in one case, but not in another. For example, throwing paint at people or on their houses with the aim of winning media coverage and influencing environmental behaviour would not be classified as a terrorist act. However, planting a bomb on a bus or in a public building in the middle of the night to reach the same aim would constitute a terrorist act. If a demonstration turns violent, with cars burnt in the course of it, one could still not say of it that it was a terrorist attack. It, however, could be labelled a terrorist act if individuals used this form of intentional violence as part of a tactic and combined it with a credible threat that the violence would be intensified in order to reach their aims if their demands were not met.[55] Thus further differentiation is necessary, yet the differentiation is not a matter of the type of target, but one of the extent or nature of the violence itself, which I have classified as the fifth definitional aspect of terrorism. Distinctions must be drawn, too, with regards to the aim with which the violence is applied, which I address in the following definitional aspect.

Ad (4) The aim of the act of violence is necessary in determining whether such an act constitutes a terrorist act. Definitions that exclude the aspect of aim altogether fail to recognize that terrorism is a tactic and that it is distinct from cases in which violence is carried out for the sake of violence itself.[56] The two important distinguishing features of an aim of a terrorist act are that the act is carried out in order to influence the behaviour of an audience and that the focus is on the public sphere, not the private sphere.

---

53 See, for example, Primoratz 2004, 21; or Teichman 1989, 512.
54 Quoted in Primoratz 2004, 21.
55 I thank Christian Walter for calling my attention to wilful damage to property in the course of demonstrations.
56 Compare also Coady 1985, 47–49.

Distinguishing between the public and private spheres in defining terrorism leads one to exclude all cases of violence carried out to reach private goals, such as bank robbery to amass private capital or blackmail carried out for private purposes. The aim of terrorism may then be described as being *to influence the political or societal*[57] *behaviour of an audience.*

The majority of definitions recognize that the intention to influence an audience is crucial for an act of violence to constitute an act of terrorism. Many definitions state this explicitly,[58] others implicitly, such as definitions describing terrorism as violence carried out for political purposes.[59] Almost all definitions that mention the matter of an aim recognize the public goal of terrorism.[60] The definition provided in this book, which incorporates the matter of the aim, is therefore in line with the predominant understanding. The definition used here, however, focuses on the public sphere rather than on subcategories such as the political realm, which, according to some interpretations, could exclude certain forms of terrorism, such as religious terrorism.

Ad (5) The extent of violence is primarily addressed in definitions intended for practical application. They commonly define as terrorism only those acts of violence thought to cause or intentionally cause '*death* or *serious* bodily injury'.[61] Similar formulations are used if attacks on property are included in the definition.[62] Theoretical studies tend to ignore the extent of violence. But a violent act must be of a certain level of severity in order to constitute a terrorist act, regardless of whether terrorism is defined for theoretical or practical purposes. In-

---

57 'Societal' refers to society in general and describes behaviour that relates to the structure of a society or groups within a society, and thus includes the political realm, but also religion, for example.

58 See, for example, *A More Secure World: Our Shared Responsibility*, UN 2004; Draft Comprehensive Convention on Terrorism (see fn. 41 in the current chapter), or the EU Council Framework Decision on Combating Terrorism (2002).

59 See, for example, Coady 2004, 5. Coady defines terrorism as 'the organised use of violence to attack non-combatants ["innocents" in a special sense] or their property for political purposes'.

60 For exceptions, see, for example, Primoratz 2004, 24. He defines terrorism as 'the deliberate use of violence, or threat of its use, against innocent people, with the aim of intimidating some other people into a course of action they otherwise would not take'.

61 For the quotation, see the Draft Comprehensive Convention on Terrorism (see fn. 41 in the current chapter), emphasis added. Identical or similar formulations can be found, for example, in the EU Council Framework Decision on Combating Terrorism (2002), or the International Convention for the Suppression of the Financing of Terrorism (fn. 36 in the current chapter). See also *A More Secure World: Our Shared Responsibility*, UN 2004.

62 See, for example, Draft Comprehensive Convention on Terrorism (fn. 41 in the current chapter), or EU Council Framework Decision on Combating Terrorism (2002).

cluding this dimension in the definition accounts for the moral repugnance exhibited towards terrorist acts, aligns the definition with a general understanding of terrorism, and serves my aim within this book, namely to identify the core of terrorism and to include actual cases of terrorism that the international community has been confronted with in recent years. While it is considered terrorism when people are deliberately killed in order to influence political or societal behaviour, the term is not employed when someone throws eggs at people in an attempt to change their environmental behaviour.

The formulation that an act *by its nature or context* has to have *the capacity to severely threaten or substantially shock people* takes into account that it is not the actual destruction caused that needs to be of a serious degree for an act to be considered terrorism. The consequences of certain acts, such as arson, can be limited if people manage to react quickly enough. Nevertheless, regardless of how quickly the fire may be extinguished, the act can still constitute terrorism, provided all other definitional requirements are met. 'By its nature' can mean that the act of violence is serious in its consequences. It can also mean that the means of violence are serious in and of themselves. The latter, for example, applies to planting bombs in general. The term 'by its context' implies on the one hand that the context can render an act of violence a terrorist act even if the violence is minor or, for example, is directed against property that is not used. An act of minor violence could, for example, constitute terrorism, if the perpetrator were to combine it with a warning that further, more harmful attacks would follow if his or her conditions were not met. On the other hand, the term 'by its context' accounts for the fact that violence against property carried out in demonstrations that turn violent differs from the use of the same violent acts as part of a series of seriously threatening acts, carried out as a means to change an audience's behaviour.[63]

I argued above that my definition captures the core of what most commentators agree to be terrorism, and I formulated it to include those cases most commonly understood as terrorism with which the international community has been confronted during recent years. Still, my definition represents an individual approach to defining the term. Two preliminary points must therefore be made before my analysis may proceed.

First, as far as is possible – and this applies to the legal justifiability in particular – I will establish the conditions that determine whether targeted killings

---

63 Given that some very sensitive people may be shocked or feel seriously threatened by minor violence, one has to focus on the question of whether the act could have such effects on the general public to decide whether the level of violence met the requirements for constituting a terrorist act.

can be justified first without reference to terrorism. The consequences that follow from this in assessing the justifiability of targeted killings of *terrorists* will then be analysed in a second step. This works to ensure that the focus is not limited to certain conditions, namely those specific to particular understandings of terrorism. This will also enable me to establish a framework which can be applied to cases of violence that – contrary to the predominant understanding referenced in this book – are regarded as constituting terrorist acts.

Secondly, the arguments that are formulated using the definition of terrorism provided here may not necessarily be transferable to cases of violence that others regard as terrorism. The arguments may apply, but they cannot be automatically applied. The limitations of the definition I develop of terrorism require that those who ascribe the term 'terrorism' to other forms of violence must elucidate the factors that make these cases comparable to the cases I discuss. Alternatively, they must demonstrate that my arguments work despite the differences identified.

1.3 Distinguishable forms and cases

Having defined the terms involved, I can now conclude by distinguishing between different *forms* of targeted killing of terrorists. It cannot yet be determined whether these forms will be assessed differently regarding their justifiability. Moreover, actual targeted killings as they are carried out by states may sometimes reflect characteristics of different forms of the practice and in some cases it may be difficult to identify to which form they belong. Regardless, for a theoretical discussion of the justifiability of the practice, categorization is important. The forms I examine may influence the decision of which aspects need to be considered in the analysis and which arguments need to be addressed. The categorization moreover enables a systematic discussion, which will also provide a basis for assessing actual cases of targeted killing.

As I demonstrated above, all forms of targeted killing of terrorists have characteristics in common. They are intentional killings directed against specific terrorists who are outside of state custody. In addition, the decision to kill these individuals is taken extrajudicially. The first important distinction among different forms of targeted killing can be drawn in relation to the purpose pursued by the specific killing as well as in relation to the deeds on which it focuses. A distinction between responsive and defensive targeted killings can in this respect be identified.

The former is carried out in response to past terrorist acts in which the targeted individual was involved. Deterrence may play a role in the decision to target an individual for his or her involvement in past deeds. The choice of the target is made, however, based on an individual's past deeds; the targeted killing does not seek to prevent the individual from engaging in future activities. These targeted killings are often fuelled by a desire for revenge or to mete out punishment.

Defensive targeted killings of terrorists, by contrast, are carried out in anticipation of future threats. Future terrorist attacks are meant to be prevented by killing terrorists held to be important in the execution of these future attacks. Defensive targeted killings of terrorists can be further differentiated into defensive targeted killings that are carried out in the face of a determinable attack and defensive targeted killings that are carried out as a preventive response to an as-of-yet abstract or indeterminable attack.

It is unlikely that all of the circumstances of a particular terrorist attack could be known prior to the targeting of a terrorist. One may speak of a determinable attack, however, if it is foreseeable that the targeted person is involved in the planning of a particular act, and if it can be anticipated what kind of attack this will be. The degree of certainty regarding the attack would depend on, for example, the source of information, the scrutiny with which the information is verified, or the accuracy of the investigative techniques. This kind of defensive targeted killing still differs from others in that it focuses on the prevention of actual harm which would result, it is held, if the terrorist could not be stopped in some manner.

The second kind of defensive targeted killing of terrorists can be described as acts of lethal force that are directed against those who are generally held to be crucial to the planning or carrying out of future terrorist attacks in the absence of specific information about any particular attack. This applies to the killing of terrorist leaders believed to be critical to ordering attacks, for the overall organization and co-ordination of terrorist attacks, or more generally for providing the ideological foundation of a terrorist organization or network. This category also applies to terrorists who are held to have special skills that are important for possible future attacks, such as a technical understanding of bombs. It applies finally to terrorists who, it is believed, will carry out further attacks themselves or who are simply involved in terrorist activity.

Depending on the moment of attack as well as the amount and reliability of available information regarding the terrorist's involvement, four *cases* of targeted killing can finally be distinguished: (1) killing of terrorists believed to be on their way to carry out an attack, e. g. driving a car to the location they are planning to attack; (2) killing of terrorists who are plotting a determinable terrorist attack, before they embark on carrying it out; (3) killing of terrorists who, according to existing information, are believed to have continuing involvement in terrorism, although there is no evidence of engagement in a determinable act; and (4) killing of terrorists who have been active in terrorist activity, although it has not been established whether they continue to pose a threat.

In the first case the attack in question is relatively close, as well as predictable to some extent. The second and third cases primarily differ in the amount of knowledge one has about the attack. They reflect, to some extent, the distinction I have introduced with regard to defensive targeted killings. Both cases could, however, involve elements that characterize responsive actions. In the fourth case, it is not clear whether the targeted individual is posing a threat at all. Strictly speaking, such use of lethal force only constitutes a case of targeted killing of *terrorists* when the targeted person, in one way or another, continues to participate in terrorist activities, regardless of whether this has been established or not. Given that this cannot always be established, and because these cases constitute counter-terrorist activity and are described as such,[64] all targeted killings which are types of case 4 shall be included in the analysis.

---

64 See for example Kasher/Yadlin 2005, 18. They allow for the 'presumption of direct involvement' for half a year after the last recorded involvement of an individual in a terrorist act or activity. Military actions in response may, according to their argument, be based on such a presumption if a thorough search has not revealed any facts to the contrary.

2 Case studies and aspects relevant for the assessment

Having defined what I understand the term 'targeted killing of terrorists' to mean, I will, in this chapter, review actual cases of targeted killings of individuals alleged to be terrorists. I will thereby illustrate the practical relevance of the issue under discussion and the context in which it is currently discussed most vividly. This chapter will highlight further the relevance of each of the different forms of targeted killing outlined above to practice. In addition, my discussion of actual cases will provide the basis for identifying the effects and implications targeted killings have in practice. These are significant in assessing the justifiability of the practice, as I will discuss in the following chapters.

2.1 Case studies

It is not possible to provide a comprehensive history of targeted killings here. While a topic that merits historical study, it does not fall within the scope of this book nor is it necessary for its purpose. I will address the contemporary cases that are most vigorously discussed: the practice of targeted killing in the context of Israel's policies since 2000, as well as in the context of US anti-terrorism policies since 2001. In addition, I will address a few other incidents in which states resorted to targeted killings in their struggles against terrorism during the twentieth century.

The fact that I discuss these different cases in conjunction with each other does not imply any assessments of their legal or moral comparability. They may be similar, or differ profoundly from one another. What they have in common, and the reason that they are addressed together in this chapter, is that they represent cases of targeted killings of individuals whom the countries responsible in each case regarded to be terrorists.

Countries and campaigns other than the ones discussed here could be addressed. Given that my aim is not to compare countries that apply targeted killings, but to analyse the practice itself, the examples I have chosen are sufficiently insightful. An additional advantage in my choices of examples is that they are relatively well-researched. This allows me to avoid speculation as much as possible and give a relatively detailed account of the incidents.

It is nevertheless the case that it is not always easy to decide, on the basis of the extant information, whether a certain act of force constitutes a targeted killing. Given that I seek to make convincing conclusions rather than provide a comprehensive review, I leave out such cases. I thus may ignore certain cases that may possibly constitute targeted killings, but this does not affect the purpose of this book in any way.

More importantly, when relevant information is available, I will detail the reasons that given individuals are targeted. I will, however, not scrutinize arguments as to whether they should be regarded as terrorists according to the characteristics I have outlined above. As expressed by the term 'alleged', I instead present cases which the relevant governments themselves regarded as targeted killings of terrorists, or which they presented as such. This is always the case when I address actual incidents of targeted killings in this book.

Finally, few states publicly admit their involvement in targeted killings. Even if they do so, they tend to keep policy details secret. Thus, information about specific cases of targeted killing or about internal guidelines for policies on targeted killing is not provided by the states themselves, but most often based on research completed by human rights activists, journalists, eyewitnesses or individuals either involved in the actions themselves or who have information owing to their position within state administrations. I will have to rely on such information. This does nothing to undermine my overall conclusions, which may be drawn from these cases and which are always based on more than one case. Nevertheless, the nature of the source of information may present complications in individual cases. When necessary, I will not only identify the source but also provide differing views. In examining each campaign of targeted killing, I will first describe the killings that took place and then enumerate crucial characteristics. This will allow me to highlight aspects relevant to any discussion of the justifiability of targeted killing of terrorists.

Over the last decade, the most vividly discussed cases of targeted killing of terrorists have been carried out by *Israel*. Israel began its current policy of targeted killing in November 2000 as a reaction to the second Intifada. In contrast to other states that have engaged in campaigns of targeted killings, Israel declared this to be official state policy.[1] Israel, however, refuses to take on the responsibility for, or to comment on, all of its operations.[2]

The first target was *Hussein 'Abayat*.[3] He was an active organizer within the second Intifada and Israel accused him of planning the killing of Israeli soldiers and of organizational involvement in attacks on the Israeli settlement of Gilo. He was killed on 9 November 2000, hit by missiles fired from a helicopter while he

---

1 See, for example, HCJ, *Public Committee against Torture v. Government of Israel*, e.g. paras. 1f.
2 David 2003a, 117/121.
3 For the information on his death, AI 2001a, 9f. See also Stein 2001, 4f.

was sitting in his car. The three missiles killed not only Hussein 'Abayat but also two women waiting nearby. Nine bystanders were injured.

On 22 November 2000 *Jamal 'Abd al-Qader 'Abd al-Razeq* was killed by IDF gunfire.[4] This Fatah leader died in his stopped car while travelling in the Gaza Strip. A fellow passenger also died in the gunfire, as did two passengers sitting in a taxi that was in front of them. The taxi driver, interviewed by Amnesty International, stated that he was stopped by a lorry pulling out, at which point he heard shots but could not identify their origin. The IDF stated afterwards that 'a senior activist in Fatah-Tazim, Gamal A-Kader Hasan A-Razak' was killed 'in an attempt to stop him, as he was travelling in his vehicle on the road between Rafah and Khan Yunis and he attempted to break through an IDF roadblock'.[5]

One day later, *Ibrahim Bani 'Odeh*, a Hamas activist, was killed by a bomb in the headrest of his cousin's car while navigating a roundabout in the centre of Nablus.[6] The previous day Ibrahim Bani 'Odeh had been released from prison where the Palestinian Authority had held him in detention. The IDF denied responsibility for the killing and argued that Ibrahim Bani 'Odeh was killed by his own bomb. According to his cousin's confession during a trial before the Higher State Security Court in Nablus on 7 December, his cousin's car had been taken by Israeli intelligence officers some days before Ibrahim Bani 'Odeh was killed. He testified further that he had been told to ensure that Ibrahim Bani 'Odeh borrow the car and to phone Israeli intelligence once he was driving, which he had done. This was not refuted by Israel.

Abbas Awaywi, an active member of Hamas, was killed by gunfire while walking from his family's shop to his car in the centre of Hebron on 13 December 2000.[7] According to eyewitnesses, the lethal shots originated from a military post about 400 metres away.

One day later, *Hani Abu Bakra*, described by Amnesty International as a 'supporter of *Hamas*'[8] who had been detained by Israel as well as by the Palestinian Authority, was killed when stopped by an Israeli tank while driving seven passengers to Gaza in his minibus taxi.[9] According to testimony by some of the surviving passengers, Hani Abu Bakra was asked to get out of the taxi, which he did about one and half minutes later. At this point, he was shot dead by five

---

4 For the information on his death, AI 2001a, 10f.
5 Quoted in AI 2001a, 11.
6 For the information on his death, AI 2001a, 11f.
7 For the information on his death, AI 2001a, 12f. See also Stein 2001, 6f.
8 AI 2001a, 13.
9 For the information on his death, AI 2001a, 13–15.

armed Israeli soldiers standing a couple of metres from the car while he slowly opened the door. The soldiers' gunshots also severely injured three of the passengers, one of whom later died. The statement presented by the IDF after the killing reads: 'During the attempted arrest of the Hamas activist at an IDF roadblock, the terrorist tried to fire the revolver that was in his possession. The force opened fire towards the terrorist, and killed him. In the exchange of fire two other Palestinians were injured, and another Palestinian was hurt from glass shrapnel.'[10] When asked by Amnesty International, the passengers consistently stated that there was no exchange of fire and that they did not see Hani Abu Bakra in possession of a gun.

On 31 December 2000, *Thabet Ahmad Thabet* was shot dead in his car, just after he had left his home for work.[11] Thabet Ahmad Thabet had been a Fatah activist and had been in detention or under town arrest orders by Israel until released in 1991. According to Amnesty International he was said to have been a peace activist and to have had many acquaintances among members of the Israeli peace-movement. According to his wife, Siham Thabet, he had even been criticized for supporting a normal relationship with Israel. At the time of his killing, the former dentist was working as a director in the Ministry of Health in Tukarem, gave classes at the university and was the secretary general of Fatah. When asked by the Israeli High Court of Justice, which Siham Thabet had petitioned after the killing of her husband, the Israeli administration, via a letter from the head of the IDF Operation Branch, explained that Thabet Ahmad Thabet was targeted as a 'commander of a Tanzim cell, who instructed his people where to carry out attacks'. They argued that this involvement 'removes him from the civilian category'.[12]

These cases of targeted killing, carried out during just the first two months after Israel adopted this policy during the second Intifada, give sufficient insight into that policy. This policy continued in subsequent years. Only some of the deaths in subsequent years, such as the killing of *Sheikh Ahmad Yassin*, elicited broad international media coverage. Other cases were covered in less detail, or not at all, by the international media. According to a list published by the Israeli human rights organization B'Tselem, a total of 252 Palestinians were targeted and killed between November 2000 and December 2011.[13]

The specific procedural steps by which Israel determines the object of targeted killings have not been made public. Based on what has 'emerged' as an 'over-

---

10 Quoted in AI 2001a, 15.

11 For the information on his death, AI 2001a, 15–17. See also Stein 2001, 7.

12 Both quotations in AI 2001a, 17.

13 For the statistics, see fn. 26 in the current chapter.

all sense of how these decisions are made',[14] the procedure involves several steps.[15] The intelligence agencies, often on the basis of agent or collaborator reports, provides a first selection of individuals whom they believe to pose a future terrorist threat. The agencies issue reports about the past and assumed future involvement of these individuals in terrorist activities. A group within the IDF, which includes military lawyers, evaluates the information and issues recommendations regarding who should be targeted; the cabinet takes the final decision. If approved, military forces act without consulting the defence minister or the prime minister unless a certain act of targeted killing could involve innocent casualties. Israel is said to have provided the Palestinian Authority with a list of potential targets and requested their arrest. Since spring 2002, however, Israel reportedly has carried out targeted killings without contacting the Palestinian Authority.[16]

Given the unofficial nature of the sources describing this procedure, concrete conclusions cannot be drawn as to who is involved in the decision-taking process or exactly how the victims are designated. It seems plausible to assume that the prime minister, possibly in consultation with cabinet members, takes the final decision, and does so on the basis of information provided by intelligence and military reports.[17]

It is worth taking note of some further aspects to do with these cases before turning to other examples of targeted killings of alleged terrorists. The human rights organization Amnesty International, after careful research, argues convincingly that in several of the cases mentioned above, arrest was a viable alternative to killing. This applies specifically to the cases of Jamal 'Abd al-Razeq, Hani Abu Bakra, and Thabet Ahmad Thabet.[18]

Amnesty International provides further evidence to support the belief that this viable alternative was available in other cases of targeted killing carried out by Israel. The organization argues that the Israeli army has demonstrated itself capable of exercising effective control by carrying out numerous arrests within the occupied territories, including the areas under Palestinian Authority juris-

---

14 David 2003a, 117.

15 The following account is taken from David 2003a, 117 f.

16 David 2003a, 117 f. For further brief descriptions of the decision-taking process, see also Byman, 2006b, 110; Meisels 2004, 308.

17 See also AI 2001c, 34; AI 2001b.

18 AI 2001c, 34–38; AI 2001a, 9 f. See also Amnesty International's statement with regard to the killing of Sheikh Ahmad Yassin, AI 2004.

diction as well as by other actions, such as the destruction of alleged Palestinian property.[19]

The facts indicate that in most cases of targeted killing, the person targeted was not on his or her way to carry out a terrorist attack, but was killed while going about daily business. In addition, many of these cases demonstrate the severe effects these targeted killings have on innocent bystanders. These effects could be attributable to mistakes or failed hits. Furthermore, the aim to avoid harming others is not always followed as strictly as official promises suggest.[20]

A case in point is the killing of the Hamas activist Salah Shehadeh. Referring to this incident, Commander Major General of the Israeli Air Force Dan Halutz said on 24 June 2003: 'We fired knowing his wife would be near him.'[21] The bomb, which was dropped 'on a densely populated neighbourhood of Gaza City' on 22 July 2002, killed 16 civilians in addition to Salah Shehadeh, injured 70 civilians, and destroyed six nearby houses.[22] The killing was later described by Ariel Sharon as 'one of the most successful operations'.[23] Two conclusions regarding official decision-taking may be derived from this description. The killing of innocent individuals was, in some cases, knowingly accepted. Additionally, the attacks took place not necessarily in remote areas, but in places where innocent people were likely to be hit. By choosing certain locations and weapons for the killings, those taking the decisions knew that uninvolved persons would die and accepted this.[24]

Amnesty International also provides reason to believe that harming other people is not necessarily avoided to the greatest possible extent on an operational level either.[25] But whether caused by the decision-taking or the realization of targeted killings, the most salient fact remains that innocent bystanders frequently die in targeted killings. According to B'Tselem, attacks up until December 2011 had claimed the lives of 175 Palestinian bystanders.[26]

---

19 AI 2003, 5f.

20 See, for example, AI 2003, 7.

21 Quoted in AI 2003, 7.

22 AI 2003, 7. Salah Shehadeh is also referred to as Salah Shehada. Daniel Byman (2006a) states that four civilians were killed. He also states that the action was called off several times in order to avoid civilian casualties and stresses the failure to achieve this aim when the operation was finally carried out on 22 July 2002.

23 Quoted in AI 2003, 7.

24 For further examples of constellations in which the use of the weapon and the place where the person is attacked make injury to civilians more than likely, see AI 2003, 7f.

25 See, for example, the report on the killing of Hani Abu Bakra. AI 2001a, 13–15.

26 Statistics available at the internet page of B'Tselem: http://www.btselem.org/English/Statistics/Casualties.asp, retrieved 5 March 2011. The names of the targeted Palestinians are

Israel's current campaign of targeted killings is not the first example of the practice in Israel's history. Apart from a few isolated reported incidents,[27] another campaign of targeted killings carried out by Israel took place in the wake of the terrorist attacks on the Israeli Olympic team in Munich that began on 5 September 1972.[28]

This early series of targeted killings was directed against members of Black September, which was responsible for the Munich attacks. The targets were, however, not limited to those involved in the attacks in Munich, but included other people thought to be involved in terrorism more generally. It has been argued that active verbal support for violence was sometimes regarded as sufficient involvement.[29] Moreover, it has been argued that some individuals who were killed for being involved in the planning or execution of the attacks in Munich – although likely to be involved in some terrorist activity – had not directly or even indirectly been involved in those attacks in Munich.[30]

In the wake of Munich, Prime Minister Golda Meir authorized the draft of a reaction plan. As Prime Minister, she decided whether a certain person should be killed or not. Several members of the cabinet, however, were also involved in the

---

listed at http://www.btselem.org/English/Statistics/Casualties_Data.
asp?Category=19&region=TER, retrieved 5 March 2011. The names of all Palestinians who died in the course of a targeted killing, including those who were objects of the action and those who were bystanders, are listed at http://www.btselem.org/English/Statistics/Casualties_Data.asp?Category=17&region=TER, retrieved 5 March 2011.

27 For example, the killing of *Sheik Abbas Moussawi*, the leader of Hizbollah, on 16 February 1992, or the killing of *Rida Yassin*, also a Hizbollah leader, three years later. For both cases, see Geraghty/Leigh 2002. Steven David (2003, 116 f.) also mentions the killing of Fathi Shikaki, head of Islamic Jihad, which was carried out in October 1995 in Malta, the killing of Yahya Ayyash, who allegedly was a skilled bomb maker, in January 1996 in Gaza, and the plan to kill the head of Hamas's political bureau in Amman, Khaled Meshal, which was supposed to take place in September 1997. See also Stahl 2010, 115.

28 Other cases of targeted killing had taken place prior to this campaign, yet these acts were reportedly few in number and isolated. The details of these cases are known, but, as far as I have been able to discover, they were not reported on in any great detail. Amnesty International (2003, 2) states that '[i]t is important to note that Israel has repeatedly used such practices for many years prior to the outbreak of the current uprising/*intifada*'. It is not clear which cases they are referring to. Aaron Klein (2005, 106/109) also mentions a few incidents, but does not provide any detail. In view of the lack of information, it is not clear what kind of force these cases involved. As a result, I am not able to determine whether these killings were targeted killing as I understand the term. Given that I seek to provide insight into different states' actual practices of targeted killing and its implications, it sufficed for my purpose to look at the cases I am addressing here.

29 Klein 2005, 137, see also 158.

30 Klein 2005, 246. See also details on the individual targeted killings below.

decision-making process. For the operational plan, a covert unit was created within the Mossad, the different sub-units of which would plan and carry out most of the killings, from 1976 onwards in a reorganized form.[31]

The Palestinian *Wael Zu'aytir*[32] was the first to be killed. He was shot dead by two Mossad agents in the entrance hall of his home in Rome on 16 October 1972.[33] Major General Aharon Yariv, who after retiring as head of Military Intelligence became the Prime Minister's personal advisor on terrorism, later stated in a radio interview that, as far as he remembered, Wael Zu'aytir was to some extent involved in terrorist support activities.[34] Zu'aytir was reportedly neither directly nor indirectly involved in the attacks in Munich. Aaron Klein holds that 'uncorroborated and improperly cross-referenced intelligence information tied him to the support network of Black September in Rome'.[35]

Mahamoud Hamshari,[36] who worked as a PLO representative in Paris, died of injuries incurred when an explosive attached to his telephone detonated in his home in Paris on 8 September 1972. The Israeli intelligence service considered him to be an active supporter of the military wing of the PLO and to be involved in the attack on a Swiss Air flight from Switzerland to Israel on 21 February 1970 in which over 50 people were killed. They also believed him to have been indirectly involved in a planned assassination of the Israeli Prime Minister David Ben-Gurion in May 1969. Moreover, they are reported to have been convinced that Black September stored arms in his apartment.[37]

On 25 January 1973 *Hussain Abu-Khair*[38] was killed by a bomb attached to his bed in a hotel in Nicosia, Cyprus. Hussain Abu-Khair is reported to have been the liaison between Fatah and the Soviet intelligence service KGB.[39]

The Iraqi *Basil Al-Kubnaisi*[40] was shot by two Mossad agents on a street in Paris on 6 April 1973. He was reportedly not affiliated with Black September or

---

31 For details on the developments, see Klein 2005, 97–109/203.

32 Also referred to as Wael Zwaiter, see Ravi/Melman 1990, 186, and Ostrovsky/Hoy 1991, 179; or as Wadal Adel Zwaiter, see Tinnin 1977, 87.

33 Klein 2005, 118–124. See also Ostrovsky/Hoy 1991, 179; Ravi/Melman 1990, 186; Tinnin 1977, 87–90.

34 Klein 2005, 122f.

35 Klein 2005, 123.

36 Also referred to as Mahmoud Hamchari, see Ostrovsky/Hoy 1991, 179.

37 Klein 2005, 130f. See also Ostrovsky/Hoy 1991, 179; Tinnin 1977, 92–94.

38 Also referred to as Hussein Al Bashir, see Ostrovsky/Hoy 1991, 179, or as Hussein Abad Al Chir, see Tinnin 1977, 96.

39 Klein 2005, 137f. See also Ostrovsky/Hoy 1991, 179; David Tinnin (1977, 96) reports the attack to have taken place on 24 January.

40 Also referred to as Basil Al Kubaissi, see Tinnin 1977, 102.

involved in the attack in Munich in 1972. But according to Mossad intelligence, he was actively aiding the PFLP with terror attacks. For example, he was believed to have been involved in the preparation of an attack that was meant to take place at JFK International Airport in New York City on 6 March 1973, the day the prime minister of Israel was to arrive. He was moreover held to having been involved in planning the attack at Lod Airport in 1972.[41]

The next operation took place three days later, in the night between 9 and 10 April 1973 in Beirut. It was not carried out by the Mossad alone but in co-operation with a unit from the IDF. The operation targeted *Muhammad Yussef Najar,* also known as Abu-Yussef,[42] *Kamal Adwan,* and *Kamal Nasser.* Muhammad Yussef Najar is reported to have been involved in the founding of Fatah and to have been second-in-command when he was targeted.[43] Kamal Adwan reportedly commanded a unit of Fatah, which was held responsible for several terrorist attacks.[44] They were reported to have been involved in terrorist activities against Israel since the late 1960s, which led Klein to the conclusion that their killing primarily served preventive purposes. While some authors describe Muhammad Yussef Najar as the leader of Black September,[45] or him and Kamal Adwan as 'Black September commanders',[46] other authors claim that the link to Black September has only been based on 'several loose, uncorroborated strands of information'[47]. Kamal Nasser was spokesman for the PLO. All three were shot dead in their apartments, which were in two neighbouring buildings. The Israeli forces also killed an old woman living in one of the buildings and Muhammad Yussef Najar's wife, as well as several police officers. In addition, two Israeli soldiers who participated in the operation died and one was seriously injured.[48]

On 9 April another man who worked for the PLO was killed. *Ziad Mokhsi*[49] was killed by a bomb that was affixed to his bed in the hotel where he was stay-

---

41 Klein 2005, 152–155. Tinnin (1977, 102) reports that the Mossad believed Al-Kubaisi to be organizing the distribution of weapons and explosives needed for terrorist attacks in Europe.
42 Tinnin 1977, 104 (he reports him to be called Abu Youssef); he is also referred to as Mohammed Yusif Najjar and Abu Yusuf, respectively, see Ostrovsky/Hoy 1991, 179; or as Mohammad Najjar, see Ravi/Melman 1990, 188.
43 Tinnin (1977, 104) describes him as being head of Black September and the third man in command of the PLO and reports that Israel intelligence held him to be responsible for several attacks.
44 Tinnin 1977, 104.
45 Ostrovsky/Hoy 1991, 179.
46 Ravi/Melman 1990, 188.
47 Klein 2005, 158.
48 Klein 2005, 157–170. See also Ravi/Melman 1990, 188 f.; Tinnin 1977, 103–105.
49 Also referred to as Zaiad Muchasi, see Tinnin 1977, 102.

ing in Cyprus. There is doubt that Ziad Mokhsi was somehow involved in the attacks in Munich, and it has been argued that he was killed because his position as a PLO representative often required that he become involved in the preparation of attacks.[50]

Two days later *Moussa Abu-Zaiad* was killed by the same means in his hotel room in Athens. Moussa Abu-Zaiad is reported to have been in Athens to carry out a terrorist attack.[51]

On 13 June 1973 *Abed Al-Hamid Shibi* and *Abed Al-Hadi Naka'a*[52] were attacked while sitting in a car in the city centre of Rome. It has been reported that this attack was carried out in order to prevent an attack on the offices of the airline El Al, which were close to where the car was parked. The two men died of injuries sustained in the explosion.[53]

On 28 June 1973 the Palestinian *Muhammad Boudia* was killed in Paris by a bomb hidden in his car seat. Muhammad Boudia is reported to have been working for different Palestinian organizations and groups such as the PFLP and Black September as well as having been involved in several attacks in various locations in Europe, such as those on oil facilities in Rotterdam (1971) and in Trieste (1972). Arguably, he was targeted not for purported involvement in the attacks in Munich, but because of his other associations.[54]

On 21 July 1973 Israeli agents in Norway sought to kill Palestinian Ali Hassan Salameh,[55] who was held to be one of the key figures in Black September and the attacks in Munich. The Mossad unit killed *Achmed Bouchiki*, a Moroccan who worked in Lillehammer as a waiter and had nothing to do with terrorism, after mistaking him for Ali Hassan Salameh.[56]

Ali Hassan Salameh was himself killed almost six years later, on 22 January 1979 in Beirut. He died of injuries he had received from an explosion detonated next to his car. The explosion also killed several of his bodyguards. He was involved in several attacks on Israel and in several countries in Europe. Conflicting

---

50 Klein 2005, 171f. See also Tinnin 1977, 102.

51 Klein 2005, 172f.

52 Also referred to as Abdel Hamid Shibi and Abdel Hadi Nakaa, see Tinnin 1977, 106.

53 Klein 2005, 173. The description does not make clear whether the explosion came from a bomb attached to the car or from some other source. Also referred to as Abdel Hamid Shibi and Abdel Hadi Nakaa, see Tinnin 1977, 106.

54 Klein 2005, 178–182. See also Ostrovsky/Hoy 1991, 202–205; Tinnin 1977, 106–108.

55 Also referred to as Abu Hassan, see Ostrovsky/Hoy 1991, 185.

56 Klein 2005, 184–198. See also Ostrovsky/Hoy 1991, 205f.; Ravi/Melman 1990, 189–192; Tinnin, 1977, 109–187/200–208.

statements exist as to whether he was involved in the Munich attacks, which reportedly was the main reason Israeli forces targeted him.[57]

After the killing of Achmed Bouchiki in Lillehammer, the targeted killings declined in number and frequency. This is true of the remaining time Golda Meir occupied the office of prime minister (until 1974) as well as of the terms of her successors until the practice of targeted killing was resurrected in November 2000.[58]

The series of targeted killings outlined above, which was begun in response to the attacks in Munich in 1972, seems to have been driven by several aims. It is not possible to distinguish among the aims that prompted each individual act.[59] This is especially true because several aims may have played intertwined roles in prompting many of the attacks. However, these examples above comprise both responsive and defensive targeted killings. More specifically, various accounts of the campaign clearly identify three crucial aims: prevention, or more generally defence, deterrence, and revenge.[60] Deterrence, of course, can be understood as a form of prevention. As addressed above, however, with regard to the targeted individual it is responsive rather than defensive.

The defensive intention behind the targeting of individuals involved in the attacks in Munich in 1972 is clearly expressed in several official statements. Klein, for example, quotes from a speech Golda Meir gave to the Knesset after she had received the plan for combating Palestinian terrorism, the creation of

---

57 Klein 2005, 211–222; Ostrovsky/Hoy 1991, 179; Ravi/Melman 1990, 189.

58 One case is reported to have taken place on 30 March 1978, when *Wadi Haddad*, a Palestinian who was charged with several airline hijackings and other attacks throughout the world, died of poisoning, which was reportedly added to his food by a Mossad agent (Klein 2005, 205–208). *Zuhir Mokhsan*, who headed the Palestinian organization A-Tzaika, was shot dead in his apartment building in Cannes on 25 July 1979 (Klein 2005, 209). On 28 October 1995 the head of the Palestinian Islamic Jihad, *Fatkhi Shkaki*, was shot dead in Malta (Klein 2005, 226 f.).

59 This is mainly due to the lack of detailed information on this issue. Moreover, given that prevention is certainly more publicly acceptable than revenge, it is not clear how public statements could be interpreted, especially with regard to the fact that different individuals involved in a single attack may have had different aims, or that several aims combined may have led to the act.

60 Klein 2005, 100–109/155/245, see also 141/157 f./164/245. Klein suggests that further factors may have played a role at some stage, including the fact that the particular person designated a terrorist was relatively easy to target since he was not a key figure. (This suggestion is also made by David B. Tinnin (1977, e.g. 89).) With regard to the killing of Ali Hassan Salameh Klein (2005, 220) reports senior Mossad officers wanting 'to close the circle'. He describes them as wanting to 'set the record straight after the disaster in Lillehammer'. See also Ravi/Melman 1990, 191 f.; Klein 2005, 141.

which she had authorized in September 1972: 'Wherever a plot is being woven, wherever people are planning to murder Jews and Israelis – that is where we need to strike.'[61] An Ex-Mossad officer is quoted: 'The goal was to intercept and prevent. We checked what he had done in the past, and what damage he could inflict in the future. We acted according to this analysis.'[62] Golda Meir reportedly said to the Knesset: 'It went all perfectly. We killed the murderer before they could murder again.'[63]

The sources on and documentation detailing Israel's policy strongly suggest that Israel also sought revenge for past terrorist deeds.[64] The facts of the cases themselves already seem to suggest this. The goal of *killing* all of the people identified as involved rather than arresting them seems to support this presumption as well – the victims were often killed in settings which, given the close contact the agents had with their victims, seem to have allowed for the possibility of arrest. Motivation by a sense of vengeance as opposed to prevention is also suggested by the aim of killing everyone involved in the Munich attacks rather than differentiating among those who were likely to be involved in future attacks from those who were less likely. The words which Klein attributes to Golda Meir also suggest this: 'I've decided to pursue each and every one of them. Not one of the people involved in any way will be walking around on this earth for much longer. We will chase them till the last.'[65]

A few additional points should be noted before turning to other campaigns of targeted killings. It appears that Israel took more care against involving innocent bystanders during the series of targeted killings that began in 1972 than it has done in recent targeted killings.[66] Death and injury of bystanders was nevertheless not successfully avoided completely. Along with the 16 people detailed

---

61 Quoted in Klein 2005, 106.
62 Quoted in Klein 2005, 133.
63 Translated by myself from Tinnin 1977, 106.
64 George Jonas' book *Vengeance* (2005), on which the film *Munich* by Steven Spielberg is largely based, primarily highlights this aspect. So do Victor Ostrovsky and Claire Hoy (1991, 178 f.), Dan Ravi and Yossi Melman (1990, 183–186, see also 188/192) and Adam Stahl (2010, 114). Other authors describe prevention and deterrence to have played a role. They, however, do not neglect that revenge played a role as a motivating factor in the campaign. Klein, for example, writes that it is likely that none of the documents produced by the government, the Mossad, the Shabak or Military Intelligence would include the term 'revenge'. Yet he asserts that revenge, to a certain extent, motivated every official involved. See Klein 2005, 107–109, see also 138/228/245.
65 Klein 2005, 100.
66 It is repeatedly reported that avoiding harm to people other than those who are targeted was a basic rule of operation. See, for example, Klein 2005, 107/179, see also 212.

above, who were targeted after the attacks in Munich, at least four people, including two Israeli soldiers, died, as did bodyguards (Beirut, January 1979) and police officers (Beirut, April 1973) of indeterminate number. At least one person (Beirut, April 1973) was seriously injured. Israel also killed a person whose identity had been mistaken by intelligence officers. In addition, Israel targeted individuals in several different countries. None of these countries were informed about the action, either prior to or following the killings.

The first twenty-first century targeted killing of alleged terrorists carried out by the *United States of America* to be widely reported on by the media and human rights organizations took place in Yemen in November 2002.[67] Reportedly with Yemen's approval and cooperation, the CIA fired a missile from an unmanned Predator aerial vehicle at a car with six men alleged to be members of Al Qaeda. The victims included *Abu Àli al-Harithi,* who was believed to hold a senior position within the network and to have been involved in the attacks on the USS Cole in 2000 in Yemen. Some sources indicate that the CIA had not known who was in the car apart from Abu Ali al-Harithi.[68]

Statements made by several US officials point at the preventive or deterrent character of this action. US Deputy Secretary of Defense Paul Wolfowitz said that the killing was a 'very successful tactical operation, and one hopes each time you get a success like that, not only have you gotten rid of somebody dangerous, but to have imposed changes in their tactics and operations and procedures'.[69] US Secretary of Defense Donald Rumsfeld is reported to have commented that 'it would be a very good thing if [Abu Ali al-Harithi] were out of business'.[70] George W. Bush said:

> [Y]ou can't hide from the United States. You may hide for a brief period of time, but pretty soon we're going to put the spotlight on you, and we'll bring you to justice [...]. We're working with friends and allies around the world. And we're hauling them in, one by one. Some have met their fate by sudden justice; some are now answering questions at Guantanamo Bay. In either case, they're no longer a problem to the United States of America and our friends.[71]

---

67 For details, see Report of the Special Rapporteur on Extrajudicial, Summary or Arbitrary Executions, Asma Jahangir, 13 January 2003, UN Doc. E/CN.4/2003/3, paras. 37–39; AI 2005, 21f.; Hersh 2002; Pincus 2003.
68 McManus 2003.
69 Quoted in AI 2005, 22.
70 Quoted in AI 2005, 22.
71 Quoted in AI 2005, 22.

George W. Bush had reportedly authorized the CIA to carry out such actions shortly after the attacks of 11 September 2001.[72] Several other targeted killings followed without much attention from the media, though they did elicit the attention of human rights organizations and other institutions, such as NGOs and the UN Special Rapporteur on extrajudicial, summary or arbitrary executions. According to several sources, the CIA under the Bush administration clearly extended this practice over the following years, both geographically and in number. An official who worked for the CIA and the State Department expressed this very clearly when he stated that they 'have plans in place to do them globally'.[73] He continued by noting that the US government would not necessarily ask for the approval of the country in which the targeted killings were to take place.[74]

Barack Obama is reported to have dramatically stepped up targeted killings immediately after taking power in January 2009, relying particularly on unmanned drone attacks.[75] Members of the Obama administration have admitted to the use of targeted killings in the fight against terrorism on several occasions.[76] Obama did the same himself for the first time in March 2012.[77] Officials have on other occasions offered legal justification for the practice without explicitly admitting to its use.[78] The extent to which the Obama administration relies on the practice of targeted killings has never been made public. Nor has information about specific campaigns and details about the decision-making procedures. In 2009, Jane Mayer reported that the Obama administration has in place two drone programmes of targeted killings. One is run by the US military and publicly acknowledged; it reportedly targets enemies of the US military in Afghanistan and Iraq, areas which at the time of reporting were recognized as 'war zones'. The other programme is reportedly declared covert and run by the CIA in collaboration with a private company; it is not limited to particular countries but operates especially in Pakistan.[79]

Given the US administration's silence on this issue, it is difficult to determine exactly how many targeted killings have taken place. In January 2006 Josh Meyer

---

72 Report of the Special Rapporteur on Extrajudicial, Summary or Arbitrary Executions, Philip Alston, Addendum, 27 March 2006, UN Doc. E/CN.4/2006/53/Add.1, 264; Pincus 2003, 227.
73 Quoted in Meyer 2006.
74 Meyer 2006. See also McManus 2003.
75 Bergen/Tiedemann 2010, 3 f.
76 E.g. Harold Hongju Koh, legal adviser to the US Department of State, March 2010 (Koh 2010).
77 Darnstädt/Hujer/Schmitz 2012, 94.
78 Jeh Johnson, General Counsel of the Department of Defense, February 2012 (Johnson 2012).
79 Mayer 2009.

reports that US officials 'confirmed at least 19 occasions since September 11 on which Predator successfully fired Hellfire missiles on terrorist suspects overseas, including 10 in Iraq in one month'.[80] According to the study *The Year of the Drone*, conducted by the New American Foundation about targeted killings carried out by drones in Pakistan, 42 attacks between 2004 and 2008 and 252 drone attacks in the years of January 2009 to March 2012 have taken place.[81] A study by the Bureau of Investigative Journalism reports that 280 drone attacks have been carried out in Pakistan under the Obama administration as of 25 June 2012.[82] Although the exact numbers and details of individual cases of targeted killing carried out by the United States since September 11 are difficult to reconstruct, several shall be discussed below.

On or around 10 May 2005, the CIA killed alleged Al Qaeda senior member *Haitham al-Yemeni*. He was hit at the border of Pakistan and Afghanistan by a missile fired from a drone. He was reportedly under surveillance in the hope that he would be of use in establishing the location of Osama bin Laden. He was eventually killed to avoid losing track of him. When approached by the UN Special Rapporteur on extrajudicial, summary or arbitrary executions about this case, the Pakistani government denied the killing. The United States did not take an official position on the killing itself, but they did justify it in principle in a reply to the UN Special Rapporteur, thus, arguably, tacitly admitting to the killing of Haitham al-Yemeni.[83]

In order to hit *Hamza Rabia*, an Egyptian citizen who was held to have been involved in an attack on President Pervez Musharraf of Pakistan in late 2003, the CIA reportedly targeted a house in northern Pakistan on 5 November 2005. The missile was fired from an unmanned aerial vehicle. Hamza Rabia survived the attack, but eight persons are reported to have died, including Hamza Rabia's wife and children, the presence of whom the CIA was reportedly aware. Hamza Rabia is reported to have been killed in a second attack, which took place on 1 December 2005 in Haisori, a village also in northern Pakistan. The missile, which was fired from an unmanned drone operated by the CIA, is reported to have killed another four people along with Hamza Rabia: the 17-year-old

---

80 Meyer 2006.
81 The study was conducted by Peter Bergen and Katherine Tiedemann and is frequently updated. It includes a list of the names of the individuals killed. The updated data is available online at http://counterterrorism.newamerica.net/drones, retrieved 19 March 2012.
82 http://www.thebureauinvestigates.com/category/projects/drones/ The Numbers are listed under the title *CIA Drone Strikes in Pakistan 2004–2012*, retrieved 25 June 2012.
83 Report of the Special Rapporteur on Extrajudicial, Summary or Arbitrary Executions, Philip Alston, Addendum, 27 March 2006, UN Doc. E/CN.4/2006/53/Add.1, 183 f.

son of the owner of the targeted house and the owner's eight-year-old nephew, as well as two other men, about whom no details are available.[84]

In the second week of January 2006, missiles fired by an unmanned aerial vehicle operated by the CIA killed 18 persons in Damadola, a village in northwestern Pakistan. Al Qaeda senior figure *Ayman al-Zawahri*[85] who is reported to have been the target of the attack, was not hit, as he was not in the village at the time of the attack. According to a written allegation sent by the UN Special Rapporteur to the US government, it has been reported that five senior Al Qaeda figures were among the victims. The UN Special Rapporteur's account states that these victims could not be identified because they had been removed from the scene shortly after the attack. The other victims are reported to have been ordinary Pakistani citizens. The Pakistani government issued a diplomatic protest, and Pakistan's prime minister is reported to have publicly condemned such attacks.[86] This was not the first error made during an attack. One is reported to have taken place as early as November 2002 at the Pakistan-Afghanistan border. The CIA is said to have been targeting Osama bin Laden. The victim, however, turned out not to be him.[87]

The killing under the Obama administration that has received the most extensive media coverage is the killing of *Osama bin Laden* in May 2011. Whether it can be classified as targeted killing is disputed. The US government initially stated that Osama bin Laden was killed in a firefight. Officials later clarified that Osama bin Laden was unarmed, though he would not have been shot had he surrendered himself.[88]

Another – officially acknowledged – targeted killing took place in September 2011. *Anwar al-Awlaki*, a cleric reported to have been strongly involved in Al Qaeda, was killed in Yemen while travelling in his car.[89]

---

84 The Pakistani government denied that the explosion that destroyed the house and killed the victims was caused by a missile, but claimed that it was due to explosives kept within the house. For details on the case, see Report of the Special Rapporteur on Extrajudicial, Summary or Arbitrary Executions, Philip Alston, Addendum, 12 March 2007, UN Doc. A/HRC/4/20/Add.1, 244 f.
85 Also referred to as Ayman (al-) Zawahiri, see Meyer 2006.
86 Report of the Special Rapporteur, Philip Alston, Addendum, 12 March 2007, UN Doc. A/HRC/4/20/Add.1, 245 f.
87 Meyer 2006. Meyer writes of two further Al Qaeda leaders who were killed by missiles fired from a remote-operated unmanned drone aircraft: Mohammed Atef in Afghanistan in November 2001 (see also Byman 2006a) and Nek Mohammed in South Waziristan in June 2004.
88 AI 2011, 1 f.
89 Mazzetti/Schmitt/Worth 2011.

The targeted killings authorized by the US administration share some aspects that characterise the targeted killings carried out by Israel. The killings not only claimed the lives of the persons targeted, but those of numerous bystanders. In some cases, the target was not even hit, but only bystanders were killed. In the time period between 2004 and February 2010, civilian deaths amount to 32 per cent of the total fatalities caused by US drone attacks in Pakistan according to the study *The Year of the Drone*.[90] It has been reported that in some cases the CIA knew about the presence of these individuals when they launched the attack and accepted that these people would likely die. Moreover, in at least one case the United States was reported to have targeted the wrong person.

Furthermore, all US targeted killings were carried out on foreign state territory and, at least in part, reportedly without the prior agreement of the state in question. The statements quoted above suggest that the killings were ordered with an eye to preventive and deterrent aims. Several officials are reported to have suggested that the targeted killings were intended to deter foreign governments and other groups from harbouring Al Qaeda members.[91] Statements issued in the wake of targeted killings, which stressed that the terrorists would be brought to justice, invoke additional considerations, such as the idea of retribution or punishment.[92]

Spain is known to have applied campaigns of targeted killing in its fight against the ETA. I will explore these targeted killings as a final example, since they illustrate the practice in a different setting. Two so-called 'dirty wars' took place between 1975 and 1987, the first in 1975–81 and the second in 1983–87.[93] Both of these dirty wars also comprised other forms of violence; still, targeted killings were crucial.

The first operation began under Franco, but it carried on after the dictatorship had ended. The operation itself and the network that carried out the campaign was apparently established by the intelligence service, SECED, which had been established to work against the resistance and which was subordinated to the prime minister. The individual acts were primarily carried out by death squads belonging to the organizational framework of the Batalión Vasco Español, the Basque Spanish Battalion. They carried out attacks both in Spain and

---

90 Bergen/Tiedemann 2010, 3.
91 Meyer 2006.
92 See, for example, White House, Ari Fleischer, Press Gaggle, 5 November 2002; or George W. Bush's statement referred to in fn. 71 in the current chapter. See also fn. 2 in chapter 7.
93 The following presentation of the Spanish involvement in targeted killings is mainly based on Woodworth 2001. See also AI 1996–2002.

in France. The second dirty war is much better researched than the first. Given the lack of information about the first dirty war, and since a focus on the second campaign will suffice for the purposes of this book, I will not elaborate further on the first dirty war.[94]

During the second dirty war, violence was almost exclusively carried out in French Basque Country and aimed at ETA members who evaded Spanish repression by taking refuge there. Spanish official agents engaged mercenaries, right-wing fanatics, and criminals of all kinds for this purpose, and created the Grupos Antiterroristas de Liberación, or in English, the Anti-terrorist Liberation Group (GAL). The GAL's activities were never official state practice, but Spanish officials in several institutions were involved: elements of both the Socialist (PSOE) government – the minister of the interior, José Barrionuevo, was, for example, convicted for involvement in the GAL activity – as were the Guardia Civil, the national police, as well as parts of the military forces. Although Spanish officials were suspected of involvement in the campaign from the beginning, and although allegations of official involvement grew in number,[95] investigations faced several obstructions and it took time to yield confessions. In 1985 the first individuals who had participated in GAL operations – mercenaries – were sentenced to prison.[96] Some mid-ranking members of the national police were charged in late 1988 and convicted in 1991.[97] These charges, however, did not reveal the structural involvement of elements of various Spanish institutions. It was not until the second half of the 1990s that members of these institutions of higher rank were convicted.[98]

The GAL carried out targeted killings. It also killed randomly, or kidnapped, tortured and killed their victims. The two latter forms of violence do not constitute targeted killings in the established understanding. In some cases it cannot be determined whether the victim was intended to be killed immediately or whether the GAL agents killed the person because he resisted an attempted kidnapping. In other cases in which individuals known to be ETA members were killed, it cannot be determined whether these persons were targeted, or whether the GAL activists sought to kill randomly.

---

94 For the details on the first dirty war, see Woodworth 2001, 44–59.

95 See, for example, Woodworth 2001, 177 f./185/189–196.

96 Woodworth 2001, 191.

97 For all details, see Woodworth 2001, 200–225.

98 For a detailed presentation of the developments, see Woodworth 2001, 174–404. He provides a detailed account not only of the individuals and institutions involved in the GAL's activities, but also of their reactions to allegations, and of the court investigations and judgments.

I point this out not to imply that one act may be legally or morally better or worse than the other, but to give a realistic picture of the GAL's activities. Without claiming to provide a comprehensive examination, I will give an overview of the activities of the GAL in 1983 and 1984, and, as far as is possible, differentiate between targeted killings and other forms of violence. The frequent killings carried out during this period are sufficient to present an investigation of an additional campaign of targeted killings of terrorist suspects.

The GAL claimed their first victims on 16 October 1983. They kidnapped *Joxean Lasa* and *Joxi Zabala*, two refugees and active ETA members in le Petite Bayonne. They tortured them and eventually killed them. Their bodies were found in January 1985.[99]

On 28 December 1983 the GAL shot *Mikel Goikoetxea Elorriaga* in front of his house in St-Jean-de-Luz in France. Originally from Spain, he had fled to France from the Spanish police, who sought him in connection with his active participation in ETA. He was active in the military wing[100] of ETA and is described as one of the 'ETA's top hit-men in the late 1970s and early 1980s'[101]. Mikel Goikoetxea Elorriaga died from his gunshot wounds on 1 January 1984.[102]

On 8 February 1984 the GAL shot dead *Angel Gurmindo Izarraga* and *Bixente Perurena Telletxea* in front of the latter's house in Hendaye. Both are described as highly involved ETA activists. Perurena Telletxea headed the commando within ETA that organized the activists' border crossing. Gurmindo Izarraga was a bodyguard for Domingo Iturbe Abásolo, who was ETA's chief of staff and known to be very close to Miguel Ángel Apalategui, who was responsible for a highly destructive attack carried out by ETA in the late 1970s.[103] Woodworth figuratively illustrates the role of the two victims by commenting: 'If the GAL's aim was to decapitate ETA, they were getting close to the jugular.'[104]

---

99 For all details, see Woodworth 2001, 72–75.

100 ETA consisted of two factions during that time. ETA came into being in 1959, to campaign for the independence of the Basque Country. Violence was used from a very early stage (1960) in pursuit of this aim. The armed struggle was intensified during and after Spain's transition to democracy. From 1974, two factions of ETA can be distinguished: the 'political-military' faction, which was in favour of pursuing their aims through political participation, and the 'military' faction, which continued to focus on violent action. When the leaders of the 'political-military' faction concentrated on political means only, most of the members of this group who still believed in armed action joined the latter faction, and from the mid-1980s this faction constituted ETA. Woodworth 2001, 451.

101 Woodworth 2001, 92.

102 For all details, see Woodworth 2001, 92–100.

103 For all details, see Woodworth 2001, 104.

104 Woodworth 2001, 104.

On 25 February the GAL killed the Spaniard *Eugenio Gutiérrez Salazar*, who belonged to an ETA commando that operated in Bilbao until a year before his death, when he went into exile in French Basque Country. He was shot from a distance while on the patio of a house rented by a group of refugees in Ideaux-Mendy, which was officially being used to teach Basque.[105]

Four days later the GAL carried out another attack in Hendaye. They killed *Jean-Pierre Leiba*, a French citizen who worked with refugees in Hendaye's railway station complex and who is not known to have had any connection to ETA or even strong political views about Basque independence. The GAL killed an innocent person.[106]

The following attack hit one of GAL's own men, *Jean-Pierre Cherid*. The bomb, which was reportedly meant to have killed a large group of ETA activists, exploded before it had been planted.[107]

The next victim of GAL was *Xabier Pérez de Arenaza*, a Spaniard who was indeed involved in ETA. He was shot dead near Biarritz on 23 April at a petrol station where he had stopped to refill his car.[108]

The next victim who died from GAL gunfire, *Rafael Goikoetxea*, was reportedly not very involved in ETA activities at the time he was killed, but he had previously carried out several actions such as robbery and was said to have commanded a unit of ETA for some time. He was shot while driving on 3 May near the village of St-Etienne-de-Baigorry. *Jesús Zugarramurdi*, who played an important role in ETA activities, was injured but survived the attack.[109]

The following attack, which took place on 15 June in Biarritz, did not resemble previous attacks in that it was carried out in a manner suggesting that the GAL was not concerned by the possibility of bystanders being hurt.[110] The GAL tried to kill *Tomás Pérez Revilla* and *Ramón Orbe Etxeberria* by detonating a bomb, which they had attached to a motorcycle, on a busy street outside a bar the two activists were walking past. Both Tomás Pérez Revilla, a former ETA leader, and Ramón Orbe Etxeberria, a refugee priest, survived the explosion. Ramón Orbe Etxeberria, however, died forty-three days later of a disease that the attack is said to have exacerbated.[111]

---

105 For all details, see Woodworth 2001, 106.
106 For all details, see Woodworth 2001, 107f.
107 For all details, see Woodworth 2001, 109.
108 For all details, see Woodworth 2001, 110.
109 For all details, see Woodworth 2001, 112f.
110 See also Woodworth 2001, 117.
111 For all details, see Woodworth 2001, 116–118.

The next attack carried out by the GAL caused only injuries, yet could have been even more destructive. On 10 July, a GAL agent tried to throw a bomb into a bar in St-Jean-de-Luz. The bomb bounced back from the window and only two of the refugees in the bar were injured from shrapnel and glass.[112] The target of the attack has not been determined, and it thus remains unclear whether the attack was a targeted killing. The incident, however, clearly shows that the GAL at that time was not concerned about whether their actions could injure innocent by-standers.

The brothers *Christian* and *Claude Olaskoaga* were shot on 18 November on their way to the village fiestas in Biriatou. Claude survived but Christian died. As they were not politically active, it was speculated that their killing was a mistake or that they happened to disturb GAL members who were waiting for someone else to target. Woodworth writes that it could also have been the case that, 'as the local French newspaper *Sud-Ouest* speculated, "some organisation" might now simply be picking targets at random, in order to create a climate of fear and mistrust in the French Basque Country'.[113]

On 20 November 1984 the GAL killed *Santiago Brouard*, a highly regarded doctor, radical nationalist, Marxist, and a senior figure within Herri Batasuna, a political coalition backing the military wing of ETA.[114] Two GAL agents shot him dead in his clinic in Bilbao.[115]

Only a few weeks later, the GAL targeted *José Ramón López de Abetxuko*, whom the Spanish media reported to be leading the units within ETA that were charged with defence against the GAL. No one died since the booby trap that had been affixed to his car was detected before it detonated.[116]

Also in French Basque Country, two more cars were booby trapped early in the next year. One of the cars belonged to *Christian Casteigts*, who did not have anything to do with ETA. The explosion seriously injured him and cost him both his legs.[117]

Not all of the actions undertaken by the GAL between the beginning of 1985 and the last attack, which took place on 24 July 1987,[118] can be classed as targeted killings. They targeted locations frequented by refugees living in French Basque

---

112 For all details, see Woodworth 2001, 118 f.
113 Woodworth 2001, 122; for all details, see Woodworth 2001, 121 f.
114 Woodworth 2001, 425.
115 For all details, see Woodworth 2001, 124–138.
116 Woodworth 2001, 139.
117 Woodworth 2001, 139.
118 The last attack does not seem to have been ordered by GAL superiors but seems to have been planned and carried out by members lower in rank. Woodworth 2001, 171–173.

Country, but the shootings often hit individuals randomly. Even if refugees who had known ties with ETA were shot, it cannot always be determined whether these persons were actually targeted specifically. However, definite targeted actions did take place. Over the course of the campaign's remaining operation, the GAL killed at least 14 individuals and injured at least 19.[119]

The GAL's targeted killings are marked by several interesting characteristics. With one exception, the killing of Santiago Brouard, the GAL's targeted killings were carried out on French soil. Several of GAL's actions hit the intended persons. In several cases, however, the wrong person was attacked and killed or injured.[120] Moreover, innocent bystanders were hit, wounded or killed.

To determine the aim behind the GAL's campaign would require extensive historical research which cannot be conducted in the context of this book. Several aims, however, have been elucidated elsewhere. Woodworth suggests that one aim was to 'convince' the French authorities to change their policies towards the ETA members who had found sanctuary in the French Basque Country. The Spanish authorities who issued orders to the GAL attempted to coerce the French into extraditing terrorist suspects and into taking action against ETA in French Basque Country.[121] It has also been said that the Spanish authorities sought to force ETA to enter into negotiations and agree to dissolve itself.[122] Another possible chief aim behind the GAL's operations was simply to end ETA's operation.[123] These aims seem to involve concerns about future terrorist threats, yet they are not necessarily defensive in the sense of seeking to prevent the targeted person from engaging in further terrorist activity and thus eliminate him as a future threat. Quite a few targeted individuals were described as no longer actively involved in ETA activity. They seem to have been chosen not with regard to their potential activity, but in response to their past activities.

The broad overview I have provided in this chapter illustrates that the issue of targeted killing of terrorist suspects is not only relevant to current anti-terrorist strategies. Moreover, it highlights the relevance of the different forms and cases of targeted killing that were outlined at the end of the last chapter.

---

119 For all details, see Woodworth 2001, 139 – 171.
120 To give one example for the several cases between 1985 and 1987 in which a person was attacked due to being mistaken for someone else: on 24 December 1985 the GAL shot Robert Caplanne, a French citizen who had nothing to do with ETA, because the agents mistook him for the alleged ETA member Enrique Villar Errasti. Woodworth 2001, 162.
121 Woodworth 2001, 168/170/411f.
122 Woodworth 2001, 412.
123 Woodworth 2001, 168.

It is difficult to precisely distinguish the aims of particular acts of targeted killing on the basis of a limited knowledge of the background of the targeted individual and the facts that triggered the decision to kill him or her. However, it seems that many examples can plausibly be described as defensive. Certain acts, e. g. acts carried out against individuals no longer known to be active in terrorism, however, seem to have been primarily responsive. Prevention, or more generally defence, will probably always prevail in public statements. Yet even in speeches or public statements, references to revenge or punishment can be recognized. They seem to have provided the incentive behind some acts and played a role in cases that also served defensive purposes.

The available facts and the settings in which the targeted killings took place, moreover, suggest that the set of examples of defensive targeted killings are dominated by those carried out in reaction to undeterminable future threats. Only one act was described as being carried out in reaction to a determinable terrorist attack. It is thus the only one which could possibly be described as exhibiting the characteristics of case 1 – that is, one in which the terrorists are on their way to carry out a determinable attack. Most examples, however, do not involve any reference to a determinable threat, and, although this cannot be definitely asserted, seem to fit the categories of case 3 or 4. In those cases, the individuals are targeted for their ongoing or past involvement in terrorist activity, which has indeed been established, but without evidence of current involvement in a determinable terrorist attack. Because I cannot establish what investigations preceded the killings, it is difficult to determine whether the case 3 or case 4 type is more prevalent.

2.2 Aspects relevant for the assessment

The key aspect of the following discussion can already be derived from one characteristic that is necessary for a certain act of force to constitute a targeted killing. This was established in the first chapter: namely, that all targeted killings of terrorists involve the targeting of a specific individual. Central to any assessment of the practice, therefore, is whether states are justified in taking the life of this particular individual.

The short presentation above of various campaigns of targeted killings of alleged terrorists illustrates additional aspects that must be taken into account if the justifiability of the targeted killing of terrorists is to be assessed in light of how this practice is applied. Although these additional aspects are not constitutive of targeted killings, they are involved in the practice or follow from it. Since this book aims to engage in a discussion of the justifiability of the practice in real life, one has to take into account these effects and implications.

First of all, targeted killings of alleged terrorists in practice often involve not only the death of the targeted person, but also harm, serious injury, or death for innocent third parties. This may be because the harming side-effects are knowingly accepted; it may be due to careless conduct, or incorrect intelligence. In other cases, the action may be directed against an individual mistaken for the intended target. Again, this may be due to lack of diligence. Even if agents act carefully, however, this type of mistake may still occur owing to wrong or insufficient intelligence. Hence, a discussion of the justifiability of targeted killing of terrorists must not only account for the killing of the 'right' targeted individual. It must also consider whether, or to what extent, the harm or killing of innocent third parties affects justifiability.

A third aspect becomes relevant when terrorists are not operating on the territory of the state that feels threatened by them and carries out the targeted killings. States carrying out targeted killings often act on foreign state territory. Hence, under certain circumstances states may interfere with other states' sovereignty, adding an additional aspect that may be relevant to the discussion of the justifiability of targeted killing of terrorists.

There are further aspects to this issue that could be explored. The aspects addressed above, however, are linked to targeted killings of terrorists in a manner that gives them particular importance. I cannot assess, at this stage, which factors will have a decisive impact on the justifiability of targeted killing of terrorists. All will meanwhile have to remain present in the discussion. The first factor mentioned above, since it is involved in all kinds of targeted killing, is central. The other two factors, which are not necessarily involved in targeted killings, gain decisive relevance only if the targeted killing can be justified with reference to the targeted terrorist(s). Therefore, the question of whether terrorists may be deprived of their lives will be of particular importance to the following discussion. That harm to innocent individuals may result and the fact that targeted killings are sometimes carried out on foreign state territory, however, cannot be ignored.[124]

---

124 In light of the increased use of drones in targeted killings discussion of the moral relevance of applying such unmanned aerial vehicles could also be relevant for the moral assessment of certain targeted killings. Given this discussion's limited relevance for the practice of targeted killings as such, it will, however, not be addressed in this book. For the general discussion, see e.g. Sharkey 2010; Singer 2009; Strawser 2010; for the discussion more specifically regarding targeted killings, see e.g. O'Connell 2010; Schmitt 2010.

One additional point needs mention before I continue. I described the term 'targeted killing' as state force applied against both state and non-state agents. I argued that it is most frequently used to describe lethal force used against non-state agents alleged to be involved in terrorism, without the term itself incorporating such limitation. Equally, the understanding of terrorism I established does not limit terrorism to non-state use of force. Non-state agents as well as state agents can apply force in a way that meets the requirements for an act of force to constitute an act of terrorism. Hence, both state and non-state agents, under such circumstances, can be terrorists. It follows that the targeted killing of terrorists includes the intentional killing of specific terrorist state-agents as well as that of specific non-state actors.

This established, I will concentrate henceforth on the targeted killing of non-state terrorists only.[125] It is in this context that the question of targeted killing arises most frequently, and it is this type of targeted killing which presents the international community with the most difficult questions. Given that international legal warfare regulations focus to a large extent on inter-state relations, it is with regard to conflicts with non-state agents that commentators demand new legal regulations or propose new interpretations of existing regulations. The focus on the targeted killing of non-state terrorists, which henceforth will be implied when I talk of targeted killing of terrorists, thus allows me to address the most vivid points of discussion. The conclusions reached regarding the targeted killing of non-state terrorists are often applicable to the questions surrounding the justifiability of targeted killings of state terrorists, whereas the reverse is not true.

---

125 This involves terrorists whose acts can be attributed to a state. For details, see chapter 4.3.2.

Part II: **International Legal Justification**

3 Human rights

The targeted killing of terrorists intentionally deprives terrorists of their lives. Hence, to assess its international legal justifiability,[1] the compatibility of the practice with human rights law and, more precisely, with the right to life, must be determined.

The right to life is regarded as the most fundamental or supreme human right.[2] It was first included in the UDHR in 1948 (Article 3). As a legally binding norm, it is incorporated in a range of human rights treaties, both on an international level (Article 6 CCPR) and on a regional level (Article 2 ECHR, Article 4 ACHR, Article 4 ACHPR). The regional treaties are of great informative value in establishing the meaning of the right to life as set out in the CCPR. Given that the obligations set out in the regional treaties are binding only for certain countries belonging to a limited region, while the CCPR, due to its international scope, involves the most universal obligation,[3] the latter will be in the focus of this analysis. The right to life also constitutes international customary law.[4] Some authors even ascribe to it the status of *jus cogens*.[5]

---

1 In this part of the book (*International Legal Justification*) the terms 'justified', 'justifiability', and 'justification' refer to *legal* justification; legality refers to international law, regardless of whether the term 'legal' or 'international legal' is used; as legal acts are considered legally justified and *vice versa*, the terms '(legally) justified' and 'justification' are used interchangeably with the terms 'legal' and 'legality'.

2 This had already been stressed during the drafting of the CCPR. UN Doc. A/2929, Chapter VI, para. 1; referred to in Bossuyt 1987, 115. Also, the HRC frequently described the right to life as 'the supreme right'. See for example HRC, General Comment No. 6, para. 1; HRC, General Comment No. 14, para. 1; HRC, *Suarez de Guerrero v. Colombia*, (Communication), para. 13.1. For affirmative statements in the scholarly literature, see Boyle 1985, 221; Dinstein 1981, 114; Nowak 2005, Article 6, mns. 1f., with further references; Ramcharan 1985a, 4f. The importance of the right to life is established by several factors, such as life being a *conditio sine qua non* to the enjoyment of any other right. See Nsereko 1985, 245. The fundamental role of the right to life is also expressed in the CCPR itself. It is the only right within the covenant described as being an *inherent* right. See Dinstein 1981, 115. Its importance is also expressed by the present tense 'has', which is used in Article 6 instead of the otherwise common term 'shall have'. See Nowak 2005, Article 6, mn. 2. Furthermore, the particular importance of the right to life is expressed by the fact that the right to life belongs to the group of rights that may not be derogated from in times of public emergency (Article 4 CCPR). This is equally the case in the regional human rights treaties. The ACHPR does not explicitly state that the right to life may not be derogated from, but it arguably must be interpreted as including such regulation. See Ramcharan 1985a, 15f.

3 At the time of writing, a total of 167 states had ratified the covenant.

4 Dinstein 1981, 115; Ramcharan 1985a, 3.

5 See, for example, Melzer 2008, 212–220; Ramcharan 1985a, 15.

3.1 Peacetime

In peacetime, human rights law is the relevant international legal framework for assessing the targeted killing of terrorists. Outside of situations of armed conflict, which I will address in detail below, the justifiability of targeted killing of terrorists, hence, can be determined in the context of this area of international law, and more particularly in the context of the right to life.

Article 6 (1) of the CCPR reads: 'Every human being has the inherent right to life. This right shall be protected by law. No one shall be arbitrarily deprived of his life.'[6] Paragraphs 2 through 6 set out specific regulations regarding the death penalty. These may be ignored at this point, as they do not apply to the issue under discussion. The formulation of Article 6 of the CCPR followed an extensive discussion throughout the drafting process.[7] Among the main controversies was the question of whether the right to life should be formulated by exhaustively listing all possible exceptions to the prohibition of deprivation of life, which was the manner chosen for Article 2 of the ECHR, or whether a different, more general formulation should be used, abstractly formulating the right to life and possible limits to it. Different reasons may have played a role in the eventual acceptance of the more general formulation, which had been criticized as not representing a generally recognized idea, as well as being too imprecise and ambiguous, and therefore avoidable.[8] Certain arguments, however, had a prominent

---

6 The relevant articles of the ACHR and the ACHPR use similar wordings. Article 4 (1) of the ACHR reads: 'Every person has the right to have his life respected. This right shall be protected by law and, in general, from the moment of conception. No one shall be arbitrarily deprived of his life.' Article 4 of the ACHPR reads: 'Human beings are inviolable. Every human being shall be entitled to respect for his life and the integrity of his person. No one may be arbitrarily deprived of this right.' Both articles correspond to Article 6 of the CCPR in that they prohibit *arbitrary* deprivation of life. Article 2 of the ECHR lists the specific cases of deprivations of life that would be deemed lawful.

7 A summary (UN Doc. A/2929) of the drafting process of Article 6 of the CCPR in the Commission on Human Rights was submitted by the Secretary-General to the tenth session of the General Assembly. The drafting process of the article in the Third Committee was summarized in a report (UN Doc. A/3764), which the Third Committee submitted at the twelfth session of the General Assembly. Both documents are referred to in Ramcharan 1985b, 42. For a brief but cogent summary of the drafting process of the right to life clause of the CCPR, see Ramcharan 1985b and Boyle 1985, 227–234. See also Bossuyt 1987, 115–146, including a detailed listing of the relevant documents of the various organs involved in the drafting process.

8 UN Doc. E/CN.4/SR.90, pp. 7f.; UN Doc. E/CN.4/SR.98, p. 6; UN Doc. E/CN.4/SR.139, paras. 16/38; UN Doc. E/CN.4/SR.140, paras. 9/14/17; UN Doc. E/CN.4/SR.309, p. 9; UN Doc. E/CN.4/SR.310, pp. 3/13; UN Doc. E/CN.4/SR.311, pp. 3f.; all referred to in Bossuyt, 1987,

role. The United States, for example, argued that an exhaustive list interfered with the domestic jurisdiction of states.[9] It, as well as other states, argued on several occasions that it was impossible to exhaustively list all possible justified deprivations of life. Unenumerated situations may occur in which states could be fully justified in depriving individuals of their lives. Moreover, the listing, it was held, would emphasize the limitations to the scope of the right to life, while the more general formulation would stress the protection of life.[10] That states were not able to agree upon the question of when killing should be permitted also played an undeniable role in rejecting the idea of listing all cases not covered by the right to life.[11]

Given that, according to Article 6 of the CCPR, only *arbitrary* deprivations of life constitute a violation of the right to life, the question crucial for understanding the scope of the right to life, and hence the justifiability of targeted killing of terrorists, is when deprivation of life may be considered arbitrary. Two aspects of this question require clarification. First, this is a matter of the systematic meaning of the term 'arbitrary'. In other words, one must determine what constitutes an arbitrary act of killing. Secondly, one must assess the material meaning of the term and hence determine what specific acts are arbitrary, according to a plausible systematic understanding of the term.

The systematic meaning of the term 'arbitrary' was not specified when the covenant was adopted in its current form; nor did the HRC provide any definition in its general comment on Article 6 of the CCPR, or in any of its general comments[12] or communications issued since concerning the right to life. Two requirements can be distinguished, however, that must be met for an act not to be arbitrary: legality and justice. In other words, any deprivation of life is arbitrary if

---

122. UN Doc. A/C.3/SR.288, para. 14; UN Doc. A/C.3/SR.289, para. 7; UN Doc. A/C.3/SR.562, para. 9; UN Doc. A/C.3/SR.809, para. 28; UN Doc. A/C.3/SR.810, para. 25; UN Doc. A/C.3/SR.812, para. 29; UN Doc. A/C.3/SR.814, paras. 13/22/31f./47; UN Doc. A/C.3/SR.815, paras. 31f.; UN Doc. A/C.3/SR.817, paras. 2/11; UN Doc. A/C.3/SR.818. para. 14; UN Doc. A/C.3/SR.820, para. 31; all referred to in Bossuyt 1987, 123.

9 UN Doc. E/CN.4/SR.90, p. 9; referred to in Boyle 1985, 229.

10 UN Doc. E/CN.4/SR.98, pp. 2f./8–10; UN Doc. E/CN.4/SR.138, paras. 7/11; UN Doc. E/CN.4/SR.140, paras. 2/13/34/42; UN Doc. E/CN.4/SR.152, paras. 4f.; UN Doc. E/CN.4/SR.309, pp. 4f./7; UN Doc. E/CN.4/SR.310, pp. 8f.; all referred to in Bossuyt, 1987, 117. UN Doc. A/C.3/SR.810, para. 16; UN Doc. A/C.3/SR.814, paras. 6/21/33f.; UN Doc. A/C.3/SR.815, para. 17; UN Doc. A/C.3/SR.817, para. 22; UN Doc. A/C.3/SR.818, paras. 3/7/9/17; UN Doc. A/C.3/SR.819, paras. 20/29/49; UN Doc. A/C.3/SR.821, para. 13; all referred to in Bossuyt 1987, 124.

11 Boyle 1985, 223f.

12 See, for example, HRC, General Comment No. 14; or HRC, General Comment No. 31.

it cannot be justified in the context of existing legal regulations. Reference to the legal order, however, only renders deprivation of life non-arbitrary if the legal norm upon which the act is based is just.

This interpretation of the term 'arbitrary' is convincing with regard to the term itself. Any act guided by an actor's will rather than a set order of law is highly subjective, changeable, and hence arbitrary. Moreover, illegal acts contradict the basic legal requirement that official acts be predictable. That said, it is self-evident that acts carried out in accordance with legal regulations may still be arbitrary. This is the case, for example, with any act carried out in accordance with a domestic legal regulation allowing for discriminatory, racist or cruel behaviour. If such an act were not labelled arbitrary, state authorities could simply introduce legal regulations justifying unjust conduct in order to act in accordance with the right to life.

The suggested interpretation of the term 'arbitrary' also makes sense in light of the drafting history of the CCPR. The meanings given to the term during the drafting process by the different delegations spanned from 'illegally'[13], 'contrary to the law'[14], 'without due process of law'[15], 'fixed or done capriciously or at pleasure; without adequate determining principle, depending on the will alone, not governed by any fixed rule or standard'[16], to 'unjustly'[17] and 'illegally and unjustly'[18]. Such diversity of interpretation suggests that there was no agreement as to the meaning of 'arbitrary' that would require limiting the meaning of the term to 'illegal'. Moreover, it would have been easy to use the term 'illegal' instead of 'arbitrary' if that was how the term was commonly understood.[19]

---

13 UN Doc. A/C.3/SR.809, para. 20; all referred to in Bossuyt 1987, 123.

14 UN Doc. A/C.3/SR.811, para. 33; UN Doc. A/C.3/SR.812, para. 33; UN Doc. A/C.3/SR.813, para. 19; UN Doc. A/C.3/SR.814, paras. 1/29; all referred to in Bossuyt 1987, 123.

15 UN Doc. A/C.3/SR.811, para. 18; UN Doc. A/C.3/SR.813, paras. 31/43; UN Doc. A/C.3/SR.815, paras. 10f./33; UN Doc. A/C.3/SR.818, para. 19; all referred to in Bossuyt 1987, 124.

16 UN Doc. A/C.3/SR.812, para. 15; UN Doc. A/C.3/SR.813, para. 43; UN Doc. A/C.3/SR.61, para. 1; all referred to in Bossuyt 1987, 123f.

17 UN Doc. A/C.3/SR.809, para. 20; UN Doc. A/C.3/SR.812, para. 1; all referred to in Bossuyt 1987, 123. UN Doc. A/C.3/SR.15, para. 34; UN Doc. A/C.3/SR.817, para. 3; all referred to in Bossuyt 1987, 124.

18 UN Doc. E/CN.4/SR.310, p. 9; referred to in Bossuyt 1987, 122. These differences in the understanding of the term 'arbitrary' continued to be evident during the discussions of Article 6 at the Third Committee, see references to UN Doc. A/C.3/SR.809–821 in fns. 13–17 in the current chapter.

19 Laurent Marcoux Jr. (1982, 358–365) interprets the preparatory works to the CCPR as revealing a shared understanding of the term 'arbitrarily' as exceeding 'illegally', with regard to the term as it is used in Articles 6, 12, 17 and 19. It is not necessary to determine whether

The suggested understanding of the term 'arbitrary' also corresponds with how the term is used in the UDHR,[20] which is of some importance. That both documents, despite the different times of their adoptions, were drafted by the same bodies, which in several cases were comprised partly of the same individuals, suggests a certain degree of connection. This connection is all the more evident from the fact that the delegations involved in the drafting of the CCPR referred to the UDHR when arguing in favour of the use of the term 'arbitrary'.[21]

Finally, the interpretation and use of the term 'arbitrary' in the wake of the adoption of the CCPR support the suggestion that its meaning may not be limited to 'illegal', but that it involves an ethical dimension. The HCR, for example, applied such meaning in its individual communication concerning *Suarez de Guerrero v. Colombia*.[22] This understanding was also supported by the Committee of Experts, which was called upon to clarify the term by the Committee of Ministers of the Council of Europe. It concluded that 'arbitrary', apart from 'unlawful', included an understanding of 'unjust', 'capricious' and 'unreasonable'.[23]

What follows from this systematic understanding of the term 'arbitrary' for the justifiability of the targeted killing of terrorists during peacetime? The systematic analysis of the term already allows for the conclusion that the targeted killing of terrorists constitutes a violation of the right to life if carried out in contravention of existing legal regulation. The second question, then, is whether targeted killing can ever be just. In other words, the material meaning of the term must be determined to assess whether cases of targeted killing of terrorists con-

---

the drafters developed such a shared understanding during the drafting process. It is enough to show that they did not agree on the view that 'arbitrary' could be limited to 'illegal'.

20 Parvez Hassan (1969) and Marcoux (1982, 348–357) provide detailed analyses of the drafting process of the declaration and convincingly show that the term 'arbitrary' needs to be understood as comprising both 'illegal' and 'unjust'. Contrary opinion in Boyle 1985, 225 f.

21 UN Doc. E/CN.4/SR.140, para. 3; UN Doc. E/CN.4/SR.309, p. 4; UN Doc. E/CN.4/SR.310, p. 8; UN Doc. E/CN.4/SR.311, p. 5; all referred to in Bossuyt 1987, 122. For this argument, see Hassan, 1969, 229 f.

22 HRC, *Suarez de Guerrero v. Colombia*, (Communication). The HRC makes clear (at 13.2 and 13.3) that legality of an act in terms of national law does not suffice to render this act non-arbitrary in terms of the right to life. With regard to the deprivation of life with which it was concerned, it stated two reasons for why this is the case. On the one hand, the deprivation of life was arbitrary because it violated explicitly stated regulations within the Covenant (due process of law). On the other hand, the HRC referred to ethical requirements that deprivations of life need to meet in order to be acceptable. The HRC, hence, did not limit the meaning of 'arbitrarily' to 'illegally' but interpreted it in terms of both 'illegality' and 'injustice'. See also Joseph/Schultz/Castan 2004, 155–157.

23 See Nowak 2005, Article 6, mn. 13.

stitute arbitrary deprivations of life, regardless of whether they are permitted by existing legislation.

Whether a certain legal regulation is unjust must be considered in view of other international legal regulations, as well as with regard to principles enshrined in international law. Nevertheless, assessments of whether an act or the legal regulation it is based on is unjust must be open to ethical considerations, possibly exceeding such principles. This corresponds to the position the HRC expressed in *Suarez de Guerrero v. Colombia*.[24] Moreover, the UDHR recognizes this in Article 29. It states that '[i]n the exercise of his rights and freedoms, everyone shall be subject only to such limitations as are determined by law solely for the purpose of securing due recognition and respect for the rights and freedoms of others and of meeting the just requirement of morality, public order and the general welfare in a democratic society'.[25]

As addressed above, the drafters of the covenant disagreed on what arbitrary deprivation of life meant in specific cases; this was one reason they chose not to adopt a list of cases, but rather a more general formulation of the right to life. That differences still exist among states as to the interpretation of the right to life, and of arbitrary deprivations of life, is evident in the differing positions they hold regarding issues such as euthanasia or abortion.[26] Some common understandings, however, existed at the time of drafting or have developed since. For example, genocide and the killing of individuals in custody without due process of law are regulated separately in human rights law and are unequivocally accepted as incompatible with the right to life. Furthermore, the use of lethal force as absolutely necessary for the defence of a person's life under acute threat is unequivocally regarded as *not* constituting an arbitrary deprivation of life. With regard to the targeted killing of terrorists, no explicit agreement can be found. That said, certain established understandings as to when state agents

---

24 See fn. 22 in the current chapter.

25 When explaining the term 'arbitrary', Daniel Nsereko (1985, 248–255) focuses on legal regulations and principles in order to assess the arbitrariness of laws and behaviour. When he assesses specific practices, this focus does, however, not dominate his discussion.
Hassan, too, sometimes seems to make such an assumption, but overall, he focuses on the fact that 'arbitrary' comprises 'illegal' *and* 'unjust', and does not define the latter term. See Hassan 1969. See also Boyle 1985, 234.

26 The acts regulated by national legal regulations on these issues concern, probably almost exclusively, acts between private individuals. Differing regulations on these issues, however, concern the right to life, for it obliges states to provide positive legal norms to protect private individuals under its jurisdiction against arbitrary deprivation of life. For Art. 6 CCPR, see Joseph/Schultz/Castan 2004, 183f.; Nowak 2005, Article 6, mns. 3–6. For Article 2 ECHR, see Frowein 1996, mn. 3.

may or may not apply lethal force, which are germane to the question of targeted killing, can be identified. These established positions do not articulate their reasoning, but they include requirements for justified deprivation of life, which express internationally shared understandings of unjust deprivation of life. They therefore allow for an assessment of the compatibility of targeted killings of terrorists with the right to life during peacetime. Due to the nature of targeted killing, one must assess the practice first in the context of those shared understandings applicable to the intentional killing of individuals who are outside state custody. Secondly, because innocent third parties are frequently killed in the course of targeted killings, those positions concerning the unintended but foreseeable killing of innocent bystanders are also relevant.

A brief examination of the list of justified deprivations of life as set out in the ECHR is helpful in determining internationally shared understandings of unjust deprivations of life. The convention specifies the measures that may justify deprivations of life. Apart from legitimate death penalties (Article 2 (1)), Article 2, in para. (2), recognizes the following exceptions to the prohibition on the deprivation of life:

(a) in defence of any person from unlawful violence;

(b) in order to effect a lawful arrest or to prevent the escape of a person lawfully detained;

(c) in action lawfully taken for the purpose of quelling a riot or insurrection.

The ECHR includes an additional limitation to lethal use of force under such circumstances. According to Article 2 (1), the use of lethal force can only be justified 'when it results from the use of force which is no more than absolutely necessary'.

It has been argued that the instances listed in Article 2 (2) (a-c) of the ECHR may be regarded as not arbitrary in terms of the CCPR.[27] The *travaux préparatoire* support such findings with regard to circumstances (a) and (b), and arguably also with regard to circumstance (c). Proposed lists of justified exceptions to the right to life commonly included instances (a) and (b), and, as far as could be determined, also incident (c).[28] Moreover, such lists, frequently submitted by Great Britain, corresponded to the solution chosen for the ECHR, and they were not opposed on the grounds that they allowed deprivation of life in too

---

27 Dinstein 1981, 119. See also Nowak 2005, Article 6, mn. 14, with further references.

28 UN Doc. E/CN:4/365; UN Doc. E/800, art. 5 (6); UN Doc. E/CN.4/188; UN Doc. E/CN.4/204; UN Doc. E/CN.4/W.21; UN Doc. E/CN.4/W.23; UN Doc. E/CN.4/W.23; UN Doc. E/CN.4/365; UN Doc. E/CN.4/398; UN Doc. E/CN.4/417; UN Doc. E/CN.4/L.140; UN Doc. E/CN.4/L.130; UN Doc. E/CN.4/L.177; all referred to in Bossuyt 1987, 115–119.

many cases. They were criticized, instead, because it was feared that they could omit justified deprivations of life. Hence, a narrower, as opposed to a wider, interpretation of the right to life was requested. With regard to exception (c), members of the HRC questioned whether lethal police force would be justified in order to quell disturbances.[29] The fact that Article 2 (2) of the ECHR requires lethal force to be absolutely necessary, however, may lead to the assumption that deprivation of life, as justified under Article 2 (2) (c) of the ECHR, would be regarded as justified under the CCPR as well.[30]

In contrast, broad agreement that deprivations of life accepted under the CCPR are limited to the exceptions listed in Article 2 of the ECHR does not appear to exist. As established above, lack of agreement on this point was one reason for formulating Article 6 of the CCPR in a more general manner. It is difficult to determine how much more limited the right to life is to be understood under the terms of the CCPR. The HRC emphasized that the right to life must not be interpreted too narrowly.[31] Nevertheless, relatively few individual communications of the HRC refer to the right to life,[32] and they only partly apply to the killing of individuals not in detention. It is, therefore, difficult to identify an established common understanding of what measures exceeding those cases addressed in Article 2 of the ECHR are compatible with the right to life under the CCPR. A comparative legal study would be required to give a precise account of common understandings and developing tendencies; this would exceed the possible scope of this book. Court decisions, decisions of international bodies, the HRC in particular, regional treaties, and other international statements about limits to the use of force by states, however, provide some basic requirements for deprivations of life not to be in breach of Article 6 of the CCPR, allowing for an assessment of the legal justifiability of targeted killings of terrorists in terms of the right to life governing peacetime situations.

With regard to the deprivation of life in the course of lawful arrest and prevention of escape, the limitations found in the ECHR are probably not paralleled by international common understanding. Article 2 (2) (b) of the ECHR is commonly understood to apply only to unintentional deprivations of life.[33] In light

---

29 Dinstein 1981, 129; Robertson 1968/1967, 30 f.
30 See also Nowak 2005, Article 6, mn. 14.
31 See, for example, HRC, General Comment No. 6, paras. 1/5.
32 Compare Nowak 2005, Article 6, mns. 12 – 17; Joseph/Schultz/Castan 2004, 154 – 193.
33 Frowein 1996, mn. 12; Grabenwarter 2005, mn. 14, p. 129. European Commission of Human Rights in *Farrell v. United Kingdom* indicates a different interpretation. The soldiers shot at the applicant's husband with the intention of killing him (European Commission of Human Rights, *Farrell v. United Kingdom*, p. 97), and the Commission, when deciding on the

of the fact that arrest or prevention from escape is the goal, which simply cannot be achieved by killing the individual concerned, this seems to be the only sensible way of understanding the provision. It is uncertain, however, whether this view is shared internationally. The HRC's decision in *Suarez de Guerrero v. Colombia* seems to indicate that intentional deprivations of life in the course of lawful arrest or the prevention of escape could also be justified.[34]

That said, one common understanding of the limits of *non*-arbitrary deprivation of life, which applies to the assessment of targeted killing of terrorists, is that deprivations of life must meet the proportionality requirement in order to not be arbitrary. This requirement is understood in a strict sense within the human rights context.[35] It allows for several conclusions that are crucial to the assessment of targeted killing of terrorists.

Proportionality requires first that the intended aim justify the use of lethal force. This, according to what seems to be an established understanding, limits the use of lethal force that is directed against individuals not in detention and is not based on an appropriate court decision to law enforcement: deprivations of life must either be carried out with the *direct* purpose of compelling behaviour in accordance with the law, i.e. preventing violations of the law, or it must be part of such *direct* law enforcement measure, i.e. occurring in the course of it. All deprivations of life that fail to meet this requirement are to be regarded as extrajudicial killings and extrajudicial executions, and, by definition, they are in breach of Article 6 of the CCPR. By prohibiting lethal force which is not based on an appropriate court decision, directed against individuals not in detention, and carried out for the purpose of revenge, punishment and deterrence, this dis-

---

admissibility of the applicant's complaint that her husband's killing violated Article 2 of the Convention, 'considers that the complaint that the killing of the applicant's husband was a breach of Article 2 of the Convention raises several issues of facts and of the interpretation of Article 2 of the Convention, mainly as to whether "the use of force was no more than absolutely necessary in order to effect a lawful arrest" (Article 2 (2) (b))'. (European Commission of Human Right, *Farrell v United Kingdom*, p. 102).

34 In para. 13.2, the HRC states: 'In the present case it is evident from the fact that seven persons lost their lives as a result of the deliberate action of the police that the deprivation of life was intentional. Moreover, the police action was apparently taken without warning to the victims and without giving them any opportunity to surrender to the police patrol or to offer any explanation of their presence or intentions. There is no evidence that the action of the police was necessary in their own defence or that of others, or that it was necessary to effect the arrest or prevent the escape of the persons concerned.'

35 This understanding differs from the use of the term in international humanitarian law. See chapter 5.2. See also Watkin 2004, 33. The ECtHR stressed the restrictive meaning of 'absolutely necessary' in Art. 2 (2) of the ECtHR in *McCann v. United Kingdom*, (Merits and Just Satisfaction), para. 149. See also Frowein 1996, mn. 10.

allows one of the forms of targeted killing of terrorists I was able to distinguish in chapter 1. It disallows all responsive targeted killings. This has been explicitly affirmed by the HCR in its assessments of the practice of targeted killing of terrorists as carried out by Israel.[36]

Additional aspects of proportionality add further limitation to the justified use of lethal force. Proportionality with regard to lethal force includes the demand that law enforcement aims cannot be reached by means other than killing and that the deprivation of life not be disproportionate to the intended aim. Any measure that fails to meet this requirement constitutes an excess of force. These two aspects of the requirement of proportionality are expressed in several documents and decisions. It has been established that it is an inherent part of Article 2 of the ECHR, which allows for deprivation of life in the cases it lists only when they result 'from the use of force which is *no more than absolutely necessary*'[37]. Article 3 of the Code of Conduct for Law Enforcement Officials, adopted by the United Nations General Assembly in 1979, states that '[l]aw enforcement officials may use force only when strictly necessary and to the extent required for the performance of their duty'. The accompanying commentary explains that '[i]n no case should this provision be interpreted to authorize the use of force which is disproportionate to the legitimate objective achieved'.[38] Similarly, the Basic Principle 5 on the Use of Force and Firearms by Law Enforcement Officials expresses that firearms may only be used if no other means are available, and that they may only be used in a manner proportional to the 'seriousness of the offence and the legitimate objective to be achieved'.[39] Principle 9 limits the intentional lethal use of firearms to those situations in which it is 'strictly unavoidable in order to protect life'. In *Suarez de Guerrero v. Colombia,* the HRC based its finding that the deprivation of life constituted a breach of Article 6 of the CCPR on the fact that it was 'disproportionate to the requirements of law enforcement'.[40] The HRC reaffirmed the requirement of proportionality in its concluding observations on Israel of 21 August 2003, where it states, in reference to Israel's targeted killings, that '[t]he State party [Israel] should ensure that the utmost consideration is given to the principle of Proportionality in all its responses to terrorist threats and activities' and that 'all measures to arrest a person suspected of being in

---

36 HRC, Concluding Observations of the Human Rights Committee: Israel, para. 15.
37 Emphasis added.
38 Both quotations from GA Res. 34/169.
39 See also Basic Principles 4 and 10.
40 HRC, *Suarez de Guerrero v. Colombia,* (Communication), para. 13.3. See also para. 13.2.

the course of committing acts of terror must be exhausted in order to avoid resorting to the use of deadly force'[41].

Several conclusions can be drawn from this regarding the compatibility of targeted killing of terrorists with the right to life, as set out in Article 6 of the CCPR. In order for lethal force to be proportionate, the act to be prevented must be of particular seriousness, such as serious harm to other people or a threat to their lives. Moreover, the use of lethal force must be strictly necessary in order to prevent such harm. As such, if arrest is possible, or if a certain terrorist act can be prevented by means other than killing, the use of lethal force cannot be justified. Finally, the fact that other means must have been exhausted or be unavailable before lethal force may be used suggests that the act against which force is to be applied must be imminent or ongoing, since until this condition is met, it is impossible to defend the absolute necessity of lethal force.[42]

It follows that neither responsive nor defensive targeted killings can be reconciled with the right to life. That responsive targeted killing cannot be justified has already been determined. Defensive targeted killing which is not carried out in reaction to a determinable terrorist act cannot be justified, because it is impossible to argue that the use of lethal force is the last means available, and proportionate in degree to the planned terrorist act and thus to the aim of law enforcement, if it cannot be determined that a particular terrorist act has been planned and will be carried out. Defensive targeted killings of terrorists known to be involved in a determined act of terrorism cannot be justified if the possibility of preventing the act by means other than killing remains. Given that such targeted killings constitute use of lethal force based on a decision triggered by a concrete, though not yet imminent, threat, they are carried out before it can be established that there will be no available means of preventing the targeted person from carrying out the act, and they thus cannot be justified with reference to the right to life.[43]

---

41 HRC, Concluding Observations of the Human Rights Committee: Israel, UN Doc. CCPR/CO/78/ISR, para. 15.
42 For further discussion regarding this argument and the requirement of imminence, see chapter 10.
43 Killing could, as I have argued, also be justified if carried out in order to quell a riot or insurrection. Such a situation, however, does not correspond to situations in which targeted killings are carried out. In a riot or insurrection, the individuals against whom lethal force is directed are actively engaged in the offensive act. As I have shown, this is not, however, what the term 'targeted killing' refers to. Killings can also be justified if they are the last available means of effecting arrest or of preventing someone who is lawfully detained from escaping. Although this is not convincing, it arguably also includes intended killings. Again,

A final look at the four cases of targeted killing of terrorists enumerated in chapter 1 allows for a more differentiated picture. The killing of terrorists held to be involved in terrorism, but whose involvement in a determinable act has not been established (case 3), and the killing of terrorists who have been active in terrorist activity, though it has not been established whether they still pose a threat (case 4), cannot possibly be regarded as being compatible with the right to life. In the absence of any idea about the particular act to be prevented, it is impossible to argue that the use of lethal force is proportionate and the last means available. Provided one has sufficient details about the planned act, the proportionality of the use of lethal force against an individual actively involved in a determinable terrorist act (case 2) could perhaps be assessed. Nevertheless, it is impossible to argue that such an act fulfils the requirement that it constitute the last resort and be absolutely necessary. The only case that leaves space for compatibility with the right to life is the killing of a terrorist believed to be on his or her way to carry out a terrorist attack (case 1). This, however, is justifiable only from the moment when there remains no possibility of stopping the individual from carrying out his or her act except by the application of lethal force. This moment arguably only exists when the act is about to be carried out, i.e. imminent. That the use of lethal force may be justified in such situations is commonly accepted. Such a case, however, should no longer be described as a targeted killing. Although it may have developed from a situation I included in the definition of targeted killing of terrorists,[44] this is no longer what characterizes the practice. One must therefore conclude that the practice violates the targeted individual's right to life, both in light of the cases of targeted killing as they commonly occur in practice and in light of hypothetical cases.[45]

---

however, this situation does not apply to targeted killings of terrorists, for it represents a situation triggered by the actual situation, and not based on a prior decision.

44 See also chapter 11.

45 My interpretation of the internationally established limits to justified deprivation of life corresponds to the position that the human right to life allows killing only in situations of imminent serious threat, as it has been formulated with a view to targeted killing of terrorists, though without extended discussion. See Kretzmer 2005, 179; Nolte 2004, 117; Ratner 2007, 267. Michael Gross (2003, 351) reports that Israel, in the beginning of its current campaign of targeted killings, held a contrary opinion in arguing that the practice was justified in terms of law enforcement. Gabriella Blum and Philip Heymann (2010, in particular 160–164) seem to argue that international human rights law as it applies during peacetime does not require imminent threat for killings to be justified under certain circumstances. They continue to argue, however, that any possible justification within such peacetime framework seems to fail with regard to continuous and systematic use of targeted killings. Melzer (2008, 239) and Schmitz-Elvenich (2008, 254) agree that deprivation of life

One final remark is required. The prohibition on arbitrarily depriving individuals of their lives protects individuals not only from intentional disproportionate use of force, but also from unintended disproportionate use of force. The HRC affirmed this position in the individual communication in *Burrell v. Jamaica*.[46] It provided remarks on the killing of Rickly Burrell, a detainee who became involved in disturbances in the prison where he was interned. The HRC accepted that the state party did not intend to kill Rickly Burrell, on behalf of whom the human rights violation was reported. Still, the HRC argued, the state failed in its duty under Article 6 of the CCPR. It came to this conclusion, *inter alia*, because, at the time of the killing, there was no longer any danger which would have justified the use of lethal force by the wardens, who carried out the killing.[47] One may conclude from this case that unintended harm to innocent bystanders in the course of a targeted killing of terrorists must always be regarded as a violation of the bystanders' right to life. This certainly applies to non-intended killings of bystanders that occur in legally unjustified targeted killings of terrorists, given that in these cases, as in *Burrell v. Jamaica*, the use of force is not necessary. Having argued that situations in which the terrorist is targeted when he or she is about to carry out a terrorist attack cannot be described as targeted killings, this applies to all cases of the practice.

3.2 Armed conflicts

Although human rights were primarily drafted with regard to peacetime,[48] they also apply in times of armed conflict. This, of course, is equally true of the right to life. In the 1970s, when the applicability of human rights law to such sit-

---

can only be carried out in response to an imminent harming act, yet disagree with my conclusion regarding targeted killing. In both cases, this is due to their wide definition of targeted killing, see fn. 9 in chapter 1. For a more extended discussion, see also Ben-Naftali/ Michaeli 2003, 284–286.

46 This position has also been formulated by the ECtHR with regard to the protection provided in Article 2 of the ECHR. It asserted that the exceptions listed in the article justify intended killings as well as the use of force that unintentionally results in the death of an individual. The court thus implicitly stated that unintentional use of force not corresponding to these exceptions equally constitutes a violation of the right to life. See ECtHR, *McCann v. United Kingdom*, (Merits and Just Satisfaction), para. 148.

47 HRC, *Burrell v. Jamaica*, (Communication), para 9.5. See also Joseph/Schultz/Castan 2004, 160 f.

48 For a brief overview of the development of the laws of war in comparison to the development of human rights law, see Schindler 1979, 327–333.

uations was discussed for the first time in reasonable detail,[49] several authors rejected the applicability of human rights treaties to international armed conflicts[50] (separatist theory) by arguing that international humanitarian law and human rights law differ conceptually in several respects, that they deal with different questions, that they protect different goods, or that they grant different rights.[51] This position is no longer accepted in the scholarly literature,[52] and several counter-arguments are convincing in their assertion that human rights law applies in both non-international and international armed conflicts.

Most importantly, the applicability of human rights in armed conflicts is exhibited by the fact that the primary human rights treaties, which involve regulations allowing for derogation from human rights in times of public emergencies, explicitly exclude certain rights, such as the right to life, from the possibility of derogation.[53] The CPPCG (Article 1) and the CAT (Article 2 (2)) explicitly state that a state of war does not render the treaties inapplicable.[54]

Moreover, API and APII explicitly recognize that human rights may apply cumulatively. APII declares in the preamble 'that international instruments relating to human rights offer a basic protection to the human person'.[55] API in Article 1 (2) generally recognizes the possibility that 'other international agreements' apply to situations to which the Protocol may apply.[56] Even more explicitly, Article 72 of the API states:

> The provisions of this Section [Treatment of persons in the power of a party to the conflict] are additional to the rules concerning humanitarian protection of civilians and civilian objects in the power of a Party to the conflict contained in the Fourth [Geneva] Convention, particularly Parts I and III thereof, as well as to other applicable rules of international

---

49 For a detailed presentation of the developments of the discussion and a convincing analysis of the arguments, see Vöneky 2001, 273 – 290. See also Fronhöfer 1994, 57 – 60; Gabriel/Kälin 1994, 15/26 – 29; Kimminich 1979, 32 – 36; Schindler 1979, 334 – 336/345 – 349.
50 The main controversies surrounding the applicability of human rights treaties did not occur with regard to non-international armed conflicts, but with regard to international armed conflicts. Partsch 1965, 912.
51 In particular, Meyrowitz 1972, 1095 – 1101/1104 f.; Mushkat 1978, 151 – 156/161; see also Mushkat 1978, 157 – 160. Dirk Fronhöfer (1994, 58) addresses this position as dualist and traditional. Compare also Schindler, 1979, 346 f.; Vöneky 2001, 279 f.
52 For others Fronhöfer 1994, 58 f.; Heintze 2004, 789 – 798; Gabriel/Kälin 1994 15/27 – 29; Kimminich 1979, 29; Kretzmer 2005, 183 – 186; Meron 1995; Vöneky 2001, 282 – 290.
53 Article 4 CCPR; Article 27 ACHR; Article 15 ECHR. Although ACHPR does not state this explicitly, it may be argued that it comprises such regulation. Ramcharan 1985a, 15 f.
54 See also Vöneky 2001, 282 f.
55 APII Preamble para. 2.
56 Partsch 1965, 912.

law relating to the protection of fundamental human rights during international armed conflict.

These references show that it is recognized within international humanitarian law itself that human rights law applies alongside it.[57] This interpretation corresponds to the practices of both individual states and the United Nations, and has been confirmed by international courts.[58] When addressed by the Special Rapporteur on extrajudicial, summary or arbitrary executions, Philip Alston, regarding the targeted killing of Haitham al-Yemeni on the Pakistan-Afghanistan border around 10 May 2005,[59] the United States questioned the applicability of human rights law in international armed conflicts.[60] The United States argued that the issue exceeded the mandate of the Special Rapporteur because it had taken place during an international armed conflict, which was governed by international humanitarian law, and review of which was outside the Special Rapporteur's mandate. This response implies the position that international humanitarian law applies to international armed conflicts to the exclusion of human rights law. Generally, however, states do not deny the validity of human rights treaties when involved in international armed conflicts.[61] Furthermore, the United States has generally not held the position it put forth in the Haitham al-Yemeni case. As Philip Alston points out,[62] the American government had, for example, advocated for the applicability of human rights in international armed conflicts in its written statement to the ICJ in *Legality of the Threat or Use of Nuclear Weapons.*[63] This corresponds to the understanding that the ICJ presented in this as well as in other cases. With regard to the CCPR, as well as human rights conventions in general, it was explicit that, although subject to possible derogation with regard

---

57 See also Fronhöfer 1994, 59; Gabriel/Kälin 1994, 26; Vöneky 2001, 286 f.; Commission on Human Rights, Report on the Situation of Human Rights in Kuwait under Iraqi Occupation, UN Doc. E/CN.4/1992/26, III A und B.

58 For further arguments in favour of the applicability of human rights alongside international humanitarian law, see Commission on Human Rights, Report on the Situation of Human Rights in Kuwait under Iraqi Occupation, UN Doc. E/CN.4/1992/26, III A und B; Vöneky 2001, 286–290.

59 For details on this case, see chapter 2.1.

60 The communication is reproduced in UN Doc. A/HRC/4/20/Add.1, 342–358. It started with the letter of allegation by the Special Rapporteur on extrajudicial, summary or arbitrary executions on 26 August 2005.

61 Vöneky 2001, 283.

62 UN Doc. A/HRC/4/20/Add.1, 347.

63 Letter dated 20 June 1995 from the Acting Legal Adviser to the Department of State, together with Written Statement of the Government of the United States of America, 44–46.

to parts of their provisions, human rights apply in peacetime as well as during armed conflicts.[64] The Security Council emphasized as early as 1967 that 'essential and inalienable human rights should be respected even during the vicissitudes of war'.[65] Since that time, different bodies of the United Nations have repeatedly addressed the applicability of human rights law in international armed conflicts, confirmed it, and demanded its observance during such conflicts.[66]

Finally, the drafting history of the right to life clause within the CCPR supports this assessment. Deprivations of life according to the laws of war were included in several suggested lists of exceptions to the right to life.[67] These references only make sense if the suggesting state assumes that the treaty also applies in armed conflicts.

Another problem regarding the applicability of human rights instruments to armed conflicts has been seen in the scope of the instruments themselves, concerning both the extraterritorial applicability and the understanding of jurisdiction, and results from the wording setting out the applicability of the different human rights treaties. This has particular relevance for the CCPR. Article 2 (1) requires states to 'respect and to ensure to all individuals *within its territory and subject to its jurisdiction* the rights recognized in the present Covenant'[68]. With regard to non-international armed conflicts in which all individuals participating in the conflict are on the territory and in the jurisdiction of the concerned state, this wording presents no difficulties with regard to the applicability of the CCPR. Yet, this wording has been considered problematic with regard to armed conflicts when the individuals concerned are neither subject to the formal jurisdiction of the state party to the armed conflict nor within its territory.[69] The regional human

---

64 ICJ, *Legality of the Threat or Use of Nuclear Weapons*, (Advisory Opinion), para. 25; ICJ, *Construction of a Wall*, (Advisory Opinion), paras. 105 f.
65 SC Res. 237. See also Meron 2000, 268.
66 See, for example, GA Res. 2443 (XXIII); GA Res. 2444 (XXIII); GA Res. 2546 (XXIV); GA Res. 2727 (XXV); SC Res. 787; SC Res. 1041; SC Res. 1059; SC Res. 1083. See also the statement of the Special Rapporteur on extrajudicial, summary or arbitrary executions, UN Doc. A/HRC/4/20/Add.1, 347–349. See also Gabriel/Kälin 1994, 15; Meron 2000, 240/247/268; Vöneky 2001, 284 f.; UN Doc. E/CN.4/1992/26, III A.
67 See, for example, UN Doc. E/CN.4/188; UN Doc. E/CN.4/204; UN Doc. E/CN.4/W.21; all referred to in Bossuyt 1987, 116 f.
68 Emphasis added.
69 Schindler 1979, 334. Karl J. Partsch (1965, 912) is sceptical about the acceptance of the extraterritorial applicability of the CCPR among states in the future.

rights treaties encounter this problem to a more limited extent, as they may refer to jurisdiction, but do not include territorial references.[70]

That the CCPR only regulates a state's conduct within its territory is no longer tenable. An understanding of the requirement of jurisdiction that is too restrictive or merely formal is likewise unconvincing. An argument which is persuasive bases the applicability of the different human rights treaties on jurisdiction established through actual authority, which protects all individuals within the power or effective control of the state concerned. This approach was taken by the ECtHR with regard to the applicability of the ECHR in several cases.[71] It was also explicitly stated by the HRC in its interpretation of the CCPR. State parties to the covenant, according to the HRC, are bound by the covenant inside as well as outside their territory. The covenant applies, the HRC argues, when individuals are directly affected by a state party's action. For the purpose of the covenant, this is sufficient for the individual to be regarded as being subject to the jurisdiction of a given state.[72] Arguably, this position corresponds to a 'trend to-

---

70 Art.1 ECHR refers to jurisdiction; Art.1 (1) ACHR refers to jurisdiction; ACHPR does not explicitly limit the applicability to any of the terms.

71 In *Drozd and Janousek v. France and Spain*, Plenary, (Merits), para. 91 the ECtHR stated that '[t]he term "jurisdiction" is not limited to the national territory of the High Contracting Parties; their responsibility can be involved because of acts of their authorities producing effects outside their own territory'. For more, see ECtHR, *Loizidou v. Turkey*, Chamber, (Preliminary Objections). At para. 62 the court holds: 'In this respect the Court recalls that, although Article 1 (art. 1) sets limits on the reach of the Convention, the concept of "jurisdiction" under this provision is not restricted to the national territory of the High Contracting Parties. [...] In addition, the responsibility of Contracting Parties can be involved because of acts of their authorities, whether performed within or outside national boundaries, which produce effects outside their own territory. [...] Bearing in mind the object and purpose of the Convention, the responsibility of a Contracting Party may also arise when as a consequence of military action – whether lawful or unlawful – it exercises effective control of an area outside its national territory. The obligation to secure, in such an area, the rights and freedoms set out in the Convention derives from the fact of such control whether it be exercised directly, through its armed forces, or through a subordinate local administration.' See also ECtHR, *Loizidou v. Turkey*, Chamber, (Preliminary Objections) para. 64 and ECtHR, *Loizidou v. Turkey*, Chamber, (Merits and Just Satisfaction), paras. 52/57. The ECtHR in *Bankovic v. Belgium*, Grand Chamber, (Decision as to the Admissibility), paras. 59–82 formulated a different position and defended a far more limited applicability of the ECHR.

72 See, for example, HRC, General Comment No. 31, para. 10; HRC, *Lopez Burgos v. Uruguay*, (Communication), para. 12. See also Kretzmer 2005, 184. Cautious regarding the effects of collective acts of war, Nils Melzer (2008, 123–139) supports such understanding of jurisdiction based on an extensive study of case law. Dietrich Schindler (1979, 334) is of

wards interpreting human rights treaties as applicable not only in the national territory of a state, but wherever it exercises power, authority, or [formal] jurisdiction over people'[73]. This understanding of the applicability of the CCPR, as well as the regional human rights treaties, corresponds to the position the ICJ expressed in particular in its Advisory Opinion in *Legality of the Threat or Use of Nuclear Weapons*. The fact that the ICJ regarded the CCPR relevant to assessing the legality of using nuclear weapons in armed conflicts implies its position that the covenant regulates the acts of a state affecting individuals outside that state's territory and not subject to its jurisdiction as formally understood.[74]

Even if one defended a more restrictive interpretation of relevant human rights treaties, one must regard states to be bound to human rights law in situations of armed conflict. Regardless of the treaties, states can, but are not allowed to, violate the human rights of individuals, irrespective of where these individuals are, by customary international law. Otherwise it would have to be accepted that states are permitted to deprive individuals of their lives in extraterritorial situations to which international humanitarian law does not apply. This is not intelligible and contradicts the idea of the universality of human rights.[75]

Having established that both human rights law and international humanitarian law apply to armed conflicts, I am able to determine more precisely the relationship between these two legal regimes with regard to the right to life as set out in Article 6 of the CCPR. As the right to life may not be derogated from, it fully applies to any situation of armed conflict. In order to determine what constitutes an arbitrary deprivation of life during an armed conflict, however, international humanitarian law must be taken into account. It is unequivocally accepted that deprivations of life that are legal in terms of international humanitarian law do not constitute arbitrary deprivations of life in terms of Article 6 of the CCPR.[76] As was already declared during the drafting of the CCPR, 'to the extent that in present international law "lawful acts of war" are recognized, such lawful acts are deemed not to be prohibited by Article 6'[77]. In its Advisory Opinion in *Legality of the Threat or Use of Nuclear Weapons*, the ICJ explicated this interpretation when it stated:

---

contrary opinion with regard to the applicability of the CCPR. He argues that it only applies in the territory of the state concerned.

73 Meron 2000, 273. See also Meron 1995.
74 ICJ, *Legality of the Threat or Use of Nuclear Weapons*, (Advisory Opinion), e.g. paras 24 f.
75 Kretzmer 2005, 184 f.
76 Nowak 2005, Article 6, mn. 11.
77 Respect for Human Rights in Armed Conflicts, Report of the Secretary-General, UN Doc. A/8052, at 104 (1970); quoted in Meron 2000, 240, see also 266 f.

In principle, the right not arbitrarily to be deprived of one's life applies also in hostilities. The test of what is an arbitrary deprivation of life, however, then falls to be determined by the applicable *lex specialis,* namely, the law applicable in armed conflict which is designed to regulate the conduct of hostilities. Thus whether a particular loss of life, through the use of a certain weapon in warfare, is to be considered an arbitrary deprivation of life contrary to Article 6 of the Covenant, can only be decided by reference to the law applicable in armed conflict and not deduced from the terms of the Covenant itself.[78]

Two conclusions as to the justifiability of targeted killing of terrorists in terms of the human right to life in armed conflicts follow from the interpretation provided. First, given that the right to life continues to apply in situations of armed conflict, individuals are protected from arbitrary deprivation, even if, under specific circumstances, international humanitarian law left a regulatory gap as to their protection. In such a situation, the meaning of 'arbitrary deprivation' must be determined by considerations not directly referring to international humanitarian law.[79]

Secondly, all deprivations of life in situations of armed conflict regulated by international humanitarian law must be considered to be in accordance with the right to life. As such, the following discussion of the compatibility of targeted killing of terrorists with the laws of war will also provide a definitive answer as to the compatibility of the practice with the right to life in situations of armed conflict.

---

78 ICJ, *Legality of the Threat or Use of Nuclear Weapons,* (Advisory Opinion), para. 25. This role of international humanitarian law is affirmed in Art. 15 of the ECHR, which prohibits derogation from the right to life, 'except in respect of deaths resulting from lawful acts of war' (Art. 15 (2)) and 'to the extent strictly required by the exigencies of the situation' (Art. 15 (1)).

79 See also Vöneky 2004, 155. Although not explicitly with regard to the right to life, Meron (2000, 267) does express this considerations when he states that '[b]ecause human rights law, or at a minimum its nonderogable core, continues to apply in times of armed conflict, gaps in protection under the law of war can be filled in some circumstances. Thus, persons who are not protected persons during an armed conflict, because their government maintains normal diplomatic relations with the power in whose hands they find themselves, would still benefit from at least the nonderogable provisions of the Political Covenant if the state concerned is a party'.

4 Legal acts of war

The analysis of the compatibility of the targeted killing of terrorists with the right to life as it applies in peacetime situations seems to explain why proponents of the practice base their arguments predominantly on the laws of war: the laws of war generally allow for killing to a much greater extent than does human rights law regulating peacetime situations. Broadly considered, proponents draw upon the structure of the laws of war to justify targeted killings of terrorists by the laws of war in two manners. One line of argument describes them as acts of national[1] self-defence; another regards them as legal acts of warfare.

Legal commentators often treat these arguments separately and focus on one or the other. Commentators who make reference to national self-defence seek to justify states in their application of force in reaction to terrorist attacks. They often seem to believe this sufficient to prove that states are entitled to use force and thereby justify targeted killing of terrorists. Other commentators do not address the fundamental question of whether the application of force is justified in response to terrorist attacks, and, if so, under what conditions. They focus instead on international humanitarian law, arguing that it applies to the situation they are considering and asserting that it justifies the targeting of specific terrorists. This dichotomy relates to the division of the laws of war into *jus ad bellum*[2] and *jus in bello* (international humanitarian law). With regard to the division between these two areas of the laws of war, it makes sense to discuss these two strains of argument separately. In this chapter, I will focus on the moral defence of targeted killing as a legal act of warfare. Before presenting the main lines of argument and analysing them, it will, however, be necessary to offer an elementary statement about the relationship between *jus ad bellum* and *jus in bello* and about the (in)dependence of the two strategies of justification both based on the laws of war. Though elementary, this issue must be ad-

---

1 It is self-evident that one speaks of *national* self-defence in a discussion of self-defence in inter-state relations. Official documents on national self-defence, therefore, generally refer to 'self-defence' only. As the concept of self-defence among individuals will play a prominent role in this book, I will use 'self-defence' for the individual context only, and, except in quotations, use the term 'national self-defence' for the collective contexts, i.e. the context discussed in this chapter.

2 The term is nowadays sometimes replaced by the term '*jus contra bellum*'. This is convincing in light of the strictly limited permission to apply force in international relations, as well the intention to limit the use of such force as widely as possible, on which this area of the laws of war is based. See, for example, Bothe 2001, mn. 2, p. 606. The terms may as such be used interchangeably. In light of the still-prevailing use of the former term, I use this traditionally used expression.

dressed in order to determine the overall justificatory force of the strategy to be discussed in this chapter as well as the strategy to be discussed in the next chapter.

4.1 The (in)dependence of *jus ad bellum* and *jus in bello* arguments

Several commentators who seek to justify the targeted killing of terrorists with reference to *jus ad bellum* or, more specifically, to the right of national self-defence do not mention the rules of *jus in bello* at all, or they merely assume the legality of the practice under international humanitarian law, without analysing whether this assumption is true.[3] Others refer only to *jus in bello,* but do not account for *jus ad bellum*. A brief look at the relationship between these two areas of the laws of war allows for an assessment of the role these arguments can play in the justification of targeted killings. This assessment will show that an isolated consideration of these arguments ignores the structure of the laws of war to a certain extent and thus fails to provide a conclusive justification for targeted killing of terrorists.

Jus ad bellum and *jus in bello* are separate areas of international law. The former determines whether states may resort to force in international relations at all;[4] the latter is crucial in deciding which measures of force may be applied in an armed conflict. *Jus ad bellum*, hence, plays a crucial role with regard to the individual acts that initiate armed conflicts.[5] If states, in resorting to force,

---

3 See, for example, Kendall 2002; Godfrey 2003. When taking a position on the targeted killing of Dr Thabet Thabet, who was killed on 31 December 2000 (see chapter 2.1), Prime Minister Ehud Barak, for example, stated that '[i]nternational law allows a strike against someone identified with certainty as being prepared to commit an attack against Israel targets. [...] This pertains to a war situation in general and to the right of self-defence specifically'. Quoted in AI 2001a, 17. See also Gross, E. 2005. Emanuel Gross' position remains slightly unclear, but he seems to argue that reference to national self-defence suffices for deciding whether targeted killings of terrorists are justified. See also fn. 3 in chapter 5.

4 The regulations for the right of national self-defence, with the requirements of proportionality and necessity, include requirements concerning the *manner* in which force may be used in national self-defence. The primary focus, however, remains *whether* force may be used at all.

5 This does not mean that, once an armed conflict has begun, the relationship between the participating parties remains a single conflict until they officially end it. There may be several 'periods of armed conflicts' (Bothe 2003, 235 f.) which have to be judged separately regarding their accordance with *jus ad bellum*. This is a consideration that is often reflected

violate *jus ad bellum,* this use of force as such remains unjustified throughout the conflict.[6] It can thus be argued with a broad view that none of the acts carried out in such a conflict can be justified. Due to the separation of *jus ad bellum* and *jus in bello*, this statement, however, applies on a general level only. *Jus in bello* applies equally to all parties to a conflict and thus provides them with equal rights and obligations. Hence, on an individual level, *jus in bello* may provide states, and warfare personnel in particular, with justification for given acts of force, despite a lack of justification for the international military force of which the individual acts form a part.

By contrast, an act of force is not necessarily justified simply because it meets the requirements set out in *jus ad bellum*. In order to be justified, it must also meet the requirements set out in the international legal norms regulating states' use of force in given circumstances. Often these will be requirements set out in *jus in bello*, theoretically, however, human rights law as it applies to law enforcement could be the relevant framework.[7] It is thus inevitable that the scope of *jus ad bellum* be examined in deciding whether targeted killings can be justified. Nevertheless, the discussion of *jus ad bellum*, or more specifically of the right of national self-defence, may not provide any conclusive justification for a certain act. The ICJ expressly states this in its Advisory Opinion in *Legality of the Threat or Use of Nuclear Weapons:*

> [T]he proportionality principle may thus not in itself exclude the use of nuclear weapons in self-defence in all circumstances. But at the same time, a use of force that is proportionate under the law of self-defence, must, in order to be lawful, also meet the requirements of the law applicable in armed conflict which comprise in particular the principles and rules of international humanitarian law.[8]

To conclude, both areas of the laws of war must be analysed to reach a conclusion as to the justifiability of targeted killing of terrorists. The argument for justification by *jus ad bellum* alone cannot possibly provide a final assessment of the practice. Justification by reference to international humanitarian law, by contrast, can theoretically offer a justification of targeted killing of terrorists. If the use of international force cannot be justified at all, however, these acts, provided they constitute international force, may under certain circumstances still be criticized as illegal use of force.

---

in actual situations and conflicts and thus needs to be kept in mind. Otherwise the idea of a continuing armed conflict may easily be abused. Bothe 2005, 234.

6 Dinstein 2005, 235.

7 See also fn. 94 in chapter 5.

8 ICJ, *Legality of the Threat or Use of Nuclear Weapons*, (Advisory Opinion), para 42.

4.2 Lines of argument

Both governments and legal commentators have taken the approach of justifying targeted killings of terrorists as legal acts of warfare. The reasoning predominantly follows two lines of argument,[9] providing reasonable reference points for a discussion of whether, and under what conditions, targeted killings of terrorists may be considered legal acts of warfare.

Both approaches refer to international humanitarian law as established in the Geneva Conventions or customary law. They thus base their arguments on commonly accepted norms. The manner in which these positions interpret the norms and apply them to the context of terrorism, however, reveals interpretations that differ from those that have commonly been formulated when conventional armed conflicts were the focus.

Both lines of arguments were addressed by the Israeli government[10] in the legal proceedings taken by the Public Committee against Torture in Israel *et al.* against the government of Israel *et al.* before the Israeli High Court of Justice.[11] It formulated arguments with reference to the Israeli-Palestinian conflict. The arguments, nevertheless, resemble those put forward in other contexts, are based on the same legal assumptions, and draw the same conclusions.

The government of Israel began its *first line of argument* by arguing that Israel is involved in an armed conflict with various terrorist groups carrying out their acts in Judea, Samaria, the Gaza Strip, and Israel itself. The government referred to these acts[12] as 'acts of combat and terrorism'[13] and stressed that the groups had killed more than 1,000 Israeli citizens and wounded many more. Initially, the Israeli government argued that the conflict between Israel and the dif-

---

9 Former US Senator Rudman stated: 'I think in the war on terrorism there are no rules. They [the terrorists] have none and we have to take whatever risks you have to take to make them fear us.' Quoted in Pincus 2003, 228 f. In view of the existing human rights regime and detailed regulations on armed conflicts, such a position does not constitute a serious legal argument requiring further discussion.

10 Given that the respondent replied as a group and that the Israeli government represented only one party in it, the argument that I will present, of course, is not limited to the Israeli government but includes all other persons and organizations that formed part of the respondent.

11 HCJ, *Public Committee against Torture v. Government of Israel*. The Court issued its judgment on 13 December 2006. The argument I will present in the following is presented in paragraphs 9 – 11.

12 In their argument they refer to the acts which have been carried out since the beginning of the second Intifada.

13 HCJ, *Public Committee against Torture v. Government of Israel*, para. 10.

ferent groups regarded as terrorist organizations constitutes an international armed conflict. They later modified this point, and argued that the conflict exhibited characteristics of different kinds of armed conflict. They furthermore asserted that a new kind of armed conflict had evolved in international law, namely one between states and terrorists. No matter what classification was applicable, the Israeli government continued, the laws of war applied and regulated the killing of terrorists. They argued that terrorists must be regarded as party to the armed conflict, of whatever type it is, since they actively participate in the fighting, and may as such be attacked and killed. The Israeli government thereby held terrorists to be *unlawful combatants*, since, they argued, terrorists do not distinguish themselves from the rest of the population and do not act in accordance with the laws of war. Owing to this status, the argument continued, terrorists may be targeted, but are deprived of the protections to which they would be entitled as lawful combatants, such as prisoner of war protection.[14] According to the Israeli government, the right to kill terrorists thereby exists for the duration of the conflict and applies to all territories in which the armed conflict takes place, be they occupied or unoccupied.

This first line of argument, as presented by the Israeli government, reflects several assumptions made about the Israeli-Palestinian conflict itself. It also, however, includes statements on the legality of the targeted killing of terrorists that apply generally. First, states can be in an armed conflict with terrorist organizations. The terrorists, then, are party to the conflict, and the laws of war apply. Second, due to their non-compliance with the laws of war, terrorists must be considered unlawful combatants. Third, the laws of war permit the targeted killing of terrorists. Fourth, this applies for the duration of the conflict; and fifth, this applies to the entire territory in which the armed conflict takes place, be it occupied or not.

This line of argument has been applied to other contexts within the general fight against international terrorism, primarily by the Bush administration of the United States and scholars defending its policy. It has been argued that the con-

---

14 The specific status that the Israeli government ascribe to terrorists and the reasons they give for this decision reveal that they hold the armed conflict between Israeli and Palestinian forces to be international in character. So do the rights, which Israel denies terrorists due to their assumed status of unlawful combatants, namely the rights of prisoners of war. Prisoner of war status constitutes a protection that the laws regulating international armed conflicts provide, but the laws regulating non-international armed conflicts do not recognize this status (for details on the laws regulating non-international armed conflicts, see chapter 4.4). Thus, to distinguish between unlawful combatancy and lawful combatancy on the basis of the reasons presented by the Israeli government only makes sense if the argument is based on the laws regulating international armed conflicts.

flict between terrorists and the US constitutes an armed conflict to which the laws of war apply in principle.[15] Because of their behaviour, terrorists are regarded as unlawful combatants who may be killed, but who are not entitled to any of the protections of lawful combatants after capture.

Although the argument runs parallel to that invoked in the Israeli-Palestinian conflict, several points regarding the understanding of armed conflict are worth noting, as they provide additional aspects not found in the argument as presented by the Israeli government. The concept of armed conflict exceeds that applied to the Israeli-Palestinian context. The conflict, described as armed conflict, is now no longer local nor does it take place between clearly defined groups. It is the *general fight against terrorism* that is described as armed conflict. As a result, the armed conflict is not limited to a specific area, but takes place worldwide. Accordingly, terrorists taking part in this conflict may be attacked all over the world, at any time.[16] Furthermore, the conflict is regard-

---

15 The Bush government and commentators defending its policies regarding terrorism appear to have regarded the conflict as an international armed conflict. This follows from the fact that they refered to international humanitarian law regulating international armed conflicts, if they mentioned any specific regulations at all.

16 In a letter dated 14 April 2003 to the Commission on Human Rights in response to the letter dated 15 November 2002 from the Special Rapporteur on extrajudicial, summary or arbitrary executions, Asma Jahangir, and to the findings of the Special Rapporteur's report, submitted to the fifty-ninth session of the Commission on Human Rights (Annex to UN Doc. E/CN.4/2003/G/80, 22 April 2003), the government of the United States wrote: 'Al Qaida and related terrorist networks are at war against the United States. [...] Despite coalition successes in Afghanistan and around the world, the war is far from over. The Al Qaida network today is a multinational enterprise with operations in more than 60 countries. Some Al Qaida operatives have escaped to plan and moun further terrorist attacks against the United States and coalition partners. The continuing military operations undertaken against the United States and its nationals by the Al Qaida organization both before and after September 11 necessitate a military response by the armed forces of the United States. To conclude otherwise is to permit an armed group to wage war unlawfully against a sovereign state while precluding that state from defending itself. International humanitarian law is the applicable law in armed conflict and governs the use of force against legitimate military targets. Accordingly, the law to be applied in the context of an armed conflict to determine whether an individual was arbitrarily deprived of his or her life is the law and custom of war. Under that body of law, enemy combatants may be attacked unless they have surrendered or are otherwise rendered hors de combat. Al Qaida terrorists who continue to plot attacks against the United States may be lawful subjects of armed attack in appropriate circumstances.' See also Dworkin 2007. Dworkin also quotes Condoleezza Rice, from Fox News, on 10 November 2002: 'We're in a new kind of war, and we've made it very clear that this new kind of war be fought on different battlefields.' Whether the armed conflict is regarded as non-international or international is rarely made clear. The reasons given for the

ed as taking place between the United States and *international terrorism* as such. It is not always made clear who precisely is considered party to international terrorism. The conflict is described as taking place between the United States and Al Qaeda. Rhetorically and practically, however, it has been extended to those who harbour terrorists[17] and to terrorists taking part in international terrorism in general, whoever this may include.[18]

Under the Obama administration, the international legal justification runs along similar though slightly modified lines, as far as it has been made public.[19] The US is considered to be 'in an armed conflict with al-Qa'ida, the Taliban, and associated forces, in response to the 9/11 attacks'[20]. It is no longer described as being in war with terrorism, i.e. a concept, but with a terrorist group and its affiliates. Whether the armed conflict is considered an international or a non-international armed conflict is not addressed. Moreover, the individuals who are con-

---

status of unlawful combatants, however, suggest that the commentators often have international armed conflicts in mind. See, for example, Ho/Yoo 2003b. Without giving any further specification, several officials also spoke of a 'new' or 'different' kind of war. This may suggest that the 'war against terrorism' is somehow different from the hitherto known classifications of armed conflicts as international or non-international. Ari Fleischer, former press secretary to President George W. Bush, described the conflict the United States is part of as 'a different kind of war with a different kind of battlefield', quoted by Johnston/Sanger 2002.

17 For practical examples, see the war against the Taliban regime in Afghanistan in 2001 and the legal arguments for these attacks. See, for example, Ho/Yoo 2003b, 2–8. See also chapter 4.3.

18 'International terrorism' and 'Al Qaeda' are terms often used interchangeably. It is, therefore, difficult to determine which is being invoked by commentators when they speak of international terrorism instead of, or in addition to, Al Qaeda. Given that the question of whether one may speak of armed conflict has hitherto been discussed with regard to specific killings of Al Qaeda members (e.g. the killing of suspected terrorists in Yemen, see chapter 2.1), the question of who else would be considered as taking part in international terrorism has not been clarified. General statements, however, seem to include members of other non-Al-Qaeda terrorist groups. George W. Bush, for example, in his military order of 13 November 2001, explicitly identifies Al Qaeda as part of international terrorism. He states: 'International terrorists, including members of al Qaida, have carried out attacks on United States diplomatic and military personnel and facilities abroad and on citizens and property within the United States on a scale that has created a state of armed conflict that requires the use of the United States Armed Forces.' Quoted in the letter by the United States to the Commission on Human Rights; see fn. 16 in the current chapter.

19 The following information on the justification is based on two speeches by the legal advisor of the US State Department under Obama, Harold Honju Koh (25 March 2010), and by John O. Brennan, Assistant to the President for Homeland Security and Counterterrorism (30 April 2012).

20 Brennan 2012.

sidered legitimate targets in this armed conflict are described as belligerents.[21] Reference to a status as unlawful combatants is not made.

The Israeli government presented an additional *second line of argument* for the legality of the targeted killing of terrorists.[22] This second line of argument differs from the first only with regard to the status of terrorists. It starts with the assertion that an armed conflict takes place and that the laws of war apply to this conflict. The Israeli government, however, then turned to the possibility that terrorists may be considered civilians. It argued that the laws of war provide that terrorists may be attacked, even if they hold civilian status, since a 'civilian who takes a direct part in hostilities loses his immunity and may be harmed'.[23]

The Israeli government differentiated between the rules of customary law and the provisions laid down in Article 51 (3) of the API, a convention Israel is not party to. The customary rules of war, it argued, allow targeting civilians who directly participate in committing, planning or launching terrorist attacks, 'at any time' before they relinquish violence altogether. It followed from this that it is permissible to prevent attacks by attacking those who are directly involved, including killing them in order to 'frustrate the intent to commit planned or *future* hostilities'.[24] Furthermore, the Israeli government argued that, correctly interpreted, Article 51 (3) reaches the same conclusion. All civilians who are planning or launching terrorist attacks, or who command a 'terrorist ring' lose their immunity from attack and only regain their immunity when they 'lay down their arms and exit the circle of violence'.[25] In other words, as long as they do not fully cease participation in the conflict, terrorists may be attacked throughout the entire duration of the conflict regardless of their actions at the actual time of attack or where they are located.[26]

To conclude, both lines of argument used to justify targeted killings of terrorists as legal acts of warfare classify the facts themselves in a specific manner. They describe the situation as armed conflict and ascribe a specific status to terrorists. Furthermore, they present specific interpretations of the status with re-

---

21 Koh 2010.
22 See HCJ, *Public Committee against Torture v. Government of Israel*, (Judgment), para. 12.
23 HCJ, *Public Committee against Torture v. Government of Israel*, (Judgment), para. 12.
24 HCJ, *Public Committee against Torture v. Government of Israel*, (Judgment), para. 12, emphasis added.
25 HCJ, *Public Committee against Torture v. Government of Israel*, (Judgment), para. 12.
26 In its judgment in *Public Committee against Torture v. Government of Israel*, the HCJ applies a similar though more differentiated line of argument. Its arguments and position will be considered in chapter 5.3.

gard to the consequences it entails for the justifiability of targeting and killing terrorists.

Some additional, more moderate lines of argument have been offered. The two lines of argument presented above, however, sufficiently reveal the primary questions which are addressed in these additional arguments, which also make reference to the legality of killing during warfare and argue that the status of terrorists in a given armed conflict makes them legitimate targets.[27] In order to determine whether targeted killings of terrorists may be justified as legal acts of warfare under international humanitarian law, it first must be established whether and under what conditions the laws of war apply to the fight against terrorists. Second, it must be asked whether and under what conditions these norms justify targeted killings. This will establish the status of terrorists and offer a conclusion regarding the justification of targeted killings of terrorists as legal acts of warfare.

4.3 International armed conflicts

International humanitarian law traditionally recognizes two kinds of armed conflicts, for which it provides different regulations: international and non-international[28] armed conflicts. As has been shown with regard to the Israeli government's arguments, commentators have introduced a third category illustrated with reference to recent conflicts. This 'new', third form denotes conflicts between states and non-state terrorist organizations and is held to be equally governed by rules of law allowing for targeted killings. In order to determine whether targeted killings of terrorists can be justified as legal acts of warfare, all three forms of conflicts will be addressed. This section focuses on the justifiability of targeted killings of terrorists as legal acts of war in international armed conflicts.

---

27 To give an example, David Kretzmer argues that conflicts with transnational terrorism may constitute non-international armed conflicts. In these conflicts, terrorists constitute combatants. Provided the use of force is proportional, and given that additional requirements set by human rights law are fulfilled, targeting and killing these terrorists is legal. Kretzmer regards far more limited cases of targeted killing as being legally justifiable than proponents of the two lines of argument I presented. Nevertheless, he also assumes the laws of war to be applicable and ascribes a status to the terrorists that allows killing them under certain circumstances. See Kretzmer 2005.

28 The term 'non-international' is often replaced with the term 'internal'. The meaning of the terms is identical.

4.3.1 Conflicts with terrorists as international armed conflicts: Preconditions

Most commonly, legal commentators base their argument on the assumption that conflicts between terrorists and states constitute international armed conflicts.[29] The requirements for an international armed conflict, and for the international humanitarian law regulating such conflicts to apply, are set out in Article 2 common to GCI-IV.[30] It requires a declaration of war or 'any other armed conflict' between 'two or more of the High Contracting Parties'.[31] Moreover, international humanitarian law governing international armed conflicts applies 'to all cases of partial or total occupation of the territory of a High Contracting Party, even if the said occupation meets with no armed resistance'.[32]

A declaration of war may be sufficient,[33] but it is not necessary for international humanitarian law governing international armed conflicts to apply.[34] The material existence of an armed conflict may equally invoke international humanitarian law, even if none of the parties involved recognizes the situation as such.[35] That said, regardless of whether the state of war is created by a declaration or through the existence of a material armed conflict, in principle, these situations[36] only entail the applicability of international humanitarian law if they take place between two or more contracting parties, i.e. between two or more states.[37]

What follows from the requirements as formulated in Article 2 of the GCI-IV for the applicability of international humanitarian law to conflicts between terrorists and states? Terrorist organizations can fulfil the second requirement. In terms of the extent and kind of force, conflicts between terrorists and states

---

29 Compare fns. 285 – 287.
30 Art. 1 (3) API sets out that the requirements of Art. 2 GCI-IV also regulate the applicability of API.
31 Art. 2 (1) GCI-IV.
32 Art. 2 (2) GCI-IV. The issue of the justifiability of targeted killing of terrorists in areas of occupation will be dealt with separately in chapter 4.4.
33 For others, Dinstein 2005, 30; Greenwood 1994, mns. 202 f., pp. 36 – 38. Focusing on a slightly different issue, yet arguably contrary, Lauterpacht 1968.
34 For others, ICRC Commentary on GCIII, 22 f.
35 ICRC Commentary on GCIII, 23; Greenwood 1994, mn. 202, p. 36.
36 The only exception to this rule constitutes Art. 1 (4) API. It sets out that API also applies to 'armed conflicts in which peoples are fighting against colonial domination and alien occupation and against racist régimes in the exercise of their right of self-determination'.
37 This is independent of whether the states and governments participating in the conflict recognize each other, but depends on objective judgements as to the status of the parties. Greenwood 1994, mn. 206, p. 39.

could constitute armed conflicts. Article 2 of the GCI-IV does not specify what kind of force constitutes an armed conflict.[38] Recourse to military force is indispensable for an armed conflict to exist.[39] What extent this violence has to reach to qualify as armed conflict, is, however, difficult to determine. The commentary of the ICRC regards any conflict involving members of armed forces, no matter 'how long the conflict lasts, how much slaughter takes place, or how numerous are the participating forces' as armed conflict.[40] The ICTY appeals chamber in *Prosecutor v. Tadic* supports this assertion by stating that 'an armed conflict exists whenever there is resort to armed force between states'[41]. State practice, however, seems to suggest a threshold that distinguishes minor and insignificant border incidents, or incidents at high sea, from armed conflicts.[42]

In the context of terrorist violence, this grey zone regarding insignificant force poses few difficulties. It is indisputable that terrorist violence can reach the extent required to constitute an armed conflict. The attacks of September 11 represent the most drastic example of this situation. In light of the targets of terrorist violence, the intention behind such attacks and the means chosen, it seems likely that terrorist violence in principle crosses such a threshold.[43]

---

38 International humanitarian law applies from the moment one state applies military force against another. It is not required that more than one state resort to military force.
39 Military force may be interpreted as limited to conventional military force, i.e. to ordinary weapons, and hence as excluding terrorist acts making use of unconventional weapons. In light of the impact the use of civilian aircraft had on September 11, this seems to be too limited an understanding. Regardless of the means, what seems decisive is whether the outcome is equal to that which would result from the use of conventional military force. (See also Stahn 2004, 857f. He discusses whether 'armed force' as used in Art. 51 UN Charter, understood as the use of military force, covers the use of unconventional weapons.) Alternatively, the term 'military force' may be limited to states' force. First, as becomes clear in the case of non-international armed conflicts, military force cannot be limited that way. State as well as non-state forces can apply military force, and the term is generally used as such. Secondly, if the term was limited to force carried out by states, force attributable to states and yet carried out by non-state actors could not trigger an armed conflict. Thirdly, if military force would be limited to states' use of force the requirement for international armed conflicts to take place between states would be redundant.
40 ICRC Commentary on GCIII, 23.
41 ICTY, Appeals Chamber, *Prosecutor v. Tadic,* (Decision on the Defence Motion of Interlocutory Appeal on Jurisdiction), para. 70.
42 Christopher Greenwood highlights that states deny the existence of an armed conflict for such incidents and, as a result, assumes that such incidents are not to be regarded as armed attacks. Greenwood 1994, mn. 202, p. 36. See also Paulus/Vashakmadze 2009, 101.
43 Terrorist attacks are acts of violence directed against innocents, or during warfare, against non-combatants. They seek to have strong psychological and physiological impact on

Terrorists could arguably also fulfil the alternative requirement of a declaration of war. A declaration of war is a formal announcement issued by the authority of a state that is constitutionally responsible for such acts[44] if it is intended to introduce a state of war, without ambiguity.[45] If the competence to speak for a group is distinguished from the necessity of a declaration being issued by a state authority, as Yoram Dinstein suggests, terrorists, theoretically, are able to issue a declaration of war, whether in the case of state-terrorism or non-state terrorism.[46]

Thus, while the first two requirements set out in Article 2 of the GCI-IV may be fulfilled with regard to conflicts between terrorists and states, the last requirement is more contentious and requires some differentiation. This is the requirement that the conflict needs to take place between two or more contracting parties. This requirement explains why only a very limited number of the conflicts between terrorists and states can be considered international armed conflicts.

Two forms of conflict must be distinguished with reference to the kind of terrorism under study: first, conflicts in which the terrorist activities are organized and carried out by non-state actors independent of any state involvement; and, secondly, conflicts in which the terrorist activities are carried out by non-state actors with state involvement, be it in terms of active participation or mere acquiescence.

The situation is clear with regard to the first constellation. Although commentators who speak of the 'war against terrorism' often seem to ignore this fact, the traditional understanding of the laws of war provides a clear answer to whether such conflicts may constitute international armed conflicts. The drafters explicitly excluded such situations from the scope of the convention

---

the attacked state and its population and are directed against life and property. The means are chosen in view of the impact they will have.

44 Dinstein 2005, 30. Given that the last requirement for international humanitarian law to apply is that the conflict takes place between states, it is questionable to make that provision also conditional for a declaration of war to exist. With regard to the outcome, this makes no difference. However it seems to be more convincing to require the declaration to be issued by an authority competent to speak for the group it is claiming to speak for, without making the link to a state obligatory.

45 Dinstein 2005, 33; Greenwood 1994, mn. 203, p. 38.

46 Osama Bin Laden, for example, issued a declaration of war, which, given his position within Al Qaeda, may arguably be regarded as such. See Lawrence 2005, 58 – 62. Given the third requirement that international armed conflicts must take place between states, the declaration of war, of course, needed to be imputable to the state in order to possibly trigger an international armed conflict. Yet if one distinguished the preconditions, terrorists may be able to issue a declaration of war.

by introducing the requirement that armed conflicts only constitute international armed conflicts if they take place between two or more contracting parties. Conflicts between states and non-state terrorist groups acting independently of state involvement, hence, cannot constitute international armed conflicts. As a result, targeted killings of terrorists in such conflicts cannot be regarded as legal acts of warfare in terms of international humanitarian law regulating international armed conflicts.

While several commentators refer to the 'war against terrorism' and justify specific treatment of terrorists with reference to international humanitarian law, John Yoo and James Ho are among the few authors who present an argument for this position.[47] Their argument, however, cannot refute the conclusion that targeted killings of terrorists in conflicts between states and non-state terrorist groups acting without state involvement cannot be justified as legal acts of warfare in an international armed conflict. A brief examination of Ho and Yoo's threefold argument makes this clear.

First, they argue that the laws of war were meant to apply to non-state groups and have always done so. They refer to the laws of war for non-international conflicts, and they argue that these provisions show that international humanitarian law is not limited to states, but that non-state actors are protected by certain minimum standards as soon as the violence carried out by them crosses a certain threshold.

Secondly, they refer to statements by 'legal authorities'[48] that one may only speak of war if the conflict takes place between states, and interpret them as seeking to distinguish legitimate conflicts from non-legitimate ones. In other words, according to Ho and Yoo, when scholars state that war must be between states, they did not mean that the laws of war were only applicable to conflicts between states. They meant rather to express that only state agents are allowed to fight in wars, and that only state agents constitute legitimate belligerents.

Thirdly, Ho and Yoo highlight that in the past, only states would have had the power to launch attacks of sufficient scope and destruction to constitute an armed conflict. The developments that allow terrorist groups to apply violence to a similar extent to that of states demand that the rules of law be applied not only to states, but also to non-state groups. They argue that:

> Simply by operating outside the confines of the traditional concepts of nation-states, terrorists cannot shield themselves from the prohibitions universally commanded by the laws of

---

47 They seek to prove that the United States are in an international armed conflict with Al Qaeda. Ho/Yoo 2003b.
48 Ho/Yoo 2003b, 7.

armed conflict. If terrorists can wield the military power of a nation-state, but are exempted from the laws of war, other groups with similar aims will be encouraged to follow the example of al Qaeda. International law does not and should not create such a perverse incentive.[49]

Ho and Yoo's arguments may easily be refuted. This is not because the assumptions on which they base their arguments are invalid, but because they conflate concepts of armed conflicts that cannot be intertwined. That there are non-international armed conflicts – a point they make when explaining that wars do not necessarily have to take place between states – does not prove that such conflicts may be regarded as the kind of war they refer to when they discuss the legality of specific treatment of terrorists, namely international armed conflicts, i. e. 'wars' to which the Geneva Conventions in their full length and the API apply.

Furthermore, in their statements, Ho and Yoo question a fundamental position in international humanitarian law without giving any reason for their assumption that the statements made by influential legal commentators are to be understood in the manner in which they understand them. They also seem, once again, to confuse international armed conflicts with non-international armed conflicts. It is manifest that humanitarian regulations governing non-international armed conflicts apply to non-state actors acting independently of state involvement. This, however, does not prove that international humanitarian law regulating international armed conflicts does so as well.

Finally, Ho and Yoo's third argument does not show that international armed conflicts may actually take place between states and non-state actors, but involves claims *de lege ferenda*. It is far from clear that the drafters would have introduced different regulations had they known the current potential for violence possible on the part of non-state groups. More importantly, by highlighting that the drafters of the Geneva Conventions were unable to predict that non-state violence would eventually be of similar dimension to state violence, Ho and Yoo merely prove that the wording of Article 2 of the GCI-IV corresponds to the intention of the drafters. Their argument, thus, supports what Article 2 of the GCI-IV explicitly states, and what the Appeal Chamber confirmed again in *Prosecutor v. Tadic* in 1999: that international humanitarian law regulating international armed conflicts does not govern conflicts between states and non-state terrorist organizations that act independently of a state.[50] Whether it is convincing to

---

49 Ho/Yoo 2003b, 7. See also Ho/Yoo 2003a, 8.
50 ICTY, Appeals Chamber, *Prosecutor v. Tadic,* (Judgment), para. 84: 'It is indisputable that an armed conflict is international if it takes place between two or more States. In addition, in case of a non-international armed conflict breaking out on the territory of a State, it may

apply international humanitarian law regulating international armed conflicts to conflicts between states and non-state terrorist organizations regardless of any state involvement on the terrorists' part, then, is a question that is *de lege ferenda*. This argument will be revisited when addressing the position that certain conflicts between states and terrorists have to be regarded a 'new' kind of armed conflict.[51] Nevertheless, it does not allow the conclusion that conflicts between states and non-state actors acting independently of any state involvement can be considered international armed conflicts.

An important insight regarding the second kind of conflict that must be analysed follows from the assertion that armed conflicts constitute international armed conflicts only when they take place between two or more states. This type of conflict is one in which terrorist activities are carried out by non-state actors, yet with state involvement, be it in terms of active participation or mere acquiescence. Such a conflict only constitutes an international armed conflict when the state's involvement makes the non-state terrorist acts imputable to that state. Only if the non-state terrorist acts are imputable to a state can the conflict be considered to take place between two states, with the result that international humanitarian law governing international armed conflicts can be applied.

The crucial question, then, is when and under what conditions private acts constituting armed attacks are imputable to states. As this question will become relevant again later in this book, and because it is highly controversial, I will turn to the requirements for imputability of non-state terrorist acts to states or, as I will also call it, their attributability to states or (legal) state responsibility for them, in a slightly more extended way. This will enable a final analysis as to whether the laws of war regulating international armed conflicts apply to conflicts between terrorists and states. It will also provide a sufficient basis for further issues in which the question of the imputability of non-state use of force to states will become relevant.[52]

---

become international (or depending upon the circumstances, be international in character alongside a non-international armed conflict) if (i) another State intervenes in the conflict through its troops, or alternatively if (ii) some of the participants in the non-international armed conflict act on behalf of that other State.'

51 Chapter 4.5. See also chapters 7 and 11.
52 See chapter 5.

4.3.2 Imputability of non-state terrorist acts to states

It is undisputed that states may be legally responsible for specific non-state acts[53] of force due to involvement in the acts themselves or, more generally, their involvement in the activities of the group carrying out these acts. The degree and nature of state involvement in non-state acts and activities required for such acts to be imputable to the state, however, is highly contentious.[54]

State involvement and support can take several forms. When states recruit, organize, pay and command the non-state groups, it is unclear whether one may still speak of state *involvement* and describe the relevant group as a non-state group. Regardless of how it is branded, it is rightly unquestioned that the groups' acts of violence are imputable to the state commanding them.[55]

Leaving aside this most extreme form of state 'involvement', the scale of state involvement or support can span from direct control to inactivity, i.e. lack of reaction to a given group's activities. Control may be understood in two ways. On the one hand, it may be understood as *effective control* over specific acts (1).[56] A state exercises effective control over a specific terrorist act if it not

---

53 Strictly speaking, one could describe non-state acts attributable to a state as state acts. I will describe all acts as non-state acts carried out by non-state agents, regardless of whether they are attributable to a state. Because this book focuses on non-state terrorism, this avoids confusion and allows for a differentiated analysis of the use of force and a clear presentation of the results. This, however, does not question the assumption that these acts are, with regard to the legal consequences for the state involved, treated as this state's acts and may be described as such.

54 The imputability of non-state violent acts to states has most often been discussed in the context of Art. 51 of the UN Charter. On a judicial level, the question was discussed in the context of *jus in bello* only in the *Tadic* case. See ICTY, Appeals Chamber, *Prosecutor v. Tadic*, (Judgment), paras. 88–145. The notion of state responsibility does not differ whether it is discussed in the context of *jus ad bellum* or of *jus in bello*. Nevertheless, it is crucial to note that claims that private acts may trigger the right of self-defence according to Art. 51 of the UN Charter do not generally mean that the non-state acts may be attributable to a state. As I will establish in chapter 5, this is due to the fact that Art. 51 of the UN Charter does not require an armed attack by a state in order to apply. (For others, see Dinstein 2005, 204–208). Hence, statements by authors who share this position, that non-state acts may have triggered self-defence, do not necessarily express claims about state responsibility.

55 In *Nicaragua v. United States of America*, (Merits), para. 114, the ICJ briefly addresses such a case and clearly indicates that such a situation makes a state responsible for all acts committed by that group.

56 The test of effective control has been established by the ICJ in *Nicaragua v. United States of America*, (Merits), paras. 106–116, see also para. 195. That such forms of state involvement in an act of violence make this act attributable to the involved state has been

only finances, trains and logistically supports the non-state group carrying it out, but also directs or enforces the perpetration of the act: the state orders and controls the act concerned.[57] On the other hand, control may be understood as *overall control* (2). A state has overall control with regard to specific acts if it is involved in the coordination and planning of the activities of the non-state group and, thus, generally participates in their activities and is able to control and influence them, yet does not order the particular act. Financial support, the delivery of equipment and training *per se* are not necessarily sufficient to establish overall control.[58]

Inactivity, the form of state involvement positioned on the opposite end of the scale of involvement from control, can also take two forms. On the one hand, it can be voluntary. In this case it may be described as *acquiescence* (5). On the other hand, in case of so-called 'failed states', inactivity can be involuntary and caused by states' *inability* to exercise control over the non-state organization (6). While acquiescence may be regarded as passive support, inactivity due to inability may not be considered support.

One can imagine several forms of active state support of non-state organizations between these two extreme forms of state involvement, *spanning from financial aid, to supply of weapons and equipment, to training and logistical support* (3). Finally, the *provision of sanctuary* (4) may be considered support. This is due to the fact that the state by providing sanctuary deliberately protects private actors who have carried out, or will carry out, violent acts.

Some consequences of these forms of state involvement are relatively easy to assess. *(Ad 1)* Non-state violent acts are attributable to a state if the latter has effective control over these acts. This is rightly and widely uncontested,[59] and it is reflected in the ILC draft on Responsibility of States for Internationally Wrongful Acts.[60] It is also consistent with the definition of aggression agreed upon in the General Assembly, according to which 'the sending by or on behalf of a state of armed bands, groups, irregulars or mercenaries, which carry out acts of armed forces against another state of such gravity as to amount to the acts

---

reaffirmed by the Appeal Chamber of the ICTY in *Prosecutor v. Tadic*, (Judgment), see particularly para. 118.

57 ICJ, *Nicaragua v. United States of America*, (Merits), para. 115.

58 ICTY, Appeals Chamber, *Prosecutor v. Tadic*, (Judgment), paras. 131/137.

59 ICTY, Appeals Chamber, *Prosecutor v. Tadic*, (Judgment), in particular para. 118; ICJ, *Nicaragua v. United States of America*, (Merits), para. 115. For others, see also Cassese 1989, 598 f.; Randelzhofer 2002, mns. 30–32.

60 Art. 8 reads: 'The conduct of a person or group of persons shall be considered an act of a State under international law if the person or group of persons is in fact acting on the instructions of, or under the direction or control of, that State in carrying out the conduct.'

listed above [in the resolution], or its substantial involvement therein'[61] constitutes acts of aggression.[62]

State responsibility may also be assumed when a state publicly approves
and endorses the non-state terrorist acts as its own after they have been committed.[63] It is unclear whether official approval of the act alone is sufficient for attribution. While the ICTY seems to hold it to be sufficient, the ICJ explicitly rejected that official approval alters 'the initially independent and unofficial character' of the act.[64] In light of the consequences that may follow from the attribution
of non-state acts to states, it seems convincing to conclude that state approval
must involve at least the clear expression of an intention to claim legal responsibility for the act in order to establish this responsibility. This result will be supported by the discussion below, which will show that some considerable degree
of involvement is necessary for acts to be attributable to the state.[65]

(*Ad 6*) As attribution is commonly accepted in case (1) and in the case of
public endorsement, it is equally unanimously accepted in the scholarly literature and state practice that non-state violent acts *cannot* be attributed to states
when the latter fail to prevent such acts due to their inability to control a non-
state group.[66]

(*Ad 2–5*) More divergent positions exist regarding the remaining forms of
state involvement. While the ICJ in *Nicaragua v. United States of America* limited
state responsibility to cases in which the state had effective control,[67] state responsibility has subsequently often been assumed for cases in which states
were involved in acts of non-state groups to a lesser degree. In *Prosecutor v.
Tadic*, the Appeal Chamber of the ICTY presented a solution more elaborate
than that delivered by the ICJ, and argues that overall control suffices for rendering a state responsible for private acts, at least under certain conditions.[68] It held
that acts of individuals not a part of state organs must be assessed by the way
they are organized. Effective control is regarded as being decisive for the imputability of acts carried out by private individuals engaged by a state to carry out a
specific illegal act, as well as for acts carried out by unorganized non-state

61 GA Res. 3314 (XXXIX), Article 3 (g).
62 See also Cassese 1989, 598 f.
63 ICJ, *Tehran Hostage Case*, (Judgment), para. 74; ICTY, Appeals Chamber, *Prosecutor v.
Tadic*, (Judgment), para. 118. This understanding is also reflected in ILC, Responsibility of
States for Internationally Wrongful Acts, draft, UN Doc. A/56/10, Art. 11.
64 ICJ, *Tehran Hostage Case*, (Judgment), para. 59.
65 See also Condorelli 1989, 239 f.
66 Cassese 2005, 470/472.
67 ICJ, *Nicaragua v. United States of America*, (Merits), para. 115.
68 ICTY, Appeals Chamber, *Prosecutor v. Tadic*, (Judgment), paras. 115–124.

groups. For the acts of organized groups – having 'a structure, a chain of command and a set of rules as well as the outward symbols of authority'[69] – to be imputable to states, however, the ICJ regarded overall control as sufficient. So did the ILC, when, in Article 8 of its draft on state responsibility, it stated that acts of non-state groups are attributable to a state when the non-state organization acts 'on the instructions of, or under the direction or control of that State'[70].[71]

In view of recent terrorist attacks, legal commentators have frequently extended the concept of state responsibility beyond these limits. The level of support that they require to make private acts of force attributable to states varies. In his dissenting opinion on the judgment of the ICJ in *Nicaragua v. United States of America*, Judge Jennings, for example, does not clearly delineate state involvement sufficient for non-state violent acts to be imputable to states from other forms of state involvement. Nevertheless, he explains, the mere provision of arms does not suffice. The provision of arms combined with logistical and 'other support', in his view, reaches an extent of state involvement which make it 'difficult to understand what it is short of direct attack by a state's own forces'.[72] Other commentators hold that allowing the use of state territory to plan and organize terrorist acts, inactivity in terms of prevention, or harbouring members of non-state groups after they have committed terrorist acts sufficient to make private acts attributable to states.[73]

Such tendencies towards a broader concept of state responsibility may also be observed in state reactions to the attacks of 11 September 2001. For several decades, states, particularly Israel and the United States, have applied military force against states on the territory of which terrorists had allegedly planned and organised their actions, and they have justified such action with the right of national self-defence.[74] The international community never unequivocally endorsed the justifiability of these acts. The reasons states gave for rejecting the jus-

---

69 ICTY, Appeals Chamber, *Prosecutor v. Tadic*, (Judgment), para. 120.

70 ILC, Responsibility of States for Internationally Wrongful Acts, draft, UN Doc. A/56/10.

71 See also in the same document the commentary to Art. 8 at pp. 104–109. Moreover, further exceptions are made for liberation movements, but these exceptions do not require discussion in this context. Walter 2004, 28.

72 ICJ, *Nicaragua v. United States of America*, (Dissenting Opinion Jennings), 543.

73 For others Bruha 2002, 400–407; Byers 2002, 409 f.; Randelzhofer 2002, mns. 30–36, see particularly mn. 34; Franck 2001, 841. See also Bruha/Bortfeld 2001, 166; they do not provide abstract criteria, yet seem to apply such criteria when assessing whether the attacks carried out by members of Al Qaeda may be attributed to the Taliban.

74 See Beard 2002, 561–565; Byers 2002, 406 f.; Cassese 2005, 472 f.; Reismann 1999, 47–49; Stahn 2004, 831–834.

tifiability of the acts did not always concern the imputability of the acts to which the counter-force was directed, yet they show a lack of consensus that states become legally responsible for acts of non-state groups if they give sanctuary to members of these groups.[75]

The reactions within the international community to the terrorist attacks of September 11 seem to reveal an opposite tendency. The North Atlantic Council regarded them to have triggered the right of national self-defence. On 12 September 2001, it was unanimously agreed that Article 5 of the NATO statute applied and that the attacks of September 11 should be considered an attack against all NATO members if it were determined that the United States was attacked from abroad. In other words, by invoking Article 5 of the treaty, the Council invoked the right to collective national self-defence.[76] Similarly, on 21 September 2001, the OAS adopted a resolution in which it declared that the 'terrorist attacks against the United States of America are attacks against all American states'[77]. While the formulation does not uniformly describe a situation of national self-defence, it arguably must be understood as invoking Article 3 of the Inter-American Treaty of Reciprocal Assistance (Rio-Treaty), the inter-American equivalent of Article 5 of the North Atlantic Treaty.[78]

The Security Council's reactions also clearly differed from statements previously issued in response to terrorist attacks from abroad or states' reactions to such attacks. In the preamble to both resolutions issued by the Security Council in immediate reaction to September 11, in which it unanimously condemned these attacks (SC Res. 1368 of 12 September 2001 and SC Res. 1373 of 28 September 2001), it reaffirmed the 'inherent right to individual and collective self-defence as recognized by the Charter of the United Nations'. Many commentators interpreted this statement as recognizing that the situation faced by the United States triggered the right of national self-defence.[79] This seems less certain than has often been stated. The resolutions do not expressively and unambiguously suggest such an interpretation. They restate the right of national self-defence, yet do not state that the attack of September 11 invoked it. Furthermore, the statement appears only in the preamble, not in the operative part. The Security Coun-

---

75 Cassese 2005, 472f. Antonio Cassese addresses several examples and quotes the relevant SC resolutions. See also Byers 2005, 62f.; Stahn 2004, 831f.
76 NATO, Statement by the North Atlantic Council, NATO Press Release (2001), 124.
77 Organization of American States, Resolution on Terrorist Threat to the Americas, para. 1.
78 Dinstein 2005, 208. See also Jinks 2003a, 87.
79 For others, see Bruha/Bortfeld 2001, 162–164 (they eventually come to this conclusion but also recognize facts that suggest the opposite opinion); Franck 2001, 839; Franck 2002, 54; Frowein 2002, 885; Jinks 2003a, 85; Tomuschat 2001, 543f.

cil does not assert that the attacks of 11 September constituted armed attacks, a precondition for national self-defence under Article 51 of the UN Charter,[80] but describes them as a threat to international peace and security.[81] These are only some facts[82] that substantiate the arguments that the Security Council, in its resolutions 1368 and 1373, was not recognizing the right of national self-defence with reference to the attacks of 11 September and, hence, that it was not applying concepts of national self-defence and state responsibility more widely than they had hitherto been accepted.

That said, reactions within the international community to the US-led military action against Afghanistan, which began on 7 October 2001, clearly reveal new tendencies. The United States, as well as the United Kingdom, justified their campaign by invoking the right of national self-defence in terms of Article 51 of the UN Charter.[83] Apart from Iran and Iraq, no state openly questioned the legality of the US-led military action against Afghanistan.[84]

So far, all of these statements and reactions do not necessarily entail an altered understanding of the imputability of non-state acts to states. There are two possible readings. First, one may argue that they illustrate an understanding of the right of self-defence that does not limit those acts that constitute armed attacks triggering the right of national self-defence to state violence, but includes non-state violence inflicted from abroad for which no state can be held legally responsible.[85] Second, one may argue that these reactions imply an understanding of state responsibility that ascribes non-state acts to states not only if these states controlled the non-state forces, but also if they supported them in other ways.[86]

---

80 See chapter 5.
81 Para. 1 to the preamble of SC Res. 1368; para. 3 to the preamble of SC Res. 1373.
82 For a detailed presentation of the position that neither SC Res. 1368 nor SC Res. 1373 recognize the terrorist attacks of September 11 as giving rise to the right of self-defence, see Stahn, Security Council Resolutions 1368 (2001) and 1373 (2001). See also Blumenwitz 2002, 105; Kirgis 2001. Thomas Bruha (2001, 393 f.) is sceptical as to absolute positions as to the meaning of the two SC resolutions.
83 Letter dated 7 October 2001 from the Permanent Representative of the United States of America to the United Nations, UN Doc. S/2001/946. See also Press Statement on Terrorist Threats by Security Council President of 10 October 2001.
84 Cassese 2005, 474.
85 Dinstein, for example, refers to the SC resolutions to make the point that non-state violence may constitute an armed attack and trigger the right of self-defence, regardless of whether they may be imputed to a state. Dinstein 2005, 204–208. For a detailed discussion of this position, see chapter 5.2.
86 See, for example, Franck 2002, 54; Jinks 2003a, 86 f./89 f.; Byers 2002, 408–410.

The statements themselves do not provide a definitive position on this question.[87] States' reactions to September 11, however, indicate a tendency to ascribe legal responsibility to states for non-state use of force on the basis of the states' active or passive support for the groups planning and carrying out these acts. The US-led military actions against Afghanistan were directed both against terrorists on Afghan territory and the Taliban as Afghan authorities. The United States argued, as did the United Kingdom, that they had the right to do so because the Taliban harboured Al Qaeda.[88] The United States in particular stated that in defending themselves, they would extend violence to all governments that supported or harboured terrorists.[89] Thus, it may be concluded that in reaction to September 11, states tended to apply an understanding of state responsibility that exceeded the findings of both the ICJ in *Nicaragua v. United States of America* and the ICTY in *Prosecutor v. Tadic*.

It remains to be seen whether these tendencies will establish a new, internationally accepted understanding of state responsibility for violent acts carried out by non-state actors against foreign states. For now, however, the described tendencies may not yet be understood as indicating the evolution of a new cus-

---

87 The NATO decision may similarly include both aspects. An explanation given by the NATO Secretary-General Lord Robertson suggests that the support provided to Al Qaeda by the Taliban played a role in the decision to regard the attacks of September 2001 as initiating the right to individual and collective self-defence. Nevertheless, it could be interpreted differently. His statement reads: 'We know that the individuals who carried out these attacks were part of the worldwide terrorist network of Al-Qaeda, headed by Osama bin Laden and his key lieutenants and protected by the Taliban. On the basis of this briefing, it was determined that the attack against the United States on 11 September was directed from abroad and shall therefore be regarded as an action covered by Article 5 of the Washington Treaty, which states that an armed attack on one or more of the Allies in Europe or North America shall be considered an attack against them all.' NATO, Statement by NATO Secretary General Lord Robertson of 2 October 2001.

88 See, for example, Press Release, Office of the Press Secretary, Bush Speaks to the United Nations, (10 November 2001): 'The allies of terror are equally guilty of murder and equally accountable to justice. The Taliban are now learning this lesson—that regime and the terrorists who support it are now virtually indistinguishable.' Quoted in Jinks 2003a, 84 fn. 4. See also Authorization for Use of Military Force: '[T]he President is authorized to use all necessary and appropriate force committed, or aided the terrorists attacks that occurred on September 11, 2001, or harbour such organizations or persons, in order to prevent any future acts of international terrorism against the United States by such nation, organization or person.' Quoted in Jinks 2003a, 84 fn. 5. See also Byers 2005, 65–67.

89 See, for example, National Security Strategy of the United States of America, March 2006, 12: 'The United States and its allies in the War on Terror make no distinction between those who commit acts of terror and those who support and harbour them, because they are equally guilty of murder.'

tomary interpretation of state responsibility. All of the decisions considered here were made in a highly emotional situation, and the timeframe in which they were made did not leave much time for deliberation.[90] Only a few of the state reactions clearly indicate a position on the issue. Moreover, given the impact the understanding of state responsibility for private acts of violence has for the right of national self-defence and, thus, for the prohibition of the use of force in international relations, two of the most fundamental regulations within international law,[91] state practice and *opinio iuris,* need to be more consistent and clear in order to amount to customary law.[92]

To conclude, the imputability of non-state acts of force to states is clear with regard to certain forms of state involvement. It is clear with regard to violent acts of non-state groups that are recruited, organized, paid, and commanded by state agents. These groups, however, can hardly be described as non-state actors. Imputability is also clear when states effectively control non-state violence. For all other constellations of possibilities, the ICJ's decision in *Nicaragua v. United States of America* and the ICTY's judgment in *Prosecutor v. Tadic* served as guidelines for some time. Positions that propagated a wider understanding of state responsibility than that presented by the ICTY existed, but did not dominate the discussion. While several states sought to apply a wider concept with regard to situations in which they were themselves involved, the reactions within the international community to such conduct pointed at a narrower rather than broader concept of legal state responsibility for non-state use of force.

Recent tendencies in the scholarly literature and state conduct have not yet established a new shared understanding of the imputability of non-state acts to states. Nevertheless, they opened the door to new interpretations and wider acceptance of legal state responsibility with regard to non-state use of force organized and planned in, or carried out from, a state's territory, and in cases in which a state supports the non-state group or acquiesced to their activities.

The situation which Antonio Cassese described in 1989 thus still proves true and does so in an even more extreme form:

---

90 Christian Tomuschat (2001, 543 f.), who concludes that the SC resolutions express that the United States legitimately reacted to the attacks of September 11 in national self-defence, supports this when he argues that the United States made deliberate use of the circumstances, since, he argues, so close after the event, no one was able to act other than in solidarity and with compassion.
91 For more details on the importance of the imputability of private acts to state for the right of national self-defence and the prohibition of force, see chapter 5.
92 Cassese 2005, 475.

It is [...] apparent that in situations (3) [the terrorist group is "independent" but supplied with financial aid or weapons by a state], (4) [such group is supplied with logistical support] and (5) [a state acquiesces in the terrorists' seeking refuge on its territory before and after terrorist acts are committed against foreign countries] these rules are far from clear and states still have plenty of room for manoeuvre.[93]

That said, the argument not to limit imputability to acts of violence over which a state has effective control is convincing. In accordance with the ICTY judgment in *Prosecutor v. Tadic*, it is also convincing to hold states legally responsible for acts of non-state groups that they could influence due to the overall control they exercise over these groups. Such control seems to exist when the state organizes, structures, and generally commands the group. Overall control can also plausibly be assumed when logistic and financial support reaches a degree rendering the state involved in areas of the non-state group so crucial to their organization that one may regard the state as being capable of influencing the behaviour of the group by its support.

The extension of the concept of imputability from effective control to overall control corresponds to the general understanding of state responsibility in international law.[94] With regard to state responsibility, international law does not rely on legal formalities, but accounts for possible realities.[95] This explains why states can be held responsible not only for acts of official state agents, when they act according to the powers they were given, but also for wrongful acts carried out *ultra vires* by official state agents.[96] It also seems to explain why wrongful acts of non-state groups ordered by a state are imputable to that state, despite the non-state group not constituting an official state organ. Thus, the official link between a state and the perpetrator is not decisive in determining whether an act carried out by the former may be imputed to the latter. Nor is a state order required under all circumstances. International law seeks rather to ensure that states assume responsibility for individuals whom they entrust with certain func-

---

93 Cassese 1989, 600.
94 For this argument, see ICTY, Appeals Chamber, *Prosecutor v. Tadic*, (Judgment), paras. 116–123, see particularly paras. 121 f.
95 The ICTY Appeals Chamber shows in *Prosecutor v. Tadic*, (Judgment), that this also applies to areas of state responsibility in international humanitarian law. It argues that Art. 4 of the GCIII is similarly based on such an understanding, in that it includes not only official state forces but also independent forces, which belong to a Party to the conflict. See particularly paras. 93–96.
96 For others, see Condorelli 1989, 234. See also fn. 97 in the current chapter.

tions, regardless of their formal legal connection to the state.[97] In view of this understanding of state responsibility, it is consistent to make acts of non-state groups imputable to the state controlling them, even when the state did not order the particular act. As long as a state generally controls a group, the difference between state forces and non-state forces acting on behalf of a state is merely formal. This also corresponds to the rationale behind rules of state responsibility to prevent states from escaping international legal responsibility by acting through private groups without giving them the formal status of state agents.[98]

The claim that this applies only to non-state groups organized to the degree the ICTY requires is not convincing.[99] To be sure, lack of organization may be of such a degree that it is impossible to argue that a state maintains overall control over a group or parts of the group. Nevertheless, as long as a state controls a non-state group overall, there is no convincing reason to hold the state's legal responsibility for this group's actions to be dependent on the group's degree of organization.

When it is understood that acts of non-state groups can be imputable to states, this imputability must be assessed on the basis of real relationships rather than formal links, which a state may generally establish or abstain from, largely depending on its own will. Any other criterion would fail to consistently reflect actual dealings of states and provide states with the opportunity to hide behind non-state groups on the basis of formalities it can manipulate itself.

That said, there seems to be good reason not to extend state responsibility to constellations in which the state exercises neither effective nor overall control, but only supports non-state groups in a non-'substantial' manner or acquiesces

---

97 This understanding is reflected in the draft of the ILC on Responsibility of States for Internationally Wrongful Acts. Art. 7 reflects that a state may be held responsible for acts carried out by persons or groups of persons formally empowered to exercise state acts, even if that person or entity acts *ultra vires* or in breach of instructions: 'The conduct of an organ of a State or of a person or entity empowered to exercise elements of the governmental authority shall be considered an act of the State under international law if the organ, person or entity acts in that capacity, even if it exceeds its authority or contravenes instructions.' Art. 5 explicitly specifies that this applies to acts of individuals legally empowered to exercise governmental authority, provided that this person or group acts in its capacity. 'The conduct of a person or entity which is not an organ of the State under article 4 but which is empowered by the law of that State to exercise elements of the governmental authority shall be considered an act of the State under international law, provided the person or entity is acting in that capacity in the particular instance.'
98 ICTY, Appeals Chamber, *Prosecutor v. Tadic*, (Judgment), particularly para. 117.
99 ICTY, Appeals Chamber, *Prosecutor v. Tadic*, (Judgment), particularly para. 118.

in the terrorists' activities on its territory. It is not always clear which arguments are being drawn upon by advocates of an extended understanding of attribution. Their positions, however, often seem to be led by considerations of the consequences for the threatened state's ability to apply force and defend itself against non-state actors in national self-defence, if non-state acts could not be attributed to the state in which the non-state terrorist groups operates.[100] Pragmatic reasons for states to be provided with greater powers to react against terrorist attacks with violence and thereby ensure their protection, however, will not suffice. I will address three arguments. All three anticipate aspects of chapter 2.2, in which I will discuss whether targeted killings can be justified in reference to the right of national self-defence. In light of the relevance of legal state responsibility for non-state acts of force for the right of national self-defence, these anticipatory considerations, however, seem to be appropriate at this point.

First, as will become clear in discussing the right of national self-defence, the fact that certain acts cannot be attributed to a state does not necessarily mean that states must accept non-state violence without being able to defend themselves. Lack of attribution primarily means that the non-state acts of force cannot be ascribed to states. This, however, does not necessarily imply

---

100 This impulse to military reaction to the attacks of 11 September 2001 seems to have played a role in state reactions taken immediately after these terrorist attacks. Albrecht Randelzhofer also seems to rely on such considerations. He starts his argument by saying: '[T]aking into consideration modern practice of international terrorism, today [as opposed to the first edition of the commentary] I am of the opinion that the statement of the ICJ [that the provision of weapons and logistical support is not sufficient for a private act to be imputable to a state] is much too sweeping and needs further differentiation. Otherwise, it would lead to the result that States were not sufficiently protected by Art. 51 of the Charter against force committed by other States in an indirect manner, thus eroding the very purpose of this rule.' (Randelzhofer 2002, mn. 33.) He provides further reasons for the imputability of private acts to states. He states that the extent to which state involvement has enabled the private group to carry out its acts is decisive. He supports this position with the argument that a state is involved in the acts of a private party if it 'knows that a private group is willing to commit acts of military force against another State *and* he places its territory at the disposal of this group to train its members *and* to offer them safe haven after they have committed these acts *and additionally* provides them with weapons and logistical support' (Randelzhofer 2002, mn. 33, emphasis added). This is a level of imputability equal to that if the state had simply sent such groups itself. His conclusion that non-state terrorist acts may be attributed to a state when this state 'was reluctant to impede these acts' (Randelzhofer 2002, mn. 34) *or* when it 'gives shelter to terrorists after they have committed an act of terrorism within another State' (Randelzhofer 2002, mn. 34) does not seem to be covered by his arguments regarding the degree of state involvement, but merely by consequentialist considerations that states need to be provided with the possibility to apply military force against terrorist attack as enormous as the attacks of September 11.

that such acts never invoke the right of national self-defence. In light of this interpretation, the pragmatic argument for widening the understanding of legal state responsibility for non-state acts of force loses argumentative weight.

Secondly, supposing great argumentative weight to the consequences of certain understandings of imputability with regard to the right of national self-defence, it is doubtful that a wider understanding would result in preferable consequences. Next to violence authorized by the Security Council according to Chapter VII of the UN Charter, national self-defence constitutes the only narrowly defined exception to the prohibition of the use of force in international relations. Extension of the imputability of non-state violent acts to a state would not only invoke the consequences claimed by proponents of a wider understanding of legal state responsibility for non-state acts of force, but would potentially also increase the number of cases in which national self-defence could be directed against foreign states. This would necessarily increase loss of life and damage to property. I am not arguing that such consequences should generally be weighed against the right of national self-defence. However, if one accepts that consequences play a large role in the argumentation, such consequences must be taken into account.

Finally, and most importantly, purely consequentialist arguments cannot replace additional theoretical reasons explaining why such a limited degree of state involvement should establish imputability. Supposing one concurred that existing legal regulations unacceptably limit the ability of states to defend themselves against current terrorism, reference to this fact alone does not nullify theoretical considerations. In other words, if one holds that the 'overall control criterion' too greatly limits states' ability to defend themselves against non-state use of force originating from foreign states, one must provide reasons that a lesser degree of state involvement justifies imputability of non-state acts of force. As long as such reasons are not given, one may argue that the legal regulations, which make the allowance of the use of force on foreign territory dependent on the foreign state's use of force, no longer suffice in light of current terrorist threats. Reference to the consequences of not changing the current understanding of legal state responsibility, however, does not nullify the theoretical preconditions for the legal rule to apply.

Proponents of targeted killings of terrorists have not provided a theoretical explanation for states being legally responsible for private acts of force over which they have no control, and to offer such an explanation seems difficult. It would require either the assertion that supporting a private group or refusing to impede their actions suffices to describe the state as a perpetrator, or a different understanding of imputability. This understanding would have to argue that the state is legally responsible for non-state violent acts even if the acts cannot be described as state acts. It would conclude that states must carry the cost of non-state violent conduct originating on their territory.

An understanding of state responsibility, as applied in the latter argument, may make sense in certain contexts. States may, for example, have to take responsibility in that manner for damage caused by their citizens in other countries. This kind of responsibility may, for example, involve a duty to compensate other states for certain damage, regardless of how the state regulates such a situation internally. This understanding of international legal responsibility, however, cannot be applied as a basis for national self-defence or in deciding the applicability of international humanitarian law. Both questions require an understanding of responsibility as strict imputability, i.e. that one may only speak of international legal responsibility for non-state acts of force if the acts, due to state involvement, could be described as that state's act of force.[101] This is convincing both in light of the purpose and the consequences of the right of national self-defence and the application of international humanitarian law. Participation in an armed conflict cannot be entered into on behalf of other groups, but necessarily exists only among those involved in the acts constituting the conflict. The right of national self-defence, as an exception to the prohibition of force, allows using force in order to ward off an ongoing attack, equally requiring force against the perpetrator of a certain act. More importantly, the severe consequences of the use of force and the fundamental role of the prohibition of force in international law[102] require a limited rather than extended understanding of imputability. These facts preclude an understanding of imputability based on a sense of responsibility due to the general role states have in international relations, but instead require that international legal responsibility understands imputability in a strict sense.

Moreover, such understanding of imputability or international legal responsibility, respectively, would require giving up profound convictions on which international understanding with regard to state responsibility for private acts of force has hitherto been based. Both the ICJ and the ICTY argued that states are responsible for acts of force carried out by non-state groups or individuals when they could be considered *de facto* state organs only. They disagree on what makes private actors *de facto* state agents. Nevertheless, both courts imply that one has to be able to describe the non-state act of force as the state's act of force or that one has to be able to regard the state as the perpetrator of the act in order to hold it legally responsible for that act.

---

101 See also fn. 53 in the current chapter.
102 See also chapter 5.

To assert that states are legally responsible for non-state acts of force over which they had no control would then require an explanation of what makes private acts of violence directed against a foreign state describable as acts *of* the state that is somehow involved in these acts. Proponents of a wide understanding of imputability have not provided such theoretical reasons. This may be because on a theoretical level it is convincing *not* to describe acts of non-state groups as acts *of* a state which lacks overall control and 'merely' harbours the non-state group. Since the state does not carry out the acts itself, but 'only' contributes to the act through some form of involvement, it can only be described as a perpetrator if it wields overall control over the group carrying out the acts in question.

This position finds theoretical support in convincing concepts of individual criminal responsibility. I will not argue that these concepts can be transferred to legal state responsibility. Nevertheless, they highlight ideas and distinctions relevant to this context; they can be drawn upon in order to explain when states that are involved in non-state acts, but do not possess overall control, can be described as perpetrators, and they are reflected in the presented understanding of state responsibility.

First, two main concepts of individual criminal responsibility must be distinguished. The first differentiates an aider and abettor from a perpetrator. While perpetrators may be tried for their actions, as can aiders and abettors, the final act is directly attributed only to the former.[103] The main alternative concept, which will be called the concept of a joint perpetrator, holds that all individuals participating in the action must be regarded as perpetrators.[104] In other words, it does not distinguish aiders and abettors from perpetrators when attributing a given act, and it understands the overall action as one act, comprising the final act and the steps supporting it or making it possible. Individuals who were aiders or abettors according to the first concept are all perpetrators according to the second.

If this second concept of individual criminal responsibility could be transferred to international legal state responsibility, it would, under certain circumstances, be possible to describe a state that 'merely' supported or harboured a non-state terrorist group as contributing to their acts and, thus, as a perpetrator.

---

103 For a well informed presentation of various positions – in particular the concept of control over the act (see below) – that accept a distinction between the category of aiders and abettors and that of perpetrators, including further references, see Roxin 2003, mns. 1– 32, pp. 5–16, see also mns. 45f., pp. 22f., and mns. 105–119, pp. 46–52.
104 In the German legal debates this concept is dicussed as *Einheitstäterlehre*. For information on the concept see e. g. Kienapfel 1971 or Engert 2005.

Overall control would then no longer be required for imputability of this group's acts. That said, regardless of the plausibility of the concept of a joint perpetrator in the context of individual criminal responsibility, one must distinguish between the category of aider and abettor and that of perpetrator when it comes to the imputability of non-state acts of force to states.

Although the concept of a joint perpetrator describes all individuals participating in a given act as perpetrators, regardless of the degree to which they are involved, and, as such, in principle applies the same threat of punishment to all of them, different degrees of punishment, in practice, can account for the differences in involvement. Hence, in the context of individual criminal responsibility, the concept of a joint perpetrator does, at the moment of conviction, account for different forms of involvement, which the first concept recognizes at an earlier stage.[105] Such differentiation, however, is not possible in situations where legal state responsibility for non-state violent acts is relevant to the issues under discussion. With regard to national self-defence and the existence of an international armed conflict, no institution, such as courts, exists that decides what reactions are to follow from states being held responsible for private acts. Differentiation of the degree of responses, corresponding to the differentiation of types of punishment, is not possible. Either the non-state act in question is imputable to a state and therefore constitutes a particular situation of national-self defence, or it does not. Similarly, the situation is either regarded as international armed conflict, or it is not. Thus, regardless of whether the concept of a joint perpetrator is convincing with regard to individual criminal responsibility, it is not applicable to state responsibility for non-state acts of force. 'Merely' harbouring non-state terrorists or supporting them to a degree that does not establish overall control, then, cannot possibly result in a state being deemed a perpetrator and thus responsible for the terrorist acts according to the concept of a joint perpetrator.

It still must be explained why overall control is required in order to describe the state as a perpetrator. In the German legal debate there is an influential, if not exclusive, concept that differentiates aiders and abettors from perpetrators on the basis of the degree to which the individuals were able to control the act.[106] In distinguishing those who have control over the act[107] as perpetrators.

---

105 Austrian criminal law, for example, which applies the concept of a joint perpetrator in paras. 33 and 34 of the Austrian criminal code, provides for aggravating and mitigating factors which must be taken into account when punishing the perpetrator.

106 In German legal discussions this is discussed as *Tatherrschaftslehre*. For information on this concept, see Roxin in fn. 103 in the current chapter.

107 In the German legal debate: *Tatherrschaft*.

This concept, which will be called 'concept of control over the act', highlights an aspect that must be taken into account by any plausible attempt to differentiate among the various participants in an act. It recognizes that there is a difference in responsibility according to whether one is able to influence the execution of the act. If one participates in an act, yet has no power to influence the situation, one may *wish* a particular act to take place, but one is unable to sufficiently direct the situation to reach the desired result. This clearly differs from a situation in which one is able to, and actually does, elicit the desired result.

The concept of control over the act makes it impossible, with regard to state responsibility, to argue that supporting, or giving shelter to, non-state violent groups renders states perpetrators. This is true even if the state was in possession of certain knowledge of the act in question, and therefore even more so if it had no specific knowledge of their particular plans and intentions.[108] This makes it impossible to extend the imputability of non-state acts to states in cases where the state is not able to control the non-state group.

It may appear that the concept of control over the act limits imputability to a more circumscribed category I rejected above, namely to those acts of non-state groups over which the state had effective control. I have given several reasons for why such a limited understanding must be rejected. These can be further supported with reference to the concept of control over the act, more particularly by clarifying aspects of a state's role and obligations in international relations.

Regardless of how the term of 'control over the act' is understood in the context of international individual responsibility, with regard to state responsibility, the external functions that states must fulfil demonstrate that a state need not have effective control over the act in question in order to be understood as a perpetrator. They show that overall control suffices in establishing such a categorization.

States must ensure that their citizens do not damage other states. In other words, they have international obligations with regard to international peace and security. Because of this, states are required to establish structures that guarantee their fulfilment of these obligations. In light of these requirements and obligations, it is only logical that states be held legally responsible for acts over which they exert overall control. Only the more general understanding of control, overall control, can plausibly correspond to the general obligations states have internationally.

---

108 Concepts that distinguish aiders and abettors from perpetrators on different grounds, e.g. with reference to the subjective interest in the act or the perpetrator's will, may come to similar results in most cases; reference to control over the act, however, seems to highlight an aspect that is convincing in particular with regard to state responsibility.

When applied to the context of state responsibility, the idea of control over the act, drawn from the context of individual criminal responsibility, provides a theoretical foundation for the position that states may be considered perpetrators of a given act only if they possess, at a minimum, overall control over the non-state group carrying it out. This provides a final reason for rejecting a wide understanding of imputability, a rejection that cannot be contested simply by pointing out possible consequences.

To conclude, there are tendencies in state practice and legal literature to extend the concept of imputability of non-state violent acts to states in view of the developments in terrorism in recent years. There is good cause, though, to reject such an extension. States can be held legally responsible for violent acts of non-state groups under their overall control. Furthermore, there are good grounds to argue that 'mere' state support or acquiescence is insufficient to establish international legal state responsibility for non-state violent actions. In a case in which a state supports non-state terrorist groups, or acquiesces in their deeds on its territory, the state may be acting in breach of its international obligations.[109] But this does not make them perpetrators of these acts, which is an indispensable precondition for legal state responsibility in the context of the right of national self-defence as well as the applicability of international humanitarian law.

4.3.3 Conflicts with terrorists as international armed conflicts: Conclusions

Given the insight gleaned into imputability of non-state acts of force to states, it is now possible to analyse whether, or under what conditions, conflicts between states and terrorists can be considered international armed conflicts. One can then draw conclusions as to whether, or under what conditions, the laws regulating international armed conflicts apply to the fight against terrorism.

The fight against non-state terrorism fails *prima facie* to constitute an international armed conflict. Hence, international humanitarian law regulating international armed conflicts equally fails *prima facie* to apply. Conflicts between states and non-state terrorists, as such, take place between states and non-state actors, and thus fail to fulfil the third requirement of Article 2 of the GCI-IV.

This finding applies as long as state involvement in the non-state terrorist acts of force is insufficiently extensive to make the acts imputable to this state and, hence, render the conflict international. More concretely, the fight against

---

109 See chapter 5.

terrorism must be regarded as taking place between two or more high contracting parties, and hence constitutes an international armed conflict, if the non-state acts were directly ordered by a state. An international armed conflict also exists if a state exercises overall control over the private group carrying out the relevant act. Nevertheless, there is no convincing argument to regard the situation to be subject to legal regulations governing international armed conflicts if a state 'solely' supported the private group to a degree insufficient for the establishment of overall control.

There is one additional conceivable constellation that may trigger the applicability of international humanitarian law regulating international armed conflicts to terrorists. While I have hitherto focused on armed conflicts between terrorists and states, terrorists can also participate in international armed conflicts between states.[110] In such a case, the conflict in which they are participating is regulated by international humanitarian law, and these regulations, under certain circumstances, apply to them. Whether and under what conditions targeted killings of terrorists are legally justified under such conditions will be examined in the following analysis.

To conclude, the justifiability of targeted killing is limited to two situations by the requirements that must be met for international humanitarian law regulating international armed conflicts to apply. The first is that in which terrorist acts constitute an international armed conflict due to their relationship with a state, and the second is that in which terrorists participate in an international armed conflict between at least two states. Targeted killings of terrorists, then, could be justified as legal acts of warfare within an international armed conflict only if these requirements are fulfilled. Whether they are justified, and under what conditions, requires an analysis of the international regulations of international armed conflicts, which will be taken up in the next section.

4.3.4 The legality of targeted killing in international armed conflicts

International humanitarian law regulating international armed conflicts allows for deliberate killing in a way that would not be acceptable in domestic or human rights law regulating situations short of armed conflict. It provides several rules relevant for the justifiability of targeted killing of terrorists. They con-

---

110 The possibility of participation in an existing international armed conflict is often ignored. This also applies to participation in non-international armed conflicts (see chapter 4.4.2). See, for example, Schmitz-Elvenich 2008.

cern the question of whether and under what circumstances terrorists participating in an international armed conflict may be deliberately deprived of their lives. At the same time, they concern how the consequences of targeted killings of terrorists for innocent third parties affect the justifiability of the practice.

I will first establish the rules that apply to targeted killing in this context. The established regulations will then be applied to the targeted killing of *terrorists*, as understood in this book, which will allow for conclusions as to its justifiability. Proceeding with the argument in this manner is reasonable in view of the complexity of relevant legal regulations and because it will provide an analytical framework that can be applied to targeted killings of individuals to whom the label of terrorist is applied in a manner contrary to the understanding of the term as presented in this book. The ambiguity in labelling individuals terrorists is relevant given the lack of an internationally accepted definition of terrorism.[111]

The first limitation on justified killing during international armed conflicts is territorial. Killing can only constitute a legal act of warfare if it takes place on the territory of one of the parties to the international armed conflict. This follows from Article 2 of the GCI-IV, which also defines the applicability of APII.[112]

In addition to this, the legality of targeted killing during international armed conflicts depends first of all on the legal status of the individual concerned. In international armed conflicts, *combatants* may in principle kill each other.[113] They may be killed as participants in warfare, regardless of whether they pose any imminent threat at the moment of attack. This is a self-evident part of warfare. This description of a positive permission was first made explicit in international humanitarian law in API,[114] which distinguishes this permitted use of lethal force from impermissible attacks, though this distinction had constituted an aspect of customary international law for quite some time prior to API.[115]

Although international humanitarian law thus generally allows combatants to kill other combatants, it prohibits the use of lethal force against enemy combatants under certain conditions. The 1907 Hague Regulations forbid combatants

---

111 See chapter 1.2.

112 See chapter 4.3.1. See also Greenwood 1994, mn. 219. For a discussion of the issue with a specific focus on conflicts with terrorists, see e.g. O'Connell 2009, who argues that lethal attacks are allowed only in a more limited area, or Blank 2010.

113 This also includes non-combatants who belong to the armed forces, but who do not participate in warfare because they, due to domestic law, are not entitled to do so. This lack of entitlement does not have any impact on their status in international humanitarian law. Inasmuch as they do not belong to medical or pastoral/counselling personnel, these persons may be targeted. Ipsen 1994, mn. 313.

114 Arts. 48 and 52 (2) API.

115 Solf 1982, 276.

'to kill or wound an enemy who, having laid down his arms, or having no longer means of defence, has surrendered at discretion'.[116] The Geneva conventions similarly exclude prisoners of war[117] and the wounded, sick and shipwrecked[118] from combatants who may be killed. Customary international law also prohibits attacking combatants who no longer participate in the fighting, who have surrendered, or who are no longer able to fight, either because they have no means of defending themselves or because they are overpowered.[119] API restates and reaffirms these exceptions to the right to kill combatants, prohibiting attacks on combatants who are or should be recognised as *hors de combat*, provided that they 'abstain from any hostile act' and do 'not attempt to escape'. It defines a combatant as *hors de combat* when he or she 'is in the power of an adverse Party', 'clearly expresses an intention to surrender', or 'has been rendered unconscious or is otherwise incapacitated by wounds or sickness, and therefore is incapable of defending himself'.[120]

Civilians – this explicitly includes the civilian population as a whole as well as individual civilians – may not be attacked. In a general way, this is expressed in GCIV.[121] More explicitly, it is codified in API.[122] It is moreover recognized in several military manuals.[123] It also constitutes an undisputed basic rule of customary international law. The parties to a conflict are required to distinguish between military and civilian targets and may only direct military violence against the former.[124]

There is, however, an exception to the prohibition against attacking civilians. It represents the second regulation in international humanitarian law

---

116 Art. 23 (c) HCIV. See also Art. 23 (d) HCIV, which prohibits against deciding that no quarter will be given, i.e. deciding that all enemies shall be killed, regardless of whether they are defeated or show the intention to surrender.
117 Art. 13 GCIII.
118 Art. 12 GCI, Art. 12 GCII.
119 ICJ, *Legality of the Threat or Use of Nuclear Weapons*, (Advisory Opinion), paras. 79/81; Eritrea Ethiopia Claim Commission, *Prisoners of War – Ethiopia's Claim 4*, (Partial Award), paras. 29/33/52f./63f.; Eritrea Ethiopia Claim Commission, *Prisoners of War – Eritrea's Claim 17*, (Partial Award), paras. 38–42/57f.; Cassese 2005, 424; Greenwood 1991, 106; Solf 1982, 220.
120 Art. 41 (1) and (2) (a-c) API.
121 See Arts. 27, 28, and 33 GCIV.
122 Arts. 48, 51 (1), (2), and (6), and 52 (2) API.
123 See Cassese (Expert Opinion), para. 6.
124 For the regulation's status as customary law, see ICTY, Trial Chamber, *Prosecutor v. Strugar*, (Decision on Defence Preliminary Motion), paras. 17–22; ICTY, Appeals Chamber, *Prosecutor v. Strugar*, (Decision on Interlocutory Appeal), paras. 9f.; ICRC Commentary on API, Art. 51, mn. 1923; Solf 1982, 276/299; Cassese 2005, 416; Greenwood 1991, 108f.

that allows for killing during times of armed conflict. The immunity that civilians are guaranteed by customary and statutory international law applies to civilians only for the time they are not actively engaged in hostilities. As with combatants, civilians may be attacked *for the time* they *take a direct part in hostilities.*[125] This is stated literally in Article 51 (3) of the API.[126] The Israeli government deny that customary international law sets any restrictions as to how long civilians who have participated in hostilities may be targeted.[127] It is, however, widely accepted that all provisions of Article 51 (3) of the API reflect customary international law, and thus bind not only states that have ratified the API, but also all those not party to the convention.[128]

Commentators, however, widely disagree both on what it means *to directly participate in hostilities* and on how long such participation deprives civilians of their immunity from attack. The understanding of the term 'hostilities' does not cause major problems. The ICRC defines hostilities as 'acts, which by their nature and purpose are intended to cause actual harm to the personnel and equipment of the armed forces'.[129] Actual harm, or hostile acts, can, according to the ICRC commentary, also be caused by means other than weapons.[130] Moreover, acts of harm constitute hostilities, regardless of whether they are directed against military personnel, military equipment, or the civilian population. This is uncontested,[131] and a more limited understanding would contradict the intention behind Article 51 of the API, which is to protect civilians from the effects of warfare.

Referring to the discussions during the preparatory work of the API, the ICRC asserts that this definition not only covers the moment of the act, but also the military deployment before and the return after the attack has been launched.

---

125 This does not contradict the general rule stated in Art. 48 of the API, since 'military objective' as used in the protocol does not only comprise actual objects that make a difference to the war effort of the enemy party and combatants of the other party but also civilians during their time of engagement in the hostilities. Solf 1982, 277.

126 It is also incorporated in the ICC Statute Arts. 8 (2) (b) (i) and (2) (e) (i).

127 HCJ, *Public Committee against Torture v. Government of Israel*, (Judgment), paras. 30/38.

128 ICTY, Trial Chamber, *Prosecutor v. Strugar*, (Decision on Defence Preliminary Motion), paras. 17–22; Cassese 2005, 421; Kretzmer 2005, 192 fn. 94.

129 ICRC Commentary on API, Art. 51, mn. 1942.

130 ICRC Commentary on API, Art. 51, mn. 1945.

131 In HCJ, *Public Committee against Torture v. Government of Israel*, (Judgment), paras. 5–7. The petitioner criticizes the respondent's interpretation of Art. 51 (3) API in several points. Yet he does not question the interpretation that hostilities include acts against enemy civilians. For other examples, see Cassese 2005, 421; Kretzmer 2005, 192.

This includes the entire period from the moment weapons are taken up before combat to the moment they are laid down after combat.[132]

What exactly distinguishes *direct* participation from *indirect* engagement in hostilities is more difficult to determine. So is the time period during which civilians lose their immunity once they have directly engaged in hostilities. Given that the arguments that support a specific position on the former question often suggest a specific stance on the latter, I will discuss these two questions in tandem.

Positions on both questions, in practice and in the scholarly literature, vary widely. In view of the difficulties in providing a definition of the term 'direct', which would provide a basis on which one could decide when civilians directly participate in hostilities, commentators tend to delineate the meaning of the term by presenting examples and classifying them as indirect or direct participation. The activities on either end of the scale of possible forms of involvement are easy to classify. This applies to civilians who take up arms against the enemy, or who carry their weapons openly and hide in a position to target the enemy at the earliest opportunity. It also applies to civilians who sell food to military forces, provide them with money, or propagate the war cause in order to improve the morale of the population and the armed forces. While the civilians in the former two examples directly participate in hostilities, those in the latter three examples may contribute to the war effort, but do not directly take part in hostilities.[133]

But what about the forms of engagement that are in between those undisputed cases? What about those cases that have to be dealt with in the context of terrorism, namely the planning and coordination of attacks, the command of a group that will carry out attacks, the preparation of explosives and weapons, the organization of equipment, or the transportation to the area of combat of those who carry out the attack? It is primarily on these forms of participation that commentators disagree. Some limit the scope of direct engagement to combat itself and to the open carrying of arms preceding it.[134] Others argue that general support does not qualify as direct participation, but include transporting combatants to the area of operation or the collecting of intelligence.[135] Others

---

132 ICRC Commentary on API, Art. 51, mn. 1943.

133 For the need to distinguish between participation in the war effort and participation in hostilities, see also ICRC Commentary on API, Art. 51, mn. 1945.

134 Petitioners' position in HCJ, *Public Committee against Torture v. Government of Israel*, (Judgment), paras. 5/7. Cassese 2005, 421; Cassese (Expert Opinion), paras. 12–17. Cassese, under strictly defined conditions, includes situations in which the individual 'manifestly' conceals weapons which he or she intends to direct against the enemy.

135 HCJ, *Public Committee against Torture v. Government of Israel*, (Judgment), para. 35.

again hold that the intention to engage in combat suffices to deprive civilians of their immunity from attack, and consider civilians gathering information in the area of operation, passing on information about objects that will be targeted, operating a weapons system, supervising or technically servicing such a system, or supporting military operations logistically as direct participation in hostilities.[136] With respect to terrorist attacks, the Israeli government similarly provides a wide interpretation of direct participation in hostilities. In addition to civilians who participate in launching attacks, the government include all civilians who participate in planning such attacks as well as those who command the terrorist organization and the members who carry out the attacks.[137] The positions on the question of what it means to take a direct part in hostilities, then, range from very narrow to very wide interpretations. A common understanding of the term has not yet evolved.

A similar discrepancy can be found among the different positions on the question of the length of time during which civilians lose their immunity for having directly participated in hostilities. While it is clear that individuals lose their immunity while carrying out hostile acts, how long this loss of immunity lasts is highly disputed. Some commentators argue that individuals who are actively involved in carrying out a hostile act regain their immunity after they have carried out the particular act. If they directly engage in hostilities again, they will lose this protection again. Yet in between attacks, they will be protected against force, as are all other civilians.[138] Other commentators disagree with the claim that individuals should be protected against attack between their carrying out various hostile acts. These commentators reject the view that a person is allowed 'to wear simultaneously two caps: the hat of a civilian and the helmet of a soldier'[139]. Some argue that civilians must stop engaging in hostilities altogether in order to return to their protected civilian status.[140] Others hold that 'once crossed the line', they will not be able to return to their protected civilian status at all.[141]

---

136 Gasser 1994, mn. 518; Schmitz-Elvenich 2008, 218 f.; Melzer (2008, 344) in addition to common activities of combat includes '"concrete" preparation, which *aims to carry out a concrete hostile act*' but excludes '"general" preparation, which *aim to establish the capacity to carry out unspecified hostile acts*'.

137 HCJ, *Public Committee against Torture v. Government of Israel*, (Judgment), para. 12.

138 HCJ, *Public Committee against Torture v. Government of Israel*, (Judgment), paras. 5 – 7, the petitioner adopts Cassese's position; Cassese 2005, 421 – 423.

139 Dinstein 2002, 249.

140 Depending on what one understands by 'direct participation in hostilities', this may mean to cut the bonds altogether with the organization with which one is fighting. This seems to be what the Israeli government holds in HCJ, *Public Committee against Torture v. Government of Israel,* (Judgment), para. 12. It argues that an individual loses his immunity as

To resume, it is clear that individuals lose the protection from attack that civilian status provides while they participate in the fighting and while they carry their arms, both prior to and after carrying out a hostile act. The different positions, however, illustrate well that it is not established whether they may also be attacked in other circumstances.

Commentators in most cases state how provisions must be interpreted, but do not provide a comprehensive argument defending or elaborating their interpretation. There are, however, good reasons to defend a narrow interpretation of the customary provision as set out in Article 51 (3) of the API, which would limit the permissibility of targeting civilians to situations in which they actively engage in carrying out hostile acts that are intended to harm the enemy. The provision has to be read with a view to its context. It is embedded in the principles central to international humanitarian law that work first to distinguish between combatants and civilians and secondly, to protect civilians as much as possible from the effects of warfare. The former principle has already been addressed. The latter has been part of customary international law for some time,[142] and has been restated in Articles 51 and 57 of the API.[143] The validity of these principles does not in any way depend on military success in the armed conflict. The outcome of the armed conflict is decided solely between the armed forces. Civilians are prevented from participating in warfare. The protection of civilians, however, does not directly depend on whether they are able to influence the conflict. It is based on the humanitarian conviction that civilians are to be protected. The commonly accepted prohibition against attacking civilians who provide the army with food or who work in an ammunition factory, without which military success would not be possible, shows this clearly.

It follows from this that the prohibition against targeting civilians taking a direct part in hostilities may not be understood in reference to the impact the individual may have on the general military success. It seems instead to be the immediate protection of military personnel and civilians that explains the exception to the prohibition against directly attacking civilians. This means, in view of the general principle that civilians must be protected, that civilian actions are tolerated even if they diminish overall military success. States, however,

---

long as he is *systematically* involved in terrorist acts. See also the court's position at paras. 39 f. See also Dinstein 1989, 105.

141 Parks 1990, 118.

142 Stefan Oeter (1994, mn. 447) is inclined to classify it not only as customary international law but also as *jus cogens*.

143 For a detailed discussion of the provision as it is incorporated in API, see Solf 1982, 296–318/357–369; ICRC Commentary on API, mns. 1923–1993/2184–2238.

no longer tolerate civilians' activities if they are to the *direct* detriment of military personnel, military objects, the population or its property. In other words, civilian activities are tolerated as long as they do not have *immediate* impact on the military or civilians.[144]

Additional arguments support this interpretation. First, the importance that the protection of civilians is accorded is reflected in Article 50 (1) of the API, which provides that in the case of doubt as to whether a person belongs to the group of civilians or represents a combatant, that person must be considered a civilian, and, as such, may not be killed.[145] Secondly, the rationale for providing an exception to the prohibition against attacking civilians, namely to protect armed forces and civilian populations from direct harm, is reflected in the commonly accepted understanding of hostilities. It comprises the entire period from the moment weapons are taken up to the moment they are laid down, including the time period during which the acting individual is able to directly harm others. Thirdly, any other interpretation would be incompatible with the central principle of international humanitarian law that civilians must be protected from the effects of warfare as much as possible. If states were allowed to target civilians in between possible engagement in hostilities, it is not only the affected individual, but the entire general population, who would be at risk. Civilians taking active part in hostilities will, in most cases, not be wearing clothing or other insignia distinguishing them from other civilians. They will be distinguishable only when they carry their arms and engage in hostilities. If attacks on individuals were accepted before or after active engagement in hostilities, the risk of escalating the conflict would be great. Suspicion is likely to lead states to target individuals who have not been and will not be actively involved in hostilities. Even states acting cautiously cannot avoid putting the population at risk, because hostile intentions are often undetectable.

---

144 Ben-Naftali and Michaeli (2003, 269/279) also apply this explanation. Note further, in contrast to the rationale for justifying the killing of soldiers, who may be targeted because they belong to a certain group regardless of whether they pose a threat as individuals, the rationale for killing civilians takes on the justification of killing in peacetime situations. (See also chapter 10). It is the threat posed by the civilian him- or herself that justifies counter-violence.

145 See also Sassòli 2004, 212. Article 50 (1) API does not restate customary international law, but goes beyond what had previously been accepted as legally binding. The requirement to distinguish between civilians and military personnel implies the duty to determine what group the targeted person belongs to. The presumption of civilian status, however, goes further and constitutes a new and supposedly widely accepted development. Greenwood 1991, 109 f.

Limiting the right to target civilians to the duration of the time period in which they actively engage in hostilities cannot exclude that mistakes will be made. In particular, if civilians participating in hostilities conceal their weapons, their conduct alone will not always make their engagement in hostile acts recognizable. (As will be addressed below, under certain circumstances this limits the right to target these individuals.) Nevertheless, certain conduct in hostilities and, at least, the carrying of arms openly make them recognizable and to limit the permission of the use of military counter-force to such moments will reduce the risk of escalation.

Moreover, understanding the term 'to take a direct part in hostilities' as limited to active engagement in hostilities reconciles the principle of civilian protection with the need to protect the adversary's military and civilian population. Active hostile activity, then, serves a differentiating purpose that cannot be overlooked if justice is to be done to the principle of protecting civilians as much as possible during warfare. The rule that civilians must be protected to the greatest possible extent thus requires limiting the right to attack civilians. This cannot fully prevent the possibility that innocent civilians could be mistakenly harmed, but it limits risk to the extent that the necessary prevention of harm to states' military and civilian population allows.

Michael Schmitt questions whether the provided interpretation corresponds to the aim of protecting the civilian population as much as possible with reference to an aspect of this provision I have not yet considered. A liberal interpretation, he argues, would create an incentive for civilians to keep away from the fighting. As a result, it would serve the law's purpose to facilitate the distinction between civilians and combatants and to protect as many civilians as possible.[146]

Schmitt's argument, however, proves to be flawed. The incentive against participating in hostilities does not vanish with a narrow interpretation. Although states cannot respond to such actions by targeting and killing the perpetrator, they can still pursue him or her. The person involved in such activities risks capture and punishment. The danger of being killed may be a greater threat than the danger of being put on trial and punished. First, however, it may be questioned whether this threat will make a difference to someone who is determined to fight the enemy. Secondly, in peacetime, trial and punishment are accepted and represent the only available deterrent measures. Furthermore, the protection of the civilian population seems to increase rather than decrease if the permission to kill civilians is narrowly construed. As addressed, the open carrying of arms is a relatively easy criterion in determining that a person is taking part in hostili-

---

146 Schmitt 2004, 507–509.

ties; it is far more difficult to determine the same when arms are concealed. The wider the interpretation of direct participation in hostilities, the more difficulties one will face with regard to evidentiary issues, such as finding reliable information on who is actually engaging in any of these activities, and in identifying the right person. The greater these difficulties, the greater the number of innocent civilians who will be targeted.[147]

A final argument can be given for the provided interpretation of the customary provision as laid down in the API. A narrow interpretation reflects a vital difference between the accepted rationale for killing combatants and a plausible justification of the use of force against civilians. This discussion anticipates a more extensive examination that will be provided below in this book. In light of a plausible explanation of the limits of (national) self-defence, it is convincing to read the right to attack civilians taking a direct part in the hostilities in a limited rather than extended way.[148]

The rationale for (national) self-defence is that states, as well as individuals, are allowed to ward off an attack. While self-defence among individuals extends the right to use force to those moments when the attack is about to be carried out, national self-defence, as shaped by international law, must be read as limiting the right to use armed force even in response to the moment when the attack occurs. In any case, defence cannot justify the use of force once the attack is no longer ongoing.

As will be discussed below, the permission to kill combatants cannot be explained on the basis of their individual actual threatening conduct but must be based on the threat emenating from the collective of the combatants to which they belong. As such the justification requires a form of collectivization. Those belonging to the group of combatants may, in principal, be killed because by belonging to that group, the individual combatant is part of the threat. This applies regardless of what a targeted combatant is doing at the time of attack and explains why combatants may be attacked during the entire time they take part in warfare. Attacks on individual combatants are not justifiable with reference to their actual individual violent acts; as part of the war threat, combatants are treated as currently engaged in an ongoing attack, namely the attack carried out by the state to which they belong, as a whole.

This collectivization does not apply in situations short of war. Neither, of course, can it explain why civilians, under certain circumstances, may be attacked. The explanation for the permissibility of attacking civilians during the

---

147 Kretzmer 2005, 194; Sassòli 2004, 212.
148 For the following results, see chapters 3, 5, 6, and 10.

time period in which they take an active part in the hostilities is grounded in the individual actions of these civilians.[149] Provided this is true, these civilians cannot consistently be considered to be taking part in an ongoing attack in between different acts of force, which could possibly justify violence against them. The time between different acts cannot be described as being part of an ongoing attack, and attacks on these civilians, therefore, must be limited to the time during which they actively engage in specific acts of hostilities.

Both what it means to directly take part in hostilities and the duration of the loss of immunity, then, must be interpreted with reference to the actual impact the civilian's action has on the enemy.[150] As a result, civilians may only be considered to be taking a direct part on the basis of their own threatening activities; membership in a hostile organization is not sufficient.[151] Furthermore, only those actions in which the individual is able to cause immediate harm to the enemy may be considered direct participation.

With regard to particular civilians, this primarily means that those taking a direct part in hostilities are those who themselves carry out hostile acts. Because hostilities include the violent act itself, but also the military deployment and the carrying of the weapon, this, however, also applies to the time preceding an attack, during which weapons are carried, and includes civilians who install a weapons system or explosives at the location from which they will be applied, even if the individual in question will not him- or herself apply or activate the weapons. The planning of an attack, general logistical support, or the sending of persons to carry out attacks may not be considered direct participation.[152] Although these activities may be necessary for the act to take place, the individuals responsible for them do not *directly* endanger the members of the adversary party. Neither may a civilian who gathers information about the enemy forces or who drives combatants to the area of operation be regarded as directly participating in hostilities.

This argument also explains why the loss of immunity is rightly limited to the time during which the civilian actually carries out the hostile act, which includes the period during which arms are carried. If, with regard to the permission to target civilians, civilian immunity has greater importance than military success, and if the reason for the loss of civilian immunity is directly related to

---

149 See chapter 10. See also chapter 3.

150 See also Sassòli 2004, 212.

151 See also Kretzmer 2005, 192.

152 The HCJ did not observe the distinction between a person who carries out an act and a person who sends this person to carry out the act or who plans the attack. HCJ, *Public Committee against Torture v. Government of Israel*, (Judgment), para. 37.

the ability to immediately harm the enemy, individuals may only be targeted while they pose an immediate threat or are able to carry out a harming act at any time, and this is the case while they are directly engaging in hostile acts. This, again, includes the act itself as well as the time during which the individual is carrying arms. Civilians thus regain their immunity when the attack is over and they have laid down their arms.[153]

Given the provided explanation and taking the provision itself into account, it makes no difference whether the given individual carries his or her weapons openly while directly engaging in hostilities. With regard to the general provision to protect the civilian population from the effects of warfare as much as possible, however, this must be modified. If civilians taking a direct part in hostilities carry their arms openly, the conclusion applies as formulated. If, however, they conceal their weapons and therefore cannot be distinguished from other civilians, civilian protection invokes additional requirements for the justified use of lethal force. It cannot be applied on the basis of mere suspicion or limited evidence. If possible, the individuals in question must be addressed, warned, and summoned to show that they do not conceal weapons, and they may only be attacked if they refuse to do so.[154] If such interaction is not possible, the requirement to protect the civilian population from the effects of warfare as much as possible requires convincing evidence of a given individual's direct engagement in hostilities before the use of lethal force can be justified.

I have so far established when combatants and civilians may be targeted in international armed conflicts only with regard to the rights of the individuals who could be targeted. Further limitations on the permission to target combatants and civilians who take a direct part in hostilities are formulated with a view to minimising harm to civilians that could result from attacks on legitimate targets. These limitations can be derived from the principle that the civilian population is to be protected from the effects of warfare as much as possible. As follows from the preceding discussion of civilians who take a direct part in hostilities, this principle refers to the protection of civilians not directly participating in hostile acts, who will also be called 'innocent civilians' in the following discussion.

Harm to innocent civilians does not *per se* render attacks on legitimate targets into illegal acts of warfare. The obligation to protect innocent civilian as

---

153 For an even more restrictive position, see Ben-Naftali/Michaeli 2003, 279. I will discuss the argument that civilians, once they have directly participated in hostilities, lose civilian status permanently when I deal with the question of whether targeted killings can be justified by referring to the status of 'unlawful combatant'. See below in this section.
154 Cassese (Expert Opinion), para. 17.

much as possible, however, requires belligerents to adhere to the principle of proportionality, which prohibits attacks on legitimate targets 'which may be expected to cause incidental loss of civilian life, injury to civilians, damage to civilian objects, or a combination thereof, which would be excessive in relation to the concrete and direct military advantage anticipated'[155]. The concrete and direct military advantage refers to the overall military advantage that can be expected from the attack. It takes into account the effects of the attack itself as well as all anticipated military consequences of the attack.[156] In other words, if an act of warfare would harm the civilian population in a manner that cannot be justified in relation to the act's military necessity, such an act is prohibited. If it can be anticipated that innocent civilians will be harmed, the obligation to protect the civilian population from the effects of warfare as widely as possible also prohibits the employment of violence that is not appropriate or necessary to reach the pursued military aim.[157] Furthermore, it requires belligerents to apply all feasible precaution to limit civilian damage as much as possible. This means, for example, that identification of the target must be carried out with thorough care and that weapons must be chosen with the aim of limiting harm to innocent civilians.[158] If it can be anticipated that innocent civilians may be harmed and if the military situation allows for it, belligerents are required to issue a prior warning to the adversary party, stating that a specific object may be attacked, a requirement that is both a part of customary and statutory[159] international law.[160]

I have now established several conditions under which targeted killings may be considered legal acts of warfare in international armed conflicts. Combatants may be targeted as long as they are not captured or *hors de combat*. Civilians may be targeted during the time they take a direct part in hostilities. In both cases, the permissibility of targeting the concerned individual is conditional upon the act not causing disproportionate harm to innocent civilians, which includes the requirement that the act of warfare is appropriate and necessary. Moreover, in order to be justifiable, it must take place on the territory of one of the parties to the conflict. Proponents of targeted killing of terrorists regard a third group as

---

155 Art 51 (5b) API.
156 Cassese 2005, 418. For a good presentation of the requirement formulated with a view to targeted killing, see Melzer 2008, 357–363/403f.
157 Oeter 1994, mn. 447.
158 Oeter 1994, mn. 447; ICRC Commentary on APII, Art. 13, mn. 4772.
159 Art. 57 (2) (c) API.
160 Cassese 2005, 417; Oeter 1994, mn. 447.

legitimate targets in warfare, namely *unlawful combatants*.[161] They argue that individuals who are not entitled to participate in warfare become unlawful combatants by doing so.[162] This view yields several legal consequences regarding the legality of targeted killing during warfare. As is the case with lawful combatants, unlawful combatants are seen as legal targets in warfare. According to this position, they lose immunity from attack not only for the time they directly participate in warfare, as would civilians, but for the entire duration of the conflict, up to the moment they are captured or *hors de combat*.[163] As long as unlawful combatants have not fully stopped participating in the hostilities, they may be targeted, no matter what their role at the time of attack. The crucial point of this position with regard to the legality of targeted killing during armed conflicts is not that this status deprives individuals of specific rights under certain circumstances. It has already been established that international law allows targeting individuals for the time they directly participate in hostilities, regardless of whether they are entitled to do so, as are combatants, or whether they are not entitled to do so, as civilians. The crucial point is that unlawful combatant status deprives individuals of protection from attack throughout the entire conflict. Thus, what is at stake is the duration during which individuals are protected from attack.

The legal analysis presented in this book did not require the existence of a status of unlawful combatant. The legal relevance that proponents of the practice of targeted killing of terrorists ascribe to this status, however, demands an analysis of how it relates to combatant and civilian status, and a conclusive response to the question of whether it constitutes an additional source of permission for targeting and killing during international armed conflicts. If it did so and

---

161 See the first line of argument for justifying targeted killings as legal acts of warfare in chapter 4.2. Instead of 'unlawful combatant' some authors use 'unprivileged combatant', 'illegal combatant', 'irregular combatant', or 'enemy combatant'. The terms are used in ways that parallel each other.

162 Strictly, one can only make sense of the statement if one understands 'combatant' in a way that differs from the understanding hitherto relied upon in this book. It requires reducing the term 'combatant' to its Latin origins: *con* (together) and *battuere* (to fight, to hit). According to this literal understanding, the term 'combatant' includes all individuals who actively participate in fighting. The question of whether they are legally entitled to do so, according to this understanding, does not affect whether they can be considered combatants. This understanding of combatant does not correspond to the way the term is used in international humanitarian law. According to international humanitarian law, the term 'combatant' does not describe all individuals who actively participate in hostilities; it only denotes those who are entitled to do so.

163 The fact that they may no longer be targeted when they are *hors de combat* is usually not addressed. That this is the case, however, necessarily follows from the regulations that apply to combatants, which have never been questioned.

if it was applied to terrorists, the extent to which targeting and killing them was justified would be substantially broadened.

International humanitarian law implicitly includes the concept of unlawful combatant. It distinguishes between individuals who are legally entitled to participate in hostilities and individuals who are not, but persist in doing so. From a descriptive perspective, it makes sense to describe the latter as 'unlawful combatants'.[164] It is, however, misleading to use the term in an international legal context, and to regard it as describing a third legal status in addition to the statuses of combatants and civilians. Analytically, international humanitarian law recognizes only two legal statuses: combatants and civilians; unlawful combatants belong to the latter.

Combatants are individuals whom international humanitarian law entitles to participate in hostilities.[165] Given that the status of unlawful combatant only applies to individuals who participate in warfare but who are not entitled to do so, unlawful combatants are by definition excluded from the category of combatants. A more detailed analysis is required to show that unlawful combatants do not constitute a third legal status, but must be regarded as civilians.

Whether unlawful combatants belong to the civilian category or whether they constitute a separate legal status has primarily been discussed with regard to the treatment to which unlawful combatants are entitled after capture. The arguments put forward focus on the question of which international legal regulations apply to unlawful combatants. Statements about which international legal regulations apply, however, are also statements about whether unlawful combatants ought to be considered civilians or whether they constitute an additional status.

Three positions on the question of which laws apply to the treatment of unlawful combatants have dominated recent discussions. By not taking into account the international legal regulations that explicitly apply to civilians, the first two positions advance the view that unlawful combatants differ from civilians. The third position regards unlawful combatants as civilians and explicitly applies GCIV to determine how they may be treated. In order to show that unlawful combatants must be considered civilians, I will briefly present the three positions. I will then show that the third position is correct in holding that the GCIV applies to certain unlawful combatants. This will be sufficient to reject the posi-

---

164 See fn. 162 in the current chapter.
165 What conditions individuals or armed groups have to fulfil in order to be combatants will be discussed in chapter 4.3.5.

tion that unlawful combatants embody a separate legal status from the statuses of civilians and combatants.

The first two positions agree that a third legal status exists, that of unlawful combatants. They differ in what legal rules apply to unlawful combatants. Some commentators argue that unlawful combatants are deprived of any protection under international humanitarian law. They argue that the Geneva Conventions, API, APII, and customary international law do not apply to them.[166] More prevalent is the view that unlawful combatants are protected by customary international law, as it is expressed in Article 3 of the GCI-IV, commonly referred to as common Article 3, or Article 75 of the API.[167] The third position holds that unlawful combatants must be considered civilians and that the GCIV directly applies to those among them who meet the nationality requirements that are set out in Article 4 (1–3) of the GCIV.[168] This view corresponds to the second position, in arguing that individuals who fail to meet the nationality requirements are protected by the customary rules, codified in Article 75 of the API and common Article 3.

Commentators who assert that unlawful combatants constitute a third legal status tend to provide thin arguments for their position. They generally refer to the conditions that international humanitarian law sets out for combatant status, assert that the individuals they are talking about do not meet these require-

---

166 With reference to the treatment of the detainees in Guantanamo Bay, Donald Rumsfeld, for example, indicates that he does not regard any of these regulations to legally limit US actions, by stating: '[A]s I understand it, technically "unlawful combatants" do not have any rights under the Geneva Convention. We have indicated that we do plan to, for the most part, treat them in a manner that is reasonably consistent with the Geneva Conventions, to the extent they are appropriate, and that is exactly what we have been doing.' United States Department of Defense, News Transcript, DoD News Briefing – Secretary Rumsfeld and General Myers, 11 January 2002. See also Brough 2003, paragraph on *The Codified War Convention Today*.

167 Inter-American Commission on Human Rights, Report on Terrorism and Human Rights, 22 October 2002, para. 74. The commission does not seem to consider the applicability of GCIV. Greenwood (2002, 316), among other things, addresses what treatment Al Qaeda members captured in the war against Afghanistan beginning in 2001 were entitled to. He does not address whether they may be considered civilians. A final statement as to his opinion is thus not possible. The fact that he does not consider the applicability of GCIV and the fact that he only refers to customary international law, however, suggest that he does not consider them civilians. Steven Ratner (2007, 259) recognizes unlawful combatants as a third legally relevant group next to combatants and civilians. He argues that the Geneva Conventions, API, and customary law provide them with a minimum of protection against inhumane treatment. See also Detter 2000, 148; Gross, E. 2005, 580f.; Ho/Yoo 2003a, 14f.

168 Cassese (Expert Opinion), paras. 7/26; Dörmann 2003; Gross, M. 2006, 329; Jinks 2004. See also Human Rights Watch 2002; Kretzmer 2005, 191f.; Watkin 2005, 50–57/71.

ments, and conclude on that basis that none of the Geneva Conventions apply. In many cases they do not consider whether GCIV could apply to unlawful combatants. In doing so, they ignore several facts strongly suggesting that GCIV applies to unlawful combatants[169] and that unlawful combatants must be considered civilians.

Most importantly, the wording of GCIV itself leaves no basis upon which one may conclude that GCIV would not apply to unlawful combatants. Article 4 of the GCIV, which sets out the personal field of application of the convention, reads:

> Persons protected by the Conventions are those who, at a given moment in any manner whatsoever find themselves, in case of a conflict or occupation, in the hand of a Party to the conflict or Occupying Power of which they are not nationals.
>
> Nationals of a state which is not bound by the Convention are not protected by it. Nationals of a neutral state who find themselves in the territory of a belligerent state, and nationals of a co-belligerent state, shall not be regarded as protected persons while the state of which they are nationals has normal diplomatic representations in the state in whose hands they are.
>
> [...]
>
> Persons protected by the Geneva Convention for the Amelioration of the Condition of the Wounded and Sick in Armed Forces in the Field of August 12, 1949, or by the Geneva Convention for the Amelioration of the Condition of Wounded, Sick and Shipwrecked Members of Armed Forces at Sea of August 12, 1949, or by the Geneva Convention relative to the Treatment of Prisoners of War of August 12, 1949, shall not be considered as protected persons within the meaning of the present Convention.

While paragraph 1 suggests a very wide application of GCIV and only excludes from its scope individuals who are nationals of the state holding them, paragraphs 2 and 3 clearly limit the scope of the convention. Paragraph 2 excludes specific individuals due to their nationality.[170] Paragraph 3 excludes all individ-

---

169 For a profound and detailed discussion of these reasons, including the reasons addressed here, see Dörmann 2003. See also ICTY, Trial Chamber, *Prosecutor v. Delalic*, (Judgment), para. 271; Aldrich 2002, 893 fn. 12; Jinks 2004, 382–386; ICRC Commentary on GCIV, 50 f./53.

170 My argument does not require specifying this provision. For details of who is excluded from the protection of the GCIV due to nationality, see, for example, Dörmann 2003, 49; ICRC Commentary on GCIV, 48–50; Jinks 2004. See also ICTY, Trial Chamber, *Prosecutor v. Delalic*, (Judgment), paras. 263–266; Meron 2000, 256–260; with reference to the armed conflict in former Yugoslavia in the early 1990s, both interpret the nationality criterion in light of the realities of an armed conflict between different ethnic groups that originally belonged to the same nation.

uals protected by GCI-III from the protection of GCIV.[171] Hence, while the convention only applies to specific individuals, the criteria by which others may be excluded from the scope of the convention are unrelated to their illegitimate engagement in warfare. In the same vein, Article 4 (3) of the GCIV explicitly excludes legal participants in warfare, namely individuals who, after capture, enjoy POW status under GCIII, but it does not address individuals who were not so entitled.[172]

The wording of Article 5 of the GCIV supports this interpretation. The article determines the conditions under which the protection provided by GCIV may be derogated from. It allows for derogation of specific protections, 'where in the territory of a Party to the conflict, the latter is satisfied that an individual *protected person is definitely suspected of or engaged in activities hostile to the security* of the State'.[173] With regard to occupied territories, it determines that 'an individual *protected person* [who] is detained as spy or *saboteur, or as a person under definite suspicion of activity hostile to the security* of the Occupying Power [...] shall, in those cases where absolute military security so requires, be regarded as having forfeited rights of communication under the present Convention'.[174] Article 5 of the GCIV thus directly addresses unlawful combatants[175] as belonging to the groups of individuals protected by the convention.[176]

The drafting history of the GCIV supports this view and will not allow a conclusion that it was meant not to protect unlawful combatants.[177] Some states sought to exclude unlawful combatants (primarily talking of spies and saboteurs) from the scope of the GCIV and argued accordingly.[178] Other powers, however, did not share this view.[179] As a compromise, in order 'to strike a fair balance between the rights of the state and those of protected persons'[180], the conference

---

[171] Richard Baxter (1951, 328) further limits the scope of GCIV. He argues that it does not apply on the battlefield.
[172] Dörmann 2003, 48–50.
[173] Art. 5 (1) GCIV, emphasis added.
[174] Art. 5 (2) GCIV, emphasis added.
[175] As pointed out, (lawful) combatants, according to Article 4 GCIV, do not count as 'protected persons' under GCIV.
[176] Dörmann 2003, 50.
[177] The discussions of this question were prompted at the Diplomatic Conference (1949) by the fact that the Stockholm Conference (1948) had included in the group of protected individuals those who participated in hostile acts but were not members of the armed forces. ICRC Commentary on GCIV, 52.
[178] Final Record of the Diplomatic Conference of Geneva, 1949, Vol. 2 Sec. A, 621f.
[179] Final Record of the Diplomatic Conference of Geneva, 1949, Vol. 2 Sec. A, 620–622.
[180] Final Record of the Diplomatic Conference of Geneva, 1949, Vol. 2 Sec. A, 796.

introduced an additional article, which was to become Article 5 in the final text, which allowed for derogations from the rights and privileges of the convention with regard to unlawful combatants.[181] This provision was adopted overwhelmingly.[182]

Finally, the wording of the API also supports the view that some unlawful combatants are protected under the GCIV. It states in Article 45 (3) that:

> Any person who has taken part in hostilities, who is not entitled to prisoner-of-war status and who does not benefit from more favourable treatment in accordance with the Fourth Convention shall have the right at all times to the protection of Article 75 of this Protocol. In occupied territory, any such person, unless he is held as a spy, shall also be entitled, notwithstanding Article 5 of the Fourth Convention, to his rights of communication under that Convention.

Both the first and the second sentences of this provision only make sense if unlawful combatants, under certain conditions, fall within the scope of the GCIV. Article 45 (3), thus, confirms that the GCIV is applicable to unlawful combatants.[183]

To conclude, certain unlawful combatants are protected by the GCIV. The term 'unlawful combatant', then, may be helpful in denoting a certain group of civilians and in highlighting the fact that individuals belonging to this group directly participated in hostilities without being entitled to do so. Unlawful combatants, however, do not constitute a third legal status that complements the two others recognized by international humanitarian law. Not all unlawful combatants are protected by the same international legal regulations. Regardless of the protections that apply to them, however, they remain civilians and are to be treated as such.[184]

---

181 The Article was introduced as Article 3 A. Final Record of the Diplomatic Conference of Geneva, 1949, Vol. 2 Sec. A, 796 f./814.

182 Art. 5 was adopted by 29 to 8 votes, with 7 abstentions. Final Record of the Diplomatic Conference of Geneva, 1949, Vol. 2 Sec. A, 798/815. For discussion of the drafting history with respect to the applicability of the GCIV to unlawful combatants, see the ICRC Commentary on GCIV, 52–54; Dörmann, 2003, 56–58. Dörmann (2003, 52–56/58) also analyses the drafting history of the GCIII and concludes that the statements made about the treatment of persons who do not meet the requirements for protection as combatants/POWs (for details on combatant/POW status, see chapter 4.3.5) do not indicate that unlawful combatants should not fall within the scope of the GCIV. See also Jinks 2004, 383 f.

183 Dörmann 2003, 50 f. Dörmann (2003, 51 f.) gives additional arguments for the applicability of the GCIV, which he draws from military manuals of different states.

184 This has been confirmed by the HCJ in its judgments in *Public Committee against Torture v. Government of Israel*, paras. 26–28.

One may conclude from the above that the prohibition against killing civilians applies to all individuals who illegitimately take a direct part in hostilities, and that their illegitimate activity does not give them a different legal status from civilians. Hence, they may only be targeted for the time they actually take a direct part in hostilities. They may not be attacked during any interim between different engagements in hostilities.

One can summarize the preconditions for the justifiability of targeted killing *of terrorists* under international humanitarian law regulating these conflicts by referring to the conclusions reached about the legality of targeted killing during international armed conflicts in general. The permission to target and kill in international armed conflicts depends primarily on the status of the targeted individual. First, terrorists may be targeted if they constitute combatants and have not ceased to participate in warfare. Provided that they are to be classified as civilians, they may not be targeted as a matter of principle. Nevertheless, their actions may result in the loss of their immunity from attack. Loss of immunity, however, is limited in time. This means that terrorists who have lost civilian immunity from attack will regain it when they stop directly participating in hostilities. If they conceal their weapons, they must be addressed, warned, and summoned to show that they do not carry arms, and they may only be attacked if they refuse to do so. If this is impossible, they may be targeted only on the basis of convincing evidence of their direct engagement in hostilities. As they belong to the category of civilians, unlawful combatants are also subjected to these regulations; this applies to all terrorists who participate in warfare and are not entitled to do so. Moreover, regardless of who is targeted, the killing can only constitute a legal act of warfare if it takes place on the territory of one of the parties to the international armed conflict in question. A final limitation on the targeted killing of terrorists follows from the requirement to protect the civilian population as much as possible from the effects of attack. Provided targeted killings of terrorist harm civilians not taking a direct part in hostilities, these killings are illegal if the harm they cause is disproportionate to the expected advantage. This necessarily includes inappropriate or unnecessary acts executed with an eye to producing an advantage in the hostilities.[185]

---

185 Though controversial, the principle of military necessity represents an additional requirement for the justifiability of targeted killings of terrorists. It, however, does not seem to have substantial practical consequences regarding the prohibition of the practice. First, this is due to the already far-reaching prohibition which I have established for targeted killings of terrorists as they tend to occur in real-life. Secondly, it is due to the difficulty of interpreting military necessity in practice and the latitude that must often be given to individual assessments of the relevant situation (Melzer 2008, 296 f.). For a detailed

4.3.5 The status of terrorists and conclusions regarding the legality of targeting and killing them

Whether targeted killings of terrorists involved in international armed conflicts may be regarded as legal acts of warfare, then, depends on three factors: (1) whether the killing takes place either on the territory of a party to the conflict or on occupied territory; (2) which status the terrorist is entitled to and the protection that proceeds from this; and (3) the manner in which the targeted killing is carried out, whether sufficient care is applied, and whether the killing is carried out in accordance with the principle of proportionality.

(Ad 1) The first requirement needs little explanation. It follows from the fact that international humanitarian law only applies to the states involved in the conflict. Nevertheless, it imposes a limit on the legality of targeted killing, one that is of particular importance in light of actual targeted killings. It is self-evident that targeted killings can be carried out in the territory of the parties to the conflict, but this is an important factor to account for when assessing actual cases of targeted killing. Taking targeted killings carried out by the United States against Al Qaeda as examples, it becomes clear that it is not necessarily the case that states carry out targeted killings in the territory of parties to the conflict in question. The overview of actual cases of targeted killing of alleged terrorists showed that the United States carried out targeted killings in several different countries, such as Yemen, Pakistan and Afghanistan.[186] The United States has never claimed that the acts of Al Qaeda can be attributed to Yemen or Pakistan. The argument that the United States is involved in an international armed con-

---

presentation of the requirement of military necessity, see Melzer 2008, 278–298. As he convincingly argues 'the principle of military necessity prohibits the employment of any kind or degree of force which is not indispensible for the achievement of "the ends of the war", even if such force would not otherwise be prohibited by IHL [International Humanitarian Law].' (Melzer 2008, 287.) For targeted killings this means that individuals who are legitimate targets during armed conflicts according to the above listed requirements may only be targeted, as opposed to e. g. being captured, where their killing is 'likely to contribute effectively to the achievement of a concrete and direct military advantage' and where there is 'no reasonable alternative which would entail a comparable military advantage while interfering significantly less with humanitarian or other values, which IHL aims to protect' including the life of the attacked individual. (Melzer 2008, 293 f.) More doubts raises the due process requirement which Richard Murphy and Afsheen Radsan (2009) introduce for targeted killings even if these acts take place during armed conflicts. Most importantly this requirement demands an 'independent, intra-executive investigation' of all cases of targeted killing.

186 See chapter 2.1.

flict with Al Qaeda itself does not hold. Such a conflict, hence, does not spread over the entire globe. As a result, targeted killings of Al Qaeda members could only be justified as legal acts of warfare in an international armed conflict if they took place in Afghanistan, provided the acts of Al Qaeda could be attributed to the Taliban, or provided Al Qaeda participated in an international armed conflict taking place between Afghanistan and the United States.[187]

(Ad 2) The second condition for targeted killings of terrorists to be considered legal acts of warfare requires more detailed discussion. It is met if the targeted terrorist is a combatant; it is also fulfilled if he or she is a civilian but, at the time of attack, takes a direct part in hostilities.

Given that terrorism is a tactic and not a kind of conflict *per se* and that all different members of (independent) armed forces could theoretically be deemed terrorists, I will establish the requirements for the attribution of these statuses relevant to assessing targeted killings of terrorists. Secondly, I will apply these provisions to terrorists, establishing the framework for analysis as well as for applying the criteria in practice, which, as I have argued above, is important because there is no internationally accepted definition of terrorism.

Civilian status requires no further explanation. Determining who constitutes a civilian can be done with reference to the requirements for combatant status. As I have argued, international humanitarian law only provides for two statuses, that of combatants and that of civilians. All persons not considered combatants must be considered civilians. In order to assess whether or under what conditions terrorists may be targeted in international armed conflicts, one must, therefore, determine the requirements international humanitarian law formulates for combatant status and ask whether terrorists meet such requirements.

Combatants are individuals who actively participate in warfare *and are entitled to do so* by international humanitarian law. Combatant status is directly linked to prisoner of war (POW) status. All combatants are entitled to POW status, when 'they have fallen into the power of the enemy forces'[188]. Not every POW, however, was a combatant before he was captured.[189] This is important to note, as the GCIII only refers to POW status. With regard to the GCIII, the provisions on POW status are, thus, decisive for determining who is entitled to participate in hostilities and, hence, who may be described as a combatant. However, not all

187 Note that the United States (under both the Bush and the Obama administrations) has not taken this line of argument, but argued that they are in an armed conflict with Al Qaeda (and its affiliates) themselves. Also note that I am not giving a legal assessment as to the actual situation in Afghanistan, but use the example to illustrate the theoretical argument.
188 Art. 4 A GCIII.
189 See, for example, Art. 4 (4) and (5) GCIII.

provisions may be considered, and the terms 'POW' and 'combatant' must, in this respect, not be used interchangeably. The API presents a wider understanding of 'combatant' than the GCIII. Moreover, it explicitly accounts for both POW status and combatant status.[190] That said, it is very unlikely that terrorists would meet the requirements for combatant status set out in any of the conventions.

GCIII generally ascribes combatant status to members of the armed forces of a party to the conflict. This includes members of militias or volunteer corps forming part of such armed forces.[191] Medical personnel and chaplains who are members of the armed forces are exempt from combatant status. They are specifically protected under Article 33 of the GCIII. However, they do not constitute combatants, and hence may not be targeted.[192]

The GCIII also ascribes combatant status to members of militias and volunteer corps, including members of organized resistance movements (independent armed forces)[193] that do not form part of the regular armed forces. These individuals, however, only constitute combatants if the armed force of which they are part belong to a party to the conflict[194] and fulfils the following conditions:

(a) that of being commanded by a person responsible for his subordinates[195]

(b) that of having a fixed distinctive sign recognizable at a distance[196]

(c) that of carrying arms openly[197]

(d) that of conducting their operations in accordance with the laws and customs of war[198]

---

190 Art. 43 API sets out who has to be considered a combatant. Art. 44 API sets out who is entitled to POW protection.

191 Art. 4 A (1) and (3) GCIII. Paragraph 3 sets out that the status of members of regular armed forces is not affected regardless of whether the government or authority to which these armed forces belong is recognized by the adversary party or not.

192 If domestic law prohibits some members of the armed forces, such as judges or civil servants, to participate in hostilities, they do not belong to the group of combatants, strictly speaking. They constitute non-combatants. In respect to the protection from attack they are entitled to, however, they belong to the group of combatants. They are not immune from attack, but may be attacked as may regular combatants. Ipsen 1994, mn. 313.

193 I will use the term 'independent armed forces' for these military organizations and groups. 'Independent' is used to express that they are not incorporated into the regular armed forces. The term should not be mistaken to mean that these forces have no relationship to the party to the conflict. Such an understanding would contradict the requirement for combatant status set out in Art. 4 (2) GCIII.

194 Art. 4 A (2) GCIII.

195 Art. 4 A (2a) GCIII.

196 Art. 4 A (2b) GCIII.

197 Art. 4 A (2c) GCIII.

198 Art. 4 A (2d) GCIII.

In order to belong to a party to the conflict, independent armed forces must be acting on behalf of that party.[199] This relationship can be based on explicit authorization of the party to the conflict, but this is not required. A *de facto* relationship suffices. While commentators make clear that government responsibility for the conduct of the independent armed forces is required, they tend not to give a clear answer as to how such responsibility is established.[200] In light of the argument I presented with regard to imputability of non-state acts to states,[201] it seems convincing that such responsibility exists if the government hold a degree of control over the independent forces, without requiring effective control. The ICRC states in its commentary on Article 4 of the GCIII that the *de facto* relationship can be established by tacit agreement, provided that the activities and operations of the militias and volunteer corps clearly indicate which side of the conflict they are on. It does not further clarify what is required for a tacit agreement.[202] Given that paragraph 2 of Article 4 of the GCIII requires 'fighting on behalf of the "Party to the conflict" in the sense of Article 2 [of the GCIII]'[203], responsibility to the extent stated here is required in order to be able to speak of independent armed groups fighting on behalf of the party to the conflict. This has been affirmed by the ICTY in *Prosecutor v. Tadic*.[204] Independent armed forces not factually linked to a party to the conflict may not be considered participants in the armed conflict, neither may they be considered as falling within the scope of the GCIII.[205]

In order to meet condition (a), independent armed forces must be under the command of a leader responsible for all acts carried out by members of 'his' or 'her' forces, whether the acts followed or were contrary to his or her orders. It appears that a formal structure of command and rank is not required, but it must be developed enough to be able to ensure respect for the laws of war.[206]

The convention does not articulate what type of sign militias and volunteer corps must wear in order to be entitled to either combatant status or POW status, as laid out in terms of condition (b) above. It is widely accepted that it does not need to be a uniform, but it must be the same for all members of the group. It must be such that it distinguishes them from civilians. Moreover, it must be rec-

---

199 Who may be considered a party to a conflict has been established in chapter 4.3.1.

200 Solf 1982, 233 f.; Dinstein 2004, 39 f.; Rosas 1976, 257 – 262.; Watkin 2005, 25 – 28.

201 See chapter 4.3.2.

202 ICRC Commentary on GCIII, 57.

203 ICRC Commentary on GCIII, 57.

204 ICTY, Appeals Chamber, *Prosecutor v. Tadic*, (Judgment), 92 – 96.

205 Compare Art. 2 GCI-IV; chapter 4.3.1. See also Solf 1982, 235.

206 ICRC Commentary on GCIII, 59; Watkin 2005, 28.

ognizable at a distance that would be sufficient to be able to recognize a uniform. When such a sign needs to be worn has been a frequent subject of discussion. The ICRC commentary on Article 4 suggests that it is to be worn 'constantly' and 'in all circumstances'.[207] This seems too strict. The provision must be read in light of its purpose, and this allows removing the sign under certain circumstances. The provision serves to guarantee loyalty in fighting,[208] and provides the precondition vital for the general humanitarian principle of protecting the civilian population as much as possible from the effects of warfare. It thus requires the members of independent armed forces to be identifiable as such whenever they could be confronted by enemy forces. No doubt this is the case throughout the course of military operations. Members of independent armed forces, however, may be regarded as likely to be confronted by adversary forces not only when these independent armed forces plan to carry out military missions; they must also be distinguishable from the civilian population when enemy forces plan to attack them. This allows them to remove the distinctive sign when they are on leave or during the night when they are in a clearly recognizable military base. It does not allow them to remove the distinctive sign immediately after military operations. It neither seems to allow removing it when carrying out administrative work or training. This is due to the fact that during such time, they would not be recognized as military personnel, and thus adversary forces would be likely to mistake civilians for soldiers or *vice versa*.[209] Finally, the condition of wearing a fixed and distinctive sign requires members of militias or volunteer corps to affix their sign to any vehicle or other means of transport they use.[210]

Condition (c) does not demand that members of militias or volunteer corps carry their weapons visibly at all time. The provision was sought to 'guarantee the loyalty of fighting'[211], and thus requires them to not deliberately hide their

---

207 ICRC Commentary on GCIII, 59, see also 60. This position is also taken by Draper 1971, 202.

208 ICRC Commentary on GCIII, 59; Dinstein 2004, 37.

209 Although he is right in limiting the time during which members of independent armed forces need to wear a fixed and distinct sign according to the regulations in the API, Dinstein (2004, 37f.) provides an interpretation of the GCIII 4 A (2b) which does not correspond to the purpose of the provision. A too limited understanding is also held by Magne Frostad (2005, 154f.).

210 ICRC Commentary on GCIII, 59f. The condition does not require military forces to choose a sign that makes them easily visible or detectable. As with uniforms which often help to camouflage, the sign is thought to make it possible to distinguish between civilians and military personnel once the person is detected. Dinstein 2004, 38.

211 ICRC Commentary on GCIII, 61.

arms and to pose as civilians in order to gain an advantage over the enemy.[212] Finally, condition (d) is self-explanatory. It requires members of militias and volunteer corps to respect international humanitarian law.[213]

Some commentators have argued that these conditions, formulated for militias and volunteer groups not part of the regular armed forces, apply to regular armed forces as well, be it directly via Article 4 A (2) of the GCIII or as customary international law. Accordingly, it has been argued that members of regular armed forces may only be regarded as combatants or POWs if these forces conform to the standards set out in Article 4 A (2) of the GCIII.[214]

The clear separation between paragraphs (1) and (2) of Article 4 A of the GCIII contradicts this view. Soviet objections during preparatory work against explicitly prescribing these conditions to regular armed forces support the argument that the distinction, as introduced by the wording of Article 4 of the

---

212 ICRC Commentary on GCIII, 61; Dinstein 2004, 38 f.

213 Some legal commentators add, as a separate precondition for combatant status, that the independent armed forces have to be organized. See Dinstein 2004, 36/39; Frostad 2005, 146/148 f. That they have to be organised is right and restated in Art. 4 A (2) of the GCIII with regard to resistance movements. Nevertheless, it does not need to be introduced as a separate precondition for combatant status. It is incorporated in the requirements set out in Art. 4 A (2a-b) of the GCIII. The delegates drafting the Article considered these paragraphs to sufficiently guarantee an internal organization. ICRC Commentary on GCIII, 56 f. 'The implication was that such an organization must have the principal characteristics generally found in armed forces throughout the world, particularly in regard to discipline, hierarchy, responsibility and honour.' ICRC Commentary on GCIII, 58. Although it is not mentioned in the GCIII, some commentators add a second condition for POW status. They deny POW status, and thus the right to participate in hostilities, to individuals who are nationals of, or owe any duty of allegiance to, the detaining power. Cassese 2005, 408; Dinstein 2004, 37/40; Frostad 2005, 146/160; contrary opinion Cerone 2002. Art. 4 (2) of the GCIII is silent on this nationality requirement. John Cerone (2002) points out that there have been precedents in US jurisdiction which accorded POW status to individuals who had been fighting against their own state. It seems convincing that these individuals do not enjoy POW status once they have fallen into the hands of a party they are nationals of or to which they owe any duty of allegiance. As with individuals who do not act according to the rules of warfare while the group they belong to does, however, it would lead to absurd consequences to oblige states to treat the legality of killing them differently from the other members of the group they are fighting in.

214 The US administration formulated this position with a view to the status of members of the Taliban captured during the Afghanistan War beginning in 2001. White House, Ari Fleischer, 58. White House Press Secretary announcement of President Bush's determination of the legal status of Taliban and Al Qaeda detained, 7 February 2002; White House, Fact Sheet: Status of Detainees at Guantanamo, 7 February 2002. See further Mallison/Mallison 1977, 44/48; Wedgwood 2002, 335; Ho/Yoo 2003a, 10–20.

GCIII, was made deliberately. They suggest that the conditions set out in Article 4 A (2) (a-d) of the GCIII do not apply to regular armed forces, in the sense that members of regular armed forces are only entitled to participate in hostilities and entitled to POW status if the armed forces they belong to meet these requirements.[215]

From this, it does not yet follow that regular armed forces may as such refuse to distinguish themselves from the civilian population, conceal their weapons, and violate international humanitarian law, and still legitimately demand POW status for their members.[216] Certain requirements seem to be incorporated in the term 'regular armed forces' itself. Armed groups only constitute regular armed forces when they meet certain requirements. Regular armed forces belong to a state. They, as a group, are distinguishable from the civilian population. Moreover, they have an organized command structure and hierarchy that allows for controlling and disciplining their members as well as ensuring that they adhere to the laws of war and, hence, fulfil the state's international legal obligations.[217] If military forces as a whole fail to meet these conditions, they may no longer be considered regular armed forces.

The threshold that must be met for military forces incorporated into the state system to be considered regular armed forces, however, must be relatively low. The command structure and the degree of organization may differ from one force to another. It would be mistaken to believe that only highly organized units or organizations could constitute regular armed forces. It is furthermore not the case that entire armed forces would be disqualified as regular armed forces if certain units do not meet the definitional preconditions of being considered regular armed forces. If any violation of international humanitarian law deprived the members of armed forces of their POW status, the provision that POWs may be tried for violations of international humanitarian law prior to detention while continuing to enjoy the protection provided by the GCIII[218] would not make sense. Furthermore, if the threshold were too high, the protection of members of regular armed forces would depend too much on the decisions of the adversary party. This neither corresponds to the intention to regulate the treatment of military personnel, nor does it correspond to the provision that POW status is to be assumed when there are doubts as to the status of a captured person.[219]

---

215 Final Record of the Diplomatic Conference of Geneva, 1949, Vol. 2 Sec. A, 465–467; Wolfrum/Philipp 2002, 597.
216 Such position seems to be implied in Matheson 2002, 355; Wolfrum/Philipp 2002, 601f.
217 ICRC Commentary on GCIII, 63.
218 Art. 85 GCIII.
219 Art. 5 (2) GCIII.

If, however, the armed forces as a whole do not display any sign – be it a uniform or a even a cap – that distinguishes them from the civilian population, for example, one could no longer speak of regular armed forces. This would also be the case for armed forces not subject to any hierarchical order guaranteeing that the members have knowledge of international humanitarian law and can be instructed to follow the rules.

To conclude, the conditions established in Article 4 A (2) (a-d) of the GCIII do not apply to regular armed forces. Nevertheless, they are to a certain extent expressed in the term 'regular armed forces'. This also makes sense of the states' agreement not to specify the requirements regular armed forces must meet to be entitled to participate in hostilities.[220]

The GCIII finally entitles the population of unoccupied territory to combatant status when they spontaneously take up arms in order to prevent enemy forces from entering and occupying their territory. This applies provided that they carry their arms openly and adhere to the laws and customs of war (*levée en masse*). This provision accounts for the fact that such situations do not allow for time to establish organized military forces and organize a recognizable sign to distinguish individuals participating in the defence action from others. Such a situation does not correspond to cases of targeted killing of terrorists and will therefore not be further addressed.[221]

API classifies a wider range of individuals as combatants. It addresses the conditions for combatant status explicitly and does not determine the status implicitly by defining POW status. It complements Article 4 of the GCIII, but does not replace it. This is particularly important given that several states, in particular those most relevant to the recent context of targeted killing (the United States and Israel), have not ratified the API.

Unlike the GCIII, the API does not distinguish between regular armed forces and independent armed forces. It formulates conditions for combatant status that apply to both groups equally. It ascribes combatant status to 'members of armed forces of a Party to the conflict (other than medical personnel and chaplains covered by Article 33 of the Third [Geneva] Convention)'.[222] All members of armed forces (with the mentioned exceptions) may take part in combat and, thus, in principle be attacked. 'Armed forces of a Party to the conflict consist of all organized armed forces, groups and units which are under command responsible to that Party for the conduct of its subordinates', provided they are

---

220 The same conclusion seems to be reached by Solf 1982, 234 f.; Aldrich 2002, 894 f.
221 Art. 4 A (6) GCIII. For details on *levée en masse*, see Ipsen 1994, mn. 313; Frostad 2005, 134–138.
222 Art. 43 (2) API.

'subject to a internal disciplinary system which *inter alia,* shall enforce compliance with the rules of international law applicable in armed conflicts.'[223]

Accordingly, armed groups must meet four requirements to constitute armed forces: they must (1) be organized; (2) belong to a Party; (3) be subordinated to a command structure responsible for the conduct of the members of the armed force; and finally, (4) be subject to an internal disciplinary system. The conditions (1), (2) and (3) match the corresponding regulations of the GCIII.[224] There are no specific criteria as to the form the organization takes. The requirement seeks to guarantee that the fighting is collective in character and not carried out by singular individuals without adequate training and preparation, fighting 'private' wars. Moreover, they must be subordinated to a command structure as well as to a party to the conflict, which equally prevents the existence of a 'private' war.[225]

Important distinctions between the API and the GCIII regarding combatant status are that the API does not make the status of individual members of independent armed forces dependent on their wearing distinctive signs or on their compliance with 'rules of international law applicable to armed conflicts'[226]. Moreover, individuals cannot be deprived of their status as combatants even if it is the case that parts of the individual's unit or armed forces do not adhere to certain rules of international humanitarian law. The armed forces, however, are bound by these requirements, and the command of such forces is under the international legal obligation to ensure that these requirements are adhered

---

223 Art. 43 (1) API. The article takes on Art. 4 A (3) of the GCIII and rules that organized armed forces, groups and units which profess allegiance to a Party to the conflict 'that is represented by a government or authority not recognised by the adversary Party' must be considered armed forces. Art. 43 (3) of the API provides that a state may incorporate paramilitary forces into its armed forces, though it must notify the other parties to the conflict of this action.

224 Other than the GCIII, Art. 43 of the API, for reasons of security, allows the command to be anonymous and collegial for resistance movements in occupied territory. Arts. 86 and 87 of the API that reintroduce personal responsibility, however, weaken the effect of Art. 43. Furthermore, the API sets out that it does not make any distinction with regard to the status of the members of armed forces, whether the state to which they owe allegiance is recognised by the adversary party. This no longer applies to regular armed forces only but also to members of independent military groups and, under certain circumstances, to individuals fighting a high contracting party in their struggle for self-determination. Solf 1982, 237 f.

225 ICRC Commentary on API, mn. 1672; Solf 1982, 237. See also fn. 213 in the current chapter.

226 Art. 43 (1) API. A definition of what those 'rules of international law applicable in armed conflicts' consist of is provided in Art. 2 (b) API.

to. In particular, condition (4) is therefore crucial for a military group to be considered an armed force, and thus for their members to be considered combatants. It guarantees that armed forces have a disciplinary system that, by way of military disciplinary law and military penal law, warrants that the members of such armed forces comply with the laws and customs of war.[227] This does not mean that individuals lose their combatant status if they do not adhere to the laws of war. The API sets out for all members of the armed forces that which the GCIII sets out for members of the regular armed forces of a party: that they, when captured, may be punished for their deeds, yet retain their status as combatants. In principle, individuals are only denied combatant status if the forces they belong to do not have an internal disciplinary system that intends to, and is capable of, preventing individuals from breaching international humanitarian law.[228]

That said, under certain circumstances, combatants forfeit their status as combatants, due to their behaviour. This applies to combatants who violate fundamental regulations by not distinguishing themselves from the civilian population.[229] An exception to this obligation is made with regard to certain specific and rare situations. Individuals retain their status as combatants in situations during the armed conflict that do not allow them to distinguish themselves from the civilian population, provided that, under such circumstances, they carry their arms openly.[230] More could be said about these provisions,[231] but they do not have any impact on the context of this book. In terms of the API, a combatant only loses his or her status as a combatant if he or she is captured while engaged in hostile acts, in preparation for them, or immediately afterwards.[232] While he or she is engaged in such hostile acts, he or she may be targeted regardless of his or her status. In the same vein, when he or she is captured, he or she may not be killed regardless of his or her status. Moreover, killing him or her under such circumstances does not constitute targeted killing. As long as he or she has not been captured, he or she cannot be deprived of his or

---

227 ICRC Commentary on API, mns. 1672–1675; Solf 1982, 238 f.
228 ICRC Commentary on API, mn. 1675.
229 Art. 44 (3) 1st sentence API. ICRC Commentary on API, mn. 1695.
230 Art. 44 (3) API.
231 The ICRC, for example, further limits the consequences by explaining that a combatant who does not distinguish him- or herself from the civilian population may be punished for such conduct, but only loses combatant status if he or she deliberately does not distinguish him- or herself in order to take advantage of the enemy for his or her hostile activities. ICRC Commentary on API, mn. 1690.
232 Art. 44 (5) API. ICRC Commentary on API, mn. 1721; Solf 1982, 256.

her status, and accordingly may be targeted as is the case with any combatant, as set out in the API.

What conclusions can be drawn from these explanations of the preconditions for possessing combatant status and, following from this, civilian status in terms of the *GCIII and the API* when it comes to the justifiability of targeted killings of terrorists? There are important differences between the GCIII and the API. They particularly concern the requirements that must be met by combatants not belonging to the regular armed forces of a state in order to be considered combatants. This is due to the particular intention of the drafters of the API to address guerrilla fighters belonging to a party to the conflict. If one applies the provisions set out in the GCIII or the API to terrorists, one finds that terrorists typically fail to meet the requirements for combatant status, and hence must be considered civilians. As a result, terrorists may be targeted only while they are taking a direct part in hostilities. Exceptions to this do exist, though these are rather theoretical situations that do not correspond to currently relevant conflicts with terrorists in general, and conflicts with terrorists that triggered the discussion about targeted killing of terrorists in particular.

More specifically, it is possible that certain units or members of regular armed forces, as addressed in the GCIII, who fight with terrorist means, may be deemed terrorists while still possessing combatant status, and therefore may, in principle, be targeted. Nevertheless, such acts carried out by regular armed forces have to be considered acts of state terrorism, and that is beyond the focus of this book. Only one, if rather specific and untypical, situation is conceivable in which *non-state* terrorists could be considered combatants and, as such, may be targeted: that in which non-state terrorist groups or individuals are incorporated into the armed forces of one party to the conflict. Being combatants, these terrorists could then be targeted throughout the entire conflict, provided they are not *hors de combat*. That said, these cases may be described as targeted killings of non-state terrorists, but the justification for targeting the terrorists is not their non-state terrorist activity, but their role as combatants. In other words, the situation of war provides justification for targeting and killing terrorists who, however, are considered terrorists for reasons other than their warfare activities.[233]

With regard to all other constellations, one must consider the rules as set out in the GCIII with respect to independent armed force and as set out in the API

---

233 If they were deemed terrorists due to their warfare activity, they could of course also be targeted. This however, would constitute the aforesaid situation of state terrorism and not fall within the focus of this book.

with regard to armed forces in general. Theoretically, terrorist groups are able to meet some of these requirements.[234] First, they may belong to a party to the conflict. The discussion of state imputability of non-state acts has shown this to be possible. If the conflict between a state and a terrorist organization triggers an armed conflict, this imputability is a precondition for international humanitarian law to apply. Terrorist groups that participate in an armed conflict taking place between two states also meet this requirement, provided that state responsibility can be established by the factual link between the non-state terrorist group and the state.[235]

Secondly, terrorist organizations could theoretically be able to distinguish themselves from civilians as well as carry their arms openly. This does not typically apply to terrorist organizations, however. It neither applies to those conflicts with terrorists that triggered the current discussion about targeted killing. This becomes clear when one recalls the terrorist acts carried out by Al Qaeda, such as the attacks of 2001 in New York, the attacks of 2003 in Madrid, or the numerous attacks on markets and public spaces in Afghanistan since 2001, as well as the terrorist attacks carried out by Palestinian terrorists in buses, cafés and other public places in Israel. Terrorists typically seek to remain unrecognized until they actually launch an attack. They hide their arms and disguise themselves as non-combatants. This decreases the likelihood of their being detected and stopped by state agents. Moreover, it maximizes fear among non-combatants, minimizing the predictability of attacks and creating a feeling of danger in arbitrary moments and places. In most cases disguise is necessary to improve the likelihood of success, and it is thus applied in terrorist groups almost throughout relevant actions. Nevertheless, terrorist violence can theoretically be carried out in uniform and while openly carrying weapons. This is particularly obvious with regard to state terrorism. The acts most often described as state terrorism, such as the dropping of the atomic bomb in Hiroshima and Nagasaki and the bombing of Dresden during World War II, show this most clearly.

---

234 Whether and how far the requirements for combatant status are collective or individual in nature has been subject to discussion. (See, for example, Draper 1971, 196 f. He argues that all criteria are collective in nature. The requirements of carrying arms openly, wearing a distinctive sign and acting according to the laws of war, however, also apply on an individual level.) This is an important question. The fact that POWs may be tried for war crimes contradicts the assumption that there is an individual perspective to the criteria. The fact that terrorist organizations as a group fail to meet the requirement, however, need not be scrutinized at this point. Regarding group denial of combatant status, see also Watkin 2005, 34–37.
235 Such a substantial link has been considered to exist between Al Qaeda units fighting in Afghanistan and the Taliban regime. See, for example, Schneckener 2006, 77 f.

Nevertheless, this also applies to non-state terrorism, and is due to the fact that terrorism is, as I have argued, defined in terms of the use of force, the extent of force, its aim (influencing the political and social behaviour of an audience) and its target (innocent individuals). Provided these criteria are met, open violence by individuals distinguishing themselves from the rest of the population would still have to be considered terrorist violence.

Finally, terrorist organizations differ regarding their organisational and hierarchical structure. Regardless of whether they are organized as large networks or as locally oriented organizations, there is nothing inherent to terrorism as such that excludes the possibility of an organizational or command structure.

That said, terrorist organizations or units fail to fight according to the laws and customs of war. As a result they fail to fulfil Article 4 A (2) of the GCIII and Article 43 (1) of the API and hence cannot be considered combatants. More specifically, terrorist acts are understood as violent acts directed against innocents. Terrorists deliberately choose this kind of violence with the aim of influencing the political or societal behaviour of an audience. This does not mean that they will not attack combatants as well. But part of their tactic is not to limit their violence to combatants.[236] They systematically and inevitably violate the prohibition against attacking innocent civilians, i.e. civilians not taking a direct part in hostilities. As such, they, as groups, necessarily violate the fourth requirement for combatant status of members of independent armed forces in Art. 4 A (2) of the GCIII, namely to act according to the laws and customs of war.[237] Equally, they necessarily lack an internal disciplinary system seeking to enforce adherence to the rules of international humanitarian law, as required by the API. As shown above, the API does not seek to deprive individuals of combatant status due to their own terrorist conduct. The API instead envisaged a disciplinary system that, among the members of a certain group, enforces conduct according to laws and customs, something that the intent of terrorist organizations – to use violence against innocent civilians – renders impossible.

With regard to the justifiability of targeting and killing a particular individual, one need not discuss the conduct of particular terrorist organizations in order to draw conclusions about the status of terrorists in international armed conflicts and, hence, about the legality of targeting them. Terrorist organizations necessarily fail to meet the preconditions for combatant status. As a result, individual members of such terrorist groups are civilians.

---

236 See chapter 1.
237 For a similar reasoning, see Vöneky 2004, 153.

The fact that terrorists are civilians does not necessarily make justification for possible targeted killings of terrorists during international armed conflicts impossible. Provided the other preconditions for describing targeted killings of terrorists as legal acts of international warfare are met, such justification is limited to targeting and killing terrorists whilst they actively participate in hostilities. This makes those terrorists who are not engaged in active participation but 'only' support terrorist activities, or those who are engaged in planning, illegitimate targets. Other terrorists may only be targeted from the moment of deployment to the moment they have laid down their weapons.

With regard to the different forms and cases of targeted killing I distinguished, this first excludes responsive targeted killing. Defensive targeted killing can theoretically be justified when the terrorist is on his or her way to carry out an attack (case 1), since this arguably may be regarded as deployment. Moreover, some targeted killings belonging to case 2, i.e. targeted killings carried out with a view to stop a determinable terrorist attack, could be justified, provided the targeted terrorists can be described as engaged in hostilities, which includes the entire period from the moment weapons are taken up to the moment they are laid down after attack: that is, the period during which they are able to immediately inflict harm.

Practically, however, ensuring the legality of such acts faces additional difficulties. One cannot normally assess a situation to be part of a hostile act based on distinctive signs the terrorist affixes to the body or a vehicle or on the weapons he or she carries visibly. An assessment is most commonly based on intelligence information, rendering the situation problematic. As addressed, mere belief or suspicion does not suffice in justifying the application of lethal force in such situations. If possible, the protection of innocent civilians requires warning the given individual and summoning him or her to show that he or she does not carry weapons. Otherwise a high degree of certainty and convincing evidence must be established before lethal use of force could be justified.

The other cases of targeted killing (the remaining situations belonging to case 2 and cases 3 and 4) cannot be justified. As follows from the antecedent paragraph, the remaining situations of case 2 are not carried out against individuals taking a direct part in hostilities. Cases 3 and 4 are carried out against individuals for whom involvement in a determinable threat has not been established. Thus these targeted individuals can also not be described as taking a direct part in hostilities.

(Ad 3) If a targeted killing only affects the terrorists against whom it was aimed, the antecedent conclusions are the final conclusions as to the justifiability of the act. As already established, if a targeted killing also harms innocent civilians, the legality of the act additionally depends on whether the harm inflict-

ed upon these individuals can be justified by the military necessity of the act. It is theoretically possible for targeted killings of terrorists to fulfil this additional requirement. In other words, it is possible for states to carry out a certain targeted killing with sufficient care. It is also possible for the act to be appropriate and necessary to achieve the intended aim, and for it not to cause disproportionate harm. These aspects cannot be determined on a theoretical level, but must be assessed on a case-to-case basis.

That said, the burden of proof is high, and this applies to several aspects involved in this requirement.[238] First, it is not clear whether targeted killings of terrorists decrease terrorist activity and, hence, whether they are appropriate.[239] Secondly, even if killing certain individuals may sufficiently add to the war effort, it must be shown that the killing of one person adds to such a degree that it renders death and injury to innocent individuals proportionate. This may depend on the importance of the targeted terrorist to the activity of the group to which he or she belongs. Given that many terrorists can be replaced, and that the expected military benefit is to a large extent speculative, however, it is all but self-evident that proportionality can be assumed for the majority of cases. If a number of innocent civilians are killed by the targeted killing, it seems rather impossible that this could be the case. Finally, targeted killings that cause great harm to innocent civilians are often executed by means of remote controlled missiles or bombs dropped from a high altitude. Moreover, they are often carried out in populated areas.[240] It is not clear whether such actions can possibly be described as carried out with sufficient care. That which Stefan Oeter formulated with regard to weapons fired from large distances in armed conflicts often seems to apply to these situation as well. He argues that this use of weapons often constitutes a particular problem for the safety of the civilian population. These weapons typically cannot be directed very precisely. If they are applied against specific military targets in a populated area, they often do not bring about great military advantage, but instead cause harm to innocent civilians in the vicinity. From the principle of civilian protection, it follows that these weapons may be applied with great care only, which means in principle that they may not be used in highly populated areas.[241] Oeter's point gains additional weight when it is not a large military post that is targeted, but a single individual.

---

238 See also chapter 6.1.
239 See chapter 8.
240 See chapter 2.1.
241 Oeter 1994, mn. 447.

This analysis allows for some final conclusions regarding the justifiability of targeted killings of terrorists as legal acts of warfare in international armed conflicts. To an extent, any theoretical assessment of the legality of targeted killing in terms of international humanitarian law regulating international armed conflicts must remain complex. However, I have provided a framework, including specific requirements, which can be applied when assessing specific cases of targeted killing of terrorists.

In order to constitute legal acts of warfare, these targeted killings must take place within an international armed conflict as regulated by international humanitarian law. Given that international armed conflicts necessarily take place between states, this requires the acts of the terrorist group to be attributed to a state. This is convincingly the case when the state has at least overall control over the non-state terrorist group. When such attribution is not possible, the laws of war regulating international armed conflicts may also apply if the terrorists participate in an existing armed conflict between two states.

In those cases in which international humanitarian law applies, terrorists can only be targeted on the territory of the states involved in the conflict. With the exception of the rather unrealistic situation in which terrorists are incorporated in the armed forces of a state but attacked for their non-state terrorist acts, terrorists may only be targeted whilst they take a direct part in hostilities. This is due to the fact that they do not constitute combatants, which is the precondition for targeting and killing them whilst they continue to participate in the conflict. Not being combatants, they constitute civilians. This limits the right to target terrorists to targeting those actively participating in hostilities. It also limits the moments at which they may be targeted. Moreover, mere suspicion of active participation does not suffice for applying lethal force in such situations; a high degree of certainty must be established. Finally, targeted killings can only be justified if they are appropriate and necessary and do not cause disproportionate harm to innocent civilians.

It becomes clear that targeted killings of terrorists cannot possibly be regarded as legal acts of warfare to the extent suggested in current scholarly and practical defences of the practice. Most often the rules regulating international armed conflicts do not apply. Even if they applied, they realistically cannot justify targeted killings in response to terrorist attacks that took place in the past. Neither can they justify defensive targeted killings against terrorists who are believed to continue to be involved in terrorism and pose a general future, or a determinable, threat, but who are not clearly determinably engaged in a particular act of hostility. Finally, because targeted killing often causes harm to innocent civilians, its justifiability in the end is highly questionable.

4.4 Non-international armed conflicts

In addition to international armed conflicts, the laws of war traditionally recognize non-international armed conflicts. It therefore remains to be asked whether targeted killings of terrorists constitute legal acts of warfare in terms of international humanitarian law regulating non-international armed conflicts. This analysis gains particular importance in light of the international legal defence of targeted killing of terrorists that has been formulated. Proponents of targeted killing tend to base their defence of the practice on international humanitarian law regulating international armed conflicts. To a more limited extent, however, they draw on international humanitarian law regulating non-international armed conflicts.[242]

4.4.1 The legality of targeted killing in non-international armed conflicts

International humanitarian law regulating non-international armed conflicts is far more limited than its counterpart regulating international armed conflicts. It comprises two different sets of rules. On the one hand, the APII sets out provisions for non-international armed conflicts. Some of them constitute international customary law, and hence bind those states that have not ratified the Protocol. On the other hand, common Article 3 of the GCI-IV sets out certain minimum humanitarian standards for non-international armed conflicts. These provisions oblige states not only on the basis of their recognition of the Geneva Conventions, but also because these provisions constitute international customary law.

In principle, the APII and common Article 3 focus on the protection of those not participating in the fighting (non-combatants). The hostilities themselves are regulated to a limited extent. As to the manner of fighting, the APII and common Article 3 only impose regulations protecting non-combatants. In contrast to the laws regulating international armed conflicts, they do not give those participating in the hostilities any rights to do so. They neither define those participating in the fighting, nor do they explicitly address how individuals still actively par-

---

242 For the Israeli government's argument in HCJ, *Public Committee against Torture v. Government of Israel*, see chapter 4.2. See also Kretzmer 2005. Derek Jinks (2003b) does not address the legality of targeted killings of terrorists, yet he argues that international humanitarian law regulating non-international armed conflicts applies to conflicts with transnational terrorist organizations.

ticipating in the hostilities ought to be treated. Implicitly, both the APII and common Article 3, then, allow for targeted killings under certain circumstances.

More specifically, *APII* explicitly distinguishes between members of armed forces or armed groups[243] and civilians, and prohibits attacks on civilians.[244] It also prohibits the killing of persons who had previously taken part in the hostilities but ceased doing so.[245] It excludes from the group of protected individuals civilians who take a direct part in hostilities for the time they do so.[246] Hence, APII does not prohibit attacks on members of the armed forces, nor on civilians, for the time they participate in fighting.[247]

Additional provisions for the application of armed force appear to be derivable from the general protection Article 13 of the APII requires for civilians as long as they do not directly participate in hostilities and from the fundamental guarantees Article 4 provides. Although APII explicitly outlaws only direct attacks on civilians, these regulations convincingly include the obligation to carry out attacks on military objectives with due care, in order to avoid harm to innocent civilians as well as the other individuals protected by Article 4. Careless conduct leading to death or injury of protected individuals contravenes the obligation to treat these individuals humanely and with 'respect for their person'[248]. Similarly, protected persons are not treated humanely when they are killed or injured in the course of military action that was not appropriate in, or was unnecessary for, reaching the intended aim. This also applies when the harm done to them is disproportionate in relation to the military aim. Any such action does not consider the individual concerned as a human being of intrinsic value who needs to be accounted for in actions affecting him or her.[249]

The basic provisions protecting the civilian population as set out in Article 13 and Article 4 of the APII restate customary international law. As the ICTY Ap-

---

243 I will in the following only refer to armed forces.
244 Art. 13 (1) (2) APII. See also Art. 4 APII.
245 Art. 4 (2) (a) APII. This prohibition applies to the civilian population but also to members of the armed forces who are *hors de combat*. The term '*hors de combat*' may be understood in the same way as in API. Partsch 1982, 640. See also Art. 7 (1) APII. The Article requires all wounded, sick and shipwrecked – this can be a military or a civilian person (ICRC Commentary on APII, mn. 4635) – to be respected and protected. The verb 'protected' means 'to spare, not to attack' and thus prohibits directing any hostile act against the protected persons. ICRC Commentary on APII, mn. 4635.
246 Art. 13 (3) APII.
247 ICRC Commentary on APII, mn. 4789.
248 Art. 4 (1) APII.
249 For the applicability of the principle of proportionality through customary law, see Kretzmer 2005, 200.

peals Chamber stated in *Prosecutor v. Tadic*, for conflicts envisaged in APII,[250] customary law prohibits intentionally bombing innocent civilians and attacking non-military objectives. Moreover, it requires taking precautions when attacking military objectives.[251]

With regard to the prohibition on killing in non-international armed conflicts, *common Article 3* of the Geneva Conventions serves a similar purpose to APII.[252] As the ICJ noted in *Nicaragua v. United States of America*,[253] and as the ITCY reaffirmed in *Prosecutor v. Tadic*,[254] the rules laid down in common Article 3 constitute customary law, and hence bind all states.

Common Article 3 prohibits intentionally killing anyone who does not 'take active part in the hostilities, including members of the armed forces who have laid down their arms and those placed "hors de combat" by sickness, wounds, detention, or any other cause'[255], under any circumstances, as an expression of inhumane treatment. Although it does not expressly reference civilians, this provision highlights a distinction between members of the armed forces and *civilians*, which is the only reasonable way of understanding the introduced distinction between those not taking an active (direct) part in hostilities and members of the armed forces who no longer engage in hostilities.

Targeting and killing those who participate in hostilities is neither addressed nor prohibited by common Article 3. The only legal limits that common Article 3 arguably places on such targeted killings follow from the possibility that such actions will harm individuals protected by the article. As I have argued with regard to APII, common Article 3 also appears to require states to take sufficient precautions during hostilities to avoid harming protected persons. Moreover, it requires the harming action to be appropriate to fighting the enemy and neces-

---

250 The ICTY does not explicitly address APII, yet the kind of non-international armed conflicts it envisaged in its judgment – non-international armed conflicts with the scope of civil wars – corresponds to the kind of non-international armed conflicts to which APII applies. For the scope of application of APII, see chapter 4.4.2.

251 ICTY, Appeals Chamber, *Prosecutor v. Tadic*, (Decision on the Defence Motion of Interlocutory Appeal on Jurisdiction), paras. 100–102.

252 Solf (1982, 667) questions that Article provides 'explicit protection for the civilian population against attacks or the effect of attack', and highlights that common Article 3, including its provision on 'violence to life and person', intended to regulate the treatment of individuals in the hands of the adversary party; yet he recognises that the prohibition to kill also applies to military attacks on civilians.

253 ICJ, *Nicaragua v. United States of America*, (Merits), para. 218.

254 ICTY, Appeals Chamber, *Prosecutor v. Tadic*, (Decision on the Defence Motion of Interlocutory Appeal on Jurisdiction), paras. 98/102.

255 Common Article 3 (1) GCI-IV.

sary to reaching the intended aim. Any inappropriate and unnecessary conduct cannot meet the fundamental requirement to treating the protected persons humanely.[256]

To conclude, targeted killings are not prohibited under the laws of war regulating non-international armed conflicts if three conditions are met: that conflicts with terrorists can be described as non-international armed conflicts in terms of the *APII and common Article 3*; that terrorists form an active part of the armed forces fighting the state, or, if they are civilians, take an active part in hostilities at the moment they are targeted; and that killing them does not constitute inappropriate, unnecessary or disproportionate use of military force.[257]

The distinction between terrorists who are members of armed forces and those who are civilians participating in hostilities is crucial to the argument of whether or not targeted killings can be justified as legal acts in non-international armed conflicts since the time period during which terrorists can be targeted depends on their classification. International humanitarian law regulating non-international armed conflicts does not provide any criteria helpful in establishing such a classification. The distinction can only be made in reference to actual situations. A few conclusions, however, can be drawn.

Provided a conflict between a state and a non-state terrorist group constitutes an non-international armed conflict, the members of that group organizing and carrying out the hostilities must be regarded as part of the armed forces, since an armed conflict by definition requires armed forces on both sides. Not all members of the terrorist organization must then be considered members of these armed forces. If a terrorist organization consists of a political and a military division, only the latter comprise armed forces.[258] Furthermore, not all individuals actively supporting the terrorists' armed activity are members of the armed force. Depending on their involvement, some of them must be regarded as civilians. An individual who, at certain points, participates in the hostilities is not excluded from the group of civilians; otherwise it would not make sense to exclude civilians from protection for the time period during which they directly participate in hostilities, as explicitly set out in the APII. It is, rather, the role of the individual and his or her affiliation that is decisive. This finding also applies to terrorists taking part in a non-international armed conflict between another non-state armed group and a state. A more precise conclusion cannot be derived from the limited regulations set out in the APII and common Article 3. In chapter 6, I

---

256 For the content of common Article 3, see Moir 2002, 58–60.
257 Consider also fn. 185 in the current chapter.
258 Compare Kretzmer 2005, 200.

will look at how civilians can be distinguished from combatants from a slightly different perspective, helpful in light of the relatively undefined international legal situation.

In those cases in which a theoretical determination has been made that the terrorists in question belong to the armed forces, an additional limit to targeting and killing them may arise in practice. Terrorist groups commonly operate in a different manner than do conventional armed forces, who are often recognizable by virtue of their uniforms. Terrorists typically hide and seek to remain unrecognized and undetected by dressing like civilians until they strike. They cannot easily be distinguished from the civilian population. What Lindsey Moir formulated with regard to guerrilla fighters applies to those terrorists: '[W]here insurgents cannot be differentiated from civilians, they must cease to be legitimate targets.'[259] This follows convincingly from the prohibition against attacking civilians, as this obligation is necessarily unfulfilled if one cannot distinguish civilians from those participating in the fighting.

To conclude, international humanitarian law regulating non-international armed conflicts allows for targeted killings under the preconditions set out. This applies when terrorists participate in non-international armed conflicts established between other groups and a state. Whether targeted killings of terrorists can be justified as legal acts of warfare in conflicts between a state and the terrorist group itself depends on whether these conflicts constitute armed conflicts in terms of the APII or common Article 3, which will be the focus of analysis in the following section.

4.4.2 Conflicts with terrorists as non-international armed conflicts and conclusions regarding the legality of targeted killing of terrorists

Common Article 3 and APII differ regarding the kind of non-international armed conflict to which they apply. *APII* sets comparatively strict requirements for its application. It only applies to armed conflicts 'which take place in the territory of a High Contracting Party between its armed forces and dissident armed forces or other organized armed groups which, under responsible command, exercise such control over a part of its territory as to enable them to carry out sustained and concerted military operations and to implement this Protocol'[260]. Article 1 (2) adds that the 'Protocol shall not apply to situations of internal disturbances and

---

259 Moir 2002, 59.
260 Art. 1 (1) APII.

tensions, such as riots, isolated and sporadic acts of violence and other acts of a similar nature, as not being armed conflicts'. In other words, the APII covers only armed conflicts that reach a high degree of intensity. It applies to 'large scale armed conflicts, that is to say civil strife presenting all the characteristics of intensity, duration, and magnitude of the Spanish and Nigerian civil wars'[261].

In view of these strict requirements for the protocol's application, conflicts between states and terrorists do not typically constitute non-international armed conflicts in the document's terms. These conflicts may be limited to the territory of the state involved, but they typically fail to meet the remaining requirements. This is due first to the fact that conflicts with terrorists do not generally manifest as large-scale armed conflicts. Terrorist violence is commonly characterized by a variety of 'hit and run' tactics. Terrorists carry out attacks that are isolated in the sense that each act constitutes a terminated action. These acts develop their impact not only via their destructive capacities but also through the fear and insecurity they provoke. Conflicts with terrorists do not typically resemble scenarios of ongoing fighting over territories and state authority, as encountered in the Spanish Civil war, 1936–1939, or in other comparable non-international armed conflicts, such as the civil war in the Congo, 1960–1968, or the civil strife in Nicaragua, 1981–1990.[262] In this respect, conflicts between states and terrorists typically differ profoundly from the large-scale civil wars that the APII applies to.

Secondly, terrorist organizations do not commonly control a certain area of territory within the state against which they are fighting. Those which confront states, such as Al Qaeda or ETA, act clandestinely. They do not establish political or factual control and, as such, typically fail to meet the requirement of territorial control as set out in Article 1 (1) of the APII. This applies even if a wide reading of the provision were accepted and an argument made that one may speak of territorial control when 'insurgents undermine the territorial control of the government whilst controlling the population and commanding its allegiance, without necessarily exercising complete or continuous control over an area'[263].

That said, it is theoretically possible for terrorist groups to fulfil the requirement set out in APII. As already noted, this is due to the fact that terrorism is a strategy that may be applied by all groups involved in armed conflicts. Given that such groups may then be deemed terrorists, it is possible that conflicts between

---

261 Cassese 2005, 433. See also ICRC Commentary on APII, mns. 4438/4453; Commission on Human Rights, Minimum Humanitarian Standards, UN Doc. E/CN.4/1998/87, paras. 78 f.
262 ICTY, Appeals Chamber, *Prosecutor v. Tadic*, (Decision on the Defence Motion of Interlocutory Appeal on Jurisdiction), para. 97.
263 Moir 2002, 106.

states and such groups constitute non-international armed conflicts as envisaged in the APII. These are not, however, valid descriptions of the examples that have been provided of the current fight against terrorism. The two current conflicts that triggered the discussion of targeted killing of terrorists, the fight against Al Qaeda and the Palestinian-Israeli conflict, for example, fail to meet this requirement. It can be stated even more firmly: overall, actual conflicts described as conflicts with terrorists do not constitute non-international armed conflicts according to the APII. In order to comprehensively assess the legality of targeted killings, the addressed theoretical situations must nevertheless be kept in mind.

With regard to such situations, applying the Protocol faces an additional difficulty. This is due to the fact that the APII requires non-state groups to be organized, under a responsible command, and in control of parts of the state territory *in order to be able to implement the Protocol.*[264] This requirement not only limits the scope of the Protocol to conflicts between states and non-state groups who, due to their organization and territorial authority, *would be able* to implement the Protocol; it requires the non-state forces to actually *be willing* to implement the Protocol. Only such willingness activates the Protocol.[265] The APII applies to a conflict once the non-state group shows its willingness to adhere to the Protocol.

This does not mean that the obligations set out in the APII apply reciprocally.[266] It means that non-state groups, on the one hand, need to fulfil the preconditions set out in Article 1 of the APII in order *to be able* to implement the treaty. Furthermore, they actually must *be willing* to do so in order to activate the APII in non-international armed conflicts.

It is possible to identify what constitutes this willingness through an examination of the drafters' intention to keep the applicability of the Protocol independent of subjective judgements of the parties to the conflict.[267] This intention

---

264 Art. 1 (1) APII.
265 Cassese 1981, 424f.; Moir 2002, 99. More generally on the legal basis of the binding effects of APII to non-state parties to a conflict, see Cassese 1981. See also Moir 2002, 96–99.
266 Arguably there exists a limited right to reprisals, i.e. to violate certain provisions of the Protocol in order to make the adversary party halt consistent and serious violations of the Protocol. The fundamental provisions, which protect the most basic human values, however, are absolute and may not be derogated from. Cassese 1981, 432–439. In light of the fundamental values affected by targeted killings – the life of the targeted individual and often the life and health of innocent bystanders – derogation from the provisions protecting these values is unthinkable. The question of the right of reprisals does, therefore, not require attention.
267 ICRC Commentary on APII, mn. 4438.

suggests that the objective existence of an organisational structure, of a responsible command, and of territorial control establish tacit compliance and make the Protocol applicable. Furthermore, non-implementation of the Protocol cannot be assumed on the basis of violations of individual provisions within it, or on the basis of single individuals' violations of it. This would make the applicability of the APII dependent on the assessment of the parties to the conflict, contradicting the humanitarian considerations behind the Protocol.

That said, tacit compliance can no longer be assumed if the non-state group's conduct indicates the contrary. It is appropriate, then, to consider that group unwilling to implement the Protocol if it systematically applies terrorist strategies and, thus, systematically violates one of the most fundamental principles of the Protocol. The terrorist strategies that characterize conflicts between terrorists and states, therefore, buttress a convincing argument that terrorist groups fail to fulfil the requirements of Article 1 (1) of the APII.

It is difficult to theoretically determine what degree of severity terrorist activity must reach before a lack of implementation can be established. The same is true of the questions of how systematic this refusal must be, and whether, and to what extent, compliance with the remaining provisions of the Protocol can change the picture. In addition, it is unclear whether one can still deem as terrorist those non-state groups that apply terrorist acts to such a limited extent that they may be regarded as implementing the Protocol. It can therefore be concluded that the argument that targeted killings of terrorists are legal acts of warfare in terms of the APII applies only to conflicts with terrorists who are able to and do implement the Protocol. As this is highly unlikely, even with regard to the theoretically possible large-scale civil wars between states and non-state parties deemed terrorist, the APII does not typically apply.

There remains only one conceivable situation in which the APII could regulate a state's treatment of terrorists. As noted with regard to international armed conflicts, terrorists could participate in non-international armed conflicts taking place between a non-state group fulfilling the requirements put forth in Article 1 of the APII and the armed forces of a state. In such situations, terrorists are not members of the armed forces on the basis of the fact that the conflict takes place between themselves and a state. Depending on their relationship to the parties to the conflict, their organization, and their manner of fighting, they constitute either armed groups or civilians who take part in hostilities. Depending on their status, they may be targeted and killed until they stop participating in hostilities altogether, or while engaged in hostilities.

Typically, such terrorists are civilians participating in hostilities.[268] As a result, they may be attacked only while engaged in hostilities. In terms of the different cases of targeted killing of terrorists distinguished above, this allows for only one of these cases: the targeted killing carried out against a terrorist who is on his or her way to carry out an attack (case 1). Moreover, targeted killings belonging to case 2 are justified if the terrorist is targeted while engaged in the execution of an attack.

Even in these cases, or if the terrorist belongs to an armed group, however, he or she may only be targeted if he or she can be distinguished from civilians not participating in hostilities. This may be possible but requires a high degree of certainty. It therefore seems rather unrealistic, generally speaking, that targeted killings of terrorists can be justified in non-international armed conflicts taking place between a non-state group fulfilling the requirements of Article 1 of the APII and the armed forces of a state.

Conflicts with terrorists, it can finally be concluded, do not constitute armed conflicts in terms of the APII. This is theoretically possible. Nevertheless, it requires the terrorist group to be sufficiently organized and to possess and control state territory. Moreover, the ongoing fighting has to reach a sufficiently substantial scale. If these requirements are met, the conflict constitutes a non-international armed conflict in terms of the APII. However, even if these requirements are met, the Protocol only applies once the terrorist group demonstrates its ability and willingness to implement it. And such ability and willingness cannot be assumed if the situation is defined by the application of terrorist tactics. It is equally unlikely that targeted killings of terrorists can be justified in a non-international armed conflict taking place between a non-state group other than the terrorist group and the state and in which the terrorists participate. With reference to the APII, targeted killings can hence be justified as legal acts of non-international warfare only under exceedingly theoretical circumstances.

This is not the conclusive answer as to the applicability of international humanitarian law regulating non-international armed conflicts to conflicts with terrorists, and hence as to the justifiability of targeted killings of terrorists as legal acts of warfare in non-international armed conflicts. *Common Article 3* applies to any 'armed conflict not of an international character occurring in the territory of one of the High Contracting Parties'. It sets the threshold for the existence of armed conflicts considerably lower than the APII, with regard to the degree of intensity of the conflict, the organizational structure, command, and territorial

---

268 For further reasoning regarding the distinction between the different groups, see chapter 6.1.

control of the non-state party to the conflict, and the territorial scope of the conflict.

Although the wording may at first suggest the opposite, it seems convincing to argue that common Article 3 does not limit non-international armed conflicts to those armed conflicts taking place in the territory of the participating state. As Nils Melzer recently plausibly argued, the territorial link to one contracting party should not be read as an attempt to limit the meaning of non-international armed conflicts to armed conflicts that take place on the territory of one state. It can be explained instead in light of the fact that common Article 3 also applies to conflicts between two non-state actors: at the time of drafting, common Article 3 required the conflict to be territorially linked to one contracting state; it required that the state via which non-state parties should be bound by the article had already ratified the treaty in order to render it applicable to such a conflict.[269] As Melzer points out, state practice supports this reading of common Article 3,[270] and the wording leaves space for such an interpretation since the article must not be read as drawing a distinction between international and territorial internal armed conflicts, but can be read as contrasting international armed conflicts – i.e. armed conflicts between states – and all other armed conflicts.[271]

The application of common Article 3, thus, does not seem to be limited to conflicts between states and non-state terrorist actors taking place on the territory of one state. As opposed to the case with APII, the matter of territorial scope does not exclude current conflicts between terrorists and states from the application of common Article 3.[272] The additional requirements that must be

---

269 Melzer 2008, 258 f.

270 Melzer 2008 259 – 261.

271 Melzer 2008, 259. For the claim that common Article 3 applies to transnational conflicts between state forces and non-state terrorist groups, see also Jinks 2003b, 40 f.; Paulus/ Vashakmadze 2009, 112/116 f.; Schmitz-Elvenich 2008, 180 – 190. Bruha (2002), in light of current transnational terrorism and consistent with Jink's position, argues that one should include among *non-international* armed conflicts all conflicts not covered by the meaning of '*international* armed conflict'. In contrast to Jinks, he formulates this understanding as a future aim to be worked towards, rather than as a clearly existing legal reality. Kretzmer (2005, 194 – 196) recognizes that common Article 3 does not formally apply to conflicts that do not take place on the territory of the state involved. Nevertheless, he ends up arguing that common Article 3 shall apply to such conflicts. He regards conflicts between transnational terrorist organizations and states as internal armed conflicts, provided they reach the required degree of violence. For a contrary opinion as to the scope of common Article 3, see, for example, Moir 2002, 31; ICRC Commentary on GCIV, 36.

272 Although this interpretation is widely accepted, the territorial limits of (non-international) armed conflicts are debated. This debate is often based on, but exceeds, the discussion in this chapter regarding the extent of violence which is required for the laws

met before common Article 3 may apply, however, make its applicability highly unlikely.

With regard to the intensity of the conflict, it is undisputed that common Article 3 covers armed conflicts that fall beneath the threshold articulated by the APII, covering armed conflicts that do not constitute full-scale civil wars.[273] There is some contention about the kind of armed clashes between non-state groups or between non-state groups and states that would constitute internal armed conflicts in terms of common Article 3. The matters under debate concern the extent of violence as well as the organizational and command structure of the involved non-state armed group.

Having agreed on the wording of common Article 3, the meaning of 'armed conflict' was subject to ongoing discussion during the drafting process, and the drafting parties did not provide a definition of the term. Different positions have been taken since. It is widely accepted that the application of common Article 3 requires the non-state armed group to have some organizational structure.[274] Furthermore, the threshold for non-international armed conflicts, in the terms of the article, is frequently set above riots, isolated and sporadic acts of violence.[275] The ICC Rome statute explicitly excludes such cases of limited force from the scope of non-international armed conflicts.[276] The ICTY has argued along similar lines. In *Prosecutor v. Tadic,* it states that non-international armed conflicts exist 'whenever there is a resort to [...] protracted armed violence between governmental authorities and organized armed groups or between such groups within a State'.[277]

The ICRC, in its commentary on the Geneva Conventions, by contrast, seeks to significantly lower this threshold. It distinguishes between a 'genuine armed

---

regulating non-international armed conflicts to apply. Depending on the position one takes in this debate, the requirements for the applicability of the laws regulating non-international armed conflicts may even exceed those presented in this chapter. See e.g. Anderson, K. 2011; and fn. 112 in the current chapter.

273 Common Article 3 also covers armed conflicts between two non-state groups. See for example ICTY, Appeals Chamber, *Prosecutor v. Tadic,* (Decision on the Defence Motion of Interlocutory Appeal on Jurisdiction), para. 70; Moir 2002, 39; Partsch 1982, 623/627. In light of the focus of this book, such conflicts do not require any attention here. Therefore, I will continue to speak of conflicts between state armed forces and non-state groups.

274 ICTY, Appeals Chamber, *Prosecutor v. Tadic,* (Decision on the Defence Motion of Interlocutory Appeal on Jurisdiction), para. 70; Kretzmer 2005, 197f.; Moir 2002, 36.

275 See, for example, Bond 1974, 54–61; Greenwood 1994, mns 210, p. 41; Jinks 2003b, 32f. See also Meron 2000, 260f.; Moir 2002, 37.

276 ICC Statute, Art. 8 (2) (d).

277 ICTY, Appeals Chamber, *Prosecutor v. Tadic,* (Decision on the Defence Motion of Interlocutory Appeal on Jurisdiction), para. 70. See also ICTR, Chamber I, *Prosecutor v. Akayesu,* (Judgment), para. 620.

conflict' and 'a mere act of banditry or an unorganised short-lived insurrection', yet argues that the article should be understood as widely as possible. Rhetorically, it asks:

> What Government would dare to claim before the world, in a case of civil disturbances which could justly be described as mere acts of banditry, that, common Article 3 not being applicable, it was entitled to leave the wounded uncared for, to torture and mutilate prisoners and take hostages?[278]

With this, the ICRC advocates that common Article 3 applies in situations that involve the use of armed force, regardless of the extent of violence, the degree of organization of the non-state group concerned, or its command structure.[279]

The intention behind construing common Article 3 as widely as possible is understandable. Nevertheless, a more restrictive reading is more convincing, owing to the consequences of a wide interpretation of common Article 3, and it makes sense in light of the drafters' intention as well as with regard to the widely shared understanding of the Article in jurisprudence and the scholarly literature.

Common Article 3 invokes the most fundamental humanitarian obligations regarding the protection of the victims of non-international armed conflicts. If one focuses on this function of the article, it makes sense to claim that this protection is applicable whenever states and non-state groups exchange violence and run the danger of ignoring these humanitarian yardsticks. Hence, with regard to this purpose of the article, the move to regard any exchange of violence between states and non-state groups as falling within the scope of common Article 3 is understandable.

From a different perspective, however, a danger appears, which the ICRC, in its commentary on common Article 3, loses sight of. To describe a conflict as an armed conflict not only invokes obligations regarding the protection of the victims of the situation, but it also invokes international humanitarian law. This is highly relevant to the justifiability of targeted killings, since this invokes an

---

278 This as well as the two preceding quotations in ICRC Commentary on GCIV, 36.
279 James Bond (1974, 54) provocatively concludes that the ICRC 'apparently believes that even one man brandishing a gun in another's face is non-international conflict within the meaning of Article 3'. See also Moir 2002, 32f./36. The ICRC commentary can be read in two ways. Either it can be understood as suggesting that conflicts of low intensity and isolated character have to be considered armed conflict, though not 'genuine' ones. Or else, it can be read as suggesting that such situations do not constitute armed conflicts but do still fall within the scope of common Article 3. The following reply equally applies to both interpretations.

understanding of legitimate force that differs from that which applies to situations short of armed conflict.[280] I will address this issue when discussing moral explanations for the distinction between justified killing during warfare and during peacetime.[281] The preceding discussion of the limits that human rights set for lethal state action in situations short of armed conflict[282] and the limits established by international humanitarian law as addressed here, however, provided sufficient insight to outline the point at stake.

In armed conflicts, the justifiability of specific armed counter-measures is based on collectivization. This applies in several respects. The ongoing attack is ascribed to the adversary group as such. Individual violent actions carried out by the armed forces add up to a single ongoing attack, and this attack is ascribed to every individual belonging to the armed forces engaged in the hostilities. As such, force directed against individuals belonging to such armed forces is no longer prohibited in terms of international law, regardless of whether these individuals themselves are about to commit an act of force or whether they have already done so, for example. The individuals' active affiliation to warfare is decisive in their becoming legitimate targets during warfare. In this respect, their individual conduct is decisive for the collective threat to be ascribed to them. However, it is not their individual threatening conduct that explains the justifiability of lethal measures during warfare, but the threat emanating from the group they belong to. As has been shown by the discussion of the right to life as regulating situations short of armed conflict, and as I will make explicit in a discussion of considerations that exceed those of the legal field, in situations short of war, such collectivization does not apply. The use of lethal force can only be justified by the actual violent conduct of the individual against whom it is directed.

This does not mean that all individuals belonging to the adversary party may be attacked or killed. As has become clear, the legality of targeted killings during non-international armed conflicts depends on several additional factors, such as the nature of the affiliation the targeted individual has with the adversary group or the determinability of such an affiliation. Nevertheless, the legality of killing

---

280 Andreas Paulus and Mindia Vashakmadze (2009, 102 f.) seem to address a similar point in stating that 'stretching Common Article 3 to include anti-terrorist measures may serve humanitarian purposes in some situations, [yet] its application to ordinary (even widespread) human rights violations would not be a desirable result, because human rights – which remain applicable – generally provide more protection and are better tailored to situations that do not amount to an armed conflict'.

281 See chapter 6.1 and chapter 10.

282 See chapter 3.1.

an individual member of the armed forces depends neither on his or her actual involvement in an attack at the time of the killing nor on his or her actual personal violent conduct, but rather on his or her affiliation with the adversary group and, therefore, with the ongoing armed attack ascribed to this group. Furthermore, the difference between wartime and peacetime reasoning does not mean that the matter of deciding how to treat individuals who participate in the hostilities is left to the discretion of the state. Human rights law applies during non-international armed conflicts, and some limits may follow from this. International humanitarian law regulating non-international armed conflicts as set out in common Article 3, however, prescribes such treatment – specifying human rights law within non-international armed conflicts[283] – and this is of particular importance with regard to the extent of force that is acceptable during armed conflicts. Finally, the difference between wartime and peacetime reasoning does not mean that states are immune from international criticism for the conduct they apply in response to non-state use of force simply by claiming that the situation constitutes a non-international armed conflict.

Nonetheless, if it is agreed that armed conflicts include small scale, isolated conflicts even with unorganized groups, the basis on which such criticism could be formulated drastically diminishes. Once it is accepted that a certain conflict constitutes a non-international armed conflict, states cannot generally question the application of armed force against individuals considered to be part of the threat being combatted. From this perspective, the intention to extend the protection of victims of armed conflict as widely as possible remains understandable. As to the legitimacy of applying armed force against members of the adversary party, the classification of a certain conflict as a non-international armed conflict in terms of common Article 3, however, cannot be extended as widely as possible. In this respect, one must require a certain degree of organization on the part of the non-state groups as well as a certain degree and duration of violence. This guarantees that non-state violence can be understood as triggering a non-international armed conflict when states are required to apply armed force in order to control the situation. At the same time, it guarantees that situations in which conventional law enforcement measures would be sufficient to control the situation can, generally, not be described as such.[284]

---

283 For details on the relationship of human rights law and the laws of war, as well as for the relationship between the right to life and international humanitarian regulations, see chapter 3.2.

284 The possibility of applying measures of law enforcement is not limited to conflicts which take place on the territory of a state participating in the conflict. It can be exercised via third

This interpretation of non-international armed conflicts is supported by several textual sources as well as by arguments derived from state practice and the scholarly literature. First, it corresponds to the concern states formulated during the drafting process that common Article 3 should not cover low-scale non-international conflicts.[285] Second, as pointed out, it corresponds to the threshold formulated by most legal scholars and international courts for the existence of armed conflicts in terms of common Article 3. Third, the requirement of a sufficient degree of organization is implied in the assertion that the non-state group must be a party to the conflict.[286] This is also required in order to be able to assume that the non-state group can implement the obligations of common Article 3, which are binding on all state as well as non-state parties to an armed conflict.[287] Finally, this understanding of non-international armed conflict makes sense of the list of criteria, distilled by the ICRC from discussions during the drafting process, that must be met for a non-international armed conflict to exist. The commentary lists criteria describing non-state groups party to a non-international armed conflict as organized, prepared to adhere to international humanitarian law, in control of a certain part of state territory or population, or as being recognized or asserted belligerents.[288] These criteria may not be regarded as having defined non-international armed conflicts.[289] Nevertheless, they all point to conflicts that exceed sporadic and isolated acts of violence, indicating instead conflicts in which states are no longer able to confront protracted violence with law enforcement measures.[290]

The understandable concern that underlies the ICRC's position in its commentary on common Article 3 carries less weight in light of the legal situation in violent situations short of armed conflict. That such situations cannot be de-

---

states and in exercise of extraterritorial jurisdiction. The *factual* ability to apply these measures is not decisive. See also fn. 290 in the current chapter; and Melzer 2008, 261.

285 ICRC Commentary on GCIV, 31/35.

286 Moir 2002, 36.

287 Cassese 1981, 424; ICRC Commentary on GCIV, 37; Moir 2002, 52. For discussion of the legal basis for the binding effects on the non-state party to the conflict, see Moir 2002, 52–58. See also Cassese 1981, 429 f.; and ICRC Commentary on GCIV, 37.

288 ICRC Commentary on GCIV, 35 f.

289 Although these criteria do not exhaustively define the term, they have been considered helpful in determining the existence of an armed conflict. The ICTR drew on these criteria in its judgment in *Prosecutor v. Akayesu*, para. 619.

290 For further support of the conclusion by further reasoning regarding the distinction between situations of armed conflicts and peacetime situations, as well as for an explanation as to the fact that the actual ability to use law enforcement measures is not required for a situation of armed conflict to exist, see also chapter 6.1.

scribed as armed conflicts in terms of common Article 3 does not leave them in a legal void; neither does it leave the victims of such conflicts without protection. The protection formulated in common Article 3 is arguably so fundamental that it must be provided whenever armed force is applied. As already addressed, the rules set out in common Article 3 'constitute a minimum yardstick' and 'reflect what the Court in 1949 called "elementary consideration of humanity"'[291]. The ICJ formulated this position with respect to international armed conflicts. Yet it seems impossible for states to argue that they may violate the fundamental protections set out in common Article 3. Moreover, in cases short of non-international armed conflicts, human rights law applies and sets limits on state conduct. Human rights may be subject to derogation in states of emergency, and, particularly with regard to judicial guarantees, this may lead to more limited protection than that provided by common Article 3. Nonetheless, the possibility of derogation does not apply to the most fundamental human rights, which to a large extent prohibit acts addressed by the humanitarian regulations of common Article 3.[292]

Applying the established understanding of non-international armed conflicts to conflicts between terrorists and states provides a strong case for arguing that terrorist attacks do not typically constitute non-international armed conflicts. The terms delineating the threshold between situations short of non-international armed conflict and non-international armed conflicts remain very vague. More clearly shaped criteria, however, cannot be derived from the legal developments that have taken place since the implementation of common Article 3. Moreover, final assessments can only be formulated on a case-by-case basis. Some conclusions, however, can already be drawn.

The requirements of organization and protracted armed violence make it impossible to regard terrorist attacks as triggering a non-international armed conflict if they are carried out by independent individuals, by small units acting in-

---

[291] ICJ, *Nicaragua v. United States of America*, (Merits), para. 218.
[292] Differences occur with regard to judicial guarantees. Given the non-derogable status of Arts. 6 (2), 15 (1), and 16 CCPR, some profound judicial guarantees, however, are provided by human rights in any situation. Given that human rights law binds states but not non-state groups, one may argue that protection for the victims of armed conflicts necessarily decreases, as these groups are bound by common Article 3 yet not directly by human rights law. This highlights the importance of common Article 3. However, implementation of the obligation requires a sufficient degree of organization, and this is one aspect of what a threshold for the existence of a non-international armed conflict as proposed by the ICTY suggests. This does not solve the problem altogether. However, owing to the fact that non-state groups do not acquire any right to carry out the fighting via common Article 3, they at least face criminal prosecution for any act that would be in breach of common Article 3.

dependently of each other, or by units that are merely ideologically or loosely linked to a greater network or group. These attacks cannot be ascribed to one organized group and must be described as isolated acts of violence.[293] Even if terrorist acts are ascribable to one group, the scale of armed force and, particularly, the frequency of terrorist attacks make it unlikely that they constitute protracted armed violence crossing the threshold for an armed conflict to exist.

It has been argued that one attack of sufficient force, such as the attacks on the World Trade Center of 11 September 2001, may constitute a non-international armed conflict, regardless of whether such an attack happens once or several times. Such an attack cannot necessarily be described as a protracted use of armed force; yet, one may argue, the scale of violence suffices to trigger a non-international armed attack, even if the attack may otherwise possibly be described as isolated. This understanding is founded on considerations regarding the existence of international armed conflicts.[294]

Transposing the understanding underlying application of international humanitarian law regulating international armed conflicts to non-international armed conflicts should be done with caution. The decisive difference between non-international armed conflicts and international armed conflicts on this point seems to be that a state's ability to defend itself internally or against non-state actors substantially exceeds the options it has internationally against other states. As the relevant discussions within this book have shown, the legal situation, as reflected in the scholarly literature, accounts for this difference.[295] Hence, although extreme extent of force seems to make it more likely that an attack constitutes a non-international armed attack, it is not plausible that the extent of violence renders the fact that an act is isolated irrelevant.[296]

It is plausible to distinguish among different possible situations. If it is estimated that the organization will continue with similar attacks, one attack of severe extent seems to suffice in constituting a non-international armed conflict. If it is clear, however, that the attack was limited to only one attack, I would argue that this attack does not trigger a non-international armed conflict. In such a case, the act is isolated, and the application of military force will not prevent further attacks. This also applies if the likelihood of repetition is low, or if it can be

---

293 See also chapter 5.3.

294 Vöneky 2004, 149 f./161 f.

295 Compare scholarly opinion about the threshold of international armed conflicts (see chapter 4.3.1) and non-international armed conflicts (see above in the current section).

296 For this result, see also Paulus/Vashakmadze 2009, 118. O'Connell (2005, 538) adds that an attack alone does not make a war – only attack with the counter-attack does.

reasonably expected that further attacks can be prevented by law enforcement measures.

In conclusion, like APII, common Article 3 justifies targeted killings under certain circumstances, but they are atypical when it comes to actual conflicts with terrorists. The conflicts we have in mind when talking of conflicts with terrorists do not reach the extent of armed conflicts and hence do not invoke wartime reasoning for the use of force. Nevertheless, as noted at several points, it is in the nature of terrorism that such cases may theoretically occur. Certain groups involved in protracted and ongoing hostilities with the armed forces of a state may apply terrorist tactics, and as such, be deemed terrorists. Common Article 3 applies to such situations and, in principle, legitimates the application of targeted killings, provided that the targeted individual belongs to the non-state armed force. Targeted killing of a terrorist can then, in principle, also be described as a legal act of warfare by common Article 3 if the terrorist does not belong to the non-state armed forces, yet is targeted while actively participating in the fighting. In non-international armed conflicts that take place between other groups and a state and in which terrorists participate, targeting and killing the terrorists may finally constitute legal acts of warfare, provided the acts are applied at a legal moment in respect to the status of the individual terrorists. Whether terrorists are members of the armed forces or civilians, in a conflict between the terrorist group itself and a state or between other groups and a state, targeted killings are not justified if the targeted person cannot clearly be distinguished from civilians not participating in the fighting. Given that terrorists typically disguise themselves, this requires clear evidence and makes it unlikely that targeted killings of terrorists can be considered legal in terms of common Article 3, even in the described theoretical constellations involving terrorists, which may be considered non-international armed conflicts according to common Article 3.

4.5 Occupied territories and a 'new' type of armed conflict

Having discussed the justifiability of targeted killing of terrorists in terms of the two kinds of conflict recognized by international humanitarian law, international and non-international armed conflicts, two remaining questions must be considered. The first concerns the justifiability of targeted killing in occupied territories. The second concerns the argument that conflicts with transnational terrorism constitute a 'new' type of armed conflict, in the context of which targeted killings of terrorists are legal.

4.5.1 Occupied territories

Territory is occupied if the occupying power is in the position of exercising authority over all or part of the territory belonging to the adversary party.[297] The regulations governing military occupation (law of occupation) are part of international humanitarian law governing international armed conflicts. In a broad sense, targeted killings of terrorists justified under the law of occupation may thus be described as legal acts of warfare. More particularly, the law of occupation is set out in the HCIV, the GCIV, and the API.

A comprehensive account of the law of occupation is not required to determine the regulations regarding the use of lethal force applying to situations of occupation.[298] If a situation of effective occupation turns into one of open hostilities, or if the occupation is paralleled by an ongoing armed conflict between the occupying power and forces of the occupied country, such armed conflicts are regulated by the international humanitarian law governing international armed conflicts. By way of Article 2 GCI-IV, all Geneva Conventions apply in times of occupation,[299] and the conclusions reached above with regard to international armed conflicts apply:[300]

---

[297] Article 42 of the HCIV reads: 'Territory is considered occupied when it is actually placed under the authority of the hostile army. The occupation extends only to the territory where such authority has been established and can be exercised.' Art. 43 of the HCIV recognizes the requirement of authority by stating that '[t]he authority of the legitimate power having in fact passed into the hands of the occupant'.

[298] For more information, see Benvenisti 1993; Dörmann/Colassis 2004; Gasser 1994, 193–225; ICRC Commentary on GCIV; ICRC Commentary on API; Roberts 1990.

[299] This has been questioned with regard to the Israeli-Palestinian conflict. It has been argued that since a Palestinian state has never existed, hostilities between Palestinian and Israeli forces would constitute a non-international armed conflict. For details, see Kretzmer 2005, 207–211; Commission on Human Rights, Question of the Violation of Human Rights in the Occupied Arab Territories, Including Palestine, UN Doc. E/CN.4/2001/121, paras. 39 f. For the opinion that the international humanitarian law regulating international armed conflicts governs an armed conflict between Israeli armed forces and Palestinian armed forces, see Cassese (Expert Opinion), introduction. For a detailed argument as to the applicability of GCIV, see Ben-Naftali/Michaeli 2003, 260 f.

[300] It may not always be clear whether a situation of occupation, which requires the occupant's *ability* to exercise authority, continues to exist under such circumstances. In many cases the former occupying state may no longer be able to exercise authority over the adversary party's territory or parts of it when open hostilities break out. Nevertheless, such states of affairs are possible. The API accounts specifically for situations in which resistance movements fight against occupation. See Cassese 2005, 407; Melzer 2008, 156 f.

Terrorists are *de facto* civilians. Like all other civilians, they are protected from direct attack unless they actively participate in hostilities, and only during that time. This renders unlawful all targeted killings carried out prior to the moment they take up their arms and following the moment they lay them down. In terms of the cases of targeted killing of terrorists used in this book, this may possibly include attacks on terrorists who are on their way to carry out an attack (case 1) and some forms of case 2. Nevertheless, this can only be the case if the terrorist is recognized as such by the weapons he or she carries, or if clear and established evidence is available concerning the engagement of the relevant individual; suspicion does not suffice. Even these acts of force are legal only if they are carried out with sufficient care not to harm protected persons. If harm is caused, the act is legal only if it is appropriate and necessary, and if the harm is proportionate to the intended military aim, conditions which are unlikely, and often impossible, to meet given the unclear effects of targeted killings as well as the interchangeable nature of many terrorists. As regards actual cases of targeted killing of alleged terrorists, chapter 2 of this book has shown that states applying the practice of targeted killing do not focus on targeting those individuals who are, at the time of attack, engaged in hostile acts. Moreover, current targeted killings have caused serious harm to protected individuals. As such, even if one assumed a situation of occupation in which the conflict is ongoing, it can be concluded already on this general basis that these acts are most often illegal.

In times of an *effective* regime of occupation, which is not one of open hostilities, lethal use of force must be applied in accordance with even more restrictive terms. Although the law of occupation forms part of international humanitarian law, there is a convincing argument that the wartime legal rationale for killing no longer applies under such circumstances. In situations of effective occupation, civilian acts of force directed against the occupying power are not rightly described as acts of hostilities in terms of the laws of war, and civilians using such force cannot be described as civilians taking part in hostilities. In other words, as long as the situation is one of effective occupation, civilian use of force does not validate the application of lethal force during international armed conflicts. It instead invokes the justification for the use of lethal force in law enforcement. This does not outlaw any use of lethal force, but acts of lethal force must be assessed with reference to human rights law which applies alongside the law of occupation. More precisely, such use of force must be assessed with reference to an interpretation of the right to life, not as it is specified by international humanitarian law, but as it commonly regulates law enforcement measures.[301]

Convincing reasons for the applicability of this interpretation of the right to life can be drawn based upon the difference between effective occupation and situations of open hostilities in an ongoing armed conflict. The occupying power manages the occupied territory for the time of occupation on behalf of the sovereign of the occupied territory. It 'shall take all the measures in his power to restore and ensure, as far as possible, public order and safety [civil life][302], while respecting, unless absolutely prevented, the laws in force in the country'.[303] If the occupying power is able to exercise authority, it possesses the means to react to the use of force, which it lacks in times of ongoing hostilities. In this respect, the situation within the occupied territory profoundly differs from a situation of armed conflict, but resembles one of peacetime. The occupying power no longer fights the enemy, but is able to exercise authority and, hence, to apply law enforcement measures. Given that human rights law generally applies alongside the laws of war, it is appropriate that the use of force be assessed by an interpretation of the right to life corresponding to such a situation.[304]

This understanding reflects the general balance that the laws of occupation seek to establish between the security interests of the occupying power and the interests and rights of the occupied population.[305] As with a conventional peacetime situation, law enforcement measures, entailing the corresponding interpretation of the right to life, suffice to preserve the safety of an authority so long as the civilian use of force does not reach the threshold of an armed conflict, which would require the occupying state to return to the laws of war regulating such a

---

301 For the relationship between international humanitarian law and human rights law, as well as for the prohibitions set by the right to life in peacetime and wartime situations, see chapter 3.

302 The original French version uses the term 'l'ordre et la vie publique'. Although the English translation refers to 'public order and safety', this should be read as meaning 'public order and civil life'. Benvenisti 1993, 9.

303 Art. 43 HCIV. This Article is generally accepted as constituting international customary law. Benvenisti 1993, 8. See also Watkin 2004, 26 f.

304 For the presented result, see also Commission on Human Rights, Question of the Violation of Human Rights in the Occupied Arab Territories, Including Palestine, UN Doc. E/CN.4/2001/121, paras. 16–19/35–43; Kretzmer 2005, 205–207; Watkin 2004, 26–28; Melzer 2008, 157–167. Melzer argues that the GCIV regulates the use of lethal force corresponding to human rights.

305 For consideration of several respects of the balance between the occupant's interests and the interests of the occupied population, see Benvenisti 1993.

conflict. This presented understanding takes seriously the occupying power's security interests.[306] In limiting the use of lethal force, it, however, also recognizes that the rights of the occupied individuals, an aspect of the laws of occupation reflected in the limits set on the argument that security requires a certain derogation of rights,[307] have acquired particular importance in the context of the right to life.

Given the already restrictive terms established for justifying targeted killing of terrorists in times of ongoing hostilities, this position does not fundamentally change the assessment of the practice. In some respects, however, it introduces even more restrictive terms for the use of lethal force and, as a result, even excludes those cases of targeted killing of terrorists that may be justified in times of ongoing hostilities. The limits the right to life imposes on the use of lethal force in situations short of armed conflicts, which are the basis for this conclusion, have been addressed in detail above.[308] A few of the differences it imposes in relation to the justified use of force against terrorists in situations of armed conflicts, however, are worth recalling. Most importantly, it allows the use of lethal force only in situations of imminent attack. This describes a time period more limited than that prescribed by the right to life as understood in terms of international humanitarian law. Furthermore, the requirement to arrest the individual concerned seems to carry more weight. Finally, foreseen harm to innocent bystanders cannot be justified in the manner in which it is accepted during times of ongoing armed conflict.[309]

4.5.2 A 'new' type of armed conflict

The antecedent arguments and conclusions allow for concluding remarks about the argument that the fight against terrorism constitutes a 'new' kind of armed conflict, to which the laws of war apply, and justifies targeted killing of terro-

---

306 This aspect of the laws of occupation is reflected, for example, in the occupants' right to derogate from certain rules if absolutely necessary for security reasons, or in the right to introduce certain regulations if security requires this. See, for example, Arts. 5, 64 (1), 75 (3), 78 (1) GCIV. See also Art. 43 HCIV.
307 See, for example, Arts. 5 (3) or 49 GCIV.
308 Chapter 3.1.
309 For a position supporting the argument made in the current section, with a particular focus on the Israeli-Palestinian context, see Nolte 2004, 124–126.

rists.[310] This discussion has shown that international humanitarian law recognizes only two kinds of armed conflict, namely international armed conflicts and non-international armed conflicts, and it is only to these that international humanitarian regulations apply. If the fight against terrorism constitutes neither of these forms, existing international humanitarian law cannot justify targeting and killing terrorists. Neither does existing international humanitarian law apply in its common reading, nor has a new understanding that would render these laws applicable to such conflicts with terrorists been developed.

This also refutes the occasional argument that international humanitarian regulations may be applied analogously, and thereby justify targeted killing of terrorists.[311] With regard to existing international humanitarian law, such a position is indefensible on the basis of the wording of the regulations or in light of the intention behind them or state practice.

The position that international humanitarian regulations can be applied analogously to the fight against terrorism can then only be understood as an argument *de lege ferenda*. With regard to targeted killings, this prompts the question of whether the wartime rationale for killing should be applied to situations other than those that have hitherto been considered armed conflicts. It also invokes the question of whether the specific characteristics of terrorism, or of the fight against it, may support such a move. I will deal with these questions in detail in chapter 11.[312]

---

310 For this position, see the example of the Israeli and the US governments in chapter 4.2. In light of my argument that they formulate a position *de lege ferenda,* the position of James Ho and John Yoo (discussed in chapter 4.3.1) could also be understood as introducing a new understanding of armed conflict and arguing that exiting international humanitarian law applies to it.

311 Emanuel Gross, for example, referencing the Israeli-Palestinian conflict, states that 'the current situation is not one of war in the usual sense – but neither is it one of peace. The current situation in the state of Israel is one of a struggle-armed conflict – in which Israel reacts in self-defense'. Gross also applies this reasoning to the American fight against terrorism. Regarding the American fight against Al Qaeda, he argues that 'a war against terrorism is a new version of war, a war of the new decade. It is a war against certain people and non-state organizations and not against states'. Both quotations from Gross, E. 2005, 582. Although international humanitarian law, according to E. Gross, does not directly apply to this new kind of war, provisions regulating the fight against terrorism may be drawn from it by analogy. He bases his argument on the right of national self-defence, yet he derives the status terrorists have from international humanitarian law and seemingly asserts that they may be killed owing to their status. For this argument, see Gross, E. 2005.

312 See also chapter 6. The moral reasoning strongly supports my legal assessment.

5 National self-defence

Proponents of targeted killing of terrorists who do not exclusively focus on international humanitarian law to justify the practice, yet still argue with reference to the laws of war, refer to *jus ad bellum* for this purpose. Some do so exclusively. They recognize the prohibition of force, a fundamental principle of international law set out in the UN Charter and recognized as *jus cogens*,[1] yet argue that the right of national[2] self-defence justifies the targeting of terrorists under certain conditions. As such, they rely on the national self-defence exception from the prohibition of force in order to justify targeted killings.[3] This argument will be subject to discussion in this chapter.

Various commentators differ on the question of the extent to which the right of national self-defence allows for targeted killings of terrorists. Their interpretations of the right of national self-defence, on which they base their arguments, vary as well. In light of these differences, I will discuss several interpretations and ask whether a convincing interpretation of the right of national self-defence justifies targeted killing of terrorists.

Before turning to this discussion, four brief points require attention. First, as established,[4] reference to *jus ad bellum* alone does not suffice to justify targeted killing of terrorists. To be fully justified, the practice also must be in agreement with international legal norms regulating states' use of force under the circumstances in question. If it can be affirmed that a state is allowed to apply force in national self-defence, then it must be determined which additional international legal rules states have to obey when carrying out acts of national self-defence, and whether these regulations permit targeted killing of terrorists.

Secondly, commentators who justify targeted killing of terrorists with reference to the right of national self-defence tend to focus on individual national self-defence. They do not usually draw upon collective national self-defence,

---

1 For others, see Dinstein 2005, 99 f.; Fischer 2004, mn. 27, p. 1086.
2 For the use of the term *'national* self-defence' in this book, see fn. 1 in chapter 4.
3 Without necessarily detailed reasoning, states have been invoking their right of national self-defence in order to justify targeted killings of alleged terrorists. With reference to the practice of targeted killing of terrorists, Donald Rumsfeld, US Defense Secretary at the time, told CNN: 'The only way to deal with terrorists is to take the battle to them and find them and root them out and that's self-defence. We're going after these people and their organizations and capabilities and to stop them killing Americans.' Quoted in Gow 2001. For scholars who claim that under certain circumstances only the right of national self-defence and customary law applying to national self-defence regulate state use of force, see e. g. Plaw 2009; Anderson, K. 2011. See also fn. 3 in chapter 4.
4 See chapter 4.1.

which, as with individual national self-defence, constitutes an exception to the prohibition of force. Neither do proponents of targeted killing of terrorists tend to base their arguments in favour of justification on the second exception to the prohibition of force recognized in the UN Charter, namely measures authorized by the Security Council in accordance with Chapter VII of the UN Charter.[5] Supposedly, the focus on individual national self-defence is due to the fact that targeted killings have been committed only by individual states in the fight against terrorism, and that they would most likely not be agreed upon collectively. Nevertheless, provided an affected state were allowed to act in individual national self-defence and it considered itself a victim of an armed attack, its right of national self-defence could, in principle, be carried out collectively.[6] Provided the Security Council authorized the use of force in response to non-state terrorist use of force in accordance with Chapter VII of the UN Charter, a state may also be exempted from the prohibition of force in order to carry out specific acts. As such, in addition to individual national self-defence, these two additional exceptions can, theoretically, provide legitimacy to states' actions involving the use of force in response to non-state terrorist force. Given their limited practical role in the context of targeted killings, I will, however, not address these exceptions in detail. Important conclusions with regard to acts of force carried out in accordance with these exceptions can, however, be drawn from the analysis in this book. As with individual national self-defence, particular acts of force need to be in accordance with international legal regulations that govern the way in which such force is carried out. As a result, the conclusions of this chapter, made with reference to these international legal regulations, also apply to the use of force carried out in collective national self-defence as well as to force authorized by the Security Council in accordance with Chapter VII of the UN Charter.

Thirdly, the right of national self-defence only regulates the use of force in international relations. It cannot, and must not, be invoked in order to justify the use of force within a state. Furthermore, though this is more controversial, it arguably cannot, and must not, be invoked when states apply force in international territory, which, for example, concerns the use of force in international airspace or on the high seas. This issue will be addressed below, but for the moment it is worth noting that the position formulated in this chapter, as a result, only fully and directly applies to targeted killings of terrorists taking place in the con-

---

5 For the development of the interpretation of the Security Council's competence and of its activities in the fight against terrorism, see Tams 2009.
6 Randelzhofer 2002, mns. 37 f. For a modification to this position with regard to one detail, see Kreß addressed in fn. 27 in the current chapter.

text of international relations, and arguably only to those that take place on foreign state territory.

Finally, the use of force on foreign state territory is not excluded by the prohibition of force and is thus regulated by the right of national self-defence if the state on whose territory the act takes place consents to the action. Consent then justifies the use of force as such.[7] Nevertheless, as applies to collective national self-defence and to measures authorized by the Security Council in accordance with Chapter VII of the UN Charter, targeted killings of terrorist are only justified if they are carried out in accordance with international legal regulations governing the way in which such use of force is applied, regardless of whether the affected state consents.

5.1 Preconditions of the right of national self-defence

Both the threat and the 'use of force against the territorial integrity or political independence of any state' are prohibited under the Charter of the United Nations.[8] Despite the fundamental and non-derogatory character of the prohibition of force, the Charter recognizes that 'nothing in the present Charter shall impair the inherent right of individual or collective national self-defence if an armed attack occurs against a Member of the United Nations, until the Security Council has taken measures necessary to maintain international peace and security'[9]. The UN Charter, hence, recognizes the right of national self-defence.

According to Article 51 of the UN Charter, states can invoke the right of national self-defence only in reaction to an armed attack. Furthermore, they are only permitted to apply force in national self-defence until the Security Council takes effective counter-measures to regulate the situation. Further conditions cannot be inferred from the wording of Article 51 itself. It is almost universally accepted, however, that the manner of force states may apply under Article 51 must be proportional and necessary in order to be justified as an act of national self-defence.[10]

---

7 Nolte 1999, in particular 543–601, examines this comprehensively and with details on exceptions to this general rule. With regard to the application to targeted killing of terrorists, see also Schmitz-Elvenich 2008, 28–35.
8 Art. 2 (4) UN Charter.
9 Art. 51 UN Charter.
10 ICJ, *Nicaragua v. United States of America*, (Merits), para. 176; ICJ, *Legality of the Threat or Use of Nuclear Weapons*, (Advisory Opinion), paras. 41f.; ICJ, *Oil Platforms*, (Judgment), paras. 43/51/73–77. For others, see also Greenwood 2002, 311; Randelzhofer 2002, mn. 42. Contrary Kunz 1947, 878.

How the different requirements are to be understood and, thus, the scope of the right of national self-defence have been and continue to be subject to discussion. Several of these issues have particular relevance for the use of force as a counter-terrorist measure, and, hence, for the justifiability of targeted killings of terrorists in terms of the right of national self-defence.[11] Several of these issues are related to the requirement that there be an armed attack. They concern, first, the extent of violence required to constitute an armed attack, and secondly, the question of whose acts of force can constitute an armed attack. Controversial issues closely related to this first requirement concern the object of counter-measures in reaction to an armed attack, i.e. against whom counter-measures may be directed. Further issues concern the timeframe during which states may react to armed attacks by violent means. This involves the questions both of whether the right of national self-defence legitimizes states to apply force prior to an armed attack, and of the length of time that states are permitted to apply force after an armed attack has taken place.

In view of these controversies, I will discuss each requirement for the right of national self-defence,[12] enabling me to determine whether, and under what conditions, states may apply violence in reaction to terrorist attacks and, hence, settle the question of whether, and under what conditions, the right of national self-defence establishes the precondition for justified targeted killing of terrorists.

5.2 Armed attack

For an act of force to constitute an armed attack in terms of Article 51 of the UN Charter, the extent of force must pass a certain threshold.[13] Massive armed force is not required, yet the threat of force does not suffice;[14] neither do minor incidents of force without substantial consequences.[15] Sporadic or isolated attacks

---

11 I will address only the issues relevant for the justification of the use of force as a counter-terrorist measure.

12 I will focus on the right of national self-defence as set out in Article 51 UN Charter, yet take into consideration the role of the customary right of national self-defence in those cases when arguments holding that customary law provides a different understanding of the right are relevant for the question of whether the right provides a precondition for justified targeted killing of terrorists.

13 ICJ, *Nicaragua v. United States of America,* (Merits), para. 191. The ICJ reconfirmed this position in ICJ, *Oil Platforms,* (Judgment), para. 51.

14 For others, Bothe 2003, 229 f., Randelzhofer 2002. 4/20.

15 For others, Dinstein 2005, 193 – 196; Randelzhofer 2002, mn. 21, he gives further references in fn. 60. For a contrary opinion, see Fischer 2004, mn. 28, p. 1087; Feinstein 1976, 529/540.

by non-state terrorists, as a result, do not meet this threshold.[16] This is widely accepted and strongly supported by the importance that international law ascribes to the prohibition of force. Any wider understanding of armed attack would contradict its fundamental and non-derogatory character, its overall aim to preserve peaceful relations within the international community and the requirement following from this, that force may only be used as a last resort.[17]

This required threshold excludes several terrorist attacks from the scope of armed attacks. Nevertheless, there cannot be any doubt that both non-state and state terrorist acts can reach this threshold. Terrorist attacks can be part of a violent pattern, and the attacks of 11 September 2001 are not the only example of the capacity of terrorist attacks for destruction.

An issue slightly more difficult to settle is whether minor terrorist attacks, which assessed separately do not constitute an armed attack, cumulate and meet the threshold if they form part of a pattern of violence.[18] The provision that national self-defence may only be applied in reaction to an armed attack deliberately limits justified use of force to situations that states cannot be expected to tolerate. Provided relief cannot be created by any other peaceful means, these intolerable situations may be resolved by the use of force. Such situations exist in cases of 'massive armed aggression against the territorial integrity and political independence of a state that imperils its life or government'[19]. That national self-defence may only be applied in reaction to actual physical force, but not in reaction to other coercive acts, such as diplomatic sanctions, exemplifies this requirement. This suggests that the mere accumulation may not *per se* transform minor armed acts into parts of one overall armed attack. Nevertheless, it also suggests that the accumulation thesis must be accepted if the frequency of terrorist attacks adds a further destructive aspect disturbing the affected state in a way that imperils the government or threatens its peaceful existence. Under such circumstances, the threat to the affected state from several minor terrorist attacks does not differ from the threat from an extensive individual armed attack. The accumulation of individual acts creates a situation for which the national self-defence exception from the prohibition of force is formulated and accepted. As such, provided the accumulation of individual minor terrorist attacks can lead to sufficiently threatening situations, there is a convincing argument that as an aggregate, these attacks can meet the extent of force required for the right of national self-defence to be invoked. As a result, both accumulated

---

16 Brownlie 1958, 731; Cassese 1989, 596; Stuesser 1987, 16 f.
17 See also Cassese 1989, 596.
18 This is, for example, argued by Dinstein 2005, 202.
19 Cassese 2005, 354.

minor terrorist attacks and extensive single attacks can meet this first requirement of the existence of an armed attack.

The second controversial issue linked to the national self-defence requirement follows from the fact that traditionally, only state acts of force were regarded as qualifying as armed attacks under Article 51.[20] As I have discussed in the previous chapter, this includes acts carried out by state agents, as well as non-state use of force attributable to a state. This seems to be what the drafters of the article envisioned,[21] and several authors still defend this view,[22] as did the ICJ in several cases. Most recently, the ICJ restated this position in its Advisory Opinion in *Legal Consequences of the Construction of a Wall in the Occupied Palestinian Territory.*[23] It, however, was strongly criticized for this position, even from within the ICJ.[24] That acts of force not attributed to a state may qualify as armed attacks has previously been argued in the literature,[25] yet the group of scholars defending this position seems to be growing with the increase in transnational terrorism.[26]

This issue is highly relevant for the question of whether targeted killings of terrorists can be justified in the context of the right of national self-defence. It is important because, in cases in which non-state acts are not attributable to a state, states may only invoke the right of national self-defence in response to these non-state acts if these acts constituted an armed attack.

Scholars support the view that non-state force may constitute an armed attack by referring to state reactions to the attacks of 11 September 2001. They point to SC resolutions 1368 and 1373, in which the Security Council restated the right of national self-defence in light of these attacks. They also point to

---

20 Compare Bruha/Bortfeld 2001, 164; Kreß 1995, 206.

21 Frowein 2002, 887; Tomuschat 2001, 540.

22 Bothe 2003, 230/233; Krajewski 2002, 188; O'Connell 2010, 14–16; Rowles 1987, 310; Randelzhofer 2002, mn. 34. Randelzhofer (2002, mn. 36), however, seems to abandon this requirement with regard to armed force carried out by non-state groups on the territory of a so-called failed state.

23 ICJ, *Construction of a Wall*, (Advisory Opinion), para. 139. See also ICJ, *Nicaragua v. United States of America*, (Merits), para. 195. Although the wording of the ICJ's Advisory Opinion in *Construction of a Wall* strongly indicates this, some commentators read the document as not involving any statement about the applicability of the right of national self-defence to non-state use of force. For such an argument, see Gray 2006, 571.

24 ICJ, *Construction of a Wall*, (Separate Opinion Higgins), para. 33. See also ICJ, *Construction of a Wall*, (Separate Opinion Kooijmans), para. 35; and ICJ, *Construction of a Wall*, (Declaration Buergenthal), para. 6.

25 Dinstein 2005, 206.

26 Bruha 2002, 394f.; Paust 2001/2002, 533–536; Paust 2010, 238–249. For further references, see fns. 35/42 in the current chapter.

the NATO and OAS decisions in which they recognize that the attacks on the Pentagon and the World Trade Center triggered the right of national self-defence. These statements and decisions, they argue, indicate that non-state force may constitute an armed attack.[27]

As the discussion about the imputability of non-state acts of force made clear,[28] the legal situation is not as clear as it is presented by some of these authors. First, it is not certain that the SC resolutions recognized the attacks of 11 September as triggering the right of national self-defence. Second, both the SC resolutions and the decisions taken by NATO and OAS can also be read as attributing the terrorist attacks to the Taliban, and, thus, as introducing a broader understanding of state responsibility, rather than as simply accepting that the acts of Al Qaeda constituted armed attacks independent of any state involvement. This is also what the United States relied on. The US did not rely on the argument that non-state terrorist acts can trigger the right of national self-defence when justifying attacks against terrorist targets in Afghanistan. It argued that it was entitled to attack Afghanistan because Afghanistan harboured terrorists and refused to hand over Osama bin Laden. The United States thus primarily based its argument on a wide understanding of state responsibility rather than on the claim that non-state terrorist acts may qualify as armed attacks. Third, in view of state practice and *opinio iuris* in the time prior to the attacks of 11 September 2001, it is too soon to determine the current legal situation on the basis of these statements and decisions. There are several examples of state practice that question the assumption that non-state violence can trigger the right of national self-defence.[29] For decades, armed counter-measures by, for example, the United States, Israel, and apartheid South Africa in response to non-state attacks on the territory of a foreign state not responsible for the acts in question were condemned by the international community. As recently as 1998, the armed response by the United States to the bombings of embassies in Kenya and Tanzania were denounced internationally. Thus, even if current acts and decisions within the international community show that non-state acts are recognized as armed attacks, these decisions may not be seen to instantly create a new and clear legal situation that would allow for only one interpretation of armed attack,

---

27 See, for example, Dinstein 2005, 206–208; Paust 2001/2002, 533–536. For an extended discussion of this question, see Kreß 1995, 215–233. He argues that the term 'armed attack' comprises non-state use of force in the context of individual self-defence, but not in the context of collective self-defence.

28 For details on the following points, see chapter 4.3.2.

29 For details on state practice, see Byers 2005, 61–68. See also chapter 4.3.2.

as some scholars assume.[30] That said, Article 51 leaves room for the argument that non-state violence qualifies as armed attack under certain conditions. Its wording does not indicate that the term applies to state force alone.

There is also good reason not to limit the right of states to use armed violence in national self-defence in this respect. The provision that only armed attacks legitimize counter-force is best understood as paying tribute to the principle of prohibition of force and to its aim of preserving peace to the largest extent possible. It seeks to prevent states from using violence in response to acts that, given their nature and the extent of violence they involve, do not justify endangering transnational peace. To make the prohibition of force against non-state actors dependent on the meaning of armed attack therefore misinterprets the requirement of armed attack, is unsatisfactory and contrary to the *telos* of Article 51.[31] Non-state actors can today apply force as threatening and destructive as that applied by state actors. This development not only supports the stated argument, but can also explain why national self-defence has been traditionally regarded as legitimizing the use of force only in response to acts of force carried out by states.

The second reason not to exclude non-state force from the meaning of armed attack is that it *per se* would prohibit states to use force in response to massive armed attacks planned, organized, and/or executed from the territory of failed states.[32] This is not to say that such practical considerations may override clear legal facts regarding the content and scope of a regulation. Nevertheless, it makes no sense to prevent states from defending themselves in such situations merely on the basis of a restrictive understanding of the requirement of armed

---

30 Yoram Dinstein (2005, 206 f.), for example, refers to the SC resolutions 1368 and 1373 as well as to the decisions NATO and the OAS took in the wake of the terrorist attacks of September 11, and diagnoses: 'However, all lingering doubts on this issue [whether "armed attack" in Article 51 does apply also to non-state acts of force] have been dispelled as a result of the response of the international community to the shocking events of 9 September 2001 (9/11)'. See also Tomuschat 2001, 540.
31 See also Tomuschat 2001, 540.
32 See also Walter 2004, 25 f. Some, such as Christian Walter, may argue that such a limited understanding of armed force would also prevent states from using force against massive non-state attacks on international territory, such as the high seas. I regard the prohibition of force and the right of national self-defence as not regulating such situations (see below in the current section). As a result, a limited understanding of armed attacks would, according to my understanding, not prevent states from using force under such circumstances. Nevertheless, for all who share this wider understanding of the right of national self-defence, this practical consideration provides an additional reason for not limiting the meaning of armed attack to state force.

attack that is deemed necessary neither by theoretical considerations, such as the purpose of Article 51 or its wording, nor by practical or scholarly agreement as to such limitation.

Analysis will show that the requirement of necessity makes the use of force against non-state actors less likely to be justified as a legitimate act of national self-defence than the use of force against states.[33] It will also reveal that the laws regulating the manner in which force may be used in response to non-state armed attacks differ from those regulating the use of force in response to state armed attacks.[34] As such, the remainder of this chapter will show that differences remain between force carried out in response to non-state acts and force applied in conflicts with other states. Nevertheless, there is no convincing argument to prohibit states from using force against non-state actors by way of a restrictive understanding of the term 'armed attack'.

To conclude, given that Article 51 and state practice do not prescribe limiting the understanding of armed attack to state use of force, the assertion that non-state terrorist acts attributable to a state as well as those that are not imputable (provided that they exceed the required threshold of force) constitute armed attacks is convincing.

What follows from this understanding of the term 'armed attack' with regard to the justifiability of states' use of force in response to non-state armed attacks? Some commentators hold that the existence of an armed attack directly triggers the right of national self-defence against non-state forces and that this right also justifies the use of force on a foreign state's territory.[35] States, too, seem to have adopted this view.[36] Such a conclusion, however, has been reached too hastily, as can be seen after an examination of the question of who is affected by the use of force to which the right of national self-defence applies.

In order to determine who is affected by such use of force, it is helpful to outline what kind of force is regulated by the right of national self-defence. Undisputedly, the right of national self-defence does not regulate the use of force on the territory of the attacked state. International legal regulations, such as human rights and, under certain conditions, specific rules of international humanitarian law, apply to such circumstances. Apart from this, the use of force is an internal state affair, to which neither the prohibition of force nor the right of national self-

---

33 See chapter 5.3.
34 See chapter 5.6.
35 Paust 2001/2002, 533–536/538–540/543 and Paust 2004, 1344. Kendall 2002, in particular 1078–1088. See also Gross, E. 2005, 586 f. For an analysis of the different positions and arguments, see Kreß 1995, 152 f./207–235.
36 Byers 2005, 62.

defence apply.[37] This also applies when non-states actors are confronted on a ship or airplane under the flag of the defending state.[38] It is equally undisputed that the right of national self-defence regulates state use of force on the territory of other states. It is less clear whether the right of national self-defence also regulates state use of force in international territory. I would argue that it does not, given that the prohibition of force, to which the right of national self-defence constitutes an exception, focuses on the relationship between states.[39]

That said, this argument has only minor relevance to the question of whether states may use defensive force in response to a non-state terrorist armed attack. If one holds that the right of national self-defence also regulates the use of force in international territory,[40] it only applies to the very theoretical case that non-state actors attack a state from the high seas or from international airspace, i.e. from territory outside any state's jurisdiction, and that force is used against them also on international territory. In all but some theoretical cases, national self-defence carried out in response to non-state acts of force necessarily takes place on foreign state territory, be it because the non-state actors against whom a state acts are based on foreign territory and carry out their acts from there, because they return to their bases on foreign state territory after their attacks, or because they are on a ship or airplane under the flag of a foreign state. As such, in all but some theoretical cases, any forceful response to non-state terrorists falls within the scope of the right of national self-defence only when it is carried out on foreign state territory. This means that in almost all realistic circumstances, self-defensive force directed against non-state actors will violate the territorial integrity of a foreign state. Territorial integrity is a fundamental part of state sovereignty. As such, force against non-state actors on the territory of a foreign state will always constitute an attack against that state.

In view of this corollary, it is difficult to uphold the position that non-state use of force qualifying as an armed attack may trigger the right of national self-defence and justify the use of force against the perpetrators on foreign state territory. Assuming that the right of national self-defence regulates the use of force in international territory, one may argue that non-state force, in such situations, may directly trigger the right to use force against them in national self-defence.

---

37 Dinstein 2005, 204 f. See also Cassese 2005, 56/476; Fischer 2004, mns. 16 – 18, pp. 1077 f.

38 Ships and airplanes under the flag of this state may in this respect be regarded as 'being a sort of extension of state territory'. Cassese 2005, 476.

39 Bothe 2001, 612; Cassese 2005, 56/476.

40 Bruha 2002, 397 – 399; Bruha/Bortfeld 2001, 166. See also Walter 2004, 25 f.; and fn. 32 in the current chapter.

This theoretical situation, however, seems to be the only constellation of circumstances under which this would apply. Hence, for almost all circumstances involving non-state force to which the right of national self-defence may theoretically apply, one must accept that force may only be applied in response if an additional justification is provided for attacking the affected state.

Scholars who recognize that non-state acts constituting armed attacks do not automatically justify the use of force on foreign territory provide different reasons for what could legitimate such use of force. Prevailing positions can be attributed to two groups. Some hold that states may use force on foreign state territory only if the non-state act triggering the violent reaction is attributable to that state.[41] Others distinguish between force applied against state institutions and force applied against terrorist targets. They hold the former to be legal only if the affected state is responsible for the act in question. According to this position, the territorial integrity of a state, however, may be violated and force directed against terrorist targets, if the state itself is unwilling or unable to combat terrorist activities on its territory and/or violates its international obligations by means concerning the non-state armed attack.[42]

If the non-state terrorist acts are attributable to the affected state, the situation is clear.[43] Under such circumstances, the discussion of whether non-state acts can constitute armed attacks loses relevance: if non-state acts are attributable to a state, they may be regarded as *de facto* state armed attacks. In such situations, the existence of an armed attack directly triggers the right of national self-defence, provided that all other requirements are met.

It remains to be considered whether, and under what circumstances, states may react to non-state armed attacks not attributable to the state affected by these counter-measures. This problem cannot be resolved by stressing that only the facilities of non-state members may be attacked in response to non-state armed attacks.[44] This is, rather, a condition *sine qua non* for legitimate use of force based upon the right of national self-defence. If a state cannot be held responsible for specific acts of force, it is impossible to argue that its mili-

---

41 Christian Tomuschat (2001, 541) seems to hold this position. With regard to situations in which non-state actors rule a certain region in a way that would enable them to set up a form of separate government without interference from the state's government, however, he seems to assume the second position addressed. See, moreover, Stuesser 1987, 19–21.
42 Greenwood 2002, 312 f.; Heintschel v. Heinegg/Gries 2000, 155–161. See also Kreß 1995, 234; Bruha/Bortfeld 2001, 164 f.; Coll 1987, 305; Frowein 2002, 887. For further references, see fn. 45 in the current chapter.
43 For the imputability of non-state terrorist acts to states, see chapter 4.3.2
44 For such a step, see, for example, Paust 2001/2002, 538 f./542 f.

tary institutions or infrastructure may be attacked. But in the absence of further explanation, this does not eliminate the problem faced with regard to the fact that interference with the territorial integrity of a state *per se* constitutes an attack against the state itself.

There are differences between attacks directed against the state's infrastructure, military institutions and facilities, and attacks carried out on a state's territory but directed against non-state terrorist facilities. In the first case, force is directed against the state to influence its own behaviour. The force, hence, threatens the state's independence. In the second, violence is used to prevent the non-state organization from endangering the defending state without deliberately aiming at the affected state's policy and independence. But do these differences sufficiently explain why attacks may be carried out in one case, yet not in the other? Why would it be justified to interfere with state sovereignty under the conditions of the latter situation? Why should such an attack not constitute an armed attack, and itself trigger the right of national self-defence?

Theoretically, two replies are possible. Firstly, one could suggest that sovereignty may not go so far as to prevent other states from protecting themselves and their populations from severe danger. This understanding of sovereignty would result in creating a grave danger of misuse. More importantly, the suggestion is unsatisfactory, as it nullifies sovereignty, one of the fundamental principles in state relations. It makes states subject to attacks even if they did not know, or could not have known, about the existence and objectives of the non-state group on their territory. Finally, it contradicts the aim of preserving peace to the greatest possible extent, as it is intended by the prohibition of force. The right of national self-defence constitutes an exception to this prohibition, but it cannot lead to the annihilation of the principle itself.

Commentators who argue that force may be directed against a non-state terrorist organization operating in a state to which the non-state attacks cannot be attributed tend to rely on a more moderate assertion. They justify the use of military force by the state's own behaviour. The use of force on foreign territory, they argue, is justified as an act of national self-defence if the state concerned, by not interfering with non-state illegal behaviour, violates or fails to meet the international obligation not to support or tolerate its territory's use for the planning or execution of acts against other states.[45]

This position is often not based on explicit arguments. Nevertheless, several points can be made to support it. It is irrefutable that states are obliged to ab-

---

[45] Stahn 2004, 864–866; Walter 2004, 40 f.; Rogers/McGoldrick 2011, 787. For further references, see also fn. 42 in the current chapter.

stain from supporting terrorist organizations, from tolerating the planning and organizing of terrorist acts against other states on their territory, or from knowingly allowing terrorist groups to use their territory as a safe haven.[46] To base the right to apply force on foreign state territory – without attacking the affected state's military institutions and infrastructure and, thus, without directly threatening the state in its political independence – on the violation of this obligation accounts for the defending state's need to protect itself, including its citizens. It simultaneously accounts for the principle of state sovereignty. If one wants to make sense of the concept, state sovereignty must be understood as being directly linked to a state's obligation to ensure that its territory is not used to endanger other states. If a state ignores this obligation, its sovereignty cannot prevent other states from protecting themselves and their citizens. They are justified to act at the expense of the former state's sovereignty. In this manner, the approach accounts for the difference between the use of force on a state's territory and attacks on that state's military institutions. While the former does not threaten the state itself and does not seek to change its policy, the latter does.

The approach also avoids some of the problems of the position that suggests that sovereignty as a concept has to be understood as not preventing other states from protecting themselves and their populations from severe danger. In accounting for the fact that a state's territory may be interfered with only if this state either decided not to combat terrorist activities on its territory or if it was unable to do so because it lacks authority and control, it does not abolish sovereignty, but articulates its limitations.

A serious risk of escalation and misuse, and a corresponding threat to peace, remains. These dangers require states to provide reasonable proof of the unwillingness or inability of the affected state to change its conduct prior to action. Involving clear limits on the right to act on foreign state territory, the presented position, then, seems to diminish the risk to an acceptable degree: it allows for the use of force on the territory of a foreign state only if this state is unwilling or unable to act, and limits allowed use of force to a degree that does not threaten this

---

46 In the *Corfu Channel Case*, (Merits), p. 22, the ICJ recognizes as a 'general and well-recognized principle' the 'obligation not to allow knowingly its territory to be used for acts contrary to the rights of other States'. Moreover, the *Declaration on Friendly Relations* reads: 'Every state has the duty to refrain from organizing or encouraging the organization of irregular forces or armed bands including mercenaries, for incursion into the territory of another State. Every state has the duty to refrain from organizing, instigating, assisting or participating in acts of civil strife or terrorist acts in another State or acquiescing in organized activities within its territory directed towards the commission of such acts, when the acts referred to in the present paragraph involve a threat or use of force.' For others, see Brownlie 1958, 734 f.; Dinstein 2005, 205 f.; Schachter 1989, 211 f.

state and its government in their political independence. Any attacks endangering the population of that state must be rejected. Neither may state institutions, infrastructure, military personnel and material be affected.

Some may find this result unsatisfactory because it strictly limits the permission to use force. Under certain circumstances, it does not allow states to defend themselves as required by the terrorist threat in question, even if the state against which they must direct force is unwilling to effectively prevent terrorist activity on its territory. Some may go so far as to argue that 'evil' states and terrorist organizations are favoured by such a solution. This, however, is not a compelling reason to broaden the allowance for unilateral use of force. First, any permission that exceeded the formulated boundaries would contradict the *telos* of the prohibition of force and the right of national self-defence as well as the idea of state sovereignty. Secondly, unilateral action is not the only form of action available to states. Nevertheless, it is the one most likely to be abused and, hence, should be strictly limited. In particular, states can resort to collective measures decided upon by the Security Council according to Chapter VII of the UN Charter. Some may argue that the Security Council will not protect threatened states sufficiently, since, due to its structure, it is often unable to come to workable decisions. This may be true. However, it does not follow that existing regulations should be stretched beyond convincing boundaries, risking damage caused by unilateral action. It rather calls for reform of the UN system and the strengthening of multilateral mechanisms to resolve such threatening situations.[47] Finally, the main solution must be to strengthen the force of regulations that avoid such situations, namely the primary rule that, with non-state terrorists from abroad in mind, it is the states' obligation not to support or tolerate terrorist activity on their territory.[48]

In conclusion, non-state terrorist acts can constitute armed attacks provided that they cross the required threshold of violence. This threshold excludes many terrorist attacks from the scope of the term 'armed attack'. Certain severely destructive attacks, as well as a series of minor attacks that, taken together, establish a sufficient degree of danger, may, however, be described as armed attacks. The claim that this applies regardless of whether they can be attributed to a state or not is convincing.

The fact that a non-state terrorist act constitutes an armed attack, however, does not suffice to justify the resort to force. The only exception to this statement occurs if one holds the right of national self-defence to regulate the use of force

---

47 See also Walter 2004.
48 Jinks 2003a.

in international territory, and if counter-force would be carried out on this territory. In the realistic circumstance that counter-force is used on the territory of a foreign state from which the terrorists operate, however, counter-force necessarily affects this state. This limits the justifiability of the use of force. Force directed against foreign state institutions can only be justified if the acts of the non-state actor are attributable to this state. If this cannot be done, force can only be justified if it is directed against the terrorist organization. This, however, is only allowed if the state affected by counter-terrorist force violates its obligation to interfere with the terrorist activity on its territory, if it is sufficiently proven that the state is unwilling or unable to change this conduct, and if the violent counter-measures do not directly affect its institutions and inhabitants. The final justifiability of the use of force under these circumstances, then, depends on the compatibility of this use of force with the requirements addressed in the remainder of this chapter.

5.3 Preventive and reactive national self-defence

Closely connected with the requirement of armed attack are the requirements concerning the timeframe during which legitimate counter-terrorist measures may be applied in national self-defence. These requirements concern the question of whether force may be applied prior to the actual attack taking place, as well as that of how long the use of force may be applied in response to an armed attack.

Both issues are controversial in the context of national self-defence and highly relevant to a justification of the resort to force as part of a justification of targeted killings. Since terrorist attacks do not typically constitute ongoing fighting, all targeted killings of terrorists are carried out either (a) prior to the attack they are intended to prevent, or (b) in response to attacks that have already taken place.

Possibility (a) characterizes all defensive targeted killings. In particular, it applies to the first and the second case of targeted killing, carried out in light of a determinable attack. Provided these acts are carried out for preventive purposes, it also applies to the third and fourth case of targeted killing, those not applied in view of a determinable threat. All of these targeted killings are carried out prior to the execution of an attack. Possibility (b) characterizes all responsive targeted killings. It also applies to defensive killings carried out in reaction to past terrorist attacks with a view to future threats.

As such, targeted killings of terrorists can only constitute legal acts of national self-defence if the right of national self-defence comprises acts carried out prior to the execution of the individual attack they seek to prevent, or if the right comprises acts reacting to an individual attack after it has taken place. I will discuss these issues in turn, starting with the justifiability of the use of force intended to prevent an attack.

Two kinds of defensive actions taken with a view to a future armed attack can be distinguished: anticipatory national self-defence and pre-emptive national self-defence. Anticipatory national self-defence is understood here as the use of force against an aggressor not with regard to an actual determinable attack, but to a situation rendering the occurrence of such an attack possible, likely, or predictable. Pre-emptive national self-defence is used to denote force applied in view of a determinable attack that is about to be carried out. Both anticipatory and pre-emptive national self-defence constitute forms of preventive national self-defence.

The rationale for preventive national self-defence is clear. If a state knows that an armed attack will take place, one cannot, so the reasoning, require this state to wait like a 'sitting duck'[49] until destruction and damage occur. States must have the right to act on the basis of their knowledge and prevent the attack.[50] The argument has more power with regard to pre-emptive use of force, yet it can also be applied to situations of anticipatory national self-defence.

That said, none of these forms of national self-defence is authorized by international treaty law. Article 51 of the UN Charter states that states have the right of national self-defence only 'if an armed attack occurs'. According to Article 51, states are prohibited from applying force, even if a state or a non-state group indicate that they may become dangerous. This position reflects the view of the overwhelming majority of legal scholars.[51] It follows from the wording of Article 51 and makes sense of the fact that the drafters of the article chose the term 'armed attack' over 'aggression', a term they knew and used at the time. It also makes sense of the fact that the drafters did not add the threat of force as they had done in Article 2 (4) of the UN Charter.[52] Finally, deriving a right of anticipatory or pre-emptive national self-defence from Article 51 would also contradict the overall aim of preserving peace and avoiding the use of military force for as long as possible; even if applied responsibly, anticipatory or pre-

---

49 Myres McDougal (1963, 601) seems to have introduced this expression.
50 Compare Cassese 2005, 358.
51 For others, Dinstein 2005, 182–187; Randelzhofer 2002, mn. 39. A different opinion is asserted in Coll 1987. Scholars who defend a right of preventive national self-defence also tend to base their argument on customary law rather than Article 51; for references, see fn. 54 in the current chapter.
52 Dinstein 2005, 184 f. For further arguments, see also Bothe 2003, 229.

emptive national self-defence carries a great risk of escalation and useless destruction.[53]

Proponents of anticipatory or pre-emptive national self-defence tend to invoke customary law to justify early use of military force, holding that Article 51 does not supersede pre-existing customary law. Either they argue that Article 51 must be read in view of these customs, or that it reflects only one aspect of it, and accordingly, that pre-existing customary law allowing for anticipatory or pre-emptive national self-defence continues to exist.[54]

As has been shown, the wording of Article 51 and its purpose preclude the reading of the article itself as allowing for anticipatory or pre-emptive national self-defence. But what about the argument that international customary law provides a broader right of national self-defence than exists in Article 51? Article 51 refers to the 'inherent' right of national self-defence. As the ICJ explicitly acknowledged in *Nicaragua v. United States of America*,[55] this expression can hardly be understood other than as referring to customary law. It is, however, misleading to argue that anticipatory national self-defence is justified on that basis. In its decision on the merits of *Nicaragua v United States of America*, the ICJ did not specify the scope of the customary right of national self-defence. It made no statement as to whether this customary rule allows for anticipatory national self-defence. The ICJ's decision thus may not be used as a reference point for any such interpretation.[56] The court's judgment and its rejection of the argument that Article 51 has wiped out all pre-existing customary law, how-

---

53 Cassese 2005, 361. In addition, for anticipatory use of defensive force in particular, it is difficult to imagine that any such use of force meets the requirement of necessity, which I will come to further below. This is because, in a situation prior to attack, there always seem to be means other than force that can be explored. See chapter 5.4.

54 Feinstein 1976, 528–533; Gross, E. 2005, 584; Kendall 2002, 1079–1082/1086; McDougal 1963, 599–601; Sofaer 1989, 91–95. See also ICJ, *Nicaragua v. United States of America*, (Dissenting Opinion Schwebel), para 88. Compare also Cassese 2005, 358; and Randelzhofer 2002, mns. 9–15/39, both including further references.

55 ICJ, *Nicaragua v. United States of America*, (Merits), para. 176.

56 Cassese 2005, 359. In para. 194 of *Nicaragua v. United States of America*, (Merits), the ICJ holds that '[i]n view of the circumstances in which the dispute has arisen, reliance is placed by the Parties only on the right of self-defence in the case of an armed attack which has already occurred, and the issue of the lawfulness of a response to the imminent threat of armed attack has not been raised. Accordingly the Court expresses no view on that issue'. Randelzhofer (2002, mn. 43) even argues that the ICJ in its ruling in *Nicaragua v. United States of America* sees the customary right of national self-defence as almost fully parallel the right under Article 51 in content and scope.

ever, is convincing.[57] This proves reasonable, as Article 51 is informed by customary law for the requirements of proportionality and necessity.[58] Nevertheless, state practice and *opinio iuris*, the two criteria crucial for customary law, cannot be established either for a right of anticipatory national self-defence or for a right of pre-emptive national self-defence.[59]

States have, on several occasions, carried out preventive acts of force, justifying them by invoking legal arguments other than a right of preventive national self-defence.[60] When states have justified their use of force by referring to the right of preventive national self-defence, other states have condemned this conduct and rejected the view that such national self-defence was legal.[61] Rejection was not in all cases unequivocal,[62] and not all acts of preventive national self-defence were officially condemned by the Security Council.[63] However, states' reactions show the lack of consensus regarding the legality of preventive national self-defence, and no customary right of preventive national self-defence can, hence, be derived from these reactions. This was reaffirmed by the international reaction to US reasoning in 2002. In June, in light of international terrorism and the fear that terrorists may be able to acquire weapons of mass destruction, President George W. Bush suggested that 'we must take the battle to the enemy, dis-

---

57 For a dissenting opinion, see Ago, Roberto, as Special Rapporteur of the ILC, Addendum to the Eighth Report on State Responsibility, UN Doc. A/CN.4/318/ADD.5–7, para. 108; Gill 1988. Randelzhofer (2002, mn. 45) rejects the idea that the customary right of national self-defence was wiped out by Article 51, yet he argues that Article 51 supersedes and replaces the customary right of national self-defence for all members of the United Nations.

58 The ICJ refers to these examples in *Nicaragua v. United States of America*, (Merits), para. 176.

59 Byers 2005, 72–81; Cassese 2005, 359–362. See also Fischer 2004, mn. 43, p. 1097. A contrary opinion with regard to situations in which clear evidence can be established as to the existing threat can be found in Franck 2002, 97–108. The facts Franck provides, however, do not reveal state agreement that preventive self-defence is justified.

60 When Israel initiated the Six Day War in 1967, for example, it argued that it had acted in response to Egypt's blocking of the Straits of Tiran. In 1988 the United States justified their attack on an Iranian civilian airplane by claiming that they had been attacked by Iranian military helicopters and patrol boats. Byers 2005, 74; Cassese 2005, 359.

61 For example, Israel's attacks on Palestinian camps in Lebanon were overall strongly condemned. Few states accepted Israel's attack on Iraq's nuclear reactor in 1981. The Security Council condemned Israel's attack 'in clear violation of the Charter and of the UN and the norms of international conduct' (SC Res. 487). The United States voted for the resolution, yet made clear that it agreed with Israel's concept of anticipatory self-defence. All other members of the Security Council rejected Israel's actions, and Egypt and Mexico expressly rejected the doctrine of anticipatory self-defence. See Cassese 2005, 360f.

62 Cassese 2005, 360. See also the example in fn. 61 in the current chapter.

63 Cassese 2005, 360.

rupt his plans, and confront the worst threats before they emerge'. He suggested that preventive military measures must be taken at an early stage, for 'if we wait for the threats to fully materialize, we will have waited too long'.[64] In the so-called Bush-doctrine, issued on 20 September 2002, the US government, at first sight, slightly moderated their approach. It limited the use of preventive force to cases in which the attack is imminent. Adapting 'the concept of imminent threat to the capabilities and objectives of today's adversaries'[65], however, the US government interpreted imminence very broadly. They understood the term as comprising not only situations in which the attack is about to be carried out, but also situations in which the attack is further away and its occurrence less certain.[66] The French president made very clear in an interview with the New York Times that this doctrine was not accepted by all other states. He firmly rejected the doctrine, a position he shared with other states.[67] All of these incidents make clear that there is no customary law of preventive self-defence. Preventive national self-defence has not been condemned in all cases in which the issue has come up, and not all states reject the idea. Nevertheless, an overall agreement as to the legality of such acts cannot be established.[68]

---

64 Both statements quoted in Byers 2005, 75.

65 National Security Strategy of the United States, issued on 20 September 2002, quoted in Byers 2005, 77.

66 Byers 2005, 78.

67 Cassese 2005, 361. For the dismissive position the EU takes regarding preventive self-defence, see Gray 2006, 564 f.

68 Cassese (2005, 361 f.) argues that state customs do not lead to a decisive judgement as to the legality or illegality of anticipatory or pre-emptive national self-defence. While state practice shows that the overwhelming majority of states hold anticipatory or pre-emptive national self-defence to be illegal, some are convinced of its legality. Cassese, however, derives from the scope of Article 51, from Chapter VII of the UN Charter, or – referring to the judgment of the ICJ in *Legality of the Use by a State of Nuclear Weapons in Armed Conflict* – more generally from 'the overall system contemplated by the Charter' that anticipatory and pre-emptive self-defence may not be held to be legal. See also Bothe 2003, 231 f. He (2003, 232) provides the additional argument that such an interpretation would ignore both the Kellogg-Briand Pact and the UN Charter in their relevance for expressing state practice and legal conviction of the participating states. This lack of agreement about the justifiability of preventive self-defence more recently became clear at a UN world summit held in September 2005, where states strongly disagreed on the justifiability of both pre-emptive and anticipatory self-defence. See Gray 2006, 566. Christine Gray (2006, 565–569) also addresses several states' reactions to the Bush doctrine and their positions about preventive, and in particular anticipatory, self-defence. Christian Tams (2009, particularly 389 f.) recognises changes regarding the required timing of actual acts of self-defence over the last 20 years, but he has not yet detected a legal change in this.

This lack of customary agreement arguably comprises both anticipatory and strictly limited pre-emptive national self-defence, i.e. national self-defence with regard to an imminent attack. The former point was made clear once again by the reactions to the Bush doctrine. With regard to pre-emptive use of force, the situation is less clear. Some might argue that the launching of an attack has never been close enough in a real-world situation from which customary law might be derived. Information that can be drawn from state actions during the past few decades, therefore, is less than clear about customary law regulating strictly understood pre-emptive national self-defence.

That said, there is good reason to assume that clear state agreement as to the acceptability of strictly limited pre-emptive national self-defence has not been established. The existence of the customary right to pre-emptive national self-defence is often based on the *Caroline* case of 1837, in which British troops boarded and destroyed the Caroline, killing two individuals on board the US steamship that had been used, though not at the moment of the British action, to support the fight of Canadian insurgents against Great Britain. Proponents of pre-emptive national self-defence tend to refer to the communication issued by Daniel Webster, US Secretary of State at the time, to Great Britain, in which he accepts the right of national self-defence if the 'necessity of that self-defense is instant, overwhelming, and leaving no choice of means, and no moment for deliberation', and argue that this statement expresses customary acceptance of pre-emptive national self-defence.[69] However, the situation is not as clear as is claimed, either with regard to the situation at the time or with regard to current customary acceptance of such a form of national self-defence. It has been pointed out in the legal literature that the conflict had been going on prior to the British military action and that the case itself was not about pre-emptive national self-defence. The Webster formula should therefore be read not as addressing preventive national self-defence, but as limiting the right to apply force in reaction to existing violent acts to what is absolutely necessary, and only when no other means are feasible.[70] A contrary position can be argued.[71] Doubts about the existence of a strictly limited right to pre-emptive national self-defence, however, are strengthened by the fact, that, as far as can be determined, the *Caroline* case was not fol-

---

69 See for others Gross, E. 2005, 584; or Gross, E. 2001, 210–212.
70 Dinstein 2005, 184 f.; Paust 2004, 1345 f.
71 See for others Stuesser 1987, 10 f. Uncertain about the absence of such limited customary right of pre-emptive national self-defence, Bothe 2003, 231.

lowed by any incident in which states unequivocally supported the existence of strict pre-emptive national self-defence.[72]

To assume a customary right of preventive national self-defence outside the Charter would, finally, be implausible. It would not make sense for the drafters to introduce clear limitations on the most obvious case of national self-defence, with, for example, the provision that national self-defence must cease when the Security Council takes effective measures, yet not regulate more ambiguous circumstance requiring limitations at least as clear.[73]

Does this absence of a right to preventive national self-defence mean that states have to wait until they are attacked before acting in national self-defence? Moreover, in the context of targeted killing, does this mean that states must await the accomplishment of terrorist attacks before they become active? Dinstein, who accepts that pre-emptive national self-defence is not authorized by international law, introduces an additional form of national self-defence, namely 'interceptive' national self-defence. By assuming a broad understanding of the term 'armed attack', he argues that states may act well before the harm occurs.[74] He includes into the meaning of the term all acts from the moment a state 'embarks upon an apparently irreversible course of action, thereby crossing the legal Rubicon'.

> The casting of the die, rather than the actual opening of fire, is what starts the armed attack. [...] Whereas a preventive strike anticipates a latent armed attack that is merely "foreseeable" (or even just "conceivable"), an interceptive strike [the use of force before the attack's destructive impact] counters an armed attack which is in progress, even if it still is incipient: the blow is "imminent" and practically "unavoidable".[75]

An armed attack, according to Dinstein, thus, begins when the final destructive act is 'in the process of being unleashed'.[76] This includes the moving of the unit executing the final destructive act to the location in question, but excludes attacks on the same unit while it is training or preparing for the attack. That the defending party has clear knowledge of the plans of the adversary party is critical to the right to interceptive national self-defence.

---

72 See Cassese 2005, 357–362. Cassese's analysis comprises both anticipatory and pre-emptive self-defence.
73 Dinstein 2005, 185. For further Charter inherent arguments for the position that there do not exist any customary permissions to apply national self-defence exceeding those regulated in Article 51 UN Charter, see Fischer 2004, mn. 43, p. 1097.
74 Dinstein 2005, 187–192. See also Feinstein 1976, 556 f.
75 This and the preceding quotation from Dinstein 2005, 189.
76 Dinstein 2005, 190.

In order to assess this argument, it is helpful to look at one of the examples Dinstein provides,[77] since this reveals an additional aspect of his understanding of armed attack. Analysing the events leading up to the Six Day War, Dinstein argues that Israeli forces had the right to fire the first shot, which they did do, in interceptive national self-defence. The aggregate steps that Egypt had taken (ejecting the United Nations Emergency forces from the Gaza Strip and the Sinai Peninsula; blocking the Straits of Tiran; positioning their troops at the Israeli border in a way they had never done before), he argues, constituted an armed attack. Dinstein reasons that none of the actions themselves qualified as armed attack, yet 'when the measures taken by Egypt were assessed in the aggregate, it seemed to be crystal-clear that Egypt was bent on an armed attack, and the sole question was not whether war would materialize but when'.[78] Dinstein seems to apply two standards for determining whether an armed attack materializes. The attacking force must be in the process of carrying out a specific armed attack. Nevertheless, this prerequisite does not seem to be required if several actions are taken that form part of the preparation for war. In view of his previous statements, this may only be understood if the entire war, rather than specific acts, is regarded as an armed attack. Then, however, most preparatory work may be seen as constituting an armed attack, given proof that the initiating strike is in the near future.

This second concept is highly problematic. It blurs or even abolishes its distinction from other forms of pre-emptive strikes of national self-defence, and it seeks to justify a form of national self-defence not authorized by international law. The meaning of 'armed attack' may therefore not be extended to that degree.

Dinstein's analysis, that the meaning cannot be limited to the mere impact, however, is convincing. Theoretically, an armed attack has begun when, in colloquial terms, the button is pushed or the trigger is pulled, no matter whether the missile is still in the air or has already hit the target. Counter-measures in such situations constitute legitimate acts of national self-defence provided the additional requirements of national self-defence are fulfilled: the extent of force predictably passes the threshold required for an armed attack; it cannot be prevented by other means but the use of force; the extent of force is predictable in a way that allows for proportionate counter-violence.

But what about acts taking place between preparatory actions and the final act of launching the attack? Does the moving of an airplane to the place whence it is to drop a bomb count as preparation, or as part of the armed attack? What

---

77 See Dinstein 2005, 192.
78 Dinstein 2005, 192.

about the sailing of a ship to the location from which the airplane dropping the bomb will take off?

Dinstein establishes his understanding of armed attack in two steps. First, he argues that acts of force do not necessarily involve the launching of the first shot. Secondly, he points at the fact that once the launch has taken place, the armed attack has started. From these two assertions he concludes that a ship *en route* to the point from which it will launch an attack constitutes the beginning of the armed attack. He requires that the defending forces know exactly what the ship is planning, yet gives no weight to the fact that the plan could still be altered.

Dinstein's first premise is convincing. The parallel between firing a gun and sailing to the point from which an attack is to be launched, however, differs in exactly the point Dinstein both addresses and disregards, namely the immutability of the course of events. This distinction constitutes the difference between preparatory work and the firing of a weapon. Nevertheless, it often also explains the difference between being on the way to carry out an armed attack and the launching of such an attack. Once the attack is launched, the impact will unavoidably occur, and this makes the launch part of the attack. Under certain circumstances, it may be possible to minimize the damage or even to interrupt the attack. Yet without such interference, the act will lead to the damaging outcome without requiring any additional action. This point has not yet been reached prior to the beginning of an attack. The example of the sailing fleet illustrates this point. When the fleet is on its way to launch an attack, the attack is not necessarily inevitable. The plans could still be changed due to internal decision or external influence.

That said, every situation reaches a point at which the likelihood for actual change reaches a minimum. Although an additional act is required to trigger the damaging event, the determination is such that it is near certain that the act will be carried out. Although the outcome may theoretically still be alterable, it ceases to be a practical consideration. Only in situations like this is it convincing to speak of a link between moving into position for a launch and the launch itself that is strong enough to assign the former action to the latter and regard it as part of the armed attack.

Does that mean that Article 51 allows for the use of force under these circumstances? The theoretical analysis of the meaning of armed attack does not seem sufficient. In view of the importance of the prohibition of force within the system of international law, more practical considerations are appropriate. An argument Cassese formulates in response to the claim that pre-emptive national self-defence is authorized under Article 51 may be helpful for appropriately replying to this question.[79] Cassese suggests considering the object and scope of Article 51, of Chapter VII of the UN Charter, or more generally the 'logic of the overall System contemplated by the Charter'[80] and highlights that the creation and maintenance of peace is considered the supreme intent, which is to be pursued as perfectly as possible. Cassese therefore argues that pre-emptive strikes should be prohibited. Given that the situation is subject to the judgement of individual states, allowance for pre-emptive strikes involves a high risk of abuse. It involves the risk that states base their pre-emptive actions on their subjective arbitrary assessment of the other state's intention.

These considerations do not lead to an outright rejection of the reasoning regarding the beginning of an armed attack. Nevertheless, they allude to an additional criterion that seems conditional to understanding armed attacks in terms of Article 51: the degree of certainty states that react to an armed attack at such an early stage must have acquired regarding the determination of an adversary agent to follow through with launching an attack. In order to act at such an early stage of an armed attack, the state has to have a high degree of certainty not only regarding the plans of the potential attacker, but also about the immutability of these plans. Knowledge of the intent to attack another state by way of, for example, intelligence gathering, does not suffice. The intent can change, and intelligence gatherings do not offer certainty, in particular because they may be flawed. States would have to address the agents in question and provide warnings of counter-measures. Only reactions to such interactions may establish certainty great enough for states to act.

With regard to the right of states to use armed force in national self-defence in the prevention of a terrorist attack that reaches the degree of an armed attack, and, hence, with regard to the justifiability of targeted killings as acts of national self-defence, the above discussion allows for some preliminary conclusions. The prohibition of preventive use of force in national self-defence proscribes the use of force prior to the execution of an attack. Theoretically, and provided all other requirements are met, the use of force is allowed if the attack has already started, which means that the terrorist organization has started acting in a manner that indicates that the final destructive act is inevitable, and the defending state, by way of communication, has established sufficient certainty of this fact. Practically, the permission to act at this point, however, has little impact on the justifiability of targeted killings of terrorists in terms of national self-defence for two

---

79 Cassese 2005, 361f.
80 Dinstein 2005, 361.

reasons. Given how terrorists act, it is relatively unlikely that any kind of communication prior an attack will be established. Unlike states, they are clandestine, and means of communication are not normally established. More importantly, the right of national self-defence only regulates the use of force in inter-state relations. The moment prior to the actual destructive act, in which the use of force may be justified will, however, most likely be on the territory of the defending state. In this situation, however, the right of national self-defence does not apply and cannot provide any justification. To conclude, the right of national self-defence can most likely not be invoked to justify preventive targeted killings.

In light of the fact that it is practically impossible to justify the use of force in terms of the right of national self-defence prior to a damaging act, it remains to be asked whether the use of force can be justified in terms of the right to respond to an individual armed attack after it has taken place. In terms of the right of national self-defence, states may respond by means of force as long as the attack continues. This is expressed by the text of Article 51. It determines that the attacked state may only act 'if an armed attack occurs'. These limits also follow from the requirement of necessity, which requires that force is necessary to repel the armed attack, as well as from the requirement of proportionality, which requires that the means and extent of force applied in response are proportional to the attack and the purpose of securing the protection of the good that is envisaged by defence. Both requirements will be addressed in more detail below.[81] If states apply force regardless, these acts of force are no longer legitimized by the right of national self-defence. They can no longer be described as defensive actions but must be described, for example, as retaliatory or punitive actions, and they are illegal.[82]

This brief explanation highlights that responsive targeted killings of terrorists cannot be justified with reference to the right of national self-defence. Responsive targeted killings are not carried out in response to an ongoing armed attack, nor do they seek to repel any attack. They are applied in response to past terrorist actions for reasons of revenge or punishment.

---

81 See chapter 5.4.

82 Randelzhofer 2002, mn. 42. This requirement is sometimes described as the requirement of immediacy. See for example, Dinstein 2005, 209 f./242 f.; Tomuschat 2001, 542. In its judgment in *Nicaragua v. United States of America*, the ICJ also seems to address this requirement within the framework of the requirement of necessity. See ICJ, *Nicaragua v. United States of America*, (Merits), para. 237. A contrary position holds Emanuel Gross (2005, 585 f.). He argues that states may react in self-defence provided the attack to which they react is sufficiently destructive, regardless of whether further acts can reasonably be expected.

With regard to defensive targeted killings, the time period during which force may be applied is less clear. It is, however, of particular importance. In light of the terrorist 'hit and run' tactic and the often long periods that pass between different attacks, determining when an attack is over is not straightforward. The duration of justified force in the aftermath of a specific act, however, is decisive with regard to whether the right of national self-defence allows states to resort to force at all in response to terrorism and, as a result, also addresses the justifiability of targeted killings of terrorists in terms of national self-defence. This issue gains particular importance given that pre-emptive and anticipatory action is not allowed and because the term 'armed attack' may only under strict conditions be understood to include actions leading up to the execution of the actual attack.

One may argue that the attack ends as soon as the strike is carried out. Different acts, the argument may continue, are carried out by different individuals, and prevention of the particular attack, hence, is no longer necessary or appropriate when the attack is over. With regard to suicide attacks in particular, one may hold that the posed threat and danger vanishes with the attack having taken place. Given that force may only be applied in order to stop the occurring armed attack, but may not be applied in the aftermath of it, counter-terrorist force would necessarily be illegal, and targeted killings could never be justified in terms of the right of national self-defence.

Such an interpretation, however, is not convincing. One may not exclusively focus on the individual terrorist action to which the defending state reacts. What seems decisive is the danger emanating from the organization behind the individual attack.[83] This is also what the understanding of the duration of armed attacks is based on when such attacks are carried out by states. It is what allows the use of force when a state attacks another state by deploying different units in different places. Even if each unit attacks only once, the first act of military force constitutes the beginning of an ongoing situation of armed attack. It is also what allows the use of national self-defence despite time passing between acts of attack. With regard to state action, the situation of armed attack continues, even if the fighting ceases between acts of military force. For an ongoing armed attack by a state to exist, one must be able to determine that the military attacks emanating from that state as a whole will carry on.

This understanding, in principle, also applies to terrorist organizations engaging in a conflict with one particular state and carrying out ongoing attacks against that state. That said, the determination that the addressed constellations

---

83 Heintschel v. Heinegg/Gries 2000, 157; Walter 2004, 28.

in inter-state conflicts can be considered cases of an ongoing situation of armed attack depends on facts about states that often do not apply to non-state terrorist organizations and which – if applicable in principle – are often far more difficult to establish in relation to terrorist organizations than is the case with states. In other words, there are several theoretical and practical differences between states and terrorist organizations which make it impossible to apply assertions that can be made with regard to states – namely that it is not the singular act, but the danger emanating from the organization which must be examined in order to determine the duration of an armed attack – to terrorist organizations in the suggested manner.[84]

The drafters of Article 51 UN Charter had states in mind, and states typically have a structure of command and relatively defined aims, formed by their governments. The state, internally as well as externally, acts as an entity. This seems to be the basis on which several attacks can be attributed to one overall armed attack. This also seems to be the basis on which attacks on a state's military units are justified even if those units have not yet themselves been actively involved in the ongoing armed attack.

This is not necessarily the case with regard to all organizational forms of terrorism. The organizational structure of terrorism encompasses everything between highly integrated terrorist units and loosely connected units that work independently while cooperating and supporting each other. Indeed, they may not have any connection that may be called organizational in a strict sense, but only have an aim or ideology in common that creates links, albeit not of an organizational manner.[85] Under certain circumstances, then, different units may in some sense belong to one network or organization, yet individual attacks of these units need not form one ongoing attack involving the entire network.

As a result, a precondition can be set for a state to invoke the right of national self-defence in the wake of a terrorist attack: that it can determine that the attack can be ascribed to a unit or organization that, like a state, acts as an entity and carries on attacking the defending state. Such a description certainly goes

---

84 Wolff Heintschel v. Heinegg and Tobias Gries (2000, 157) accept that attacks that have already taken place and attacks that are expected to take place have to be related in terms of organizational structure and time frame, in a way that can be determined. Nevertheless, they seem to underestimate the difficulties related to such a requirement and, thus, fail to see the practical consequences that follow from their statement.

85 For an excellent analysis of different organizational forms of terrorism, see Mayntz 2003. Though problematic in his classification of current terrorism as 'new' terrorism, for an account of the organizational setting and command structure within the terrorist network Al Qaeda and other less trans-national but rather regional or international organizations or networks, see also Schneckener 2006, 49–100.

too far if the activities are carried out by different units in a loosely associated organizational structure.

This points to a second difference between terrorist organizations and states that highlights a difficulty with regard to the determination of an ongoing armed attack. In order to determine that an act constitutes the beginning of an ongoing armed attack, which may only be stopped by force, the act must be clearly attributable to the organization. It also requires clear knowledge of the organization's intention.[86] While such attribution may be relatively easy to determine with regard to states acting with their military forces, both facts are difficult to establish with regards to non-state terrorist organizations. Among other things, they act clandestinely, their organizational and hierarchical structure is not clear, their membership is neither openly declared nor visible in any way, and they do not generally engage in negotiations.

There is a third difference between how terrorist organizations and states engage in aggressive conduct, which brings into question the idea that the former engage in one ongoing armed attack against a state. Terrorist organizations or networks, in particular in their transnational form, often direct violence against several states. They attack different countries in sequence. And even if they attack one country several times, these attacks may be years apart, making it implausible to argue that they form one ongoing armed attack. These facts not only support the statement that clear evidence must be established before an individual attack may be interpreted as being part of an ongoing attack. They also highlight that an attack which a specific state encounters typically ends with this single attack.

To conclude, national self-defence may only be carried out if it is still required to ward off an attack. If the situation of attack has ended, the use of force is illegal. Armed attack, that by a terrorist organization and that by a state, does not necessarily end with a single attack. Single attacks can, in principle, be part of an ongoing attack, and the use of force in response can, in principle, be justified as act of national self-defence. Individual acts may be described as such if the act is not isolated. Because differences exist between states and non-state terrorist organisations, arguments made regarding attacks by states may not simply be translated to situations involving terrorists in order to describe acts undertaken by terrorists as part of an ongoing situation of armed attack. Provided it reaches the extent required to classify it as an armed attack in the first place, an individual terrorist attack can only be regarded as the beginning of an ongoing armed attack if it can be attributed to an organ-

---

86 Walter 2004, 28.

ization or unit that may be described as organized and integrated, and if it can be determined that this organization will continue to attack the state concerned in a manner that lets the individual act appear to belong to an ongoing attack rather than being an isolated act.

5.4 Proportionality and necessity

The requirements of proportionality and necessity further limit the justifiability of such acts. Several examples show that both criticism and support of individual acts of national self-defence are often based on these requirements.[87] The requirements for national self-defence discussed up to this point have to do with the question of whether states may resort to force against non-state terrorist organizations on foreign territory. The requirements of proportionality and necessity have an impact on answering this question, in particular with regard to the determination of the time period during which states may apply force after the accomplishment of an individual terrorist armed attack. They exclude any act that is not defensive, but retaliatory or punitive, and thus exclude all forms of responsive targeted killings. They are, however, of particular importance regarding the kind of defensive force that may be justified in response to terrorist armed attacks. They are crucial to the justifiability of targeted killings of terrorists as means of national self-defence.

A certain act of defence is proportional if the means and extent of force are not disproportionate to the gravity of the attack or the defensive effect reached through it.[88] It does not make sense to further elaborate the principle of proportionality on this general level,[89] but one point crucial to the context of targeted killing of terrorists is worth mentioning. Lethal force may only be applied if the attack to be repelled involves lethal damage or its equivalent.

The requirement of necessity means that force may only be used when strictly necessary and to the extent necessary to repel an armed attack. As has been established, this entails the prohibition of anticipatory or pre-emptive national self-defence as well as the prohibition of use of force in response to past terrorist attacks. It also includes limitations as to the kind of force to be applied.

As with the requirement of proportionality, concrete limitations as to the kind of force that is justifiable in terms of necessity can only be determined on a case-by-case basis in light of the particular attack to be fended off. A few

---

87 Schachter 1989, 220 f./223.
88 Feinstein 1976, 537; Randelzhofer 2002, mn. 42.
89 For some criteria of the requirement, see, for example, Fischer 2004, mn. 39, pp. 1094 f.

general points regarding the limits it involves for targeted killing of terrorists, however, are possible.

In order to be necessary, targeted killings of terrorists must be appropriate to repel future terrorists attacks. The effectiveness of targeted killings is controversial.[90] States, then, have to convincingly demonstrate this efficacy in order to claim that such acts are necessary.

Further general statements as to the justifiability of targeted killings as a necessary means of national self-defence may be derived from the differences that are implied regarding the need to forcefully respond to state-force and non-state attacks. Other means of repelling an attack are available in response to non-state violence when compared to the situation of responding to state force. Although the possibilities available to a state may be more limited on foreign state territory than they are internally, the means of redress against non-state actors still exceed those it is able to apply in a conflict with another state.

Internally, states have established a wide set of measures to deal with non-state violence. Most of these are law enforcement measures, and law enforcement measures involve force. However, minor forms will be, and have to be, applied long before the state may resort to the most extreme kind of force, namely lethal force. Even in highly violent situations, special police forces will be deployed rather than military units. It is the overall aim to detain and convict the persons involved and to establish the rule of law and order. This is different in conflicts with other states. It is not the police forces who engage in these conflicts, but the military. The primary aim is not to capture enemy forces, but to weaken them to an extent that makes the other state change its policies, surrender, or, in the most extreme cases, lose its power all together. Law enforcement is not a consideration. The aim is not to convict certain persons, but to prevent the other state from interfering with the other's interests and existence. Structural factors seem crucial for these differences. While a state does, at least formally, have authority over non-state actors, the relationship between states is one of equals. Moreover, in an inter-state armed conflict, the entire militaries of the states are potentially involved. The number of people able to fight leaves no choice but to attack the other state's army rather than to capture individual members of it. Necessity, triggered by the manner states relate to one another and the structure of conflicts between states, requires the use of substantial force; minor use of force, equivalent to internal law enforcement measures, such as detention, is not a feasible option.

---

90 See chapter 8.

Neither of these factors that apply to inter-state armed conflicts necessarily (or typically) characterizes conflicts between states and non-state terrorist groups. The formal relation between states and non-state terrorist groups differs from that between states. Moreover, non-state terrorist groups or organizations do not generally have military capacities resembling those of states. As a result, to repel attacks by non-state actors, states generally have a range of measures that are not available to them when confronted with the forces of another state. This also applies, via third states or extraterritorial jurisdiction, to situations where terrorists are situated on foreign state territory.

It follows from this, in the context of justifying force against terrorist groups abroad, that the requirement of necessity obliges states applying such force to explore all measures before they resort to the practice of targeted killing. Whether means other than targeted killing are available depends on the given circumstances. Whether these means are appropriate to repel the attack, and therefore legally necessary, also depends on the circumstances. In general, however, in conflicts between non-state terrorist organizations and states, regardless of whether they take place on foreign state territory, states are provided options that exceed those available in inter-state armed conflicts. These must be explored before targeted killings can be justified as a last resort.[91] The requirement of necessity, then, sets a very high and typically insuperable barrier for justifying targeted killings of terrorists as acts of national self-defence, not only with regard to the question of whether force may be used in response to terrorist attacks, but also with regard to the kind of force implied in targeted killings.

5.5 Legality of targeted killing in terms of the right of national self-defence

The discussion of the different requirements directly related to the right of national self-defence makes clear that targeted killings of terrorists on foreign state territory can rarely be described as justified acts of national self-defence.

---

91 Carsten Stahn (2004, 872–874) argues that the capture of terrorists on foreign state territory, or as he rightly addresses it, abduction, may be justified in terms of the right of national self-defence only if the terrorist is captured while 'engaged in action that directly precedes or leads to an armed attack'. Only in such situations may states have the right to prevent an impending attack. Stahn's position is convincing for all situations that cannot be described as an ongoing armed attack. In the arguably very rare case that the situation can be described as an ongoing armed attack, capture of terrorists is justifiable as an act of national self-defence, provided it can reasonably be argued that such an act is necessary to repel the ongoing armed attack.

First, the use of force in response to terrorist attacks can be justified with reference to the right of national self-defence only to a very limited extent. It requires a terrorist attack to reach the extent of force necessary to constitute an armed attack and for it to be more than a sporadic or isolated act of force. It must be reasonable to assume that the act to which the attacked state reacts will be succeeded by further attacks that aggregate to form an ongoing situation of armed attack. If the situation of attack is still present, force may be used before as well as after individual armed attacks. If there is no ongoing situation of attack, force may under no circumstances be applied after the individual attack has finished. Prior to the attack, i.e. prior to the realization of the attack, force may only be applied in a moment that can be described as being part of the attack. Moreover, the terrorist acts have to either be attributable to the state on the territory of which the act of national self-defence will take place, or that state must have violated its international obligation to prevent terrorist activity on its territory and be unwilling or unable to change this situation. In the former case, the situation is relatively clear, as it corresponds to national self-defence as it has commonly been discussed. In such a situation, the use of force must be necessary and proportionate in order to be justified in terms of the right of national self-defence. In the latter case, acts of force may only be applied against the terrorist facilities themselves without affecting the state's institutions or population. Moreover, the manner of force must be strictly limited to acts necessary to fend off the attack and proportionate to an established aim.

These strict limitations exclude the justification of any responsive targeted killing of terrorists. Defensive targeted killing of terrorists is, in principle, possible. In order to be justified in its action, the acting state, however, must be able to provide convincing proof that the act to which it responds forms part of an ongoing attack. This faces difficulties largely alien to the context of inter-state relations, particularly in conflicts between states and terrorist organizations whose acts cannot be attributed to a state. Moreover, states must convincingly posit that the targeted killing of individuals is necessary to repel the attack and proportionate to the defensive purpose. It is not a foregone conclusion that these requirements may be met with regard to targeted killings of terrorists. It is far from clear that the targeted killing of individual terrorists is appropriate to fend off ongoing attacks. Moreover, states generally have options in these situations which are not available to them in conflicts with other states.

5.6 Applicable international law and limits to the use of targeted killing in self-defence

The requirements emanating from the right of national self-defence, which have been established above, substantially limit the justifiability of targeted killings of terrorists and render it a rather theoretical possibility. Apart from those set by the requirements of necessity and proportionality, these limitations concern the question of whether force may be applied in response to non-state terrorist acts at all. They concern the justifiability of targeted killings of terrorists, since the practice cannot be legally justified if the use of force itself is not justifiable. What is often ignored is the fact that whether terrorists may be targeted and killed is also dependent on international legal regulations governing such a use of force. If the resort to force is justified, the justification of targeted killings of terrorists then depends on which international legal regulations govern the use of force in the relevant situation, and on the allowance for targeted killings that these rules comprise. The previous chapters provide the relevant discussions and allow for the following conclusions.

Given that national self-defence has traditionally been discussed in light of inter-state conflicts, the kind of force that may be applied in national self-defence is generally discussed with reference to international humanitarian law regulating international armed conflicts. As the last chapter has shown, this applies to conflicts between states and non-state terrorist groups if the non-state acts are attributable to the state on the territory of which they operate, plan and organize their deeds. If this can be determined, targeted killings of terrorists under such circumstances must, in order to be justified, be in accordance with international humanitarian law regulating international armed conflicts. If the use of force as such is justified, targeted killings of terrorists can, under such circumstances, only be justified as a means of national self-defence if they are carried out against terrorists who actively participate in the hostilities and only during the time they do so. In view of the cases of targeted killing examined here, this, realistically, limits justifiable targeted killings to lethal acts directed against terrorists who are on their way to carry out an attack or involved in a determinable attack, the deployment for which has started, provided there is sufficient proof that this is the case. Targeted killing can also be justified in the theoretical case in which the targeted terrorists, deemed terrorists owing to non-state terrorist activity, are incorporated in the armed forces of the state involved in the international armed conflict. If the targeted killing affects innocent individuals, it requires the killing to be of such importance that it renders the harm done to these individuals proportional to the military advantage reached by the act.[92] It is clear that these requirements render the legality even more unlikely than has already been concluded with regard to the requirements derived directly from the right of national self-defence.

The conclusions regarding the justifiability of targeted killing is little changed even if the situation constitutes a non-international armed conflict in terms of common Article 3. (APII is not applicable at all to these situations because of its territorial limitations and because it requires the non-state forces to be willing to implement the Protocol.) In the rather unlikely situation that lethal force may be justified with regard to the requirements directly linked to the right of national self-defence, e.g. proportionality and necessity, the legality of targeted killing of terrorists faces further burdens. Terrorists who belong to the non-state armed forces that are part of the armed conflict may only be targeted and killed if this is appropriate in fighting the enemy and necessary for reaching the intended aim. Terrorists not belonging to the non-state armed forces, but who do take an active part in the hostilities, may only be attacked during the time they do so. Most importantly, in as much as terrorists are not recognizable as taking an active part in the hostilities or belonging to the armed forces, they do not constitute legitimate targets. This follows from the strictly required protection of civilians not taking an active part in the hostilities. In light of typical terrorist strategies, these requirements make the legality of targeted killings of terrorists in typical conflicts highly unrealistic,[93] even in the already rather theoretical case where the right of national self-defence may legitimately be invoked and does not exclude targeted killings from the legitimate available means.[94]

---

92 For details, see chapter 4.3.

93 For details, see chapter 4.4.

94 If states have the right to act in national self-defence and are allowed to apply lethal force according to this right, the situation seems to be governed by international humanitarian law, be it by the regulations applying to international armed conflicts or by the regulations applying to non-international armed conflicts. In case there may be circumstances to which none of these regulations apply, the human rights regulations, or more specifically the right to life, as applicable to peacetime situations, regulate whether targeted killings of terrorists can be applied. (See chapter 3.2. With regard to conflicts between terrorists and a state on the high sea, see also Neumann 2003, 291f.) The right to life then is best understood as prohibiting any use of lethal force against individuals not in detention – this is by definition the case with targeted killing of terrorists – that is not absolutely necessary to prevent serious harm to other people and if not occurring in the course of arrest or prevention of escape. This excludes justification as legal acts of national self-defence for all genuine forms of targeted killing of terrorists. (See chapter 3.1.) Some authors argue that there are situations in which neither human rights regulating law enforcement nor the laws of armed conflict apply. See e.g. Paust 2010, 263 – 269/279 f.;

This result may not be satisfactory to everyone. It may be argued that it un-justifiably limits a state's ability to react to transnational non-state force. As such, the argued limitations to the use of state force against non-state actors may give reason to discuss whether measures exceeding those recently allowed in international law should be accepted. Such a discussion could reasonably in-volve the question of whether international humanitarian law should account ex-plicitly for conflicts between states and non-state transnational terrorist organi-zations. It could also involve the question of whether certain acts of lethal force exceeding those accepted under human rights law should be accepted as not constituting arbitrary deprivations of life, and respectively, whether international humanitarian law should allow the use of lethal force in cases exceeding those currently accepted. All of these questions, however, go beyond existing interna-tional law and address its future development. Responding to these questions requires a thorough discussion, accounting not only for the needs states may claim for their security, but also for the rights individuals must reasonably pos-sess, as well as for the principles that could justify legalizing the use of lethal force beyond the limits established. In the following part of the book (*The Moral Justifiability*), I seek to provide some answers to these questions.

Anderson, K. 2011. See also fn. 3 in chapter 4. In light of the reasoning about the applicability of human rights law laid out in chapter 1, there is however no reason to believe that there are situation in which the right of national self-defence including the customary regulations applying to acts of national self-defence regulate state conduct alone.

Part III: **Moral Justification**

The arguments for the moral justifiability[1] of targeted killings of terrorists put forward in academic literature and in practice are not always attributable to only one approach; often several approaches are drawn upon. It still seems possible to differentiate different lines of argument. Discussing these, as well as additional conceivable approaches, will not only allow for the assessment of their justifying force; it will also help to better understand the principles that distinguish justified killing from unjustified deprivation of life. Based on these principles I will try to give a plausible explanation as to whether, when and why targeted killings of terrorists can be morally justified. I will thus be able to develop an argument as to the justifiability of targeted killing of terrorists as well as to answer to the moral arguments which states and scholars put forward to justify state practice, and hence to adequately react to the current debate.

The philosophical argument will also complement and strengthen the international legal argument. In particular, this regards three points, to which I referred in the preceding part of the book: the question of whether the fight against terrorism needs to be regarded as a new form of warfare to which the laws of war apply; the distinction between members of armed forces and civilians in non-international armed conflicts; and the question of whether, or under what conditions, targeted killings of terrorists constitute unjust, and hence arbitrary, deprivations of life.

In order to analyse the different conceivable approaches to justifying targeted killing of terrorists, it is helpful to restate some points previously made as to the meaning of 'targeted killing of terrorists' and the problems for the justifiability of the practice. First of all, targeted killings of terrorists can be divided into defensive killings and what I called responsive killings. The former are carried out in defence against future terrorist attacks. The latter are carried out to avenge terrorist attacks that have already taken place or to punish terrorists involved in past acts. Individual cases of targeted killing may often pursue more than one of these purposes. Nevertheless these two purposes must be kept in mind as being possible aims of the practice since, as will become clear, they constitute a morally relevant distinction.

This also applies to the distinction I made between different cases of targeted killing of terrorists. So secondly, defensive targeted killings can be distinguished into killings carried out in view of a determinable threat – that is, carried out in order to prevent a specific terrorist attack that is held to be predictable – and

---

1 While in the preceding part on the international legal justification of targeted killing of terrorists the terms 'justified', 'justification', and 'justifiability' referred to *legal* justification, I in this part on the moral justification use these terms to refer to *moral* justification.

killings in view of the terrorist threat as such – that is, that the killing is *not* carried out in reference to a *specific* terrorist attack that is held to be determinable.

Thirdly, I introduced an additional distinction regarding the moment of attack and facts acquired prior to attack. This resulted in four cases: (1) killing of terrorists that are held to be on their way to carry out an attack; (2) killing of terrorists prior to that moment, though in view of a determinable terrorist attack; (3) killing of terrorists who, due to existing information, are suspected of continued involvement in terrorism, without evidence of engagement in a determinable terrorist attack; and (4) killing of terrorists who had been involved in terrorist activity, though it has not been established whether they still pose a threat.

Fourth, looking at the occurring cases of targeted killing, I identified three key issues that have central impact on the justifiability of acts of targeted killing: that the *targeted* person is deprived of his or her life; that innocent third parties are harmed; and that state borders are crossed in carrying out the killing. The international legal part of this book addresses all three aspects. This part will focus on the first question involved. The principles developed during the course of the discussion will, however, also enable me to address the impact that killing innocent third persons may have on the justifiability of individual acts of targeted killing of terrorists. The question of how moral justifiability may be influenced by a situation in which the killings are carried out on foreign state territory would go beyond the scope of this book and, thus, will not be discussed.

This focus corresponds to the public debate on the morality of targeted killings. The public as well as the academic philosophical debate focus on the questions addressed in this part. The discussion will hence allow for an adequate reply to the different arguments given in these debates. Moreover, as concerns the legal debate in this book, the questions that require further discussion are directed at aspects crucial to assessing whether terrorists – i.e. the targeted person – may be targeted and killed. I will discuss the moral question independent of the legal debate. I think the legal relevance of the discussion has become clear, however, and it suggests the focus I will be taking. This coincides with the fact that the question of whether the targeted person may be killed is the morally pivotal question attendant on the targeted killing of terrorists. It gets at the core of the practice. Other than harm to innocent bystanders and crossing state borders, targeted killings are just that: the targeted application of lethal force. Targeted killings do not necessarily take place on foreign territory. Moreover, as apparently was the case in the targeted killing that the United States carried out against alleged Al Qaeda members in Yemen in November 2002, the governments concerned may agree to such action, and hence dismiss the problem of state sovereignty.

6 The rationale for killing in war

Many proponents of the targeted killing of terrorists base their arguments on the rationale for killing in war. This is because wartime reasoning justifies killing on the basis of some form of collectivization. In comparison to moral assessments of peacetime activity, this broadens the justification of killing in respect to the object of attack and with regard to the time period during which this target may be attacked. Drawing on wartime reasoning further broadens the justification of the use of lethal force that causes harming side-effects. This is relevant for the justifiability of targeted killings under certain circumstances, because, as has been established, the practice often involves harming third parties.

6.1 Morally accepted means of warfare

One conceivable argument for morally justifying targeted killings of terrorists, on the basis of wartime reasoning, is that terrorists may be targeted as combatants[1] in a war against terrorism.[2] Paralleling the legal debate, this argument plays a predominant role in the discussion of the moral justifiability of targeted killings of terrorists.[3]

The argument gains its justifying relevance from the traditional or orthodox just war position on justifiable killing during warfare. According to this position, one must strictly distinguish between combatants and non-combatants. Non-combatants must not be attacked intentionally and have to be spared from the effects of warfare as much as possible. Provided they are not in detention, sick or wounded, combatants, in contrast, are not generally protected from attack. They may principally be attacked at any time during warfare, regardless of whether they are about to kill enemy combatants themselves or whether they will actually kill other individuals in the course of war.

The argument, however, generally also works on the basis of a non-orthodox position that argues that there are moral differences between killing combatants fighting a just war and those fighting an unjust war. This position, which questions the orthodox claim that *jus in bello* is independent of *jus ad bellum*, has

---

1 It is important to note that the term 'combatant' here, unlike in the international legal discussion, does not imply a statement as to whether the individual is permitted to participate in the fighting.

2 This term is often substituted for the terms 'war against terror' or 'war against terrorists'.

3 For such argumentation, see, for example, David 2003a, 121; Gross, M. 2010, in particular 100–121; Meisels 2004; Statman 2004.

convincing force and does not make a difference with regard to the argument presented here. If terrorists were combatants, they would not belong to the group that is protected from attack. This is not necessarily because they would always have to be regarded as fighting an unjust war, but because they, by definition, attack innocent individuals, non-combatants in the terms of warfare, and hence systematically violate *jus in bello*, which equally abolishes their protection from attack. Hence, for everyone who questions the independence of *jus in bello* and *jus ad bellum* and claims that only some groups of combatants could justifiably be attacked, the argument discussed in this chapter equally applies. It then has to be read with regard to terrorists as fighting with means that violate *jus in bello*.[4]

It is far from easy to explain why combatants may be killed during warfare regardless of their behaviour at the time of attack and the threat they individually actually pose. Given the fact that combatants often do not threaten anyone at the time of attack, and that some may never personally pose any actual threat in their role as combatants, it is impossible to justify targeting them with reference to their actual individual threatening behaviour. I hold that killing them can only be explained with reference to their role in the war effort. Their relation to the war effort makes them part of the threat posed to the enemy, which during the course of the war allows the use of force. They are part of the continuous threat, and this renders them both a part of the group of combatants and, in principle, liable to attack at any time as long as they can be considered combatants.[5]

---

4 Most powerfully, Jeff McMahan recently questioned the independence of *jus in bello* and *jus ad bellum*. He a.o. questions that all combatants may generally be attacked during warfare. (For his account of justified killing in war, see McMahan 2004 and 2006b; see also McMahan 2006c). Those who do not fight according to *jus in bello*, however, are in his view liable to attack, regardless of whether they fight a just or an unjust war (McMahan 2008, 228). Holding that wartime reasoning equates to peacetime reasoning, McMahan would not subscribe to the collectivizing reasoning presented in this chapter to determine the justifiability of targeting combatants (see also below fn. 34 in the current chapter). This however does not yet question the argument discussed in this chapter, as long as it is accepted that in wars only those combatants may be attacked who fight an unjust war or – as terrorists – (systematically) violate *jus in bello*.

5 Walzer 1977, 138–147. Walzer argues that combatants may be attacked regardless of whether they fight a just or an unjust war and that guilt is not ascribed to combatants of either side. As I have already discussed, I do not need to go that far, in order to make my argument. The crucial point which I take from Walzer's reasoning is that the justification for killing combatants during warfare cannot be explained on the basis of the combatant's actual individual threatening conduct, as is the case during peacetime, but must be explained with reference to the overall threat that justifies the use of force and killing during warfare. In other words the justification is based on some form of collectivization.

I will say more about the distinction between combatants and non-combatants, but the given explanation suffices in order to make sense of the argument for targeted killings of terrorists. The argument that conflicts between states and terrorists constitute warfare develops its justifying relevance in light of this justification of killing during warfare. If it can be argued that the fight against terrorism constitutes war, it can be concluded that terrorists are combatants. After all, war without combatants is a contradiction in terms. It may then still be asked what it means to belong to the group of combatants, and this designation as combatant may not be applicable to all individuals who are somehow active on behalf of a terrorist group. But the groups that actively carry out the conflict may be regarded as combatants. Hence, if the fight against terrorism can be considered war, it seems to be arguable that (certain) terrorists may be targeted due to their role as combatants, and hence independently of any additional justification referring to their individual threatening conduct.

This would provide states with a broad justification of targeted killings of terrorists. It would legitimize killing terrorists, whether they are currently and directly involved in a terrorist attack, or whether they are alleged to be involved in the planning or organizing of a terrorist attack. To target them, it would suffice to establish that they are sufficiently affiliated with the group of terrorists against which the state is fighting the war.[6]

---

6 Michael Gross (2006, in particular 325–327) questioned this conclusion. He argues that the justification for killing combatants does not apply to targeted killing, in his words, named killing. According to Gross, the fact that certain individuals are selected and killed assigns guilt to them, which is not assigned to them when they are killed as 'nameless' combatants. In so doing, the named soldiers are declared 'outside the law' and the orthodox justification for their killing no longer applies (Gross, M. 2006, 326). Gross's argument hits upon three important points. It highlights a difference that can be recognized between targeted killing and warfare strategy. (See below in the current section.) More drastically, Gross's argument may suggest that the argument that terrorists may be killed since they constitute combatants is hypocritical. Terrorists are killed for guilt assigned to them as individuals for their terrorist activities. The orthodox warfare rationale for killing combatants, however, is that combatants are killed for being part of the warfare threat, while personal guilt for actual violent deeds is not ascribed. The third point also concerns the justification of killing during warfare. In view of the fact that not all combatants are threatening the enemy personally or ever will, justification for killing combatants during warfare abstains from giving decisive weight to the threat the individual poses at the moment of attack or in the future. Selecting and killing a specific individual, due to his or her personal deeds, therefore appears to re-introduce individuality and hence abandon the collectivizing justification of killing combatants during warfare. Still, Gross's argument does not convincingly challange the argument made so far. First, it does not convincingly rebut the relevance of the orthodox wartime rationale for killing combatants to the targeting of

I have already discussed from an international legal perspective whether conflicts with terrorism constitute wars – in legal terms, armed conflicts.[7] I concluded that, theoretically, this is possible. Yet the cases that have taken place in practice, and that come to mind when discussing the targeted killing of terrorists, do not commonly represent armed conflicts.

To restate, international law distinguishes between international armed conflicts and non-international armed conflicts. International armed conflicts are inter-state conflicts. Given that terrorism is a tactic and a form of violence, but not *per se* a form of conflict, one can speak of war against terrorism, in the case of an armed conflict taking place between two states, one of which may be deemed terrorist, e.g. for attacking the civilian population. This, however, is not parallel to states' conflicts with terrorism that have triggered current debates about the justifiability of targeted killings of terrorists. Moreover, it is not relevant to this book, which discusses the killing of non-state agents only. Legally, one may also speak of an international armed conflict if the terrorism triggering the conflict is attributable to a given state. The conflict between a state and a terrorist organization can then be described as a conflict between two states, and hence as international armed conflict. In light of the requirements for imputability of non-state acts to states, this is, however, also atypical for current conflicts considered to be conflicts with terrorists. An international armed conflict also exists during open hostilities constituting an armed conflict in a situation of occupation. In light of the fact that acts directed against the occupying power, however, must not be considered to trigger an armed conflict, provided the use of force does not reach the required extent and the authorities continue to be in the position to exercise authority, this also does not typically apply to conflicts with terrorists.

---

terrorists. Provided one can speak of war, as long as an individual is picked with reference to the role he or she has in warfare, it is not clear in what way loss of anonymity can make a difference. In this sense, loss of anonymity does not necessarily ascribe guilt for actual personal harming deeds. Second, given that the aspect of the orthodox reasoning, which Gross addresses is not necessarily required for the reasoning provided in this chapter (see fn. 5 in the current chapter) the argument could still be made, even if Gross's point were convincing. For a different criticism of Gross' argument, see also Meisels 2004, 302 f.; Statman 2004 190; Statman 2003, 776 f. In his book *Moral Dilemmas of Modern War* Michael Gross (2010, 107 – 109) questions his own point. He argues that naming does not necessarily ascribe guilt but may establish that individuals are combatants, when they cannot be recognised as combatants because they do not wear uniforms.

7 See e.g. chapter 4.3.1. I will in the following not distinguish between wars and armed conflicts, a distinction that is necessary under certain circumstances in international law.

Equally atypical for current conflicts with terrorists are civil wars or other forms of non-international armed conflict. Legally, non-international armed conflicts take place between armed forces of a state and an entity, or else between two such entities (within a state). If any of these groups can be deemed terrorist, such a conflict could be described as war against terrorism, and targeted killings could potentially be justified with reference to the argument under discussion. This, however, is not the situation states are typically and currently facing. Conflicts relevant to the current debate did not, according to the legal analysis, constitute non-international armed conflicts. Depending on the legal regulation focused on, this is due to a lack of territorial control on the part of the terrorists, their organizational structure, their strategy, or the scale of the conflict. As regarding international armed conflicts, it is theoretically possible that groups involved in a non-international armed conflict could be deemed terrorist by their methods alone. In such a case, this non-international armed conflict may be regarded as war against terrorism. This term, however, is not generally applied to such situations and is in most cases wrongly ascribed.

This international legal assessment was formulated with reference to the preconditions required for the application of international humanitarian law, which, in international legal terms, is decisive for whether an armed conflict exists. Given the potential argument that these regulations were agreed to prior to the appearance of current forms of terrorism, the legal assessment can be bolstered with other factors. These will show that the fight against terrorism is not regularly understood as warfare, and, most importantly, that it should not be discussed in those terms.

Two reasons are commonly given for attributing terrorism and the fight against it to warfare. The first is that terrorism has highly destructive capacities, and the second is that states are not able to effectively combat terrorism with normal law enforcement measures.[8] Even if this were held to apply to terrorism as such,[9] these facts alone do not suffice to describe terrorism and the fight against it as warfare. In situations short of war, violence can have a dominant impact on day-to-day life. Serious crimes that harm individuals may occur. As was the case with the Mafia in the south of Italy, criminality may even threaten

---

8 See e.g. Statman 2004, 183–185. Seumas Miller (2009, 132–139, see in particular 137–139) also makes the status of the situation dependent on the effectiveness of the (domestic or international) criminal justice system – in his words, on whether the state or parts of it are 'well ordered, i.e. the domestic criminal justice system is unable adequately to contain the terrorist activities' (Miller 2009, 137) as well as on the extent and duration of the terrorist threat.
9 For problems with this view, see chapter 11.1.

public order, forcing individuals to question their day-to-day safety. Moreover, states may be highly ineffective in fighting these crimes with conventional law enforcement. As with Germany's engagement with the RAF, or again, as with the Mafia, states may be unable to prevent attacks or control criminal structures for varying periods of time. Still, states and the public distinguish such situations from war and identify the individuals carrying out such acts as criminals, even if they act in an organized manner. Their acts of violence are understood to be criminal acts, but not acts of warfare. Criminality is fought, but this fight against such behaviour is perceived to be a matter of law enforcement rather than warfare.

Furthermore, several differences between wars and relevant conflicts with terrorism can be pointed out. The characteristics of war, as well as those of conflicts with terrorism, which will be addressed in order to establish these differences, necessarily function as cornerstones. Not all wars have all of the characteristics to be presented here, nor are all conflicts with terrorism characterized by all of the factors that I give as typical for conflicts between terrorists and states. Nevertheless, I think that all conflicts with terrorism relevant to the debate on targeted killings of terrorists involve some of these various factors. This illustrates that conflicts with terrorists, as they are relevant to this discussion, commonly differ from warfare and may not be described as such.

Terrorism can most clearly be contrasted with conventional wars. Conflicts with terrorism do not involve clashes between professional and uniformed organizations of combatants, fighting on 'battlefields', largely territorially separated from the civilian population. They typically take place in populated areas,[10] between states and non-uniformed individuals, who blend into civilian society.

These differences are not sufficiently persuasive to definitively separate the combat against terrorism from warfare. Certain strategies recognized in war, such as guerrilla warfare, for example, stand in equal contrast to the conventional characteristics of warfare. Some slightly more convincing characteristics can be pointed out. Conflicts between states and terrorists are not, of necessity, limited by time or space. Moreover, terrorists do not generally belong to an organized fighting unit, but – perhaps with the exception of certain key figures – engage in terrorist activities whilst simultaneously going about civil day-to-day business, living with their families, and maintaining non-terrorist-related employment. More importantly, as Joan Fitzpatrick points out, in conflicts with terrorists, 'progress is measured by the absence of attacks, and success in applying control measures (arrest, intercepted communication, interrogations, and asset

---

10 See also Kasher/Yadlin 2005, 7.

seizures). The duration of "hostilities" is measured by the persistence of fear that the enemy retains the capacity to strike.'[11] Terrorist hostilities are not characterized by consistent or ongoing combat, and the end of a conflict with terrorists cannot be determined by the absence of lethal attack. These factors are, however, most often formulated as being decisive in a conflict being classified as warfare.[12] Moreover, despite the destructive potential of terrorist activity, terrorist strategy differs significantly from warfare strategy. Destruction is crucial for terrorist power, but it is so primarily because it is instrumental for instilling fear within the population.

All of these individual factors seem to point out differences between terrorism, the fight against it, and war as hitherto recognized. Apart from these individual characteristics, however, one can point to a structural and more general explanation that seems to distinguish war from other conflicts. This difference bolsters the argument that it is misleading to regard the terrorists' highly destructive capacities and the claimed inability of states to effectively fight terrorism by law enforcement measures as reasons decisive for attributing the fight against terrorism to warfare.

The differentiation drawn between wars and the fight against criminal behaviour, as well as between the means available in these different struggles, seems to depend on the relationship between the groups involved in the conflict and, *depending on* this relationship, the ability of states to react effectively. This is most evident in inter-state conflicts. Such conflicts take place between two entities facing one another as equals in terms of the formal authority they exercise. They face each other as independent and sovereign. Neither is entitled to give orders to the other. Lacking authority over the other state, the only means of countering ongoing, armed aggression is to eliminate the threat with armed force.

---

11 Fitzpatrick 2003, 251.
12 Definitions of war on which organizations that map and analyse wars and armed conflicts base their analysis most commonly require conflicts to exhibit a certain continuity in fighting, often measured in the number of battle-related deaths occurring per year, in order to be considered wars. Both the time period during which the hostilities must be below a certain threshold, and the threshold itself, differ. The fact that terrorist attacks may not claim a certain number of victims per year, or over a certain period, nevertheless, does not necessarily mean that the conflict has ceased. For relevant definitions, see Arbeitsgemeinschaft Kriegsursachenforschung (AKUF)/Forschungsstelle Kriege und Entwicklung (FKRE), Aktuelle Kriege und bewaffnete Konflikte; Political Instability Task Force (PITF), Problem Set Codebook; Centre for the Study of Civil War at the International Peace Research Institute, Oslo (PRIO)/Uppsala Conflict Data Program (UCDP), Armed Conflict Dataset Codebook, Version 4–2007.

This explanation also sheds light on why non-international armed conflicts, e. g. civil wars, are also regarded as war. Civil wars between two groups within a state, or non-international armed conflicts between the state and a certain organized group, also take place between two entities that do not exercise authority over the other. Neither entity possesses the power to control the other's behaviour by authoritative measures, rules or regulations. State authority, involving executive, legislative, and judicial power, no longer rests with the state itself in any practical way. The relationship between the state and the contravening entity, or between two other entities, is not one of hierarchy and dependence. Practically, although not necessarily legally, the relationship instead evolves into a conflict between independent entities. State authorities cannot but fight the contravening power by force.

In light of this observation, two factors seem to be decisive in regarding these conflicts as wars: the combating parties are independent in terms of authority, which can, of course, also exist via third states, and the states' options in fighting the opposing party are reduced to armed force. These factors are interdependent. It is important to note that it is not the state's lack of ability to reduce the danger other than by armed force, alone, that renders the conflict a war. The relationship between the entities conditions this inability. This is illustrated by the common understanding of conflicts with criminals, which consist of conflicts between states and 'subordinates'. States confront criminals with measures that are at their disposal due to their position relative to these individuals. Although these measures may sometimes not suffice to get rid of the problems emanating from criminal activity, authority – executive, legislative and judicial power – is in the hands of the state.

The measures taken by states to combat terrorism, as well as the general characteristics of these conflicts, finally support that conflicts with terrorists differ from wars, and that they are perceived to be different. First, most counter-terrorist state measures take cues from crime prevention (e. g. tracking individuals, wire-tapping, video surveillance, detention), revealing states' perception of relevant conflicts with terrorists. (This could also indicate that terrorism, due to its characteristics, can best be prevented by law enforcement measures.) Secondly, even the practice of targeted killing does not resemble typical warfare strategy. In warfare, it is legally and morally justified to target and kill specific members of enemy forces under certain circumstances.[13] Individual members of the military, however, are commonly killed as an aspect of attacking the enemy. It is un-

---

13 A contrary position is offered by Michael Gross, e. g. in Gross, M. 2006. See fn. 6 in the current chapter.

common in warfare to plan for *certain* individuals to be explicitly targeted. Substantial differences between wars and relevant conflicts with terrorists can also be observed regarding the decision-making processes that preceed the targeted killing of terrorists. As far as can be discerned from the few descriptions available, the process of deciding to execute a targeted killing falls within the political rather than the military sphere. Military personnel may be involved, as may be intelligence services. The head of government and possibly other members of government, however, ultimately authorize the killings.[14]

It may be concluded at this point that the line between wars and conflicts short of war are not always easy to draw. However, the characteristics of wars that contrast with those of the fight against terrorism, as well as the general explanation of what arguably distinguishes wars from situations short of war, help to identify why conflicts with terrorists, in their currently relevant forms, constitute conflicts with criminals rather than wars. This conclusion corresponds to the results dictated by international law: certain wars may be described as wars against terrorism due to the terrorist strategy that one of the parties to the conflict applies. However, conflicts with terrorists relevant to the debate about the justifiability of targeted killing of terrorists are commonly mislabelled as wars. They lack the characteristics ascribed to war and *vice versa*.

This provides us, too, with a conclusion regarding the argument discussed in this chapter. If conflicts with terrorists do not constitute wars, terrorists are not combatants in these conflicts, and targeted killings of terrorists cannot morally be justified with reference to justified killings of combatants during warfare.

I have not yet covered all of the conceivable circumstances that could render the justification for killing combatants during warfare applicable to the targeting of terrorists. In order to apply, the argument does not require the conflict with terrorists to be war. Terrorists may be active in wars that take place between other groups. If the terrorists can be considered combatants in such existing wars, the justification for killing combatants in warfare would apply in cases where they are targeted. A relevant example is the terrorist activity of Al Qaeda in the war in Afghanistan beginning in 2001. Such participation begs the question of whether or not terrorists can be considered combatants in such situations or whether they must be considered non-combatants.

The legal discussion revealed that terrorists in international armed conflicts are generally civilians by virtue both of their clothing and their means of fight-

---

14 The available information is largely limited to the Israeli decision-making processes, both in current cases of targeted killing and during the campaign in the wake of the Munich attacks in 1972; see chapter 2.1.

ing. This classification can be explained in light of the aim to protect civilians from the effects of warfare as much as possible, as well as the intention to provide *legal* combatants with specific protections.[15] Other reasons, exceeding these conventional considerations, support the legal classification of terrorists in international armed conflicts. Given that international humanitarian law regulating non-international armed conflicts does not provide criteria for such a distinction,[16] these other reasons also complement the legal analysis of these conflicts. Provided the self-evident assumption that not everyone who ever participates in a war may be classified as a combatant in that war is true, I argue that terrorists do not normally constitute combatants. Depending on their involvement, they more resemble civilians than combatants.

Before I engage in this argument, a few preliminary clarifications as to the different terms denoting various groups of individuals during warfare are necessary. I will distinguish between combatants, non-combatants, civilians, and civilians participating in hostilities. These terms largely parallel the terms and differences established in the legal discussion of the justifiability of targeted killings of terrorists during international armed conflicts. In some aspects, however, they differ. This first concerns the distinction between combatants and civilians. This distinction will be addressed in the next paragraph, which will clarify that it refers not to institutional affiliation, but to roles in warfare. The term 'civilians participating in hostilities' is rather self-explanatory. Structurally, it corresponds to the way the term was used in the legal discussion of the justifiability of targeted killings in international armed conflicts, even if the meaning here does not entirely encompass the same group of individuals as the legal term did. It denotes civilians for the time they actively engage in hostile acts, but who are not thus included in the group of combatants, but remain civilians. During the time they do not participate in hostilities, they are non-combatants. Non-combatants, then, are civilians who do not engage in hostile acts.

To show that terrorists are commonly civilians, not combatants, establishing what it is that distinguishes these groups is required first. This becomes clearer in recalling the justification for killing combatants during warfare.[17] Combatants may be targeted because they are part of the enterprise that constitutes a threat to the enemy. Their role is decisive in attributing them to the category of combat-

---

15 See chapter 4.3.4; see also chapter 4.3.5.
16 As established, international humanitarian law regulating non-international armed conflicts does not distinguish between combatants and civilians, but between members of the armed forces and civilians.
17 See fn. 5 in the current chapter. Recall that this reasoning can be read with reference to combatants fighting an unjust war. See also fn. 4 in the current chapter.

ants. They are not subject to elimination because of their actual individual harming conduct: they are liable to attack in their role in warfare, and only their role allows for considerations which draw on the collective. It is uncontested that all who are part of the military forces allotted to the military engagement are combatants: they are trained, equipped, and provided with food and quarters to participate in the fighting. They remain in their role even while eating and sleeping, and they may be attacked while living in this role as military personnel. The line between someone remaining in his or her role, which justifies killing him or her, and someone who no longer lives in this role is not always easy to draw. With regard to military personnel, this is not linked to a given place, e.g. military camps they are living in. Even if soldiers go back home every night, eating and sleeping in their families' homes, they remain soldiers. Killing them while they are at home would probably not be justified. This is, however, due to the fact that the harm done to their families in most situations would render the attack unjustifiable, rather than the notion that soldiers in these situations would be killed as non-combatants. They remain combatants even if they do not sleep in military camps. They are prepared to return to fighting at any time, and even if they are back home, they retain their military identity and remain part of the threat the military poses, and as such, they keep their role as combatants.[18] However, there are occasions in which military personnel no longer live in their role as combatants, despite technically still being part of the military. This includes, for example, when soldiers leave their occupation during furlough. During that time, the collective context no longer exists, and they must be considered civilians. Strict individual responsibility comes back into play, and the justification for killing which is based on collectivization no longer applies. This does not mean that they may no longer be targeted; nevertheless, targeting them must be justified with reference to individual behaviour at the time of attack.

The distinction between the two forms of justification for killing can thereby be illustrated with reference to the status of civilians. Civilians are defined as not being part of the threat posed by the enemy. Most clearly this applies to individuals who oppose the war and refuse to provide any support for the war effort. But this can apply even to individuals who engage in hostilities for a certain limited time. They do not preserve the right not to be attacked during the time of their engagement. This, however, can be explained by individual responsibility. They do not lose the right not to be attacked due to a role they have. But they are liable to attack because they pose a threat by their specific individual behaviour.

---

18 See here specifically Walzer 1977, 146.

On the basis of this explanation, two conclusions can be drawn to resolve the question of the combatant status of terrorists active in an existing war. First, clearly only those individuals who participate in the war effort of one or the other party to the conflict can be regarded as combatants. Hence, terrorists active in a war, but pursuing their own aims independently of the parties to the war, do not constitute combatants. The collectivizing moral reasoning applicable during warfare does not apply to them. This does not mean that (lethal) force is never allowed in reaction to their deeds, but they may not be considered combatants. With regard to terrorists siding with one of the parties to the conflict, the second conclusion, which can be drawn from the justification of killing combatants during warfare, applies. Becoming active on one side of the conflict is not sufficient for combatant status. A certain degree of affiliation to and activity in the war effort must be established in order to justify killing based on collectivizing reasoning.[19]

What does this mean with regard to the status of individuals who apply terrorist force in support of the war effort of one of the parties to the conflict? Ultimately, this can be decided only with reference to individual cases. A few general assessments, however, are possible. Certain terrorists, in a moral sense, seem to belong to the group of combatants. A conclusion as to their status depends on the form their participation in warfare takes. Those terrorists organized in fighting camps, where they live in their role as participants in warfare, for example, may, under certain circumstances, be regarded as combatants. It is not their residence in camps that is decisive, but rather whether they live in their role as combatants, and this is most clearly indicated by their institutional organization. Many terrorists active within certain conflicts, however, seem to live a different life, much closer in nature to that of civilians. They live with their families and have 'normal' jobs. They engage in terrorism at a certain point, yet do not live their lives in this role. To classify terrorists as civilians, then, does not mean that they may never be killed. It points to the difference be-

---

19 One may question the position that some form of collectivization is at all relevant to the killing of combatants in warfare and argue that justified killing in warfare can always be explained with regards to the individual threatening conduct of the attacked individual. This, however, would weaken rather than strengthen the argument that terrorists may be targeted and killed as combatants taking part in a war. It would beg the question of why terrorists had to be described as combatants in the first place rather than as individuals carrying out violent actions (during warfare). Moreover it would fatally weaken this argument because, as becomes clear in chapter 10, this would rule out killing prior to the point at which the attack is imminent, and hence targeted killings of terrorists, in war altogether. See also fn. 34 in the current chapter.

tween combatants and civilians and suggests that the same rules be applied to these terrorists that are applied to other civilians.

As has also been established concerning the legal justifiability of targeted killing of terrorists, distinguishing combatants from civilians and non-combatants, respectively, involves an additional limit to the justifiability of targeted killing, even if the targeted terrorist is a combatant. The strict prohibition against intentionally attacking non-combatants implies that only those combatants may be attacked who are recognizable as such. Mere suspicion not supported by clear facts does not provide sufficient grounds for carrying out such an act. This is implied in the prohibition against attacking non-combatants itself.

That non-combatants are mistakenly attacked may not always be avoidable. Such mistakes may occur because certain facts may not have been accessible to the agent carrying out the attack or because circumstances might have changed. That said, any regulation requires due diligence and sufficient safeguards to prevent mistakes due to negligence or recklessness. Moreover, the required degree of certainty increases with the value of the goods at risk. This also applies to the prohibition against attacking non-combatants. The fundamental role of the prohibition against attacking non-combatants, thus, proscribes carrying out attacks unless sufficient care has been taken not to harm non-combatants as well as prohibits acting on the basis of uncertain facts. This proscribes targeted killings of terrorists who are suspected to be combatants but who cannot clearly be distinguished from non-combatants. This does not seem to prohibit acting on the basis of intelligence; nevertheless, in light of the fundamental principle involved and the fact that life and health of non-combatants are at risk, intelligence is only sufficient as a basis for action if it convincingly proves that the targeted individual is a combatant.

To conclude, it is possible for terrorists during warfare to be considered combatants. As combatants, they may be targeted during the time they act in this role, provided they can be distinguished from non-combatants. Regarding conflicts with terrorism relevant to the debate on the targeted killing of terrorists, however, this only realistically applies to a specific situation: namely, that terrorists participate in an existing war, i.e. in a war between two groups, neither of which is the terrorist group, and that they are organized in a manner that mirrors military unity. Overall, states are typically confronted with terrorists independent of existing wars. The justification for killing combatants could then only apply to these conflicts if they qualified as wars themselves. This, however, is not realistically the case.

The preceding argument explains that reference to the warfare rationale for killing combatants provides justification for very restricted and rather unrealistic cases of targeted killing of terrorists. In spite of this, the second aspect of the argument that conflicts with terrorists constitute wars must finally briefly be addressed.

Reference to warfare in comparison to peacetime substantially broadens the justifiability of killing. It does so regarding the killing of the targeted individual. However, it also broadens the justifiability of acts that cause harm to non-combatants as a side-effect, what is euphemistically called 'collateral damage'. This is relevant to the question of the justifiability of targeted killings of terrorists because it concerns the second aspect relevant for the assessment: that the practice often causes harm to non-combatants. The question of whether non-combatants may be harmed in the course of warfare is thus relevant in deciding whether those targeted killings that not only kill the targeted terrorists but also harm innocent third parties, or in terms of warfare, non-combatants, may be justified. Regardless of whether the killing of the targeted person can be justified, the action is only morally acceptable if the harming of the affected non-combatants can equally be justified.

To what degree and on what basis non-combatants could justifiably be harmed during warfare is subject to wide debate. Within the just war tradition, this issue is commonly addressed in terms of the doctrine of double effect, allowing for unintended but foreseen harm to non-combatants under strictly limited circumstances. Not everyone agrees with the doctrine of double effect. And giving justice to the contentious issues would require extensive discussion, which cannot be provided at this point. That said, it seems possible to draw sufficient conclusions.

Strict immunity from indirect harm is irreconcilable with warfare under realistic circumstances. Either one accepts some modification to the immunity principle, or one must subscribe to contingent pacifism and oppose any realistically possible war.[20] This is not to say that harm to non-combatants does not matter. It means that it is inevitable that non-combatants will be harmed during warfare and, therefore, the extent to which such harm is acceptable must be strictly regulated. Not accepting such principles setting out limits to harm caused as a side effect to fighting jeopardizes the principle of non-combatant immunity as such.[21]

Provided it is accepted that harm to non-combatants cannot be fully avoided during warfare and that clear limits must be formulated with respect to acceptable harm, it is unquestioned, as well as confirmed by the internationally shared legal understanding expressed in international humanitarian law,[22] that an act of

---

20 See also Coady 2008, 136.

21 See also Coady 2008, 142.

22 See chapter 4.3.4.

force causing such harm can only be justified if the harm (a) is neither intended nor (b) disproportionate to the morally acceptable benefit sought by the harming act. Moreover, (c) the harming act and the intended aim must be morally acceptable.[23] If non-combatant immunity is taken seriously, it also follows (d) that the harm to non-combatants must be kept as minimal as the intended aim allows – in legal terms, that the harming act must be necessary. Intended harm corresponds to a direct attack and, hence, ignores non-combatant immunity as such. As it sacrifices human life and health for a relatively minor benefit, disproportionate harm would equally contradict the fundamental role of non-combatant protection. Unintended but foreseen harm that cannot be reasonably expected to lead to the intended aim must also count as disproportionate. This is because harm caused by an act that, to use the legal term, is inappropriate cannot possibly be justified with reference to its outcome.

These preconditions alone, which are often complemented by additional requirements, set strict limits to the justifiability of targeted killings of terrorists that cause unintended but foreseen harm to non-combatants. As I now only analyse those targeted killings of terrorists that can be justified with regard to the killing of the targeted individual, the condition (c) does not require further attention. As pointed out in the above discussion of the legal justifiability of harming non-combatants as a side effect of attacks on legitimate targets,[24] the other conditions, however, in fact strongly question the justifiability of these acts.

This is due to a set of uncertainties about the benefits of targeted killings of terrorists, some of which have been addressed above. To recapitulate some of the points,[25] it is unclear whether the practice is appropriate at all, which questions substantially whether it can ever be proportionate. Moreover, provided the killing of a certain individual adds to the war effort at all, it can only be justified if this benefit renders death and injury to a (greater) number of individuals proportionate. Given the ability to replace many terrorists and the uncertain benefit, proportionality seems unlikely with regard to targeted killings of most individuals involved in terrorism; it seems impossible as soon as a number of non-combatants are harmed and killed in order to kill one of those terrorists, probably regardless of the role of the targeted individual. This is almost necessarily the case if terrorists are targeted with heavy weaponry in closely populated areas. These latter cases point at an additional obstacle to the justifiability of targeted

---

23 Coady 2008, 137.
24 See chapter 4.3.5.
25 See chapter 4.3.5.

killings that harm non-combatants which is difficult to overcome: necessity.[26] The use of heavy weaponry certainly cannot be considered the least destructive means available for killing one individual. This conclusion cannot be drawn with equal certainty regarding targeted killing in general. Nevertheless, targeted killings aim at killing one particular person; a limited extent of force is required to achieve this clearly defined aim, and, in principle, it is possible to achieve it with means that avoid harm to non-combatants and which are otherwise often inaccessible in warfare.

To conclude, the requirements that constitute a minimum provision of protection to third parties call the justifiability of targeted killings substantially into question. This is true even provided that it is acceptable that harm to non-combatants cannot be avoided as long as wars exist and that the targeted killing is justified in terms of its actual target. There may be targeted killings of terrorists, including harm to third parties, that fulfil all of the above requirements, but the burden of proof is very high.

6.2 Analogous application of the wartime rationale for killing

Given that most conflicts with terrorists that are relevant to the question of whether targeted killings of terrorists can be justified do not constitute wars, and given that the justification for killing combatants therefore does not directly apply, one may argue that terrorist activity necessarily constitutes peacetime activity. As such, terrorism would be considered criminal activity and be assessed with reference to the principles governing law enforcement measures. This step, however, is logically compelling only if the wartime rationale for killing combatants applies only during warfare. One may argue that terrorism, although not constituting a situation of war, does exhibit substantial similarities to warfare activity. This and the characteristics that distinguish terrorism from criminal peacetime activity, one may argue, make the wartime rationale for killing combatants applicable to the fight against terrorism. In other words, due to the characteristics that terrorism shares with warfare activity, the rationale for killing combat-

---

26 Tony Coady (2008, 114) convincingly points out that most of those cases are problematic not only in terms of proportionality or necessity. He refers to the killing of Salah Shehadeh (see chapter 2.1), which destroyed six nearby houses, killed 16 bystanders and injured well over fifty, and argues that this action cannot be presented as intending 'only to kill a Hamas leader'. He very convincingly disqualifies some important misinterpretations of intention, leading to hypocrite application of the justification of collateral damage. See Coady 2008, 137–142.

ants should be applied to conflicts with terrorists, even though these conflicts do not constitute wars.

The argument can be formulated in two different ways, and different conclusions as to the justifiability of concrete measures, including targeted killings, can be drawn. In both understandings, the justification used in killing combatants during warfare substantiates the argument for the justification of targeted killings of terrorists. On the one hand, one could argue that terrorism and the fight against terrorism, due to its specific characteristics, correspond to warfare without, however, being warfare. If the fight against terrorism is regarded as paralleling wars, a terrorist can be described as constituting a form of combatant, and wartime rationale for killing combatants can be applied to the group of terrorists. Given the fact that justification for killing during warfare is based on the conduct of the collective and allows for killing regardless of whether the given individual threatens someone else at the time of attack, this, if applicable, allows states to target terrorists at any time, as long as they continue to be involved in terrorism, because they play an ongoing role in the threat posed by the terrorist organization or network. Moreover, if the fight against terrorism is regarded as paralleling wars, targeted killings causing foreseen but unintended harm to third parties are justified if they fulfil the moral requirements set out for such acts during warfare.[27] On the other hand, one could argue that the warfare rationale for killing combatants applies to the fight against terrorism only to a limited extent. The rationale for killing combatants during warfare does apply, but due to the fact that relevant conflicts with terrorists do not constitute wars, requirements must be fulfilled that are unknown, to this extent at least, in warfare. This, for example, could mean that killing should be allowed in conflicts with terrorists as a last resort only. The legitimacy of killing, if detention is impossible, is then derived from the warfare rationale; the requirements to turn to targeted killings as a last resort could be defined by the similarities terrorism shares with criminality and the differences between terrorism and warfare proper, respectively. Similarly, targeted killings causing foreseen but unintended harm to third parties would be justified under conditions exceeding those regulating such harm during peacetime.[28]

Despite the differences, both arguments face severe difficulties due to the rationale they have in common. Though formulated differently, both arguments seek to establish the fight against terrorism under varying circumstances as a

---

27 Statman 2004, 179–188. See also Meisels 2004.
28 Kasher/Yadlin 2005. Walzer (1977, 10f.) holds such a claim with regard to specific situations in the fight against terrorism.

general situation that extends the justifiability of killing. In order to establish such a position, the wartime rationale for killing is used.

I will not at this point offer a conclusion as to the convincing force of the claim that it is morally acceptable to extend the justifiability of killing in (certain) conflicts with terrorists to an extent unknown in law enforcement. The final answer to this question will have to be postponed to chapter 10, i.e. after the principles governing the use of force in law enforcement will have been established. Rather, I will argue that the reasoning provided for such an extension, i.e. that the warfare rationale may be transferred to terrorism because of its resemblance to warfare, is not convincing.

This is not due to the assumption the arguments are based on. The assertion that terrorism, although not warfare, sometimes shows characteristics that may call into question the classification of terrorism as criminal activity, and that it, in fact, in some respect more closely resembles warfare has some force. Terrorists themselves often understand their struggle as warfare.[29] Osama bin Laden's explicit declaration of war on the United States is a powerful example of this.[30] Moreover, the other two reasons that have already been mentioned and which are commonly given to show that the fight against terrorism resembles warfare cannot always be dismissed categorically. First, terrorist attacks in their immediate destructive power often exceed in destruction individual criminal acts with which states are commonly confronted. And second, measures that states conventionally apply in their fight against criminality are sometimes ineffective in the fight against terrorism, particularly when the attacks are planned and carried out from abroad or from areas that are not under effective state control.[31]

That said, the fact that the fight against terrorism sometimes and in some respects resembles warfare is not a sufficient argument for applying the warfare rationale for killing combatants. On the contrary, it is the idea that pointing out these resemblances suffices to defend the analogous applicability of warfare regulations and the warfare rationale that I find unconvincing. Warfare is a distinct concept; it evolved historically, and the fact that a wider justification of killing is accepted is limited to this phenomenon. This does not mean that warfare is exempt from moral considerations,[32] nor does it mean that moral reasoning about war and warfare must merely seek to justify the behaviour encountered during warfare. But warfare reasoning, to some extent, differs from peacetime reason-

---

29 Meisels 2004, 303.
30 Lawrence 2005, 58–62.
31 Asa Kasher and Amos Yadlin (2005, 7) add that terrorists are usually not party to the 'social contract' of which the citizens are part, who are protected against terrorist violence.
32 Michael Walzer (1977, 3–20) convincingly rejected this position.

ing, and this makes it impossible to simply transfer wartime reasoning to situations other than war.

Walzer visualized this difference between principles governing warfare and those governing peacetime by stating that '"justice" in the [just war] theory lives, so to speak, under a cloud'.[33] If this means that there is a fundamental principled distinction between warfare morality and peacetime morality, I would disagree with this description. Yet it is convincing that there are differences regarding the reasoning, which to a large extent come down to alternative interpretations of the same principles.[34] Most importantly, the justification of killing combatants

---

[33] Walzer 2006c, 43.

[34] McMahan (2004, 2006b and 2006c) rejects the idea that killing in warfare can be justified in light of principles differing from those that justify killing in self-defence during peacetime and with regard to collectivizing reasoning in particular. The discussion of principles governing killing in peacetime situations will reveal why I do not share his propositions about when killing is justified in situations short of armed conflict and why I accept the described difference between wartime and peacetime reasoning. It will explain, for example, why I believe the permissibility of causing harm to non-combatants cannot be explained along the lines justifying the use of lethal force in self-defence. Also with regard to the justifiability of killing the person intended to be killed, McMahan himself, in my view, has to depart from peacetime reasoning in order to be able to explain the justification of the killing of unjust combatants. For McMahan the fact that one may kill all members of a certain group of unjust combatants despite not knowing whether each is actually taking part in the threat does not represent a departure from the morality applicable to peacetime, but represents an epistemic limitation that does not have any moral impact. This, however, is difficult to understand. For it is this certainty that is inevitable in relations among individuals. Self-defence is justified only in reaction to an imminent harming act, for only the highest degree of certainty possible that an individual seeks to inflict harm allows reaction. (See chapter 10.) One can never be entirely sure that a person pointing a gun is actually planning to kill. By requiring that an act of force is imminent, however, one has reached a degree of security that is not paralleled in McMahan's argument that individual members of certain military forces may be killed, because their being members provides the counter-forces with sufficient grounds to assume that these individuals may be targeted (in McMahan's words, for they may be assumed to be personally morally responsible for the threat one reacts to). Hence, McMahan seems to give up the requirement of certainty to a degree that lacks any equivalent in peacetime understanding of justified killing. Secondly, even if one accepted his explanation, it does not account for the fact that soldiers may be killed at any time, regardless of their involvement in a threat at the time of attack – another departure from peacetime reasoning, as it contradicts the moral limits to killing during such times (see chapter 10). It is not the soldiers' individual harming act that justifies the use of force against them, but their being part of the overall threat, and this seems to be the relevant collectivization. (For the criticism that McMahan himself reverts to collectivization, see also Walzer 2006c, 43 f.)

requires reference to some form of collectivization in a manner that is not accepted as morally right during peacetime. The difference is readily apparent in the justifiability of killing civilians participating in hostilities during warfare. I will discuss the justifiability of killing during peacetime in subsequent chapters, and this discussion will explain why and under what circumstances killing is justified in situations short of warfare. That killing cannot be justified with reference to the conduct of some collective, but must instead be addressed with reference to the individual's concrete harmful conduct, responsibility and liability, however, seems to be so commonly accepted that, here, it may be assumed without detailed discussion. This is not to argue that the grounding principle differs. In peacetime, however, lethal force against an individual requires him or her to be about to carry out a severe attack, i.e. the harmful conduct with reference to which counter-force can be justified must be the individual's actual conduct.[35] In war it is sufficient that he or she forms on the basis of his or her role a part of an ongoing overall threat. It does not require him or her to be engaged in an actual harming act him- or herself but ascribes the overall threat to him or her. Moreover, some differences seem to apply to permissible harming side effects. If one seeks to argue about morally right behaviour in warfare at all, one must accept that foreseeable but unintended (lethal) injury to non-combatants does not necessarily render warfare activity wrong, reasoning which in peacetime is commonly (and rightly) not accepted.

Now, that claims and arguments apply that differ from those that apply in situations short of war can only be understood in light of the existence of war. Either one has to reject war altogether as morally wrong, or provide for the basic facts of warfare.[36] Wartime reasoning exists because of the phenomenon of war itself and is therefore limited to this phenomenon. In other words, extended forms of violence are accepted because the situation is regarded as warfare.

What does this mean with regard to the claim put forward that the warfare rationale for killing can be transposed onto the fight against terrorism? It underscores that authors holding such a position seek to allow for a general situation that extends the justifiability of killing. Yet it does not explain why the justifiability in the fight against terrorism should be extended in a manner similar to

---

Daniel Statman's reasoning (2004, 185–187/195) also relies on the collective and he is unable to show that the same principles permit killing during warfare and in situations short of war. This particularly applies to the justifiability of harming innocents and to the extent to which his argument allows killing combatants who are not engaged in actions threatening other individuals.

35 See chapter 10.

36 See also Coady 2008, 136.

warfare, and it requires recognizing that resemblance to warfare as such is insufficient for purposes of justification.

To be sure, this does not yet make implausible the position that targeted killings can be justified to the extent claimed, i.e. that principles differing from law enforcement apply. Though I have argued that the rationale for killing during warfare may not simply be applied, this does not mean that it cannot still be argued that the necessities triggered by terrorism require accepting different standards. Yet it is this that must be argued. In order to formulate such arguments, one is bound to begin by establishing moral considerations regulating situations short of armed conflicts. From there, one can look at how relevant characteristics of certain forms of terrorism may be for the justification of targeted killings of terrorists. This will reveal what limitations would have to be surrendered, and whether it is morally acceptable to do so. In other words, in reference to factors specific to terrorism as such or for certain forms of it, the moral requirements in situations short of armed conflict may be questioned, as may the applicability of the moral assessment relevant to other forms of criminality. This, however, requires establishing first whether targeted killing of terrorists can be justified within the rubric of peacetime reasoning. The discussion of the addressed claims may therefore be postponed until after an examination of justifications of targeted killing of terrorists that do not draw on the idea of warfare.

7 Revenge and punishment

Justifications of targeted killings of terrorists drawing on the ideas of revenge or punishment, as opposed to all other approaches that justify targeted killing with reference to situations short of war, focus on only one specific form of the practice: responsive killing. They require attention not primarily because a few scholars have drawn upon these ideas in order to justify the targeted killing of terrorists. They are of importance because the ideas of revenge and punishment have motivated states to apply the practice of targeted killing,[1] and because they are evident in statements made by state officials[2] – though the few existing official justifications of targeted killings of terrorists are not based on any of these ideas.

Revenge and punishment are not necessarily always strictly kept apart, in particular because the concepts of revenge and retributive punishment are similar in some respects. Nevertheless, they describe different things, and it therefore makes sense to separate them in the following argument.

7.1 Revenge

Revenge can be described as being 'essentially a requital by an agent for a perceived injury'[3]. It is motivated by resentment, which triggers the desire to retaliate against an individual for a perceived injury or harm for which this individual is held responsible. The perceived injury or harm need not be a wrong. It may be something to which the other person is entitled, yet which is resented for some reason. Satisfaction is thereby gained by the suffering of the other person.[4]

Steven David in particular has drawn upon the idea of revenge to justify the targeted killing of terrorists. He addresses two aspects of revenge.[5] On the one hand, he regards revenge to be a natural desire on the part of individuals and societies for obtaining justice if no other means are available. On the other hand, David regards revenge as expressing the government's power and ability to protect society. If terrorist acts are not retaliated, both aspects may trigger neg-

---

1 See chapter 2.1.

2 See, for example, White House, Ari Fleischer, Press Gaggle, 5 November 2002. For Barack Obama referring to the idea of justice when announcing the death of Osama bin Laden, which presumably, but not with absolute certainty, constituted an act of targeted killing, see White House, Remarks by the President on Osama Bin Laden, 2 May 2011.

3 Uniacke 2000, 62.

4 For these characteristics, which were established in distinction to retribution, see Nozick 1981, 366–368; Uniacke 2000, 62 f.

5 For David's justification of targeted killings as revenge, see David 2003a, 121 f.

ative developments, such as frustration and anger. Furthermore, if the state does not retaliate in response to terrorist acts, this may be interpreted as the government's impotence and inability to provide the society with protection and security. The attempt to avoid such negative developments justifies seeking revenge by way of targeted killing. In both cases, abstaining from revenge may substantially weaken the government, lead to its downfall, and to the society's inability to protect itself. Given the fact that states have 'a moral right to exist', according to David, '[o]ne of the greatest immoralities a State can commit is to behave in a way that results in its own destruction'.[6] Provided that states establish criteria for deciding who may be targeted, thereby avoiding 'arbitrary revenge', revenge morally justifies the targeted killing of terrorists, because it meets the desire of individuals and society, and reassures them.

Several assumptions within David's argument could be questioned: for example, the conviction that every state has a right to exist, that it is one of the greatest immoralities for a state to act in a way that leads to its own destruction, that defeat of a certain government questions the existence of the state, that revenge rather than state action in accordance with civil rights and fundamental guarantees would strengthen the state, or that unsatisfied desire for revenge can endanger a state. I will not engage in these discussions. Neither will I focus on the general consequentialist idea that David's argument is based on. Whether consequentialism as a general concept can provide justification for targeted killings will be discussed in the next chapter. I will, however, make a few points in reply to David's argument concerning the idea of revenge as such, and make clear that revenge cannot provide any justification for targeted killings, regardless of what follows if this desire for revenge is not satisfied.

First of all, a population's desire cannot, as such, justify state action. Certainly, if this desire involves limiting individuals' rights or harming other people, it has no justifying force at all. Societies and individuals may and have developed diverse desires. They may desire more public parks or better infrastructure. They may, however, also desire the expulsion of any foreign individual from their society or the elimination of certain groups of people owing to race, colour, religious affiliation, disability, sexual orientation, etc. Apart from the fact that it is questionable that societies as such share one desire, these few examples show that certain desires are acceptable and may, or even shall, if expressed democratically, direct political decisions, regardless of their specific terms. Certainly, however, if desires, provided they were acted upon, would affect given individuals' rights, then the mere existence of these desires cannot be relevant to state action.

---

6 Both quotes at David 2003a, 122.

Desires have to be judged according to their content. And if their content is not morally acceptable, states are not only unjustified in acting on them: they are duty-bound to act against them.

This leads to the second point, which concerns the desire *for revenge* more specifically. In non-consequentialist terms, seeking revenge could only justify the targeted killing of terrorists if revenge itself were intrinsically good. Recalling the meaning of revenge, there is no reason to ascribe intrinsic value to such desire. There rightly seems to be little disagreement on this point. Revenge does not proceed from a certain understanding of justice, but follows a personal emotional desire to '[return] a perceived humiliation, insult or injury'[7]. The avenged act is not, by definition, a wrong. The person against whom revenge is directed may have been entitled and right to act the way he or she did, yet the avenger may perceive the act as humiliating, invidious or offending. Revenge is triggered by an emotional reaction, such as resentment, bitterness, or anger, and based on this resentment, the avenger seeks or gains satisfaction from making the other suffer, rendering revenge morally wrong. A reaction that simply materializes – regardless of whether or not it is justified in light of the act that it concerns – is contingent and cannot provide a moral basis for action. It is then the drive to make the other suffer and the fact that the act is carried out in order to gain satisfaction through this suffering that render the revenge *qua* revenge morally wrong. This is not to say that all acts carried out in revenge are unjustifiable; they may be justified on different grounds. But reference to revenge cannot provide such justification.[8] Hence, it cannot provide any justification for the targeted killing of terrorists either.

7.2 Punishment

To describe targeted killings as punishment avoids the problems faced by an approach drawing on revenge. For punishment, it does not suffice that someone's action is perceived as injustice: he or she has to have committed a wrong in order to be liable to punishment. Punishment is not motivated by an emotional frameset of resentment, such as anger or hatred. It is not based on a *desire* to pay someone back for what he or she did. Neither is it the suffering of the punished

---

7 Uniacke 2000, 62.
8 Uniacke 2000, 63–68.

individual that fulfils the purpose of the act. In order to be called punishment, an act has to be based on normative considerations.[9]

Punishment is explained with reference to different theories. While some scholars explain it in terms of retribution, others explain it on consequentialist grounds. Other concepts of punishment combine aspects of the two positions, or seek to reconcile them.[10] Retributive punishment, despite a variety of different understandings of the theory, may be summarized as justifying acts of punishment with reference to justice. The offender may be punished, since the act of punishment resolves injustice. For example, he or she may be punished because he or she deserves punishment for the wrong he or she committed, or because the injustice that occurred due to his or her behaviour needs to be evened out. Unlike revenge, satisfaction from retribution, if satisfaction is involved at all, is derived not from the suffering of the punished person but from the pleasure that justice has been done.[11] Consequentialism justifies and regulates punishment in terms of the consequences that follow from a certain form of punishment for the overall good of the society. Punishment thereby commonly serves preventive purposes. Accounts that seek to combine or reconcile these two theories argue, for example, that the fact that punishment is allowed at all is based on some idea of justice. They continue to argue that the degree and form of punishment are determined by the preventive effects that can be ascribed to different kinds of punishment.[12]

---

9 These differences have been formulated as between revenge and retributive punishment. See Nozick 1981, 366–368. See also Uniacke 2000, in particular 62f. Contrary, Zaibert 2006. The application of these characteristics may be argued to not be applicable to consequentialist accounts of punishment. I, however, regard them as essential to speaking of punishment. Accounts that do end up justifying acts as punishment with different characteristics may be held to not provide a convincing account of punishment; yet they do not show that punishment lacks these characteristics (see also the following discussion about consequentialist accounts of punishment). This distinction also corresponds to the way in which revenge and (retributive) punishment are used in the context of targeted killings of terrorists.

10 For a discussion of several such positions, see Primoratz 1987. For a brief insight into different aspects to different ideas of punishment, see also Hart 1968, 230–237.

11 For the last differentiation, see Nozick 1981, 366–368. Depending on the specific account, states, due to the demands of justice, *have to* punish the offender to a degree equivalent to the deeds of the offender, or else are *merely allowed to* punish the offender. See, for example, Primoratz 1989. For classifications of different approaches of this type, see Cottingham 1979; this work has been updated and commented upon by Walker 1999.

12 For a discussion of several accounts of this 'third' kind, see Primoratz 1987.

Regardless of how punishment is justified and explained, I argue, targeted killings cannot be described as justified punishment.[13] This is due to the fact that acts declared to be punishment only constitute justified punishment if they 'recognize' the actual facts surrounding the deed. This, however, is possible only on the basis of due process of law, something that is absent from the manner in which states currently decide whom to target. Even if targeted killings were based on court decisions, which, as I have established, would not in a strict sense constitute targeted killing, this would not be possible, and hence targeted killing could not be justified in terms of punishment.

The argument is based on the assumption that any act of justified punishment needs to give justice to the specific circumstances under which the deed was committed. This means that an act carried out in reaction to a wrong can only be deemed justified punishment if it first is directed against the individual who committed the act, and if it secondly thereby accounts not only for the deed itself but also for the circumstances under which it was committed.

Retributivist accounts have this precondition necessarily built into their theory. Since justice is referred to in order to justify punishment in the first place, the act of punishment necessarily needs to give justice to the specific circumstances. In other words, the damage done must be known exactly in order to even out the situation or to provide the degree of punishment an individual deserves. If this is not the case, the act of punishment itself would not be able to achieve justice and would therefore not be justified.

Consequentialist accounts, by contrast, are often criticized for not paying attention to the circumstances of the deed. Consequentialism, it is argued, does not even limit punishment to those who have actually committed a wrong, but under certain circumstances justifies punishing innocent individuals. This is a serious criticism which certainly does not apply to all forms of consequentialism. However, it is not necessary to look more closely into the different consequentialist accounts of punishment. If accounts justify using force against individuals who have not committed a wrong, then they allow states to exploit the term 'punishment' for the sake of the greater good. Still, these states would not *punish* this individual but harm him or her *under the label of* punishment: punishment requires some deed for which the individual may be harmed. If one accepts this, one necessarily must establish that the individual being punished has committed the punishable offence. Punishment cannot be separated from what actually

---

13 The position that targeted killing can be justified as punishment has most recently been spelled out by Steven David (2003a, 122 f.), and by Daniel Statman (2004, 188 f.). Both base their argument on retribution.

happened. Moreover, if one accepts this understanding of punishment and accordingly focuses on state force that constitutes punishment, one is bound, even from an internal consequentialist perspective, to establish what the individual subject to punishment actually did and under what circumstances the act was carried out. If the degree of punishment does not aim at resolving injustice, but is derived from the consequences following an act of punishment, the specific circumstances are equally crucial. For example, if a sufficiently mentally ill person committed a wrong, yet acted without fault, punishment would not be justified, because it would not have any preventive effect on the behaviour of the individual. Provided he or she were sentenced to a punishment, after serving the sentence, he or she would be just as likely to re-offend – or not – as he or she was before serving the sentence. The experience of punishment would have no impact on the individual's mental state or behaviour. Punishment of such an individual would not be justified by its consequences for others either. Other equally mentally ill people would not be deterred, as they are unable to evaluate their own behaviour with deliberation in the first place. Neither would it influence others' appreciation of a certain norm or prohibition if a severely mentally ill person was not punished for violating it. Given the differing circumstances, it would not give the impression that they themselves could violate the prohibition without consequence. Punishment, in order to be justified on consequentialist grounds, hence, requires factual evidence regarding what happened and why.

This argument may not have been substantial enough to convince everyone. However, if this is the case, the remaining argument can be read with only a retributive account of punishment in mind. The next chapter will deal with consequentialism at greater length and identify its inadequacies in distinguishing justified killing from unjustified deprivation of life.

Now, if it is accepted that justified punishment must account for the circumstances of the deed, it can be based only on an objective and impartial decision, which itself is based on an objective and impartial understanding of the relevant situation. In this case, however, targeted killings of terrorists cannot be justified as punishment, as objective and impartial facts can only be provided by due process of law. Due process of law does not guarantee an undoubtedly right decision. Nevertheless, it provides procedural safeguards, adheres to fundamental legal principles and is carried out by an organ that, designated to jurisdiction, is institutionally independent from a political context. And these factors in combination make the realization of the objective being sought and an impartial decision as likely as possible.

Targeted killings of terrorists are, as established, not based on a judicial decision. Little is known about how the decision-making process takes place, but it is sufficiently evident that this process has little in common with due process of law. It deprives the individuals concerned of procedural rights necessary to render a decision sufficiently objective and impartial to be able to consider an act based on it a justified act of punishment. The decision is taken on the basis of information gathered by intelligence services. The decision-making process denies the accused the possibility of defending him- or herself. There are no public hearings, no objections, no appeals, and no amnesty. It does not grant, or even allow for, the appointment of a legally competent, experienced, and, most importantly, independent person to make the decision. Moreover, it does not guarantee the recognition of any additional principles or regulations established to guarantee a just decision, such as equal treatment, or the principle *in dubio pro reo*. Lacking a defence, public accountability and procedural structure, the fact-finding process cannot guarantee justice either to the deed or to the accused. Finally, there is no room for questioning decisions.

Even if governments set up strict procedural safeguards,[14] these could not possibly ameliorate such deficiencies. That the decision is made by a political body, and not by independent judges, suffices in and of itself to reject the decision as insufficiently impartial and objective. Judges may be influenced by public opinion, and one cannot be certain that legal decisions are always completely unbiased. Unlike political bodies, however, whose day-to-day decisions are necessarily political, judges are not bound by a political position.[15] Finally, even if courts made the decision, which by definition would render the act following such a decision different from targeted killing, it seems impossible to organize the process in a way that justifies the killing of an individual. It is difficult to imagine how such a case would look, given that the accused person is necessarily absent, that the defence would likely not be able to face the offended person, etc. It is generally highly problematic to try an offender *in absentia*. Because the decision, if it establishes the guilt of the accused, allows killing the individual, it certainly cannot be accepted, in particular because it leaves the alleged offender no possibility of questioning the decision.[16]

These few considerations show that targeted killings cannot be justified in terms of punishment. It is questionable whether the death penalty can be justified at all. But even if a death penalty of any description were held defensible,

---

14 David (2003a, 123), for example, introduces two requirements that punishment (he refers to retribution) must fulfil in order to be justified. First, the act of retribution must fit the crime'. Second, the act of retribution must focus on the offender and avoid harming innocent bystanders. These requirements, however, do not diminish the problem. It is the ability of extrajudicial decision-making processes to fulfil the first requirement that I deny.
15 See also Meisels 2004, 310.
16 See also Meisels 2004, 305.

such acts can only possibly be justified in terms of punishment if the decision-making process sufficiently guarantees that the decision rightly distinguishes between the guilty and the innocent, and that the final judgment does justice to the offender in a way that accounts for·his or her individual circumstances. These criteria can be fulfilled by due process of law only.

The requirement of due process of law does not thereby lose its power through reference to the difficulties states face in bringing an offender to trial.[17] The impossibility of detaining terrorists, to bring them to trial and to punish them does not give other bodies, such as the military forces of the injured states, the legitimacy to punish them with targeted killings. Punishment may, under certain circumstances, be deemed important. In view of this, states are required to actively seek detention and trial. They are not, however, required to act swiftly and punish offenders without due process of law. Given that punishment is directed against actions that have already taken place, the urgency to act, which can be ascribed to defensive acts, is absent. The fact that it is impossible to detain an offender, to put him or her to trial, and to punish him or her, therefore, cannot possibly justify carrying out punishment by different means. If the necessity to act is invoked to justify punishment, this merely points out that the argument of punishment has been corrupted to justify defensive action, to which arguments of punishment *per se* do not apply.

Neither does the argument that most terrorists do not hide their active involvement in terrorist offences or terrorist organizations, but openly admit it, diminish the necessity of due process of law in justifying retributive punishment.[18] First of all, this hardly applies to the majority of targeted killings. Targeted killings are mainly based on information gathered by intelligence agencies, establishing the role a given individual plays in terrorist activities. Furthermore, and more importantly, even if the offender openly admitted his or her involvement, such general statements fail to suffice as a basis for any just, objective, and impartial judgment. The reasons for this are myriad and independent of the position held on the justifiability of capital punishment. Public statements may have several motives, and cannot necessarily be regarded as factual. Even accepting the worth of public statements as such and then determining that a certain individual was involved in a certain act on the basis of them is insufficient. Participation in an act can take several forms, and the specific circumstan-

---

17 This is what Statman (2004, 188 f.) argues. That he argues for retribution within the context of war is insignificant, at this point. This is because, in Statman's account, retribution does not gain its justifying force from the status of terrorists in war but from the idea of justice itself that he propagates.
18 Statman 2004, 189.

ces of a given deed will never be sufficiently clear to describe any act based on such statements as justified punishment.

It can be concluded that, for different reasons, neither revenge nor punishment can provide the basis for justifying targeted killings of terrorists. While revenge cannot justify state action, being morally wrong, an act of punishment, to be justified, requires guarantees that only due process of law can provide. Presenting any extrajudicial decision-making process on which a targeted killing is based is insufficient.

This result also allows for a distinction important to the further discussion of the justifiability of targeted killing of terrorists. Targeted killings of terrorists are either defensive or responsive. The former are carried out with a view to defend against future terrorist attacks, be these attacks determinable or otherwise. The latter are carried out in light of past deeds. They can be explained in terms of revenge or retribution, or otherwise justified by consequentialist considerations. Consequentialist considerations thereby respond to past deeds, yet they can equally have preventive aims. This is the idea that is evident in consequentialist accounts of punishment. Having argued that neither reference to revenge nor reference to punishment can justify responsive targeted killings, the only remaining possibility for justifying these 'backward-looking' targeted killings of terrorists, then, would be if consequentialism provided justification for such acts without reference to punishment. Whether and to what extent consequentialism provides convincing justification of targeted killings, both with regard to past terrorist deeds or to future terrorist deeds, will be discussed in the next chapter. The justifiability of targeted killings of terrorists carried out with regard to past terrorist attacks thus depends on the conclusions of that discussion. Either they can be justified in terms of consequentialism, or else they cannot be justified at all. If the latter is the case, only targeted killings that are carried out to defend against future terrorist attacks should be dealt with in the remainder of the book. A rejection of responsive targeted killing also has consequences with regard to the different cases of targeted killing of terrorists that were laid out in chapter 1. In a case of the targeted killing of a terrorist who had been active in terrorist activity, though it has not been established whether he or she still poses a threat (case 4), justification necessarily depends on whether a case for a responsive targeted killing can be sufficiently made. If responsive targeted killings cannot be justified, such cases can similarly not be justified, since killing him or her cannot possibly be justified in terms of defence if it cannot be established that the targeted person is still involved in terrorism.

8 Consequences (i): Consequentialism as a general moral theory

In statements made by state officials and in arguments put forward in public, but also in academic debates, targeted killings of terrorists – if they are not justified with reference to armed conflicts – are often defended based on considerations such as the need for them in effectively fighting terrorism. The situation is illustrated by examples that highlight the loss of life that may be prevented through the killing of a terrorist.[1] It is argued that there is no choice but to target and kill terrorists.[2] In situations in which a terrorist is on his or her way to carry out an attack, it is argued, it is necessary to kill the terrorist in order to prevent loss of life and injuries among the population.[3]

Such statements and arguments may be based on different normative approaches: different rights may be taken into account and balanced against each other, not with regard to the actual consequences in a particular situation, but instead to the importance of the rights themselves. A terrorist's right to life may be regarded as less important than the security of others or of the society as a whole. There may also be a theory to support such statements that explains why terrorists may be killed in reference to their behaviour and their rights. The strong reference to necessity as well as the choice of examples, however, suggest that consequentialist considerations are essential for such justifications of targeted killings.

Two different consequentialist approaches may underlie these statements. The first is wholehearted consequentialism. With regard to the moral justifiability of targeted killing of terrorists, this means that targeted killing is morally justified whenever the overall consequences of killing terrorists are preferable to the overall consequences of not applying the practice. The second approach is reflected by the conviction that under 'normal' circumstances one must distinguish moral behaviour from immoral behaviour on deontological grounds, yet that under certain circumstances – the fight against terrorism as such, or specif-

---

1 See, for example, Rami Gershon, one of the founders of an IDF unit carrying out targeted killings, quoted in Stein, 2.
2 See, for example, the statement the Prime Minister Ehud Barak made in a meeting of the Foreign Affairs and Defence Committee that '[i]f people are shooting at us and killing us – our only choice is to strike back. A country under terrorist threat must fight back'. Quoted in Stein 2001, 1; for further quotes, see page 2. See also David 2003b, 139; Boot 2002. Boot also refers to the argument that killing is allowed in wars, yet the consequentialist argument dominates his statement.
3 AI 2003, 2.

ic, particularly threatening situations – consequentialist considerations gain prevailing justifying power and justify the targeted killing of terrorists. In this chapter, I will focus on the genuine consequentialist position only. The discussion of the second position will be postponed for the moment. In order to make sense of any version of the argument, one first must determine on what grounds targeted killing of terrorists may generally be assessed.

Consequentialism can take several forms, depending on what good constitutes the benchmark for assessing the consequences. What this highest good is does not necessarily become clear in the statements referred to at the beginning of this chapter. Security for a certain society certainly plays a crucial role. However, security alone cannot be the basis on which the consequences of a certain act must be assessed. The members of any society need security, but they also need freedom, for example. I will assume a plausible understanding of a just and functioning society as a reference point for the assessment of possible consequences, and, despite the different approaches that the term consequentialism comprises, I will speak of consequentialism as if it were one theory only. This is acceptable because it is one aspect that all possible attempts to justify targeted killings of terrorists on consequentialist grounds have in common – namely, that one is able to justify this practice in light of the *consequences* – which the main objections against such approaches address.

These approaches all face an internal empirical objection, on the one hand, and an external theoretical objection, on the other. First, it is highly questionable whether and to what extent any plausible consequentialist approach would actually justify targeted killings. Second, it is not the consequences that distinguish justified from unjustified killings and describe this distinction in convincing terms. The discussion will instead suggest that justified killing may only be explained and described in reference to the rights of the individual concerned.

As regards the *internal empirical objection*, in order to justify targeted killings of terrorists on consequentialist grounds, one first needs to show that targeted killings of terrorists actually lead to the expected consequences. In other words, the practice of targeted killing of terrorists cannot be justified if it does not effectively fight terrorism. It can only be justified if it increases overall security and thus leads to an outcome that is better for the majority than the result if targeted killings were not applied. This, however, is difficult to prove and highly contentious, both if one assesses the overall development of terrorism in specific conflicts and if one considers the consequences in view of individual cases of targeted killing of terrorists only.

The empirical consequences which targeted killings produce in the overall development of terrorism in specific conflicts seem not to have been determined yet.[4] This presumably is due to the obvious difficulties such research faces. First, terrorist attacks that are foiled by targeted killings can hardly be measured. Second, states apply different measures in their fight against terrorism, all of which may have an impact on the extent of terrorist violence. Furthermore, developments within terrorist groups may influence the terrorist activities that are carried out by these groups. Hence, even if a decrease of terrorist attacks were noted, it seems impossible to determine whether this is due to the practice of targeted killing.

Existing assessments of the efficacy of targeted killings of terrorists cannot replace the absence of convincing empirical research. Assessments differ depending on the conflict looked at. This can be seen most dramatically when comparing the American assessment of Israel's practice of targeted killing to the American assessment of the targeted killings carried out by the United States itself.[5] Assessments also contradict each other with regard to specific conflicts.

The most extensive discussion on the efficacy of targeted killings of terrorists has taken place with regard to Israel's current policy of targeted killing. But contradicting assessments have also been formulated regarding the American context.

The fact that the United States and Israel apply targeted killings indicates that the countries' administrations consider the practice to be productive. More specifically, authors highlight that it is more effective to eliminate the source of the terrorist threat than to try guarding potential terrorist targets, something which, given the number of these targets, turns out to be very difficult.[6]

---

4 Asaf Zussman and Noam Zussman (2005) sought to measure the effectiveness of targeted killings of senior members of Palestinian terrorist organizations in reference to the effects these killings have on the stock market. The study comes to the conclusion that the killing of alleged terrorist military leaders positively affects the stock market, while the killing of alleged terrorist political leaders negatively affects it. I will only point out one problem of this study: the research is based on the assumption that effective countermeasures should have positive effects on the stock market, while counterproductive measures would influence the reactions at the stock market negatively. Given the many psychological factors that may influence stock market reactions, it is highly problematic to use these reactions as indications for the effectiveness of counter-terrorist measures. See also Avi Kober 2007, who challanges the result of Asaf and Noam Zussman; Jones/Libicki 2008; Wilner 2010; and compare Daase/Spencer 2010, 413–416.
5 See, for example, US Department of State, Richard Boucher, Daily Press Briefing, 2 July 2001; or White House, Ari Fleischer, Press Briefing, 3 August 2001.
6 Betts 2002, 33. With reference to the American context, Betts recognizes that targeted killings may risk mobilization and alienation against the state carrying out these countermeasures, but argues that, even if one takes these effects into account, it is more effective than any other measure, provided it hits a significant number of relevant terrorists.

Moreover, it is argued that targeted killings destroy the structure of terrorist organizations. The practice is believed to weaken these organizations because it is difficult and time-consuming to replace central and experienced figures in such organizations or networks, because it demoralizes the members of such organizations, and because central figures, out of fear, are not able to work as effectively as they would be if not forced to act covertly.[7] Commentators highlight that targeted killings may have deterrent effects on potential terrorists.[8] To strengthen their point, some add that terrorist groups would attack regardless, or that the extent of hostile and adversary emotions have reached such a degree that the pursuit of revenge triggered by specific targeted killings is negligible. Targeted killings of terrorists, it is argued, thus, have all the aforementioned positive disrupting effects, yet do not increase the number of terrorist attacks or substantially decrease the prospect for peaceful settlement of the conflict.[9] Authors point out that in the Israeli context the victim rate among Israelis has decreased since Israel started its policy of targeted killings.[10] Commentators assert in the American context that the people who replaced the targeted persons were inferior in quality and training.[11]

A similar range of arguments has been put forward for the position that targeted killings do not improve, but worsen, a given situation. Commentators point to the mechanism of revenge. They argue that targeted killings increase the desire for revenge, and hence the number of victims.[12] They hold that targeted kill-

---

7 For the different reasons, see e.g. Byman 2006b, 104; David 2003a, 120; Eisenstadt 2001; Statman 2003, 778; Statman 2004, 192.

8 David 2003a, 120. See also David 2003a 118 – 121/125 f. David provides arguments for and against the effectiveness of targeted killings of terrorists. However, '[i]n sum,' he argues, 'the policy of targeted killing has prevented some attacks against Israel, weakened the effectiveness of terrorist organizations, kept potential bomb makers on the run, and deterred terrorist operations. It has not prevented all acts of terrorism, nor can it. But as part of a larger array of policies, including blockades, checkpoints, and incursions, it is a successful response to an intolerable threat'. (David 2003a, 121.) Although he initially states that targeted killings do not have a clear benefit with regard to the numbers of victims on the Israeli side caused by terrorist attacks, he argues that the practice may have longer-term effects. He therefore holds it to be too early to 'declare targeted killings an ineffective or failed policy'. (David 2003a, 125 f.)

9 See, for example, Luft 2003. See also Meisels 2004, 323; Ephraim Sneh, Israel's former Defence Minister, quoted in O'Sullivan 2000.

10 See, for example, Byman 2006b, 103; Statman 2004, 192.

11 Gellman 2002.

12 See, for example, Gross, M. 2003, 357; Byman 2006b, 99 f. Byman argues that the benefits of targeted killing outweighs its costs.

ings increase the popularity of terrorist groups.[13] They point out that targeted killing creates resentment that helps terrorist groups to raise money and recruit individuals willing to take part in terrorist activities. Counter-violence leads to a spiral of violence and increases death and destruction.[14] With regard to Israel in particular, it has been argued that the structure of organizations that support and promote terrorism against Israel is decentralized in such a way that attacks on one group have little, if any, impact on others.[15] In other cases, authors hold that Israel supports a radicalization by killing relatively moderate leaders, with whom negotiations may have been possible, and who are then succeeded by more radical individuals.[16] As regards the US practice of targeted killing, Lee Strickland, a former CIA counsel who became head of the Center for Information Policy at the University of Maryland in 2004, is quoted as having commented: 'Paradoxically, as a result of our success the target has become even more decentralized, even more diffused and presents a more difficult target – no question about that.'[17]

Overall, some situations may be more predictable than others. Targeted killings certainly have greater effect on strongly centralized organizations than they may ever have on decentralized networks. However, even in such situations, consequentialists must meet a high burden of proof in order to justify targeted killings of terrorists. It is equally difficult in such situations to come to an indisputable conclusion as to whether targeted killing may be regarded as an effective practice in the fight against terrorism. None of the assessments can claim to be based on unquestionable facts, and all arguments can be opposed by equally comprehensible counter-arguments. Even if individual aspects of the arguments are held to be more convincing than others on a theoretical level, any assessment must judge the importance that the individual factors have for the overall outcome compared to other factors, and this involves a high degree of personal belief.

The possibility of justification of targeted killings on consequentialist grounds thereby decreases when the threat the targeted individual poses is less determinable. With regard to killings belonging to case 4, a conclusive consequentialist justification seems impossible. These targeted killings are carried

---

13 See, for example, Byman 2006b, 100.
14 See, for example, US Department of State, Richard Boucher, Daily Press Briefing, 27 August 2001; David 2003a, 118.
15 David 2003a, 118.
16 Gross, M. 2003, 357.
17 Quoted in Meyer 2006. For further assessments of the situation, see, for example, Gellman 2002.

out without any knowledge as to whether the previously active targeted person will become active again, and hence with a limited understanding of whether he or she will endanger innocent individuals. If he or she is no longer active, he or she poses no threat to others, and killing him or her does not directly influence any terrorist network. Only two positive effects are possible: deterrence and/or a decrease in effectiveness due to hiding, changing whereabouts, etc. In these situations, it seems unlikely that the positive consequences ever outweigh the fact that such targeted killings may increase hatred and desire for revenge.

That said, one may argue that under certain circumstances, the consequences of not killing someone may in *individual cases* be so severe that the terrorist must be prevented from acting, regardless of what follows. This argument has no force with regard to targeted killings not carried out in light of a determinable threat, but instead in light of an undetermined future threat (case 3), or merely in reaction to terrorist activities (case 4). In these cases, it does not make sense to separate the individual case from the overall development. These targeted killings are carried out solely with regard to the overall development. Given that the benefits of such acts cannot outweigh the loss of life, they can never be justified if assessed as individual cases. The argument, however, seems to have some weight with regard to targeted killings of case 1 or case 2. In contrast to other cases of targeted killing of terrorists, these cases prevent a realistic danger, the extent of which, under certain circumstances, may be determined. If the threat is determinable to the extent that the degree of destruction is predictable, and if this destruction is expected to reach a certain dimension, one may conclude that the benefits of a targeted killing outweigh the destruction caused by it to such an extent, that a targeted killing is the right thing to do, even in light of the future consequences which at that time may not yet be predictable.

To conclude, if one comes to the conclusion that consequentialist approaches are convincing in general, it is not clear whether they actually justify targeted killings in their different forms and cases. Under certain circumstances, i.e. that the likelihood is high that the targeted killing prevents severe harm, consequentialism may justify the targeted killing in case 1 or 2. Under all other conditions, it is questionable whether targeted killings could be justified in terms of consequentialism, since it would have to be shown that the killings are in fact effective measures in the fight against terrorism. This has hitherto not been done, and it seems to be a burden which is almost impossible to meet.

This leads to the *external theoretical objection* against a consequentialist justification of targeted killing of terrorists. If extreme situations are considered, such as killings with a view to prevent a predictable severe threat, consequentialism, at first sight, seems to provide a convincing explanation for why a certain person may be killed. However, the explanation is insufficient in light of further examples of killing in general. Consequentialism is neither able to convincingly distinguish justified from unjustified killing, nor does it describe and explain this distinction in convincing terms. Overall it can thus not be used to assess the morality of *targeted* killings.

Five examples will help to illustrate these conclusions: (1) a ticking bomb scenario (it will be referred to as *ticking bomb scenario*); (2) and (3) two slightly altered ticking bomb scenarios (they will be referred to as *altered ticking bomb scenarios a* and *b*); (4) a common one-on-one situation of self-defence (it will be referred to as *one-on-one self-defence*), and (5) a situation of self-defence in which several people attack one innocent person (it will be referred to as *several-to-one self-defence*).

Ad (1) Ticking bomb scenario: A person planted a highly destructive bomb which, if it detonates, will kill hundreds of thousands of people. The attacker has the remote control to detonate the bomb. Apart from the attacker, no one knows where the bomb is located or is able to defuse it in a way that makes the attacker unable to detonate it. The attacker is on his or her way to detonate the bomb in a place out of reach of the area of destruction. The only way to save the potential victims is to immediately target and kill the attacker so that he or she will not be able to detonate the bomb. The attacker is an independent attacker, i.e. he or she is not part of a terrorist network. His or her killing will not have any destructive consequences other than his or her death.

Ad (2) Altered ticking bomb scenario a: This scenario is identical to the ticking bomb scenario, with one exception. The bomb will go off if the attacker is killed, so the only way to stop the destruction is not to kill him or her, but to kill a class of twenty primary school children. Why the death of the children will stop the detonation is not important for the scenario. The attacker may, for example, have set this as a condition for not detonating the bomb.

Ad (3) Altered ticking bomb scenario b: This scenario is a variation of the altered ticking bomb scenario a. In order to prevent the destruction, one child, rather than a group of children, would have to be killed.

Ad (4) One-to-one self-defence: A is walking along the street. B, with whom A had no prior contact, stops A, pulls out a gun, and intends to kill A. A can only save his or her own life by killing B.

Ad (5) Several-to-one self-defence: This scenario is a variation of the one-to-one self-defence. A is walking along the street. Not one, but several people approach him or her, take out guns, and intend to shoot him or her dead. A can only save his or her life by killing all of the people who are threatening him or her.

With regard to the ticking bomb scenario, consequentialist approaches would justify the killing. This may be in accordance with many people's intuition. It may also appear to be easy to understand that the consequences explain these intuitions and justify the outcome. *One* guilty person has to die for *hundreds of thousands* who happened to be at the wrong place at the wrong time, and no further destructive consequences will follow from the attacker's death. Fewer people may share the intuition that it is right to carry out a killing in the case of the altered ticking bomb scenario a, namely to kill children in order to save many more lives. The reason for this does not seem to be the fact that not one, but several individuals have to be killed in order to prevent the attack. If just the overall outcome is considered, in view of the enormous number of people saved, the difference between one and twenty individuals changes the result only minimally.

A comparison between altered ticking bomb scenarios a and b supports this assessment. If the number of the targeted persons made the difference, one would have to think identically about the killing in the ticking bomb scenario and the killing in the altered ticking bomb scenario b. And one would only think differently about the altered ticking bomb scenario a. I, however, argue that many people would see a difference between the altered ticking bomb scenarios a and b – probably due to the numbers of victims that the killing would claim – yet they would still not equate the ticking bomb scenario to the altered ticking bomb scenario b.

Three replies seem to be possible from a consequentialist position. First of all, one may argue that there is no difference between these two cases. It makes no moral difference whether the person *endangering* hundreds of thousands of people is killed in order to save the latter, or whether an *innocent* child is killed to reach the same aim. If one wants to avoid this highly counterintuitive result, one may accept that there is a difference between the ticking bomb scenario and the altered ticking bomb scenario b, and try to explain this difference on consequentialist grounds. The consequences for a society which would kill innocent children in order to resolve security issues, one may argue, would be so severe that the overall good would be greater if hundreds of thousands of people died than if children were deliberately killed. This may be the first step on a slippery slope, leading to more killing of innocents in less extreme situations. Moreover, the killing of children may implant a feeling of insecurity that heavily disrupts day-to-day life and may end in mistrust of politicians and of the state.

Regardless of how much force is ascribed to these arguments, they do not resolve the problem with a consequentialist explanation for the difference between the ticking bomb scenario and the altered ticking bomb scenarios a and b. If the described consequences made the difference, my assessment of the different ticking bomb scenarios would have to be identical if one altered the scenario a and b in a way that excluded all these consequences. This could be done by assuming that no one will find out about the real facts behind the killings. The killing would be presented as an accident, the politician who ordered it would not inform anyone of the facts, and he or she would leave office afterwards. This, however, leaves only the counter-intuitive first option. One may also argue that both forms of killing may be justified, yet that there is a difference as to the morality of these two cases, which comes down to the attacker's guilt versus the child's innocence. That this does not lead to a convincing solution will become clear in the remaining two examples.

Before turning to these examples, however, a few remarks on the fact that seems to distinguish the ticking bomb scenario from the altered ticking bomb scenarios would be appropriate. If the intuition that the ticking bomb scenario and the altered ticking bomb scenarios differ is taken seriously, and if it is accepted that the consequences cannot explain this difference, one must note one outstanding difference: while the terrorist actively endangers a large number of people, the children are innocent. While the killing of the terrorist is a reaction to his or her own behaviour, the killing of the children is not. As such, it does not follow that the killing of the terrorist in the ticking bomb scenario is justified. Regardless of the conclusion finally reached, the difference intuitively made between the killing of the terrorist and of the children sounds plausibly described in reference to their behaviour. And, I would argue, many would describe it in reference to the right to life of the individuals – entailing their right not to be killed – as relates to their behaviour. It sounds plausible to say that the children may not be killed because they, due to their innocence, have *the right* not to be killed. From a different perspective, it could be said that the state does not have the right to kill the children.

Regardless of how the situation is intuitively assessed, the justifiability of killing the terrorist in the ticking bomb scenario also seems plausibly described in the rubric of the right to life. If his or her killing is held to be justified, it sounds plausible to say that he or she may be killed because he or she, due to his or her conduct, lacks the right not to be killed. If one has doubts about the justifiability of killing the terrorist, it could be said that one is not entirely sure whether the terrorist has the right not to be killed, because he or she him- or herself endangers a large number of individuals. Hence, if the number of victims does not explain the difference, it seems plausible to argue that the behaviour of the individuals in reference to their rights does.

A look at the remaining two scenarios will support the conclusions drawn with regard to the ticking bomb scenarios. The discussion will not only illustrate that consequences are not decisive for convincingly distinguishing between justified and unjustified killings. It will also show that a consequentialist approach would require accepting situations which contradict widely established under-standing, and, in fact, situations that are far less rare than the altered ticking bomb scenarios. Finally, it will also strengthen the assumption that the behaviour of an individual and his or her rights, related to this behaviour, are relevant to explaining justified killing and hence for assessing targeted killings of terrorists.

A look at the one-on-one self-defence scenario already illustrates some of these points. Any consequentialist approach needs to demonstrate why the loss of life of the attacker is a more palatable consequence than the loss of life of the attacked if it does not want to ignore the basic moral conviction, which is also broadly legally institutionalized, that the attacked person may defend him- or herself with violence, and if necessary, kill the attacker. On the level of number of victims, which only accounts for the two individuals involved, it makes no difference whether it is the attacker or the victim who dies. A strictly consequentialist approach is, thus, not able to decide what is morally right in this common situation of self-defence. Moreover, if one accounts for the overall consequences and includes the consequences such an act may have for others, a consequentialist, under certain circumstances, must conclude that the victim is not justified in reacting, but must accept that he or she will be killed. That is because the overall consequences may be preferable if the attacker rather than the attacked person survives. For example, this may be the case if a famous surgeon, who will cure many individuals during the rest of his or her life, attacks an individual who would have less positive impact on other people if he or she survived.[18]

A comparison of the one-on-one self-defence and the several-on-one self-defence supports this argument. It illustrates a few points, which David Rodin recently formulated.[19] It is commonly accepted that in both scenarios the person who is attacked may defend him- or herself, even by killing the attacker(s) if necessary. It is also commonly acknowledged that the number of attackers does not influence the justifiability of appropriate counter-violence. But it seems plausible that the victim, because he or she is the one who was attacked, has the right to defend him- or herself; similarly the attacker, owing to his or her own behaviour, does not have the right not to be killed. From a consequentialist perspective, the only answer to this seems to be that the attacker's life counts for less than the life of the attacked, because he or she, by attacking another person, is morally at fault, while the attacked person is not. It is difficult to understand how such

---

18 Rodin 2002, 53f.
19 Rodin 2002, 52–54.

moral assessment fits within a consequentialist approach. It requires a non-consequentialist framework to an extent that questions the basic consequentialist assumption that morality is to be derived from calculating the overall benefit. Morality in this case is dependent on the moral value of the individuals concerned, and this moral value is not explained by a consequentialist account. However, even if this is accepted, one may ask why the moral impact of the actual attack is decisive for the moral worth of someone's life, rather than his or her *overall* behaviour. Yet, if the overall moral value is taken into account, this approach would, under certain circumstances, lead to results that are incompatible with a commonly accepted understanding of self-defence. Rodin clearly illustrates this:

> A victim who has just committed attempted murder does not forgo the right of self-defense if he is unjustly attacked, though his moral worth is presumably no greater than that of his assailant (it should be remembered that the only crime an aggressor who is killed in self-defense had committed is *attempted* murder [in other legal systems, e. g. the German legal system, it is not even necessarily murder, but homicide]).[20]

To conclude, an analysis of different self-defence scenarios – the core circumstance of justified killing – supports the conclusions drawn with regard to the killings in light of the different ticking bomb scenarios. Consequences are not decisive for the justifiability of killing in self-defence, of killing in general and, thus, of targeted killing in particular.

One may argue that I presented a rather crude version of consequentialism. If other consequentialist approaches were taken into account, rule consequentialism in particular, it would be more difficult to reject the approach. Rule consequentialism no longer applies the principle of the overall good to individual actions but to rules of action. The morality of a certain act no longer depends on the actual consequences of a particular act but on the utility of a certain moral rule according to which the act is carried out.

Rules, however, do not seem to improve the situation. It is possible to argue that the rule that innocent individuals may not be killed leads to the best overall outcome. *Prima facie*, this would resolve the problem faced with regard to consequentialist accounts hitherto addressed, i.e. act consequentialist accounts. It is, however, difficult to argue on rule consequentialist grounds that one has to stick to such a rule if in a particular situation the killing of an innocent individual guarantees the best result and if no one knew about the incident.[21] This,

---

20 Rodin 2002, 52.
21 Rodin 2002 54 f.

however, leads back to the initial problem. Moreover, what would such rules have to look like in order to justify targeted killing? In light of the difficulties in determining the overall consequences of targeted killings, the formulation of rules does not improve the situation but rather worsens it. Given that the consequences of individual cases of targeted killing cannot be securely determined, it cannot be argued that the majority would benefit from the endorsement of a rule that allowed states to kill terrorists.

On the basis of these few arguments, it may be concluded that consequentialism, neither as act consequentialism nor as rule consequentialism, would, within its own terms, clearly justify all forms of targeted killing of terrorists. More importantly, it fails to provide a convincing distinction between justified and unjustified killing as well as to express this distinction in convincing terms, and can hence not be applied to justify targeted killings of terrorists.

In light of this discussion I would like to recall the conclusion of the last chapter. Having argued that responsive targeted killing of terrorists can only possibly be justified in reference to revenge or punishment, or on a consequentialist basis, it may now be concluded that such form of targeted killing cannot be justified. With regard to the different cases of targeted killing of terrorists distinguished, this concerns all killings of terrorists of case 4, that is killings of terrorists who had been active in terrorist activity, but whose continued threat has not been established. As such, the remainder of this book focuses on defensive targeted killing of terrorists.

9 *Feindstrafrecht:* Forfeiture of the right to life

So far, the arguments against possible consequentialist approaches to justify targeted killing suggest that the behaviour of a person relating to his or her right to life does play a central role in reasoning whether and when killing – including targeted killing – may be justified. If one takes these suggestions seriously, one must explain, with reference to a behaviour-relative right to life, why the targeted person may be killed and why other people may not. One conceivable argument would be that by behaving in a certain manner, some individuals – in this context, the targeted terrorists – have fewer rights than others. While everyone possesses the right to life in principle, by behaving in a certain way, some forfeit this right and hence may be attacked.

Günther Jakobs draws upon such reasoning with his concept of *Feindstrafrecht* (criminal law for enemies). Jakobs himself does not discuss the justifiability of targeted killing at great length, though he affirmatively addresses the topic of targeted killing at a few points.[1] In principle, his concept allows for this practice. This makes his approach, which offers a possible means of justifying targeted killing, highly relevant to the question under study.

Jakobs introduced the term '*Feindstrafrecht*' as primarily descriptive. Normatively, he initially legitimizes it, if at all, in situations of national emergency and regards it as contradicting a state order that respects and guarantees freedom.[2] Ultimately he applies it affirmatively in a general normative sense.[3] In view of the present concern, I will not question whether the concept of *Feindstrafrecht* is useful in analysing existing legal regulations, but will focus instead on its normative worth.[4]

Jakobs distinguishes between citizens (or persons) and enemies (or sources of danger). Citizens, he argues, are all individuals who cognitively accept the legal order to which they belong. They guarantee to some degree, through their attitude and behaviour, that they by and large will abide by established laws. By so doing, they create and maintain their status as persons, and thus

---

1 Jakobs 2004, 92f. See also Jakobs 2005, 848f.
2 See Jakobs 1985, in particular 783f.
3 See for example Jakobs 2000, 2004, and 2005.
4 Critical regarding its normative value, yet positive in view of the analytical worth of the concept of Feindstrafrecht to analyse criminal law, for example, Aponte 2004; Cancio Meliá 2005; Prittwitz 2005, in particular 224–228. See also Albrecht 2005, 856f.; Sauer, D. 2005. For a critical assessment, see, for example, Roxin 2006, mns. 127f., pp. 55f.; Saliger 2006, 760f.; Saliger (2006, 757/759–761) also gives a brief overview over different positions on Feindstrafrecht as analytical category.

have rights *vis-à-vis* the state. Enemies do not accept the laws regulating the community of legal order to which they belong. They 'probably forever, but at least decisively disregard the law'.[5] Enemies thus do not provide a minimal cognitive guarantee that they will carry out the duties they have as members of society and, as such, are no longer citizens, but manoeuvre outside of the community of legal order. Enemies forfeit their status as persons, and therewith their claim to be treated as such. They turn from persons to mere sources of danger, which must be fought.

Not every criminal, Jakobs argues, undergoes this transformation. Criminals may have violated certain norms, yet this does not necessarily exclude them from the community of legal order. 'The enemy is an individual, who, to a not merely casual extent, but supposedly permanently or on long term renounced the law.'[6] This can be due to the individual's attitude, which can be the case with regard to, for example, sexual offences, or how the individual earns his or her living. This applies to economic or organized crime, drug crime in particular. Finally and most importantly, the fact that the individual no longer accepts the legal order is expressed through his or her involvement in certain organizations. This applies to terrorism, organized crime or drug crime.[7] Although the line between citizens and enemies cannot always be easily determined, terrorists, understood as individuals who deny the legitimacy of a certain legal order on principle and therefore seek to destroy it, according to Jakobs, are undoubtedly enemies.[8]

While citizens are punished for their deeds, enemies are fought for their behaviour. The main function of punishment, alongside force and prevention, is to stabilize the violated norm. The perpetrator's violating act questions the norm. Punishment contradicts the perpetrator and reaffirms the norm and its validity.[9] Measures applied against enemies do not involve any such meaning. They do not aim at norm-stabilization. They do not seek to redress norm violations. They are applied in order to effectively fight the danger emanating from a dangerous individual.[10] According to Jakobs, the state is not even free to choose whether it wants to treat enemies as persons and allow them corresponding rights:

> Everyone who does not provide a sufficient cognitive guarantee that he will behave as a person may not only not expect to be treated as a person any longer, but the state *must*

---

5 Jakobs 2004, 92. All quotations from Jakobs' texts are translated by myself.
6 Jakobs 2000, 52. See also Jakobs 2004, 92.
7 Jakobs 2000, 51f.
8 Jakobs 2004, 92.
9 Jakobs 2004, 88f.
10 Jakobs 2004, 88f.

not treat him as a person any longer. If it were to do so, the state would violate the right to security of other people.[11]

This brief presentation of Jakobs' reasoning makes the relevance that the concept of *Feindstrafrecht* has for justifying targeted killings of terrorists clear. If accepted, the concept seems to justify the practice in all of its different forms. It deprives the terrorist of all rights he or she may have against the state. Degraded to a source of danger, according to the concept, he or she faces 'physical force, which may go so far as war'[12]. Jakobs illustrated the extent of force applicable when he formulated that the state is not only allowed to, but required to force a terrorist to provide information about planned attacks, and the prohibition of torture may thereby not set a limit.[13] Having said that, Jakobs introduces limits as to how extreme state measures may be. He argues that a state may only apply necessary measures. This prohibits excessive actions, yet does not limit the use of force to actions applied in reaction to imminent attacks – as the requirement is understood in other contexts[14] – but allows for preventive application of force.[15]

It is not clear how Jakobs comes to the limitations of necessity. Although it is a widely accepted requirement for the use of force, it cannot easily be derived from his account. One cannot derive any requirements as to the means an enemy is to be confronted with from the assertion that he or she is to be treated as source of danger no longer possessing any rights. These questions, however, may be left aside since *Feindstrafrecht* cannot be drawn upon to justify targeted killings of terrorists. It must be rejected, mainly because the full forfeiture of rights is incompatible with basic and non-negotiable convictions and values. It must be rejected additionally because Jakobs does not provide a convincing argument for his concept. The first objection thereby explains why there can be no convincing argument drawing on the idea that individuals, due to their behaviour, can fully and absolutely forfeit human rights.

---

11 Jakobs 2004, 93.
12 Jakobs 2004, 90.
13 Jakobs 2005, 849.
14 The requirement of necessity as it is generally understood in the context of self-defence will be addressed in chapter 10.
15 Jakobs 2000, 51; Jakobs 2005, 847–849. Also prudence – abuse and the possibility for peace may, for example, be prudential reasons not to apply all possible means – may prohibit the application of certain measures. Jakobs 2005, 849; Jakobs 2004, 90. This however does not seem to be a normative limitation deprived from normative assumptions but rather from pragmatic considerations that should be taken into account.

First of all, the notion of full and absolute forfeiture contradicts the idea of human rights itself. There is no uncontroversial and common understanding of human rights. Many aspects are subject to debate. However, if the existence of human rights is accepted, they are accepted as applying *universally*. This follows from the idea of *human* rights itself and is incorporated in all relevant international declarations and treaties on human rights.[16] Universality of human rights may include different aspects. It certainly means that human rights apply to *all* human beings, *unconditionally,* depending neither on the individual's 'race, colour, sex, language, religion, political or other opinion, national or social origin, property, birth or other status'[17], nor on their attitude and behaviour. These basic tenets of human rights are incompatible with the idea that rights, including human rights, are conditional on the attitude and behaviour of the individual concerned.

Looking at what state action is accepted as justified in response to criminal activities, one may argue that rights do not apply universally in legitimate state systems, but depend on one's behaviour. This argument, however, does not hold up to a closer examination of counter-criminal activities. The way certain rights may influence the life of a given individual depends on his or her behaviour. Someone who is sentenced to prison may not choose his or her place of residence in the manner that non-criminal citizens can. This, however, may not be described in terms of full and absolute forfeiture of rights. The individual who is justly sentenced to prison may not be put in prison because he or she forfeited his or her rights. This already becomes clear by the fact that no one may be imprisoned twice for the same criminal action. It is also expressed by the fact that only certain crimes carry prison sentences, as well as by the fact that a criminal who may be sentenced to jail must be sentenced to a specific and appropriate, rather than indefinite or arbitrary, period of time in prison.

Feindstrafrecht contradicts human rights in at least one other respect. It describes rights, including human rights, as being valid with regard to states only. According to Jakobs, any state may, and has to, deny the status of a person, and thus his or her rights, to an individual who does not accept the legal order. The concept of *Feindstrafrecht* does not allow additional rights, either extra-state rights that have actual protecting effects or extra-state rights to which one may refer in order to claim further protection. The contradiction becomes evident immediately when this concept of rights is contrasted with human rights. Human

---

16 Consider, for example, CCPR, Preamble, Article 2 and 3. See also UDHR, Preamble, Arts. 1 and 2.
17 CCPR, Art. 2 (1).

rights first of all require *states*, i.e. politicians, state officials, or generally those responsible for the political order, to ensure and respect human rights and to implement legal and other measures required to give effect to these rights. However, the validity of human rights is not limited to a certain society. Human rights are not at the disposal of state officials, but continue to exist even if states fail to give effect to them. And this is the case if human rights are understood as moral rights or as political rights, but equally if described as legal rights as set out in international law.[18] Even from a positive legal perspective, human rights continue to exist and continue to formulate claims towards states to ensure them regardless, in particular if the state does not fulfil this obligation.

The second objection to the concept of *Feindstrafrecht* is closely linked to my first objection, in describing it from a different, state-focused, perspective. The concept of *Feindstrafrecht* is incompatible not only with the idea of human rights, but also with any plausible understanding of a state governed by the rule of law, in particular, because it does not accept the presumption of innocence. By legitimizing countermeasures against enemies on the vague basis of their attitudes, it jettisons the presumption of innocence. It does so not only in the case of individuals who Jakobs describes as enemies, but also to all other citizens.

The state decides who fulfils the minimal cognitive guarantee that is required for the status of citizen and person: 'But if the state is able to withhold the presumption of innocence from anyone who it holds to be its "enemy" then the presumption of innocence loses its validity.'[19] The problem is additionally aggravated by the fact that the decision to reject the applicability of the presumption of innocence is a political decision, and by the fact that this decision may be taken on the *assumption* that an individual does not accept the legal order.[20] While the annulment aims at the presumption of innocence, it, in light of the fact that enemies in principle lose all of their rights against the state, applies to other rights and principles crucial to a state governed by the rule of law, such as equal treatment under the law. Any state that applies such considerations dissolves these principles as such.[21]

Jakobs sees and addresses this problem. He admits that a state perfectly governed by the rule of law cannot treat its enemy as a mere source of danger. He rejects the idea of this perfect state, however, and argues that one needs to imagine a state that, in a *practical optimal* manner, is governed by the rule of law. In

---

18 For this distinction, see e.g. Menke/Pollmann 2007, 25–41.
19 Bielefeld 2004, 10. Translated by myself.
20 Sauer, D. 2005, 1704.
21 Bielefeld 2004, 10. See also, Roxin 2006, mn. 129, p. 56; Sauer, D. 2005, 1704.

other words, Jakobs regards this to be the best possible degree of rule of law if one takes into account the fact that states have to defend themselves against enemy attacks. According to Jakobs, the situation becomes problematic only if the state applies *Feindstrafrecht* while claiming to apply *Bürgerstrafrecht* (criminal law for citizens).[22] Jakobs underestimates both the consequences of his concept and the importance of a state governed by the rule of law. As I have shown, *Feindstrafrecht* severely weakens the rule of law because it denies the principles of a state governed by the rule of law to enemies and because in so doing, it questions the validity of these principles in general, with regard to all citizens.

Two additional objections follow from this second objection. The fact that the state decides who is to be regarded as an enemy gives it enormous power. This is problematic because it allows for drastic misuse. The fact that the limitation of rights is justified by the prevention of 'supposed danger from the supposed majority'[23] makes this point all the more serious. The argument presents the limitation of rights as politically justified, and it ignores that the points of reference are highly arbitrary and can easily be manipulated.[24] Independent of any possible abuse of this power, the fact that *Feindstrafrecht* puts the basic rights of individuals at the disposal of the state must be rejected because it dissolves the safeguards that protect individuals against endangerment and violation by the state itself. This last argument points to a misunderstanding governing the concept of *Feindstrafrecht*. Jakobs either misunderstands the right to security, which he refers to in order to establish that states *must* treat individuals who reject the legal order as enemies, or his concept fails to give justice to this right. One aspect of the right to security is that the state protects individuals from the danger emanating from other citizens, other individuals, or entities outside the state. This aspect is what Jakobs draws upon. Another aspect of the right to security, however, is the protection from threat or danger emanating from

---

22 Jakobs 2005, 850 f. In his early writings (see Jakobs 1985, 783 f.), Jakobs regards *Feindstrafrecht* to be less compatible with a state governed by the rule of law, or as he puts it, with a state that respects freedom. He states: 'The existence of enemy criminal law is, hence, not a sign of strength of a state that respects freedom, but a sign of the fact that it [such a state] does not exist at all, in this respect.' (Jakobs 1985, 784.) Although Jakobs adds that *Feindstrafrecht* may be legitimate under certain circumstances, he accepts that it would contravene the principles of a state that fully accepts freedom. Since this implies a state governed by the rule of law, Jakobs implicitly accepts at this point that *Feindstrafrecht* is incompatible with a state governed by the rule of law. In his more recent publications, however, he gives up this position.
23 Albrecht 2005, 854. Translated by myself.
24 Albrecht 2005, 854.

the state itself.[25] It is this profound aspect of security that a state system must honour which Jakobs ignores in his concept if he reasons, on the basis of the right to security, that certain individuals, at the state's decision, forfeit their status and their rights against the state.

All of these objections carry additional weight because Jakobs does not provide any plausible reasoning for the conviction on which he bases his concept, namely that certain individuals, due to their attitude or behaviour, cease to be persons and thereby lose their rights against the state. He argues by drawing on a parallel between the validity of a norm and the validity of personality:[26] 'A norm is valid if it achieves what it seeks to achieve: to safeguard the expectation.'[27] If norms are to determine a society, Jakobs argues, the members of this society must be able to expect the other members to act within these norms. In other words, in order for a norm to be valid and to exert real influence, the members of this society must provide a certain cognitive guarantee that they will follow this norm. A norm which is not based on a certain cognitive fundament degrades to an 'empty promise'. In such a situation, citizens could not rely on other people acting according to the norm and would no longer model their lives as though they expect the norm to protect them. Hence, a norm requires this fundament in order to provide for a 'liveable' society. According to Jakobs, the validity of norms parallels the validity of personality. In order to be a person, one needs to be able to expect that he or she acts like a person. The individual must provide a certain cognitive guarantee that he or she models his or her life on right and wrong.

Jakobs's reasoning fails in two respects. First, his understanding of the validity of norms is not fully convincing. And secondly, the parallel that Jakobs draws between the validity of norms and the validity of personality is not plausible.

With regard to the first point, according to Jakobs, a norm that no longer provides orientation for the society is no longer a norm. Jakobs, in other words, regards the validity of a norm to depend primarily on the effect it has on the lives of the individuals protected by the norm.[28] This, however, is an unconvincing description of the validity, or the absence of validity, of norms. In order to illustrate

---

25 Jeremy Waldron (2003, 205–208) made this point very strongly in pointing out that diminution of civil liberties involves a security issue in that it increases power of the state prone to abuse.
26 Jakobs 2004, 90–92. See also Jakobs 1985, 775; Jakobs 2005, 841–843; Jakobs 2000, 51.
27 Jakobs 1985, 775.
28 Jakobs addresses this most clearly in Jakobs 1985, 775 f.

that a norm can only contribute to forming a society if its members can expect compliance with it, Jakobs refers to the example in which a person will not enter a public park voluntarily if he or she expects to be hurt, robbed or killed when entering this park, regardless of whether he or she is convinced that he or she has the right and ought to be able to enter the park. The example clearly demonstrates that individuals may change their behaviour if they cannot expect that other people will act according to a certain norm. The conclusion that the norm no longer determines the form of society because individuals avoid a public park, however, is exaggerated. Violence must spread much more widely – the necessary extent may not be determined on an abstract level – for the norm to fail to provide for a 'liveable' society. Moreover, the example demonstrates that the validity of norms may not merely be reduced to the influence the norm has on actual life, but that it depends on additional factors. A norm will have lost its validity if the majority of citizens no longer regard it as legally binding them in their behaviour. This, however, does not follow from the mere disregard on the part of some people for the norm. It seems to depend, for example, on how the state reacts to the violation of the norm. If it investigates a case and penalizes the norm violation, and by so doing restates the validity of the norm, the fact that the norm was violated and that individuals may be influenced by fear of further violations does not devalue it. This can be shown by considering a norm that is ignored on a day-to-day basis, the prohibition of theft. In a state where theft is a common crime, citizens protect themselves by securely locking their flats, by holding their handbags tightly on public transport, or by not walking on certain streets in certain areas. In other words, as evidenced by their behaviour, many people are not guaranteed to act according to the norm against theft. The state does prosecute the crimes but does not fully control it. Nevertheless, this does not mean that the norm forbidding theft has lost its validity.

Jakobs replies to this argument. He argues that the violation of a norm does not necessarily destroy its validity. If the violation of the norm is treated as such, the norm continues to be valid and provide orientation. How much violation a norm can withstand depends on the value of the good that it protects. The more important the good, the more secure it must be if the norm is to survive. It may then be that property, such as handbags or money, which some individuals regularly steal from others, are not important enough for the frequent violation of the norm to devalue it. Conversely, bodily integrity is. A slightly changed example can be offered in which the thefts not only involved the loss of money or similar goods, but also bodily harm. In this example, the police prosecute the crimes but are not able to fully control the situation, and affected individuals, for example, avoid certain streets. This, again, does not invalidate the norm. If the state, however, accepted these activities and did not investigate or prosecute, the validity under such circumstances may be seriously questioned. Hence, it may be maintained that the influence the norm has on people's lives alone – at least if it does not cross an extreme line – is not the factor decisive for the validity of a norm.

The explanation Jakobs provides for the preconditions of the validity of norms, questionable in several respects, does not provide a convincing basis for the argument that the status of personality depends on the cognitive guarantee an individual gives for it. Yet even if Jakobs's analysis of the validity of norms were accepted, it is not clear how this may lead to conclusions regarding personality and the possession of rights or the possibility of losing this status. The fact that legal norms may lose their validity does not allow for any conclusions regarding the validity of personality. Norms may lose their validity under certain circumstances, not only owing to given citizens' behaviour, but also because the abolition of legal norms is part of the normal development of a legal order. The loss of validity, however, is highly contentious with regard to personality. An explanation for the former, thus, does not explain the latter, even less so if it is not made clear why these two issues should equate in this respect, a notion which is not self-explanatory, but instead implausible at first sight.

To conclude, *Feindstrafrecht* as it is presented by Jakobs fails to provide a justifiable reply to terrorists. Several objections with regard to the concept of *Feindstrafrecht* as presented by Jakobs apply generally to the idea that individuals under certain circumstances fully and absolutely forfeit (some of) their rights against the state, including their right to life. It fundamentally contradicts the idea of human rights and the rule of law. Hence, the first response a rights-based approach to justifying targeted killings of terrorists might give must be rejected: the idea that individuals under certain circumstances forfeit absolutely their right to life cannot possibly justify targeted killings of terrorists. This is not to say that the idea of forfeiture has lost all of its power. Accepting that individuals have a right not to be killed, it intuitively remains appealing to argue that an individual may be killed in self- or other-defence because he or she does not have the right not to be killed, in this particular situation. Certainly, however, the radical version of forfeiture is not convincing.

10 Self-Defence: Limited forfeiture of the right to life

The predominant peacetime justifications of targeted killing of terrorists were not convincing. I will, therefore, turn finally to a justification of killing that is not typically applied for the purpose of justifying the practice of targeted killing of terrorists: self-defence (or other-defence).

This is plausible because self-defence (or other defence) is a morally widely unquestioned, as well as legally commonly institutionalised, justification for certain forms of killing and, as such, requires attention as a potential justification for targeted killing of terrorists. More importantly, it must be addressed because a plausible account of self-defence (or other-defence) will reveal principles explaining why and when killing is allowed in defence during peacetime, which apply to defensive targeted killing of terrorists, the form of the practice that has yet to be assessed. This will then provide a useful starting point for discussing and assessing the arguments for the justifiability of targeted killing of terrorists that were hitherto postponed, leading to a final assessment of the practice.

I will start from the preconditions to which self-defence is commonly bound. This will provide a foundation from which to discuss the applicability of the different preconditions to the practice of targeted killing of terrorists, and, if necessary, to question their validity. Therewith, an analysis of the moral reasoning behind the concept of self-defence (or other-defence) will be possible.

The paradigmatic situation of justified self-defence[1] is when one individual of sound mind (the aggressor) attacks another individual (the victim), and when

---

1 Some authors argue that self-defence comprises myriad defensive actions that are not all necessarily justified. Such a position may be based on two different assumptions. One may argue that the term 'self-defence' comprises all actions that resist or ward off a threat. This would not only comprise the victim's use of force, but also force used by the attacker to ward off his or her victim's justified response. Such an understanding forces one to distinguish between justified and unjustified self-defence (see Uniacke 1994, 172). I will interpret the term 'self-defence' as comprising justified defensive actions only. I am not sure whether the force the attacker uses in the example can be described as defensive action at all. If it was described as such, then one should distinguish justified defensive action from unjustified defensive action. Self-defence, however, in equivalent terms in other languages (e. g. in German *Notwehr)*, can be limited to defensive force which refers to the concept of justified self-defence. I will, therefore, in the following no longer speak of justified self-defence but of self-defence only. Conversely, one may argue that the concept of self-defence reveals which acts are just. Yet one may hold that not every just act is necessarily justified. According to this position, an act of self-defence could be unjustified despite not being unjust. Most importantly, this would be the case if, all things considered, it seems that

the victim attempts by force to avert this attack. Self-defence is, then, the justified use of force to avert the harming act. Under certain circumstances, self-defence allows warding off such harming act with *lethal force*. It is thereby commonly bound to three preconditions. In terms of the use of lethal force[2] in self-defence, these requirements are as follows. First, individuals may only use lethal force if the goods attacked are of such value that it is proportionate to kill in their defence (requirement of proportionality). Second, individuals may only kill in self-defence if they are not able to ward off the attack by means that have less harming effects (requirement of necessity). It is logically involved in this requirement, though not always explicitly recognized, that the force applied in self-defence must be capable of fending off the harming act. Finally, lethal force can only be justified in terms of self-defence if the threatened harming act is imminent or ongoing (requirement of imminence of the harming act).

In light of these requirements, the justification of defensive targeted killings of terrorists in self-defence faces three difficulties:
(1) Targeted killings of terrorists are carried out not by individuals who are threatened, but by states in order to fight terrorism on behalf of their citizens.
(2) Defensive targeted killings of terrorists are not necessarily directed against individuals who carry out terrorist attacks themselves. They can be directed against terrorists who are held to be involved in the planning or execution of determinable attacks, or against terrorists held to be involved in the planning or execution of undeterminable attacks.
(3) Defensive targeted killings of terrorists are carried out prior to attack. Moreover, they are not carried out in the face of a terrorist attack that is about to be carried out. Advocates of targeted killings of terrorists often highlight that they are directed against terrorists who are on their way to carry out attacks. I included these cases among targeted killings, but noted that they do not represent the majority of cases. Even so, if constituting a targeted killing,

---

better consequences would result from not carrying out an act in self-defence, even though this act, according to the concept of self-defence, constitutes a just act. An act could also be justified according to this position if it were unjust in light of the concept of self-defence, and yet, all things considered, it would result in better consequences than would come about if it were not carried out (see Uniacke 1994, e.g. at 182/211f.). The next chapter will explore whether consequences under certain circumstances can justify killing contrary to the findings of a right-based account. Given the general authority I ascribe to deontological right-based approaches, I will, for now, understand defensive killings carried out in self-defence, and only those, as being justified.

2 Given the focus of this book, I will focus on lethal self-defence, and hence largely forego discussing the role that self-defence plays with regard to the protection of other goods.

the killing in such situations takes place before the attack is about to be carried out.

Ad (1) The applicability of the concept of self-defence to defensive acts of state agents: The first difficulty is easily dismissed. It concerns *the subject* of the right of self-defence. Although self-defence refers first to private individuals who apply force to defend themselves, it can be applied to third parties, including state agents, defending the victim. This becomes clear in asking where defence rights come from. David Rodin, on whose account my understanding of self-defence is based in many aspects, provides a convincing explanation.[3] Following Joseph Raz,[4] he distinguishes between 'derivative rights' and 'core rights'. The former gain their normative force from the latter or from other 'normative features'. The latter have normative force independent of any prior rights. Defence rights are of the former kind. This is because acts carried out in self-defence, e.g. killing, are not intrinsically good, but in contexts other than self-defence, are condemnable and wrong. The relationship between the subject and the end of the right of self-defence is crucial for explaining the right. Three such relations can be determined. The first follows from the individual's right to the good that the defensive action protects. As rights to things in general, the right to this good entails a claim against other people not to violate it. With regard to the right to life this means that the individual possessing this right has a claim against other people that they not interfere with his or her bodily integrity and that they not take away his or her life; put differently, that they not attack these goods.[5] From that follows the individual's liberty right to defend his or her life and bodily integrity if other people interfere with it.

The right to defend a third person is not derivable from the victim's right to defend him- or herself.[6] Although one's right to life is a precondition for anyone else's right to defend it, additional considerations are necessary to explain why

---

[3] Rodin convincingly develops his account of self-defence in his book *War and Self-Defense* (2002), 17–99. For the following normative foundations of defence rights, see Rodin 2002, 36–39.

[4] Raz 1984, 197f.

[5] In the following I will refer to both the right to life and the right not to be attacked. As this relation shows, the latter is entailed in the former.

[6] The individual's right to defend him- or herself may in most, if not in all, cases coincide – Uniacke (1994, 179–181) is doubtful with regard to this point – yet this does not show that the defence rights of third parties derive from the right to defend the victim. As Rodin (2002, 32) rightly points out, it does not generally follow from the fact that an individual has the right to do something that others automatically do also have the right to carry out that action.

third parties may act in defence of the victim's life. The right of third parties to defend the victim can be based on two additional normative relations. Hence, the second normative foundation for defence rights may be derived from the duty to care, which some possess due to an 'established moral relationship'[7] between given individuals. For example, the relationship parents have with their children implies the parents' duty to care for their children and provides the liberty to defend their lives.

The third normative foundation for defence rights is the general duty to protect goods and individuals. These '"duties of rescue" arise from the fact that the end (being a particular good or value) is in danger, combined with the fact that one is situated so as to be able to assist'.[8] Provided an individual is able to help without having to sacrifice anything of comparable moral value, individuals have the right and duty to defend others with whom they have no established relationship, even those whom they may not have met previously.

Based on these normative foundations of defence rights, the right of states, and state agents, to defend their citizens and individuals who find themselves on their territory, then, follows from the morally relevant relationship they have with these citizens, or the duty to protect the good or valuable. A state's legitimacy is inevitably bound to the protection it provides for its citizens. Given that citizens in turn generally abstain from enforcing their claims and rights independent of state authority, this state's duty to protect carries particular weight. Hence, the fact that targeted killings are carried out by state agents to protect certain individuals, rather than by the victims themselves, does not constitute an obstacle to justifying this practice in terms to the concept of self-defence.

If it is not the victim who applies defensive force, but a third party who defends him or her, it no longer constitutes self-defence, but is more correctly called other-defence. That said, since both are concepts of defence rights, they correspond in their moral foundation. Given that self-defence constitutes the paradigmatic concept of defence rights and, therefore, allows recourse to strong intuitions and convictions, I will establish the moral foundation and scope of defence rights relevant to the issue under discussion with reference to the right of self-defence, which then equally apply to the right of other-defence.

Ad (2) The object of self-defence: The second question concerns the object of self-defence. In order to assess whether targeted killing may be justified as self-defence despite the different status of the individuals who are the objects of such practice, it must be explained why and under what conditions an individual be-

---

7 Rodin 2002, 38.
8 Rodin 2002, 38.

comes a legitimate object of self-defence. The antecedent discussion of conceivable and formulated approaches to justify targeted killings of terrorists has underscored several factors that a plausible distinction between justified and unjustified killings must take into account. Most importantly, it cannot consider consequences a distinguishing factor. Rather, the discussion suggested a justification of killing within the rubric of the rights of the aggressor, relating to his or her conduct. With the concept of *Feindstrafrecht*, I have addressed one possible right-based approach: the idea that individuals, due to their behaviour or convictions, forfeit their rights, including their right to life, and therefore may be attacked and, under certain circumstances, killed. I did not reject the idea of forfeiture as such, but concluded that the idea that certain rights, including the right to life, can be forfeited fully and absolutely is unacceptable. Therefore, to explain in terms of rights why an individual may be killed implies, on the one hand, that one regards the victim in a situation of self-defence as justified in defending him- or herself due to the *right of self-defence* he or she possesses. On the other hand, to account for the right of self-defence, one must start from the statement that everyone has rights, including the right to life. Thus, the fact that lethal force may be directed against the object of the right of self-defence, despite his or her generally possessing the right to life, must be accounted for. In addition, a plausible account of self-defence must account for the 'moral asymmetry' between the aggressor and the victim.[9] In other words, it must take into account first, that the victim has the right to defend him- or herself against the aggressor and second, that the aggressor, provided the defensive force is appropriate, may not respond to the defensive action with force.

The fact that the aggressor poses a threat to the victim is not sufficient alone to make sense of self-defence. If one were justified to act in self-defence whenever threatened, both the victim and the aggressor have the right of self-defence against the threat they face. In order to account for the moral asymmetry, it must be explained *why* the aggressor's behaviour gives the victim the right of self-defence and, under certain circumstances, allows him or her to deprive the aggressor of life, despite the aggressor's general right to life, while the victim's appropriate counter-force does not provide the aggressor with the right to defend him- or herself. The idea of limited[10] forfeiture of the right to life most plausibly fulfils these requirements. While both the aggressor and the attacked person generally possess the right to life, the aggressor, by his or her behaviour, forfeits this right

---

9 Rodin 2002, 50.
10 When, in the following, I speak of forfeiture, I speak of this limited forfeiture, which, as will become clear, strictly differs from the idea of full and absolute forfeiture as envisioned by the concept of *Feindstrafrecht*.

– or, expressed differently, the right not to be attacked in this particular situation. He or she forfeits the right not be attacked in this context of the particular relationship between him or her and the victim, the particular time, space and circumstances.

In more detail, and in terms of justified killing in self-defence, this general idea prevails: everyone has a right to life, or, expressed differently, a right not to have his or her life attacked. If an aggressor carries out an attack on someone's life, he or she violates the victim's right and hence wrongs him or her. Due to violating conduct, the aggressor loses his or her own right not to be attacked in relation to the situation he or she has created. If the victim – or any third person – defends him- or herself against the aggressor by appropriate lethal force, he or she does not violate the aggressor's right not to be attacked. The victim does not wrong the aggressor and therefore does not forfeit his or her own right not to be attacked.

This explanation describes the general structure convincingly explaining the right of self-defence. Different right-based accounts of self-defence share this basic understanding.[11] The idea of forfeiture can thereby equally be expressed by the idea that the right to life is conditional upon conduct, and hence individuals, who all posses this right as human beings, no longer have it under certain circumstances.[12] This, however, is a different formulation rather than a different theoretical concept. In both cases, the attacker, as a result of his or her conduct, does not possess the right to life in the relevant situation. This also applies in a third manner in which the formulated idea can be expressed, one in terms of the scope of the right to life.[13] One could argue that the right to life does not protect against appropriate reactions in response to a violation of another's right to life in the first place. To avoid circularity and still give such an account, however, one must provide an explanation as to the limits on the protection given by the right to life, and this reintroduces the relationship between the attacker and the victim.[14]

---

11 David Rodin spelled out this reasoning very clearly in Rodin 2002, 70–99. Judith Jarvis Thomson (1991), though not focusing on forfeiture but on the possession of the right to not be attacked, has also explained self-defence with this general structure.

12 Uniacke 1994, 194–201. She recognizes the idea of forfeiture, yet prefers to express it in terms of a conditional right to life.

13 This is what is applied in legal formulations of the right to life. See chapter 3.

14 See also Uniacke 1994, 211f. The circularity is evident if one argues that one is allowed to kill in self-defence since the right to life is limited in scope in a manner that it allows self-defence. Critique by Thomson 1986a.

This explanation corresponds to the suggestion formulated in discussing consequentialism: that an individual who acts in self-defence has the right to do so, while the aggressor does not posses the right not to be attacked. Moreover, it accounts for further suggestions that the discussion has hitherto revealed. It explains the right to kill in reference to the behaviour of the individual to be targeted. Finally, it gives justice to the argument that rights cannot be forfeited absolutely. Given the relationship between the aggressor and the victim, the aggressor does not forfeit his or her right to life in general. The forfeiture depends on the particular relationship between the aggressor and the victim. The aggressor forfeits his or her right only due to the threatening harming act with which he or she confronts the victim, and he or she does so only with regard to the protection of the victim. Hence, the forfeiture is dependent on the specific situation. The aggressor may not be killed for any reason other than the protection of the victim, and only for the time this protection requires his or her killing.[15]

One point, however, needs to be examined more closely. The victim logically need not wait until the harming act is carried out. He or she may use force prior to the actual damaging act. Accounting for that fact in terms of forfeiture, one must argue that the aggressor forfeits his or her right to life prior to the actual lethal act of force. Upon first glance, this seems to be explicable by the meaning of 'harming act'. The violation of the right to life, one may argue, starts with the threat prior to the application of lethal force. Hence, when the aggressor threatens to kill the victim, he or she violates the victim's right to life and forfeits his or her own right not to be attacked. The forfeiture of the right to life, however, cannot clearly be linked to the threat prior to the accomplishment of the harming act.

Consider the following hypothetical circumstance: an aggressor *will*, unless thwarted, kill an individual in one week's time; the aggressor can only be thwarted by pre-emptive lethal force; and the aggressor will not be thwarted unless lethal force is applied immediately. Given indisputable knowledge of these aspects of the situation, I hold that killing the aggressor is justified because if not stopped, he or she *will* kill the victim and hence violate the victim's right to life. As such, the fact that the aggressor, if not stopped, *will* violate the right to life of his or her victim seems decisive for the forfeiture of the right to life, and therefore for the determination of the object of the right of self-defence.[16] This is a necessary, yet not necessarily sufficient, condition for forfeiture of the right to life.

---

15 Rodin 2002, 73 f.

16 See Thomson 1991, 308. She argues that you, as victim, may kill other individuals because 'they will otherwise violate your right that they not kill you'.

Two points must be addressed to finalize the concept in order for it to apply to targeted killings of terrorists. First, as will be shown, the requirements of proportionality, necessity, and imminence of the harming act, requirements not derived from the relationship between the aggressor and the victim, influence the description of the scope of forfeiture, and this influences the description of the moment in which an individual is an object of the right of self-defence as well as the circumstances under which this occurs. These requirements add additional limits to forfeiture, yet they do not question the idea presented at this point. They will, hence, not justify self-defence extending beyond the limits on targeted killings that follow from the hitherto formulated reasoning.

Secondly, different positions are possible with regard to the question of the requirements for rights violations as well as the question of whether violation alone is sufficient to forfeit one's rights. On one hand, the position depends on whether the violation of rights is held to require fault, or at least agency. On the other hand, some accounts, though they may argue that the violation of rights is possible without fault, require the aggressor to be at fault in order to lose the right not to be attacked.[17] The position held on these issues affects any assessment of the justifiability of defensive action against what is widely known as an innocent aggressor. This is an individual who actively threatens another individual, but who cannot be held morally responsible for his or her behaviour. It also affects an assessment of the justifiability of defensive force against an innocent threat, someone who without fault constitutes a threat.[18] Both issues that are at stake therefore concern details of the account of self-defence which are relevant for a comprehensive understanding of self-defence. However, the position one holds on these issues does not force one to question the concept as such. Whether it is asserted or denied that fault and/or agency are required for forfeiture of rights, it remains true that only those who would violate the other person's right not to be attacked may justifiably be attacked in re-

---

17 Thomson (1991) and Uniacke (1994, 175 f.) are in favour of the justifiability of self-defence in both cases. They hold neither fault nor agency necessary for violation of rights and for forfeiture. Rodin (2002, 77 – 99) requires fault, and hence rejects justifiability of self-defence against both innocent aggressors and innocent threats. He pictures the relationship between aggressor and victim by saying that 'at the critical moment, the aggressor's *fault* for the aggressive action puts him at a moral disadvantage in respect to the victim and the victim's innocence allows him to reap the advantage'. Rodin 2002, 78, emphasis added. Although he requires fault, he applies an understanding of fault that differs from the way the term is most commonly understood, e. g. in criminal law systems. In Rodin's terms, mentally ill individuals, for example, could legitimately be attacked in self-defence. For details, see Rodin 2002, 88 – 99.
18 The term was first introduced by Robert Nozick (1974, 34 f.).

sponse. The question of fault may, therefore, be left open. There seems to be no reason to regard the violation of rights to depend on fault of the aggressor. Moreover, there seem to be good reasons to reject the notion that fault is required for forfeiture, at least if the term is understood in its strong and most common sense, as lacking the ability either to form a moral position or to act according to it. However, even if fault were required in this sense, it would not affect the assessment of targeted killings of terrorists. Although the question of whether terrorists may be objects of self-defence, no matter what role they play in organizing, planning or carrying out terrorist attacks, remains to be discussed, they cannot possibly be fully excused for their behaviour. They do not happen to pose a threat, but rather intentionally apply force as part of their terrorist strategy. Moreover, they generally do not act under circumstances which diminish their individual responsibility or fully excuse them. Terrorists do not act in the heat of a moment, but choose to be involved in terrorist activity. They may be fanatic, but they are not generally mentally ill in a way that fully absolves them of moral responsibility for their deeds.

Neither does the question of whether agency is required for possible violation of rights affect the assessment of defensive targeted killings of terrorists. This is because terrorists are killed for actively engaging in terrorist activity. In certain interpretations, however, it may affect the assessment of whether the killing of innocent bystanders can be justified.[19] Innocent bystanders are individuals who would be harmed in the course of warding off the attack though they are not actively involved in it. Given the fact that targeted killings often involve the killing of innocent bystanders, the question of whether agency is required for violation of rights hence calls for attention. The term 'forfeiture' itself does not seem to demand active agency on the part of the individual who forfeits his or her rights. Although it would be at the expense of expressing the connection between characteristics of the individual and his or her loss of life, forfeiture of the right not to be attacked could be replaced by other terms, such as loss of the

---

19 This would be the case if one argued that innocent bystanders endanger others because they, by virtue of their very existence, exposed others to attack: e.g. if a bystander's presence prevents one from running away and hence evading the attack, or if one could defend oneself by simultaneously causing harm to innocent bystanders, it is not inconceivable to describe innocent bystanders as causal for the danger to which one is exposed. Such situations differ from situations which I described as innocent threats. As Rodin rightly points out, the former is an 'indirect cause' while the later is a 'direct cause'. Given, however, that none of them actively endangers the victim, there also is crucial similarity between them. This is that they are both causal for the situation to be endangering. Some people may hold this to call the moral impact the difference has into question. Rodin 2002, 82. See also Uniacke 1994, 164/167–171.

right not to be attacked. The argument that the violation of rights requires agency, however, is compelling. Just as it does not make sense to think that an object such as a stone could violate someone's rights, it similarly makes no sense to regard someone who merely as an object threatens an individual as violating this individual's rights.[20]

What does this account of the object of self-defence mean for the justifiability of targeted killings of terrorists who are involved in terrorism in various manners? I anticipated that the requirements of proportionality, necessity, and imminence do have impact on who may be described as having forfeited the right to life. Hence, from what has been argued thus far, it does not follow that these individuals may be attacked. Yet the analysis allows some conclusions as to possible objects of attack. Given that only those who will violate someone else's right not to be attacked can become the object to the right of self-defence, only those individuals who do something that can possibly fulfil this requirement can become the object. This is clear for terrorists who carry out attacks themselves. Planning and organizing, or even leading a terrorist organization, cannot as actions be described as violating someone's right to life; as such, individuals ordering, planning, and organizing terrorist attacks can only become the object to the right of self-defence if their conduct makes these attacks ascribable to them. This seems to be the case with regard to terrorist leaders who order an attack, and who can call it off at any time. By doing so, they hold responsibility for the attack, and thus the attack may be ascribed to them. With regard to any other role, the situation is less clear. Other terrorists participate in the attack, but whether they can be described as aiders and abettors, or as perpetrators, depends on the theory held regarding the accountability of acts. Most plausibly the deed and hence the violation of the victims' right to life may only be ascribed to them if they are able to control the execution of the attack. If they cannot, they may be held responsible for morally wrong conduct, and yet, it seems, not for the violation of the victim's right to life, which is caused by the harming act. Such reasoning corresponds to theories of accountability that distinguish perpetrators from aiders and abettors, and that refers to the control over the act. Other theories recognize only perpetrators, and hence argue that everyone who sufficiently adds to the execution of the final harming act is a perpetrator. As addressed above, such theories may be acceptable in the context of punishment,

---

20 For this argument, though with a slightly different focus, see Rodin 2002, 85–87. Rodin argues that one only has a moral duty to abstain from violating others' rights in one's capacity as moral subject. Anyone who is not acting voluntarily merely resembles an object which cannot violate someone's rights and hence who cannot forfeit their own right not to be attacked. For an opposing opinion, see Uniacke 1994, 162–166/175 and Thomson 1991.

since one can still take into account the degree of involvement when deciding in what manner a certain perpetrator should be punished. Yet these theories do not seem to be acceptable regarding any situation allowing for only one form of reaction, namely killing.[21]

Given that the requirements of necessity, imminence, and proportionality will have impact on when individuals forfeit their right not to be attacked, I may stop at this point and turn to a second important corollary of the account as it has been presented up to this point. It does not concern the killing of the individual terrorist, but the justifiability of those targeted killings that harm innocent bystanders. The explanation given hitherto explains why any harm caused to innocent bystanders, or more generally to third parties, violates their right to life. They have not done anything, and thus they have not forfeited their right to life and any harm done to them is unjust, regardless of whether the harm is carried out intentionally or not. With regard to targeted killings of terrorists, this shows not only that targeted killings of terrorists that cause harm to third parties may be described as unjust, but also explains why. This applies even if the possibility of violations of a right is regarded as depending on the fault of the attacker. I can only think of one situation in which state agents could be excused for harming innocent individuals in the course of targeted killings of terrorists. In this example, those targeting the terrorist could not have known that targeting terrorists would violate other innocent individuals' rights, despite thorough investigation and care. This, however, is not what characterizes targeted killings of terrorists that harm innocent bystanders. Despite this harm being the result of negligence, perhaps, rather than calculation, the examples in chapter 2 have shown that the cases under discussion did not carefully avoid any involvement of innocent bystanders.

Ad (3) The requirement of imminence of the harming act: The third problem faced when seeking to justify targeted killings in terms of self-defence results from the requirement of imminence of the harming act.[22] According to this requirement, defensive use of force can only be justified as self-defence if it is applied in view of an imminent or ongoing harming act. It is questionable whether targeted killings of terrorists can meet this requirement. Targeted killings, by def-

---

21 See also chapter 4.3.2.

22 The position I took on the question of whether agency is required for the possibility of rights violation makes sense of the fact that I refer to an imminent harming act rather than to an imminent threat. Imminent threats comprise imminent acts. Even if 'act' is understood in very broad terms, it excludes situations from the scope of self-defence in which an individual becomes a threat due to something that happens to him or her rather than due to something he or she does in a wide sense of the word.

inition, are not triggered by, or carried out in response to, the (sudden) occurrence of a present harming act. Neither are targeted killings carried out after the harming act has begun. Most commonly, they are applied in response to an undeterminable abstract harming act for which the targeted individual is held to be responsible due to his or her involvement in terrorism. Less frequently, yet conceivably, targeted killings are carried out with a view to prevent a determinable harming act. This may involve the killing of terrorists held to be on their way to carry out an attack. More generally, it may involve the killing of terrorists held to be involved in the planning and organizing of a specific terrorist attack, though prior to the moment in which the attack could be said to be about to be carried out. In light of these characteristics, targeted killings can only be justified as self-defence if imminence may be understood in a way that is compatible with the practice of targeted killing, or at least with some cases of it. The practice could also be justified as self-defence if the requirement of imminence were abandoned altogether and the argument made that preventive self-defence can be justified.

Four interpretations of the requirement of imminence are conceivable if one seeks to understand it in a way that is compatible with targeted killing of terrorists. They differ regarding the scope of the justification they offer, both as to who may be targeted and the time period prior to the physically damaging event during which individuals may be targeted. This said, what specific cases of killings these interpretations would justify is of secondary importance; it first must be discussed whether the interpretations are convincing in the reading they provide of the requirement of imminence of the harming act.

The first manner in which the requirement may be interpreted draws on the fact that self-defence may be invoked while an attack is ongoing. This interpretation does not require extensive discussion. It may be argued that certain terrorist groups are so frequently involved in terrorist attacks that the entirety of their activity can be described as an ongoing attack. This, one may conclude, ascribes the ongoing harming acts to all terrorists involved in the organization, and hence forces them to forfeit their right to life. Even if this does not apply to the entire organization, one may argue, it does apply to terrorist leaders who frequently instigate terrorist attacks. Much could be said about the collective aspect of the argument. Even if this argument were applied only to terrorist organizations or small units, in order to work for all members of a certain group, it requires a defence of such a crude form of collective responsibility, that it may be rejected on this basis alone. The interpretation, however, also fails to be convincing if applied to terrorist leaders only, for it fails to give justice to the fact that attacks are necessarily limited to specific aggressor-victim constellations. I established that the aggressor forfeits his or her right not to be attacked only under the specific preconditions of the situation, and even then, only in his or her relationship with the victim. This makes it impossible to combine individual actions into one ongoing attack that continuously invokes the right of self-defence.

The three remaining interpretations of the requirement of imminence as being compatible with targeted killing of terrorists are initially more conceivable. The second interpretation of the requirement highlights the continuous danger that emanates from individual terrorists. One may argue that certain terrorists, once they are determined to act at the appropriate moment, pose a constant abstract danger that at some point *will* transform into an actual harming act: this transformation will necessarily take place, since terrorism often comprises fanaticism and vigorous determination. The timing of the transformation cannot be determined; it could be at any time. From this perspective, any moment is imminently prior to a harming act. Imminence is disconnected from the accomplishment of an actual concrete nameable harming act, or at least from a moment in which the attack will take place. But it refers to a real, though not yet (in terms of exact time) determinable, attack. The entire period, from the determination to act or to carry out a specific act to the actual accomplishment of the act, constitutes a situation of imminence.[23]

A third means of understanding targeted killing as a reaction to imminent terrorist harming acts is to focus on the term 'harming act'. One could argue that the terrorist harming act begins long before the final act of destruction is carried out. This argument draws on Dinstein's argument about the possible extension of armed attacks to situations prior to what most authors hold to be the beginning of such attacks.[24] Certain networks or organizations, one may argue, are organized in such a way that, once the planning of a terrorist action has started seriously, it can be guaranteed that the attempt to inflict harm will follow. Like clockwork, one cog moves the next, and together, they produce the result. One may add that fanaticism nurtured by ideology and, possibly even more powerfully, by religious convictions, enforces this course of action and creates watertight commitment. In whatever terrorist organization this fanaticism is generated, the harming act may be regarded as beginning once a given enterprise is initiated since this will necessarily lead to the accomplishment of the harming act.

Neither the second nor the third interpretation can be dismissed straightforwardly as unrealistically describing any form of terrorism. In the second interpre-

---

23 Either Meisels (2004, 310f.) abandons the requirement of imminence when she takes the position that self-defence can be invoked for killing someone who 'is more than likely to instigate or command an attack in the near future', or the statement has to be read as interpreting the requirement along the lines presented.
24 See chapter 5.3.

tation, for example, a suicide bomber equipped with an explosive device and theoretically ready to carry out a terrorist attack poses a constant threat that can immediately become a concrete act of harm, as is the case with all terrorist attacks that are prepared and are waiting to be carried out. The fanaticism often involved in terrorism may thereby deprive certain individuals of space for deliberation, doubts, reconsideration, and reversal of course. In the third interpretation, it is arguable that this fanaticism and determination may, under certain circumstances, control individuals to such an extent that they would not reconsider their role in a given terrorist act. Hence, neither interpretation of the requirement of imminence of attack is *per se* indefensible. Nevertheless, both must be ruled out as applicable interpretations, since neither gives justice to the functions on which the existence of the requirement of imminence is based in the first instance. To show this, I must return to the concept of self-defence. The moral grounding of the requirement that a harming attack be imminent, commonly accepted as crucial to determining an act of self-defence, necessitates a specific interpretation which, by definition, rejects other conclusions.

As with the requirement of proportionality and necessity, the requirement of imminence of the harming act sets limits on defensive action. All three requirements are based on the normative relation between the good that the defensive action seeks to preserve and the content of the defensive action.[25] In contrast to proportionality and necessity, imminence of the harming act, however, cannot be directly derived from this relationship. It follows from the requirement of necessity, as it is instrumental to its fulfilment.[26] The requirement of imminence of the harming act also serves an additional instrumental purpose. This is to sufficiently determine that the individual attacked in self-defence indeed is an object to the right of self-defence, i.e. that he or she may be attacked in terms of the right of self-defence.

Given their relationship, it is necessary to briefly establish the reason for the requirement of necessity in order to explain the first part of the justification of the requirement of imminence. As Rodin clearly pointed out, the justification for such a requirement rests in the fact that the life and bodily integrity of the aggressor do not lose their value through the harming act. Any defensive action carried out to preserve a given good *ipso facto* also harms a certain good. The defended good and the good affected by defensive action, then, form the normative relation that entails requirements necessary for a defensive action to be morally acceptable. In view of the continuing value of the good affected by the de-

---

25 Rodin 2002, 40.
26 Rodin 2002, 41.

fensive action, the protection of the defended good sets the ultimate limit on defensive force. In addition, the protection of the defended good may not be achieved by violating goods disproportionate to the defended good (requirement of proportionality). As Rodin puts it, proportionality 'requires us to balance the harmful effects of the defensive action against the good to be achieved'.[27] Finally, if it is accepted that the good affected by the defensive action remains valuable and that it is worth protecting as much as possible, the defending act may only cause such harm as is required to protect the defended good. In short, in reaching the required outcome against an aggressor, the requirement is to use the least destructive defensive action.[28]

With regard to the killing of individuals, this means that lethal force is justified in self-defence only if killing is the least destructive measure available. This requirement involves a rather self-evident but often unmentioned addendum: to be necessary, a defensive act must be capable of warding off an attack. Any act incapable of fulfilling this purpose fails to reach the requirement of necessity, regardless of what other means are available.

---

27 Rodin 2002, 41. Proportionality does not only allow for killing if the aggressor's act is life threatening. Other serious attacks, such as rape or serious bodily harm, justify the killing of the aggressor. In other circumstances, such as theft of minor property, the requirement of proportionality clearly prohibits killing. How serious an attack must be to justify the killing of the aggressor depends on one's understanding of proportionality, from which several disputes may arise. This, however, does not negate the requirement itself as entailed in a proper interpretation of the right of self-defence. Not all legal orders recognize the requirement of proportionality. For example, the German legal order, according to prevailing legal opinion, does not recognize proportionality as limiting use of force in self-defence. This seems to be a political legal rather than a moral consideration (Roxin 2006, mns. 47f., pp. 679f.); it is only to a certain extent a question of content. Defensive attacks on the life of an aggressor are unjustified if the attack is minor, owing to the requirement of *Gebotenheit* (acceptability), which states that defensive actions are justified only if they do not cross certain 'social ethical limitations'. (For details, see Roxin 2006, mns. 55–60, pp. 683–685, particularly mns. 73–82, pp. 586–590). With regard to certain individuals, e. g. police forces, the German legal order knows the requirement of proportionality. Federal state laws regulating the use of lethal force by the police allow the application of firearms in a way that could kill the attacker only if the attacker threatens to kill or severely harm. In any case, a lethal act of self-defence clearly requires limitations via the value of the protected good. It affects life, regardless of the circumstances, which is one of the highest goods. Although the aggressor's behaviour provides the precondition to justify his or her killing under certain circumstances, that he or she may actually be killed necessarily depends on the relationship between the good preserved by an act of self-defence and the good harmed by that act.
28 For the presented explanation of the requirements of proportionality and necessity, see Rodin 2002, 40–43.

At this point, the requirement of imminence of the harming act gains importance. Only imminence determines whether or not lethal force is the least harmful means of defence available. As such, it is only at this moment that it is sufficiently clear that the aggressor may be killed in self-defence. If a victim, or an individual defending him or her, were a clairvoyant and knew that an attack could not be prevented except by killing the aggressor before he or she starts carrying out the attack, the requirement of imminence could be dissolved. The requirement of necessity would be fulfilled, and the time period between the act of self-defence and the act of attack would not render the defensive action morally wrong.

Nevertheless, changes may arise due to human involvement. Even the most determined human beings may change their minds. External factors may also influence developments. The harming act may be called off or, due to external factors, become impossible. In all such situations, defence is not necessary. The harming act may also be postponed, creating space for unexpected developments that may render the act preventable by means other than lethal force. As a result, in the absence of clairvoyance, without the requirement of imminence of the harming act, the certainty necessary to justify lethal force is lacking.[29]

This is one function which the requirement of imminence of the harming act fulfils. The requirement has an additional function, which independently explains why it is required for self-defence. I argued that only those who, if not stopped, *will* violate someone else's right not to be attacked are objects of self-defence. Now, in the absence of clairvoyance, until the harming act is about to be carried out, there is not sufficient certainty that the harming act will take place, and hence, it is impossible to determine with sufficient certainty if the individual who would be attacked actually is an appropriate object to the right of self-defence. This applies in two respects. If defensive force is applied prior to the attack being about to be carried out, there is a risk of harming someone who never intended to commit a harmful act. This may occur due to bad intelligence, or because the agents carrying out the defensive act mistake someone for an aggressor.[30] Moreover, if defensive force is applied to someone who had planned to harm others before the harming act is imminent, there is a similar risk of targeting someone who is not an object to the right of self-defence. It is not planning a harmful act that makes an individual liable to attack, but the

---

29 Rodin 2002, 41.
30 This is what happened to the Moroccan waiter Achmed Bouchiki during the campaign of targeted killings that Israel carried out in the wake of the Munich attacks of 1972. See chapter 2.1.

fact that he or she *will* violate one's right not to be attacked. What makes imminence of the harming act such a vital precondition for justified use of force in self-defence, then, is that it provides the required certainty that the right person is targeted. Therefore, what I stated in respect to the first function of the requirement of imminence applies equally in respect to its second function. If it were possible to determine at a certain point prior to the execution of a harming act that the act *will* take place, then the requirement would become less important, or would even lose its relevance altogether. Such a determination, however, is virtually impossible to make.

To conclude, the requirement of imminence of the harming act gains its importance from the two functions it fulfils: providing the required certainty that an attack cannot be prevented by means less harmful than killing; and providing the required certainty that the individual to be attacked is an object to the right of self-defence. These functions are required by the value of the good affected by the act of self-defence and by the right to life, which protects anyone from attack who has not forfeited this right.

Before analysing the interpretations offered for describing targeted killing of terrorists as meeting the requirement of imminence, the idea of forfeiture can be further specified. The requirements of proportionality and necessity detail the formulation gleaned from considerations of the normative relations between aggressor and victim. The aggressor does not forfeit his or her right not to be attacked, but rather his or her right not to be attacked *in a proportional and necessary way.*

Moreover, a substantial limitation of the cases of targeted killing that can possibly be justified in self-defence follows from the provided reasoning. The fact that the good at stake in a defensive action remains valuable and worthy of protection, as well as the requirements of proportionality and necessity following from it, explain why self-defence can only be applied in the context of a determinable harming act. In the case of undeterminable attacks, these requirements simply do not make sense. For the remaining discussion, those cases of targeted killing carried out in reaction to an undeterminable future attack may then be excluded. In the case of targeted killing of terrorists, this limits any possible justification to those cases carried out in view of a determinable harming act.

In light of the functions of the requirement of imminence, it is now also clear why both the second and the third attempt I made to describe targeted killing as fulfilling the requirement fail. Although it seems arguable that the described situations can occur, they are not common to all terrorist attacks. Actual situations are often quite the reverse: changes occur as soon as human behaviour is involved. While certain forms of fanaticism may regularly create a relatively strong determination to stick to a plan, individuals are not immune to other influences. Changes in conviction may be triggered by diverse and contingent factors. Similarly, external factors may influence or foil plans. As such, certain terrorist attacks, once planned or prepared, will be carried out with certainty, but this does not apply to all terrorist attacks. Given that these cases cannot easily be distinguished, 'imminence' may only be understood as describing the moment just prior to the accomplishment of the harming act. For the same reasons, the term 'harming act' cannot be stretched in the manner suggested by the second interpretation. To conclude, force applied in the described situations cannot be justified in terms of self-defence. Killing the potential aggressor in these situations must be regarded as violating his or her right to life.

There is a fourth arguable interpretation of certain targeted killings of terrorists as compatible with the requirement of imminence. It differs from the previous interpretations as it does not provide an extended understanding of the requirement. It draws on the meaning of imminence, as heretofore established, and questions the initial assessment that targeted killing in general does not correspond to this understanding.

One could argue that certain terrorists, due to the role they play in terrorist organizations, are continuously involved in harming acts. This primarily applies to terrorist leaders, who ideologically or organizationally lead a terrorist group, organization or network. Their leading role, one may argue, makes them responsible for all terrorist attacks carried out from within 'their' organization. They formulate the overall aims and strategy of the terrorist organization. They motivate individuals to carry out terrorist attacks. They order the execution of terrorist acts. Seen in this manner, all terrorist activity is a function of its leadership. Leaders continuously engage in terrorist attacks. If they are not involved in a current terrorist attack, they are constantly involved in an imminent one. As a result, they continuously create situations through their deeds that justify the use of force in self-defence.[31]

Under certain circumstances, such an argument seems powerful. In extreme situations, this description seems to justify the killing of certain individuals as self-defence. For example, once the systematic killing of innocent people began during the regime of terror in Hitler's Germany, the killing of leaders, cer-

---

31 Gad Barzitai is quoted with a position which can be read as somehow following this line. He is quoted as stating that self-defence can be invoked even if the attack is not about to be carried out, as in the case of a terrorist leader who continuously instigates terrorist attacks. To some extent, it also fits interpretation one above. Barzitai, Islands of Silence, Democracies Kill?, presented at Annual Meeting of the Law and Society Association, Budapest 2000, 6, referred to in Meisels 2004, 310 fn 42.

tainly of Hitler himself, seems justified. Germany had created a system of such enormous and systematic destruction that any moment could be described as a lethal attack on innocent individuals, or alternatively, as the moment immediately prior to such an attack. Hitler, without doubt, can be held responsible for this destruction. Moreover, from a given point in time, the situation left no doubt that no other means besides the killing of Hitler were available to stop the machinery of destruction.

The differences between the terror regime in Hitler's Germany and terrorist activities as contemporary states encounter them are evident: the extent, continuity, and system of destruction, which render every moment a situation of attack or of imminent attack; the certainty with which responsibility can be ascribed; and the certainty with which one can determine that no means other than killing will prevent the next attack. Therefore, though it may apply to some extreme situations, this fourth interpretation also fails to give justice to the role of the requirement of imminence. I may thus conclude that the strategy of justifying targeted killing of terrorists as self-defence, by way of interpreting the requirement of imminence of the harming act in a way compatible with this practice, fails.

The explanation for the requirement of imminence does provide strong reason to believe that the second possible means of facing the difficulty of justifying targeted killing in terms of self-defence, namely to give up the requirement of imminence of the harming act, equally fails. If the functions the requirement fulfils explain why imminence has to be understood in a certain way, one equally cannot dispense with it. However, this, some may argue, is drawing a conclusion too quickly. First, it may be right that the term, due to the general functions it must fulfil, must be interpreted in the described way. But under certain circumstances, one does not require imminence of the harming act for these functions to be fulfilled. The requirement may then be abandoned for these circumstances. Secondly, one could point out that the requirement of imminence still leaves a degree of uncertainty. This uncertainty, one may add, is paralleled in the context of targeted killing. Given that uncertainties are accepted in the context of self-defence, they must also be accepted with respect to targeted killings of terrorists.

I can think of only one potential situation which, in the absence of imminence, could, at first sight, be regarded as providing a sufficient degree of certainty regarding both an aggressor's forfeiture of the right to life and the conclusion that he or she cannot be stopped by any means short of killing: the widely discussed case of terrorists hijacking an airplane and intending to crash it in a populated area for a maximum of casualties.[32] As opposed to the details of the case as it is usually discussed, in this example there are no passengers on board. What distinguishes this situation from others of a similarly threatening nature taking place on the ground is that any attempt to stop the terrorists by means other than persuasion will necessarily lead to their deaths.

If one requires the degree of certainty provided by imminence of the harming act, the fact that terrorists have hijacked an airplane *en route* to harming others seems insufficient for justifying targeting the terrorists in terms of self-defence, as the plan is being enacted, but the harming act is not yet imminent. (Imminence, in this case, would be reached when the plane is close to reaching the populated area.) These facts do not suffice to establish that the persons in the plane seek to inflict harm; furthermore, even given such a plan, it may be possible to persuade them to abstain from carrying it out.

Nevertheless, one may argue that the situation allows the government to establish the required degree of certainty prior to the act being imminent. State agents could communicate with the individuals flying the aircraft in order to clarify their plans, as well as warn them that they will target the aircraft if the plan is not aborted. In this way, one may argue, state agents establish the required degree of certainty as to the development of the situation. Provided the individuals on board are not persuaded, despite sufficient communication and warnings, there is a point at which it is certain enough that there is no way to prevent the harming act but to target the aircraft. At this point, the airplane may be attacked.

This seems convincing. Nevertheless, it does not necessarily question the requirement of imminence. As long as state agents see potential in waiting and continuing with persuasion, this course is required. And in such a situation, this course of action is possible until the harming act can be described as imminent. In other words, regardless of what communication takes place, the explanation behind the requirement of necessity demands that the aircraft is not targeted hours before it reaches its populous destination. If the aircraft is sufficiently

---

32 The issue was widely discussed in Germany when the government issued an Aviation Security Act (*Gesetz zur Regelung von Luftsicherheitsaufgaben*) (LuftSiG) of 11 January 2005), which, under certain circumstances, allowed the air force to shoot down a hijacked airplane. The Federal Constitutional Court (Federal Constitutional Court, *H. et al. v. §14 para. 3 Aviation Security Act,* (Judgment)) ruled that the law violated the constitution because the killing of the innocent passengers on board could not be justified. The number of individuals that would be killed or seriously harmed if the airplane hit the area is irrelevant for my argument. If the situations allowed for killing in self-defence, the terrorists were justified targets, even if only one person would be seriously harmed or killed by their harming act.

close to the populated area, targeting it can possibly be justified; then, however, the harming act simultaneously is imminent – and as such targeting the aircraft can no longer be regarded as targeted killing.

The second and final argument for the justifiability of preventive self-defence remains. One could highlight that the imminence of the harming act does not provide absolute certainty regarding the fulfilment of necessity or regarding the fact that the individual actually forfeited his or her rights. Despite this uncertainty, the victim is regarded as justified in reacting, and, under certain conditions, even killing his or her opponent. Targeted killings of terrorists may equally involve some degree of uncertainty. One may argue, however, that this uncertainty must be accepted, just as a degree of uncertainty is generally accepted in self-defence. This argument requires more detailed discussion.

I introduced the requirement of imminence as a means to establish as much certainty as possible in a given situation. Nevertheless, even in situations when the harming act is imminent, a degree of uncertainty is accepted in several criteria. An individual at gunpoint is justified in acting defensively, even though the presence of the gun does not impart absolute certainty that the aggressor will actually pull the trigger. Self-defence is justified despite a lack of clarity regarding whether the individual will actually violate his or her victim's right to life, and hence whether he or she has actually forfeited his or her right not to be attacked. One can even take it one step further: if the aggressor points a toy gun at his or her victim which looks sufficiently like a real weapon, and threatens to kill him or her, one would regard the victim's defensive action as justified. Similarly, the application of lethal force is justified despite not knowing whether the use of force applied in defence is truly necessary. It may be the case that an aimed gun's machinery fails, or that the aggressor dies of a hard attack before he or she is able to shoot; or, indeed that it would be sufficient to shoot the aggressor in his or her leg to ward off the attack. Conversely, the aggressor may carry out his or her attack despite the application of lethal force. In all of these cases, lethal force would not have been necessary. Nevertheless, the victim remains justified in applying defensive force in these situations. If it transpires that the aggressor did not seek to kill the victim, or that the applied force was otherwise unnecessary, the defensive action is similarly regarded as justified, provided any reasonable individual would understand the situation at the time of defence as requiring such use of force.

The *prima facie* easiest way to reconcile these observations with the presented concept of self-defence would be to argue that the right to life embraces not only the right not to be killed but also the right of not having one's life threatened, regardless of whether a harming act follows or not. Both the attack on someone's life and the violation of his or her right to life, one could hold, begin with the moment of concrete threat. As such, the moment at which the aggressor points his or her gun at the victim violates the victim's right to life, and the aggressor forfeits his or her own right not to be attacked in a proportionate and necessary way. Regardless of how this suggestion is assessed, however, this argument does not explain why the victim may act despite the remaining uncertainty. In particular, it does not explain why self-defence should be justified against an individual who threatens someone else with a toy gun that appears to be authentic or an unloaded weapon. If there is no real threat to someone's life, this non-existent threat cannot be a violation of the right to life. Moreover, the argument does not account for accepting a certain degree of uncertainty, not only with regard to the behaviour of the aggressor, but also with regard to proportionality and necessity. If an aggressor forfeited his or her right not to be attacked by threatening someone else, he or she still only loses this right in accordance with the proportion and necessity of the situation. If the aggressor's intention was never to kill the victim, lethal force would be neither necessary nor proportional.

An understanding of the term 'harming act' as it informs the concept of self-defence thus does not explain why the application of defensive force is justified under such circumstances. None of the relevant normative relationships explaining the concept of self-defence can account for such situations. Defensive killings are justified despite uncertainties, and even despite the fact that preconditions theoretically justifying self-defence are not fulfilled. The reasons for this are the epistemological difficulties faced in reality, which contradict the ideal situations used to explain the concept. Reference to the epistemological circumstances alone, however, does not actually explain why it is right to justify such action, except to a limited extent.

If it is accepted that self-defence has to be action-guiding and that it has to explain morally justified behaviour with regard to reality, moral reasoning must correspond to the epistemological limitations faced in reality. This then affects the description of the preconditions for becoming an object of the right of self-defence. In order to be satisfying, however, the answer requires an additional consideration regarding the aggressor's behaviour. The aggressor, by his or her deeds, creates a situation in which the victim reasonably believes that his or her right to life will be violated. If the aggressor goes so far as to threaten the victim in a way that induces the victim to believe that he or she will die if he or she does not defend him- or herself with lethal force, the aggressor must face the consequences of this conduct.

This explanation makes sense of the addressed examples and makes sense of the limits set on what may be interpreted as a life-threatening situation. Self-defence is justified in situations that may reasonably be interpreted as life-threatening attacks, e. g. a threat posed with a toy gun that appears to be a real weapon. This, however, does not apply to situations unreasonably interpreted as life-threatening. For example, if someone interpreted children playing with a yellow toy gun, recognizable as a toy, as a threat to life, and reacted by killing the children in question, the act could not be justified in terms of self-defence. Such a situation cannot be reasonably attributed to the perceived aggressor. Depending on the circumstances, the individual who reacted wrongly may not necessarily be held fully or even partly responsible for what he or she did, yet a lack of responsibility cannot be mistaken as a justification of the act.

On the basis of this explanation, one may now argue that it is morally acceptable to carry out targeted killings of terrorists, despite an uncertainty regarding first, whether the targeted person, if not stopped, *will* actually violate someone else's life, and second, whether it is possible to prevent the harming act by means other than lethal force. Terrorists are not incidentally destructive. They act highly systematically, developing strategies in order to have (as much) impact on society (as possible). They train to carry out such acts and seek to be destructive. They do not act spontaneously, but deliberately. Moreover, as addressed before, they follow their aims vigorously. Fanaticism and the beliefs that often accompany terrorism do not necessarily render insight impossible, nor do they preclude the re-consideration of plans on the part of the terrorists, but they do make it likely that terrorists will adhere to their plans. In addition, at least certain terrorist groups or units are active in areas that are not effectively controlled by state authority. They live and operate in areas that leave states seeking to confront these individuals unable to effectively react. Based on this description, it may then be argued that terrorists, by becoming part of a terrorist organization or network, and by becoming involved in terrorist activity, assume the risk of being mistaken as individuals who, if not stopped, will violate other individuals' right to life. Due to the above explanation of the forfeiture of rights and the requirements of necessity and proportionality, this description applies only to terrorists who are taking part in a particular determinable attack. The attack does not need to be determinable to the extent that time and place is known, but it must be reasonably certain that the targeted individual is sufficiently involved in an attack that will be destructive enough that killing is a proportionate response. Terrorists involved in such a determinable attack, one may continue, may be attacked preventively. While in the context of self-defence it becomes obvious at the threatening moment that an aggressor is dangerous to others, terrorists, through their known involvement in terrorism, make this threat obvious at an earlier stage. As with 'normal' aggressors, they thereby make it reasonable to believe that, if not stopped, they will violate other individuals' right to life. As a result, just as 'normal' aggressors must carry the burden of the remaining uncertainty, terrorists must assume the remaining risk. Through involvement in terrorist organizations and their activities, terrorists carry the risk of being mistaken for individuals who have forfeited their right to life. If doubts remain that this argument applies to all terrorists, one may argue that, at a minimum, it applies to terrorists who operate in areas where the structural incapacity of states provides a high degree of certainty that few means other than killing are available to stop the terrorists.

This argument is not convincing for several reasons. Pragmatic considerations point to the high risk of abuse that such an understanding would entail. Moreover, unlike common self-defence situations, the targeted killing of terrorists puts at risk a greater number of people than just the individual who provokes the situation, uninvolved individuals not involved in terrorism and who hence cannot be required to assume any risk for their behaviour. Most decisive among these reasons, however, is that the argument misinterprets the reason for which self-defence in situations of imminent harming acts is justified despite lingering uncertainty.

The idea that people, under certain circumstances, may kill in self-defence, despite a certain degree of uncertainty, may not be reduced to the *extent* to which the potential aggressor is required to assume the risk for his or her own behaviour. Self-defence must be understood in terms of the theoretical explanation above. An individual may only be killed if he or she forfeited his or her right to life. This means he or she may only be killed if he or she forfeited his or her right not to be attacked in a proportionate and necessary way, and if killing him or her would meet these latter requirements. This, and only this, allows the application of force in self-defence. Given the *de facto* presence of uncertainty, established procedures must secure these facts. The limits faced in doing so are not established on the basis of considerations of how much uncertainty can arguably be accepted. They are established on the basis of factual abilities. If one does not want to give up the possibility of defence, one has to act before the harming act takes place. As such, one must act when the harming act is imminent. Imminence is thereby the most accurate means through which to minimize the degree of uncertainty. The remaining risk must plausibly be assumed by the aggressor. Nevertheless, it is not this fact that defines the moment at which the use of defensive force is justified. This moment is defined by the normative relations on which the right of self-defence is based, and by a reality which cannot be overcome.

This reasoning not only finally rejects the argument that the requirement of imminence can be abandoned in certain situations of targeted killing, but also provides for finalizing the concept of self-defence as presented. I presented an explanation for what makes individuals object to the right of self-defence by use of a hypothetical situation in which it is possible to know exactly how matters will develop in the future. The explanation for the requirement of imminence now highlights the difference between this hypothetical situation and reality: reality makes certain facts about future developments inaccessible. If it is accepted that self-defence has to be action-guiding and that it must morally justify behaviour within an understood and realistic context, moral reasoning must correspond to the epistemological limitations faced in reality. This affects the description of the preconditions for becoming an object of the right of self-defence. Based on the hypothetical situation, I argued that someone forfeits his or her right of self-defence, and hence becomes an object to the right of self-defence, once he or she, if not stopped, *will* violate someone else's right to life. When it comes to real situations, this explanation of forfeiture may be read in light of the epistemological difficulties, requiring its reformulation with consideration of the requirement of imminence. This means that an individual forfeits the right not to be attacked in a proportionate and necessary way when he or she *is about* to carry out a harming act.

This reformulation does not question the initial theoretical explanation for the forfeiture of the right not to be attacked in a proportionate and necessary way. Still, it is decisive to the forfeiture of the right not to be attacked in a proportionate and necessary way that the individual concerned, if not stopped, *will* violate someone else's right not to be attacked. Nevertheless, it reformulates the explanation in a manner that gives justice to the fact that the principles explaining the right of self-defence must be action-guiding and applicable to reality.

To conclude, the requirement of imminence must be read as referring to the moment directly prior to the actual harming act. Given the functions it fulfils, it cannot be interpreted in any other sense; neither can it be abandoned altogether. Preventive use of force, and hence targeted killing, cannot be justified in terms of self-defence.[33]

The above discussion explains why no one may be attacked prior to the moment in which the harming act is imminent: any such attack would violate the targeted person's right to life. It also explains, if these rights are taken seriously, why harm to innocent bystanders cannot be regarded as morally right: these individuals do nothing to give reason to believe that they have lost their right to life. Hence, any act depriving them of life would violate them in this manner.

---

33 A contrary opinion is offered by Meisels 2004, 310 f.; Meisels (2004, 310 f.) also refers to Barzitai, G., 'Islands of Silence, Democracies Kill?', presented at Annual Meeting of the Law and Society Association, Budapest 2000, 6.

There is no final conclusion regarding what is required to violate someone's right to life. This, however, is not problematic. Any targeted killing has to be described as action. Therefore, whether, and to what extent, agency is crucial for a violation of rights is irrelevant in this context. This also applies to the question of whether fault is required for a violation of rights. If active state agents did everything possible to ensure that innocent third parties would not be affected, and yet harm innocent individuals due to an unavoidable mistake, one may exclude fault, and the question of whether fault is required for a violation of rights would become relevant. However, this is not relevant to the targeted killing of terrorists that actually occur. At best, states attempt to minimize the danger of innocent casualties and call off targeted killings if they are sure that innocent individuals would die. But they do not investigate the situation in a manner that would make it possible to describe the killing of innocent individuals as an unavoidable mistake.[34] This is, of course, theoretically possible. But it is very rare. Hence, regardless of what one concludes as to the impact of guilt and agency, states generally violate innocent victims' right to life by harming them in the course of targeted killings, and hence wrong them.

One argument remains before I may turn to arguments that depart from the right-based framework of defensive action. It does not draw on the concept of self- or other-defence. It however shall be discussed in this chapter because it in a broader sense relates to the concept of defence right and because its discussion is required to conclude the right-based accounts to defence. The concept of defence rights as hitherto presented justifies defensive action whenever the aggressor, due to his or her conduct no longer possesses the right to life. Generally, however, within the concepts of rights, justified defensive action is not necessarily limited to situations in which the affected individuals do not possess the right that would otherwise be infringed. In practice, rights may conflict with one another. It is then possible to fulfil one of the rights only by infringing the other. Theories of rights must account for such conflicting situations.

One can account for them by referring to the importance of the goods, rights and duties concerned. This, for example, justifies violating someone's property rights, e.g. entering someone's property or even destroying vital parts of it in order to save someone else's life. Other than in self-defence, the individual who owns the property does have a right against someone walking onto his or her property or damaging it. Nevertheless, in this case, the individual entering or damaging the property is justified in infringing this right. This is because the right to life of the person who is to be rescued through the violation or dam-

---

34 For details, see chapter 2.1.

age of property, and the good it protects, are more important than the infringed property right and the good protected by it. The rights infringement, which would have to be described as a violation of the right to life based on the given explanation of defence rights, would then no longer be described as such. The less important right would be described as having been overridden, meaning it has been justifiably infringed.[35]

Can targeted killings of terrorists be explained in terms of such conflicts of rights? This question may be asked with regard to the killing of the targeted person, as well as to harm done to innocent bystanders in the course of targeted killing. Ultimately, the question must be answered negatively in both constellations.

It may first be argued that the targeted person's right to life conflicts with the parallel right of his or her potential victims. In other words, either the terrorist dies or the potential victims are deprived of their lives. Both rights cannot be protected at the same time. Arguably, the situation cannot be properly described as a conflict of rights. The causal relationship between the killing of a terrorist and the protection of potential victims is often unclear. The lives of potential victims are not actually threatened at the time of the killing, and the effect targeted killings have are uncertain. The situation probably comes closest to a conflict of rights when the targeted terrorist is held to be on his or her way to carry out an attack. Nevertheless, given that the possibilities for establishing certainty regarding the circumstances in such situations necessarily remain limited, it is unclear whether the situation can be described as a conflict between different individuals' right to life.

The answer to this question may be left open, since the targeting and killing of the terrorist would not be justifiable, even if a given situation is described as a conflict between the right to life of this terrorist and that of the potential victims. Two equal rights protecting equally important goods are involved, and, thus, such conflicts cannot be settled in terms of the importance of the rights and goods involved. The mere fact that the right to life is involved on both sides does not allow for the choice of infringing on the terrorist's right to life on the basis of weighing the rights involved against each other. Thus, even if the situation were described as a conflict between different individuals' right to life, a solution by deontological accounts does not apply.

It may be argued that this is too simple a description of the rights involved. At least one consideration remains for justifying the killing of terrorists in terms of a conflict of rights. The argument asserts that it is wrong to describe the rights involved on both sides of the conflict as being of equal weight. The fact that the

---

35 These terms have often been applied. See e.g. Gewirth 1981, 92.

terrorist is responsible for the situation, and hence guilty, or that he or she is morally worse based on his or her deeds, tips the balance towards the decision to kill him or her rather than to accept the death of fully innocent potential victims.[36]

This reasoning, however, is dangerous and false. It is true that the terrorist concerned is less innocent than his or her potential victims in some respect. The terrorist, for example, is guilty of planning the terrorist attack and for creating the situation that the state faces. However, as the discussion in the first part of this chapter made clear, the terrorist remains innocent of possible killing until the point of imminent attack. Any other description would disturb the presented account of defence rights, if not any limits to state action.

First, the concept of defence rights as it has been presented in this chapter makes clear that the right to deprive someone of his or her life inevitably depends on this person's violation of goods of comparable value. No other wrongdoing may lead to any justification of such severe action. Secondly, the discussion of the requirement of imminence demonstrates the failure of the argument that the right to life of the individual concerned loses importance in a manner that, balanced against another individual's right to life, would justify killing the former individual over the latter. Because the life of the attacker is valuable, the harming act must be imminent. An attacker may be killed because if it were not done, he or she will violate the victim's right to life; it is not because the attacker's life loses value as such.

The harming effects that such reasoning would have regarding limits to state action is obvious. Accepting that certain individuals are less innocent than others, and allowing this to influence decisions regarding their rights in general, dissolves the notion that state actions must advert to the deed they are reacting to in order to be justified. Most problematically, to extend the guilt of a certain individual to his or her status, and to describe him or her as generally less innocent, suggests that an individual, by committing serious wrongs as a person, loses his or her value. This leads back to the discussion of *Feindstrafrecht*, and it is, as I have discussed, unconvincing and fully incompatible with any plausible rubric of human rights and a just state order.

---

36 This is what Michael Moore seems to base his consideration on, when he argues, 'perhaps it is *less* wrong to torture the blameworthy than the innocent. Put crudely', he continues, 'their lives and rights are worth less precisely because they are morally odious individuals deserving of punishment, even if we are not their rightful punishers and even if death or torture is not their rightful punishment'. Moore, Michael, 1997, 717 f., see generally 717–719/724.

Hence, even if the situation is described as a conflict of different individuals' right to life, the terrorist's right to life cannot be described as having been overridden by that of potential victims. The rights exist with equal weight until the point at which the attacker no longer possesses the right at all. Given that the attacker, at this moment, no longer possesses a right to life with regard to the particular situation of defence, the idea of overriding rights loses its relevance. Until this specific point, however, the conflict cannot be resolved in terms of the importance of the rights and goods involved.

The situation state agents face could, however, also be described as a conflict between other kinds of rights. One may argue that the situation represents a conflict between the right to life of the terrorist and the right of the potential victims to be protected by the state. To speak in Hohfeldian terms, this is the conflict between the claim right citizens have against the state to be protected from harm and the claim right not to be actively killed. Expressed in corresponding state duties, it is the conflict between the negative duty of the state to abstain from violating individuals' rights and the positive duty to protect them.

Such a description, however, does not strengthen the argument in favour of targeting and killing the terrorist. It instead weakens it. If this is how the conflict between rights is to be described, the right not to be killed necessarily prevails. This is so because the right to be protected by the state necessarily entails the right not to be actively killed by that same state. The state's duty, corresponding to the right to protection, is, hence, not thinkable without the right to not be attacked and, hence, the fulfilment of the duty to not actively violate an individual's right to life. In other words, justifying the killing of a certain individual with reference to another's right to protection questions the existence of the right to protection as such. Formulating the situation faced by states with certain terrorist attacks in terms of conflicts of rights, hence, cannot possibly lead to the justifiability of targeting certain terrorists.

Given that the killing of terrorists cannot be justified in terms of a conflict of rights, I must not engage at great length with the question of whether certain conflicts of rights can justify harming and killing innocent third parties in the course of targeted killings. The answer I gave to the idea that the killing of the terrorist could be explained in terms of a conflict of rights already provides a response to the question of whether or not harm to third parties can be justified in terms of conflicts of rights. Nevertheless, certain points must be addressed.

Depending on how the situation is read, such a conflict of rights would involve the right held by the third parties not to be killed, as well as the right held by the victim not to be killed, or their right to be protected, respectively. The answer given with regard to killing the targeted person explains that such a conflict cannot be resolved in terms of the importance of the individual rights involved, regardless of a given interpretation of the conflict. In other words, infringement of the innocent third party's rights in order to protect the lives of potential victims cannot be justified in the context of the rights and goods involved. The third parties' right to life cannot be overridden by the less, or, at most, equally, important rights of the potential victims.

Some may hold this conclusion to be unsatisfactory. Situations may come to mind in which killing an individual cannot be justified with reference to an absence of rights, or by a conflict involving a right more important than the right to life, yet which for many people would justify killing or accepting the death of one individual in order to avoid that of others. An example of such a situation is the famous trolley case. Similarly, rescue situations may come to mind, in which the rescuer, due to lack of resources, can save only some of the affected individuals and seems justified in turning to the larger group, to the detriment of the smaller. One may wonder whether the reasons for the conviction that numbers, or more generally consequences, are important in such situations may influence the assessment of the justifiability of targeted killing of terrorists.

I will turn to such examples in the next chapter. For now, it suffices to say that no argument of justification in these situations can bear directly on the rights of the individuals affected or on the relative importance of the rights themselves. Given that consequences play a role, I will come back to this position in the next chapter, despite the fact that the reference to numbers or consequences may arguably be justified by a deontological account of morality.

At this point I may conclude that the targeted killing of terrorists cannot be justified by a plausible concept of defence rights, with respect either to the killing of the terrorist or to that of innocent third parties. Any such action would violate the right to life of the individual concerned, a right that cannot be overridden by other more important rights in the relevant circumstances.

The right to life sets clear limits on state action in this respect. Further arguments seeking to justify the targeted killing of terrorists may be possible, and they will be dealt with in the following chapter. Nevertheless, any further argument must take into account that the killing infringes on the right to life of the individuals involved, and that such infringement cannot be justified in terms of the rights of the individuals themselves.

11 Consequences (ii): The situation-dependent justifying force of consequences

In light of the proposed right-based account of defence rights, I can assess the hitherto postponed, but conceivable, arguments for the justifiability of targeted killing of terrorists. All of these are to some extent based on the conviction that, under certain circumstances, the targeting and killing of terrorists is morally justified in light of the consequences of failing to do so.

The first conceivable argument to be discussed in this part of the book, which was also reflected in legal arguments *de lege ferenda*,[1] became apparent in discussing whether the rationale for killing during warfare could be transferred to conflicts with terrorism that differ from war (chapter 6). The fight against terrorism, one may argue, cannot be assessed within the strict principles of 'normal' peacetime situations. It invokes principles that, to some extent, differ from those governing peacetime as well as those governing war. This is due to the specific characteristics of terrorism and the fight against it. This position does not necessarily question the validity of the justification of killing formulated in the previous chapter. It rather holds that the strict limitations for killing following from it do not apply to the fight against terrorism. The normative foundation for the justifiability of killing in such situations, then, need not be consequentialist. As with warfare, it may be explained on different grounds. Nevertheless, principles differing from those established for 'normal' peacetime situations must be accepted because of the predicted consequences of not allowing for targeted killing.

The second conceivable argument is normatively based on the consequences themselves. It asserts that consequences generally have no impact on the distinction between morally justified killing and morally unjustified deprivations of life. Nevertheless, it questions whether the provided deontological theory of defence rights always sets the final limits for justified defensive killing. In fact, this general argument can be presented in terms of different positions, which must be distinguished. At the most general level, however, they similarly argue that consequences, under certain circumstances, may have or gain justifying relevance.

---

1 See chapter 4.5.2.

11.1 'Counter-terrorism principles'

The argument that principles differing from those regulating peacetime behaviour (heretofore 'counter-terrorism principles') apply to the fight against terrorism can be formulated with varying degrees of radicalism. It may be held that the fight against terrorism in general is governed by these principles,[2] or else that they apply only to certain forms of terrorism and the fight against it.[3]

What form these 'counter-terrorism principles' take has an impact on which cases of targeted killing can be justified. The different positions do, however, share some attributes regarding what such principles comprise. As regards the person targeted, they both hold that killing is allowed not only in response to imminent harming acts, but also for involvement in the planning, organizing or carrying out of terrorist attacks, provided that killing constitutes the last resort. It is not clear what 'last resort' means under these circumstances. Strictly understood, to speak of a last resort makes sense only in terms of an imminent harming act. Only at this point can it be known that the situation cannot be resolved but by killing. This would, however, eliminate the benefits of specific 'counter-terrorism principles' in contrast to principles governing state conduct in 'normal' peacetime situations. 'Last resort', then, must be understood in a wider sense. In this wider sense, killing seems to be the last resort if, at a certain point in time, it is held to be unlikely that the individuals concerned can be detained.[4]

The second substantial alteration from the regulations governing justified killing during 'normal' peacetime situations concerns the potential risk imposed on innocent bystanders in the course of fighting terrorism. Innocent third parties may still not be directly attacked. Injuring them, however, is not prohibited to the extent it is restricted in 'normal' peacetime situations. The different positions formulating the applicability of 'counter-terrorism principles', of varying degrees of radicalism, differ regarding the accepted degree of risk and injury to innocent bystanders. Kasher and Yadlin differentiate between innocent citizens of the acting state and innocent non-citizens. Provided the damage is proportional, however, they accept some degree of collateral damage with regard to both. Walzer, in contrast, requires a higher level of protection for innocents. He argues that

---

2 For such a general position, see Kasher/Yadlin 2005. They present a concept regulating the fight against terrorism that they hold to apply to any fight against terrorism 'within the framework of a democratic state' (Kasher/Yadlin 2005, 7). For further critique of individual principles Kasher and Yadlin propose, see e.g. Miller 2009, 142–145.
3 Walzer 2006a, 10 f.
4 Walzer 2006a, 11.

state agents carrying out targeted killings 'can't avoid imposing some degree of risk to innocent people, and the risks will certainly be greater than those imposed by police in a city at peace, but we must insist on a strenuous effort to minimize the risks'.[5] Though differing in degree, Walzer, too, accepts that, under certain circumstances, harm to innocents can be justified beyond the strict limits set by the principles I have developed, and that Walzer himself formulates,[6] for peacetime situations.

Both variants of the argument must refer to some characteristics of terrorism that justify accepting 'counter-terrorism principles'. As encountered when discussing whether the rationale for killing during warfare may be transferred to the fight against terrorism, there are two characteristics that are predominantly highlighted. First, there are the destructive capacities that are ascribed to terrorism. Second, authors refer to the inability of states to effectively combat terrorism with conventional measures applied in their fight against crime.[7]

I argued that these characteristics cannot be dismissed outright for all forms of terrorism. They alone, however, are insufficient to be able to conclude that the principles normally applied to defensive action no longer govern states' fight against terrorism. Neither destruction, nor the inability of states to react, invokes a change of principles under normal circumstances.

In a hypothetical scenario, a state has severe problems with adults abusing children in an organized way, or with rape crimes; it is unable to apprehend the offenders, and the number of incidents increases rather than decreases. In another scenario, the incidence of bribery, organized crime, or tax fraud is abnormally high in number. These crimes can severely impact states and their populations. Tax fraud, for example, can deprive a state of money, substantially weakening that state's ability to maintain its social system and, as a result, one may argue, to provide the needy and sick with state support. The Mafia, to which I have referred previously, constitutes a further example. It can dominate entire societies, forcing innocent individuals to pay protection money or live under the threat of being financially ruined or otherwise harmed. Corruption can undermine entire state systems, including the efficiency of its police and legal systems. When it occurs to a sufficient degree, it deprives citizens of protection and exposes them to crime and danger.

---

5 Walzer 2006a, 11.

6 Walzer 2006a, 11.

7 Walzer does not explicitly mention these factors to be decisive, but his reference to the characteristics of Yemen, and his reference to the necessity of applying more extreme measures in the fight against terrorism than in the fight against other crimes, imply some factors along these lines. I will account for his specific reasons below.

In the context of these different forms of crime, it is reasonable to question whether the presented characteristics of terrorism have a moral impact to the extent claimed. The consequences of all of the crimes addressed are severe. Moreover, states often cannot effectively fight these crimes. Nevertheless, this does not lead to the abandonment of moral rules normally regulating state action. Instead, the examples of these other crimes show that destruction and danger, and states' inability to react to them, must, to a certain extent, be accepted. By 'acceptance', it is not suggested that such dangers should not be counteracted; however, they do not invoke a set of moral rules complementing the principles governing the two situations commonly recognized, peacetime and wartime.

Only characteristics that distinguish terrorism from other forms of crime, then, could justify the introduction of 'counter-terrorism principles'. Or otherwise, one would have to be able to establish that the addressed characteristics are connected to terrorism in a manner that exceeds their manifestation in the context of other crimes.

The fact that terrorism is, by definition, directed against innocent individuals does not render terrorism unique. It can equally apply to all addressed crimes. It is that terrorists *deliberately use* innocent individuals for their purposes that makes terrorism so morally appalling. Yet does this distinguish terrorism from other crimes in a way that justifies giving up accepted moral rules? With regard to counter-measures, it seems instead to be the consequences for the individual victims that count. Terrorism would be less threatening if it did not severely harm individuals in order to use them, but only implied minor economic damage for the same ends instead. The desire to apply other principles would, then, certainly be diminished. It thus seems to be the impact rather than the motivation that is decisive for the question of whether differing rules should apply.

The fact remains that terrorism often instils fear in the population, another serious aspect of terrorism. Terrorism influences the conduct of the population; it deprives the people of a life without fear; it makes them avoid using public transport, spending time at public places, and conducting other day-to-day activities. As such, terrorism, under certain circumstances, substantially limits civilian freedom. This again, however, is a potential consequence of myriad forms of crime. Provided the crime rate is high enough, individuals live in fear, avoid walking along certain streets, no longer use public transport, and leave home less frequently. The factor of fear does not sufficiently distinguish terrorism from other crimes and, hence, does not justify different principles for counter-action.

This is not meant to trivialize terrorism. Terrorism is so morally appalling due to all of its characteristics. However, these particular characteristics do not distinguish terrorism from other crimes sufficiently enough to argue that principles should apply to the fight against terrorism that do not apply in combating more conventional forms of crime. The position that specific 'counter-terrorism principles' apply to the fight against terrorism as such, then, can only be maintained if terrorism can be described as exceeding other forms of crime in destruction, and if it can be established that states substantially fail to react to terrorism with conventional means. This, however, evidently applies neither to all forms of terrorism, nor to all states.

First, terrorism has occurred and still occurs in various forms. Not all terrorist organizations have similar destructive capacities. This may be due to organizational and financial capacities. It may also be due to the strategy to which different terrorist groups subscribe. Not all terrorist groups or organizations seek to kill as many individuals as possible. Neither are all of them prepared to carry out suicide attacks.

Secondly, and often closely related, states are not necessarily unable to fight terrorist threats. History has shown that states have defeated terrorism by means other than killing the members of terrorist groups. This applies to Germany's conflict with the RAF; it also applies to the conflict the United Kingdom faced with the IRA.[8] Moreover, states are able to react to current terrorist threats by way of intelligence discovered about the planning of certain terrorist attacks. Several examples demonstrate this. Intelligence services, police forces, and legal systems enable states to react to terrorism and ward off terrorist attacks. Hence, if one accepted that a sufficiently extreme degree of destructive capacity and an inability on the part of states to effectively fight a terrorist threat justify the application of 'counter-terrorism principles', one must conclude that this neither applies to all forms of terrorism, nor to normally structured states.

If this argument applies at all, it applies to highly destructive forms of terrorism and, more importantly, to states that, due to substantial structural deficiencies, are not able to effectively react. This is the more moderate version of the proposal that 'counter-terrorist principles' apply to the fight against terrorism, as Walzer suggested. Walzer argues that principles differing from those applying to warfare and common law enforcement apply in the fight against terrorism *under certain circumstances.*[9]

This version of the argument has fundamental advantages over the first version. It recognizes that danger *per se* cannot possibly justify giving up principles normally governing state conduct. Moreover, it recognizes that this also applies

---

8 The UK is reported to have applied targeted killings in this conflict at some stage. These actions, however, did not lead to the present settlement of the violent conflict.
9 Walzer (2006a, 10f.) argues that certain areas, due to the structural deficiencies of the state concerned, resemble neither war zones nor peace zones, yet constitute some in-between form, to which these principles apply.

to the inability of states to react to certain threats. It corresponds to the oft-held idea that terrorism, under certain circumstances and due to its structure and transnational scope, evades state authority to an extent that requires the application of more extreme measures.

Ultimately, it is a question of deciding whether such reasoning is accepted or rejected. Some will insist that extreme circumstances do not justify giving up the normative foundation of state conduct. Others will hold that the danger is so severe, and that a given state's means are so limited under these circumstances, that such a step must be accepted. There are, however, good reasons to reject such reasoning, even in its more moderate form, as applying to states substantially lacking effective power. The basis for such a decision is too vague, the principles involved too fundamental, and the infringements on the rights of individuals too severe. This becomes apparent in light of the normative consequences of such a step and illustrates the vagueness of the concept.

None of the authors suggesting the acceptability of 'counter-terrorism principles' provides normative reasoning for how targeting and killing terrorists, as well as collateral damage, are justified under these 'counter-terrorism principles'. In order to explain why targeted killing is allowed under such circumstances, it must be made clear why the attacked individuals are liable to attack. Furthermore, it must be made clear why harm to innocent third parties is acceptable under certain circumstances. Both explanations seem possible by referring to the interpretation of moral principles accepted during warfare. Terrorists, one could argue, may be regarded as liable to attack because they participate in the threat that states combat. Innocent bystanders, one could argue, may, under certain strict conditions, be harmed because the doctrine of double effect, as during warfare, justifies foreseen though not directly intended harm to innocents. This, however, does not suffice. In order to provide a convincing position, one must also make clear why justified harm to innocents is limited more strictly than during warfare. It must also be explained why, unlike the situation during warfare, terrorists may only be killed as a last resort. This is a profound, but missing precondition for any acceptability of altered principles.

I will not enquire how this could be done in more detail. The consequences stemming from the introduction of 'counter-terrorism principles' for the individuals' rights are evident without additional explanation. In terms of the proposed 'counter-terrorism principles', the argument that terrorists, if not stopped, will violate others' right to life or bodily integrity is no longer decisive in determining the justifiability of killing terrorists. Killing them is allowed not only in response to a determinable terrorist attack, but also on the basis of their involvement in terrorism. Moreover, intelligence information, rather than imminence of the harming act, suffices to establish the required certainty of the targeted individual's involvement. The mistakes that occur in the application of defence rights in 'common' situations would potentially increase. Even if states, through intelligence, discovered who is involved in terrorism, this practice risks misidentification. Additionally, innocent individuals are no longer protected from harm by abiding by laws. They must accept potential injuries that cannot be explained in the context of their own right to life and bodily integrity. Overall, fundamental principles of peacetime reasoning are given up, and protection provided by legal systems is abandoned in several respects.

In light of these implications and consequences, the vague terms on which the shift in principles is based gives compelling reason to reject it. Neither what it means to be sufficiently dangerous, nor what it means that states are structurally unable to react effectively can be clearly determined to a sufficient degree.

What does it mean to be very dangerous? I have already argued that other forms of criminal activity can have severe consequences. These consequences may not present themselves as immediately as do the consequences of terrorism; nevertheless, they often profoundly affect societies. Moreover, as I have argued, not every form of terrorism presents such a threat of danger. But what frequency of attack, extent of attack or organizational structure is required to establish such a situation? What kind of damage does the terrorist organization have to plan in order to warrant new principles? Does the death toll play a crucial role, or do other dangers and harms also constitute a sufficient degree of threat? How many dead individuals are required to abandon the moral prohibitions and securities accepted in peacetime situations? What degree of danger makes the need to act urgent enough to accept changes to rules regulating conduct?

Moreover, what structures count as sufficiently weak to justify giving up peacetime reasoning? Walzer refers to Yemen in order to illustrate such situations:

> In large sections of Yemen, the government's writ doesn't run; there are no police who could make the arrests (14 soldiers had already been killed in attempts to capture the Al Qaeda militants) and no courts in which prisoners could expect a fair trial. The Yemeni desert is a lawless land, and lawlessness provides a refuge for the political criminals called terrorists.[10]

From what moment is the structure sufficiently disrupted that it must be accepted that the existence of such a structure requires altered rules? Do seriously corrupt structures, which gravely undermine effective counter-measures, suffice to establish a zone differing from 'normal' circumstances? Under these circumstan-

---

10 Walzer 2006a, 10 f.

ces, police forces may exist, yet may not work effectively. Does speaking of a law-less land require that no rules be enforced? Can a land be described as lawless when police forces or military forces exist, yet only rarely manage to detain crim-inals? What about countries that work relatively well as such, yet exert little im-pact on certain areas of their country, such as mountainous regions, because they are, due to their topology, difficult to control? How large do such areas have to be in order to establish insufficient government authority? What about police or military forces that, in spite of having access to these different areas, cannot secure dangerous individuals because they are badly trained and badly equipped? Walzer's conclusion, which he formulated with a view to his example of Yemen, seems to apply equally to all these situations:

> The best way to deal with the refuge would be to help the Yemeni government extend its authority over the whole of its territory. But that is a long process, and the urgencies of the "war" against terrorism may require more immediate action.[11]

These questions demonstrate that reference to either a destructive capacity that imposes an urgency to act, or to insufficient state structures introduces very vague terms. In light of the serious implications and consequences of introduc-ing 'counter-terrorism principles' regulating the justifiability of killings, refer-ence to these highly interpretable terms is unsatisfactory. It exposes human rights to the manipulation of states and questions the validity of rights as such. The vagueness exposes them to arbitrariness, which may result in deliber-ate misuse or lead into an unintended over-stretching of the acceptance of differ-ent regulations. This is dangerous not only in the context of terrorism. Once ac-cepted in the context of terrorism, it can be applied to any other form of crimi-nality held to be sufficiently dangerous and in response to which certain states are held to be unable to act. A step toward a third set of rules, complementing peacetime and wartime reasoning, then, opens the doors to a fundamental rup-ture of (human) rights, and ought, therefore, to be rejected. And this point carries additional weight in light of the uncertain effectiveness of the practice of target-ed killing.[12]

This assertion is not to belittle the problems that states face with regard to terrorists who evade state authority by planning and organizing their actions in areas where states lack control. Moreover, it must be recognized that by adhering to normal law enforcement, one must, in some respect, account for risks that are

---

11 Walzer 2006a, 11.
12 For details about the profoundly differing claims on the effectiveness of targeted killing, see chapter 8.

arguably higher than those run if different principles regulating state conduct were accepted. Nevertheless, this is for the benefit of human rights, and thus of general protection. Though he rejects it as insufficient, Walzer addresses the only way to react to such a situation and minimize risk: states must co-operate and improve their ability to control terrorist activity, and the associated risk must be shouldered. In the same way as this applies to ineffective police forces in otherwise 'well-functioning' countries, this applies to states where authority is limited due to geographical circumstances or other factors.

11.2 Consequences 'regain' normative force

The argument against generally relaxing the prohibition to kill does not specify that targeted killings cannot be justified under any circumstances. It primarily requires taking into account the reasoning I provided for justified killing in 'normal' peacetime situations. As such, it can still be argued that targeted killings of terrorists can be justified in view of specific situations. One may argue that the moral regulations for defensive force have profound normative weight, generally apply, and cannot be overridden by ordinary consequentialist considerations. In certain situations, however, consequences, so one may argue, do play a decisive role. More concisely, at least three positions, differing as to their underlying normative concept, must be distinguished as subsumed under this general statement.

First, there are agent-based deontological positions, briefly mentioned at the end of last chapter. They assert that agents potentially face situations in which the consequences of their actions have decisive impact on these actions' justifiability.[13] What these still-differing positions have in common is an understanding that numbers make a difference under certain circumstances, as sometimes argued explicitly, also according to deontological positions. These positions do not argue away the rights of the individuals involved, neither do they argue that rights may justifiably be overridden because a conflicting and more important right requires and justifies this. Moreover, none of them is based on consequentialism. Rather, they argue that individuals may face situations in which

---

13 This is not to argue that consequences cannot generally play a role in deontological accounts. If the conduct, however, impacts on other's rights, deontological accounts must generally be able to justify it in terms of rights and duties rather than with reference to the consequences. Given that killing, as shown, strongly affects rights, this is the situation relevant for the issue under discussion and, hence, to what I refer.

they must decide what to do, and in which they may, or even ought to, act to the detriment of a smaller group of individuals.[14]

In order to work out the differences that give reason to accept the relevance of numbers in some cases, but not others, the debate about this question pictures several different scenarios. Given the circumstances states face with regard to targeted killings of terrorists, the only case that requires discussion is the famous trolley case, as it was first invented by Philippa Foot,[15] and extended by others, most prominently so by Judith Jarvis Thomson.[16] As is well known, in its original form, it describes a trolley driver who faces the choice of killing five individuals on a trolley track by not interfering with a trolley on this track that, due to a brake failure, cannot be stopped; or of redirecting the trolley to a second track, by which he or she would kill one individual on that track who would be unable to leave in time to evade death.

It is not necessary to discuss whether it is convincing that individuals are justified to act to the detriment of the few under such circumstances.[17] Even if it were justified, the reasons that the authors provide for such justification in the trolley case do not apply to targeted killings of terrorists. Targeted killing resembles the scenarios which these authors provide as counter-examples in which killing is morally strictly prohibited. A brief look at Foot and Thomson's explanation of the difference between justified killing in the trolley case and unjustified killing in other cases is sufficient to make this clear.

Foot justifies killing in the trolley case by arguing that actively killing one individual is better than actively killing five.[18] Using counter-examples, such as the case in which five seriously ill patients can be saved only if another person is killed and a life-saving serum extracted from the dead body,[19] in which acting to the detriment of the one is not permissible, Foot, however, highlights that kill-

---

14 There is of course a challenging debate about whether it is true that numbers may be, or must, be taken into account in reasoning about any of such situations. Since the argument I make in this section works regardless of whether one holds this to be true, I will not engage in this discussion.

15 Foot 2002, 23.

16 Thomson 1986c; see also Thomson 1986b.

17 Intuitions may also differ as to whether individuals *may* act in favour of the larger number of individuals and to the detriment of the one individual, or whether one *ought* to do so. This, however, is irrelevant at this point. If any of these or similar cases is applicable to the situation of targeted killings of terrorists, it would suffice to argue that states *may* target terrorists. Whether they ought to or merely may kill terrorists is, morally, highly relevant and interesting, but not essential for the aim I am pursuing.

18 Foot 2002, 27.

19 Foot 2002, 24.

ing, in her words 'inflicting injury', is worse than letting die, in her words failing 'to bring aid'.[20] This, however, is exactly what states face in the question of targeted killing. They kill one in order not to let many die, or in Foot's word in order 'to bring aid' to many. Thomson explains the difference between the examples on different grounds. Introducing further examples, she argues that the trolley case is justified because it simply requires redirecting the existing threat. The transplant case, which requires killing one in order to enable five to survive by using the killed person's organs, however, is not justified. Saving the five patients requires the introduction of a new threat, and this is what is prohibited.[21] The conclusion drawn with regard to Foot's reasoning applies equally to Thomson's. The targeted killing of terrorists corresponds to the examples in which killing is regarded as morally impermissible, but not to the trolley case, as the reasons given for a justification in the trolley case do not apply. Targeted killings cannot be justified on any such deontological account.

One may object that the situations states face with regard to targeted killings differ from the transplant example in that the young, healthy person, whose body would be used for saving the life of the five patients, has nothing to do with the life-threatening conditions of these patients. The terrorists, by contrast, are responsible for the fact that there is a threat to the potential victims at all. As argued in the last section, this is a misleading interpretation. To recall, it is correct that the terrorist is responsible for the threat states react to. Nevertheless, to follow from this that terrorists may be killed ignores that targeted killings are carried out before the threat itself can justify the killing. Arguing that the terrorist is less innocent and can therefore be killed ignores the previously elaborated explanation of defence rights.

Two positions directly applicable to the killing of terrorists remain. These do not base their arguments on a deontological consideration which under certain circumstances, however, must account for numbers or consequences. They argue that, at a certain point, when consequences that would follow from a certain act become too severe, these consequences justify action, even when this means actively inflicting harm on innocent individuals. With regard to the targeted killing of a given terrorist, this means that sufficiently severe consequences following from not targeting and killing him or her would justify the act, regardless of a deontological assessment of the situation.

---

20 Foot 2002, 23–30, see in particular 27–29.
21 Thomson 1986c.

If one accepts that the non-consequentialist prohibitions to kill constitute not only *prima facie* prohibitions[22] but profound moral prohibitions, there seem to be two conceivable ways of normatively making sense of such position. First, one may argue that from a certain point 'the consequentialist principle outweighs competing moral principles'[23]. In other words, while the moral rightness or wrongness of actions can, under 'normal' circumstances, be assessed with reference to the affected individuals' rights and duties, if the consequences of adhering to such rights and duties cross a certain threshold, consequentialist considerations are decisive for morally appropriate behaviour. This normative concept is often debated as 'threshold deontology'.[24]

Second, one may argue in terms of the 'dirty hands' tradition, best understood as the distinction between unjust behaviour and unjustified behaviour. Accordingly, one could argue, the account of defence rights provides important insight into the principles commonly regulating conduct. It comprises central and fundamental moral prohibitions and accounts for unjust acts. Nevertheless, it is not unjustified under all circumstances to carry out unjust acts. This leads to the slightly complicated idea that while killing in such situations violates the concerned individual's right to life and is thus unjust and morally wrong, in view of the consequences, it is justified to get one's hands dirty.

The justifiability of killing innocent individuals in order to avoid extreme consequences has been addressed in the 'dirty hand' literature, for example, with regard to the question of whether terrorist acts can ever be justified.[25] Under the term 'supreme emergency', Walzer proposed that under certain extreme circumstances, state terrorist action can be justified.[26] He argues that in war, states are permitted to attack the enemy's civilian population if no other

---

22 Coady (2008, 285–287) discusses this position as 'balanced exceptionalism'. It argues that moral principles do not reveal absolute and final prohibitions but only provide *prima facie* or presumptive obligations and duties. What is morally wrong depends on the balance between *prima facie* obligations, which, under certain circumstances, involves considering the consequences in the balance.
23 Moore, Michael 1997, 723.
24 Moore, Michael 1997, 719–726.
25 The present issue does not require an extended discussion on the theory of 'dirty hands'. For a general discussion, see, for example, Coady 1993 and 2001. Stephen de Wijze (2009) has recently tried to justify targeted killing of terrorists on the basis of dirty hands reasoning, under certain, seemingly rather extended, circumstances. He, however, basis his argument on a rather hypothetical description of the practice.
26 Walzer 1977, 251–268; Walzer 2004, 33–50. Walzer himself does not in this discussion describe these acts as state terrorism. According to his own definition of terrorism, however, it has to be described as such.

means are available to ward off a supreme emergency, which is a close, extraordinarily serious, 'unusual and horrifying'[27] situation.[28] Igor Primoratz, whose argument also seems attributable to the 'dirty hands' tradition, argues that state as well as non-state terrorism may be justified, provided 'that terrorism is indeed the only method available and likely to succeed, and that what is to be prevented by its use is an evil so great that it can be termed a moral disaster'.[29]

At first sight, threshold deontology and the 'dirty hands' tradition may seem identical. Both threshold deontology and the tradition of 'dirty hands' argue that there is a certain point from which consequences justify a certain act. Depending on the point from which the positions ascribe justifying force to the consequences, they may correspond in the result they reach as to what actions they regard as being justified. The 'dirty hands' tradition, however, gives more weight to the fundamental force of the relevant moral prohibitions. The idea that consequentialist considerations take over from a certain point expresses that otherwise applicable moral prohibitions are rendered inapplicable. The disregarded moral prohibition loses not only its force but, it seems, its applicability. The force of consequentialist considerations is, as a rule, part of the theory.[30] According to the 'dirty hands' tradition, by contrast, disregard of the moral prohibition is treated more like a real exception. Moreover, the act carried out in reaction to otherwise unavoidable consequences remains unjust and morally wrong, yet it is necessary, and carrying it out is thus justified.[31] This expresses more clearly the burden of carrying out acts that conflict with profound moral prohibitions. In this way, the 'dirty hands' tradition seems to better express how one who

---

27 Walzer 1977, 253.

28 Walzer 1977, 252.

29 Primoratz 2007, 49.

30 Threshold deontology has been criticized particularly for basing a theory on the idea of a threshold, the determination of which, so the criticism goes, is necessarily arbitrary. The discussion is philosophically very interesting, yet not crucial to the issue here. For details, see Ellis 1992 and Alexander 2000.

31 Uniacke (1994, 212) seems to accept the idea of distinguishing between unjust und unjustified and just and justified behaviour, respectively, in a more general way than the 'dirty hands' tradition. Next to the right-based justification of action, she accepts the justification 'all things considered'. Different situations could be imagined in which reference to all things considered justified killing, despite the fact that the harmed individual possessed the right not to be killed. Uniacke, for example, argues that an old person who knows that he or she will die soon may not be justified in acting in self-defence against a small child threatening him or her. Uniacke is unclear as to considerations of how consequences gain justifying power. It therefore remains unclear whether her account can actually be read as accepting that certain 'absolute' moral prohibitions in such situations are overridden. I will therefore focus on the two accounts I introduced.

was ordered to act, or acted according to consequences, would evaluate these actions. Even holding the act to be justified, and otherwise convinced of a deontological account of morality, one would, it seems, still feel regret about having to disregard a profound moral prohibition. One would, I believe, argue that one did something terrible and morally wrong, yet that one had to act.

Some may consider this distinction between threshold deontology and the 'dirty hands' tradition sophistic. Eventually, both positions argue that it is justified to act contrary to profound moral prohibitions in light of the consequences any other conduct would cause. Moreover, one may argue, similar words could be used to describe an act justified by reference to threshold deontology. Nevertheless, I hold there to be a real distinction. The following will, therefore, focus on the 'dirty hand' tradition, which, in my opinion, is more convincing due to the profound moral weight of the right to life and the consequent obligation not to kill except in moments of definable self-defence or other-defence. That said, both positions are eventually confronted with the same difficulties. Hence, anyone who does not share this evaluation of the difference between threshold deontology and the tradition of 'dirty hands' may read the remainder of this chapter in respect of both positions.

If 'dirty hands' positions are not to turn into genuine consequentialist positions, they must accept the justifying force of the deontological grounds of defence rights. If the justifiability of most acts is ultimately judged in light of its consequences, the distinction between unjust and just behaviour, as well as any deontological account of killing, are deprived of their normative relevance. Hence, if one is to make sense of the 'dirty hand' tradition, the consequence-based justification can only apply to certain distinguishable cases. Accordingly, targeting killings could then only be justified under certain extraordinary circumstances.

Such an extraordinary situation could be described by the following hypothetical scenario.[32] A state discovers that a certain terrorist unit is planning a terrorist attack. The attack, if carried out, will result in an enormous number of casualties. To make such scenarios most horrible, ticking bomb scenarios, which are frequently referred to in discussions, for example, about justified torture, describe terrorists as being in possession of nuclear devices. The detonation of such devices will kill hundreds of thousands of individuals or wipe out an entire

---

32 I am not arguing that Primoratz or Walzer would accept this scenario as a moral disaster or supreme emergency. At least with regard to the killing of innocents during wartimes or with regard to the use of terrorism in general, they seem to require even more extreme threats to abandon the prohibition of directly attacking innocents. See Primoratz 2007, 49; Walzer 2004, 46 f.

city. Intelligence reveals who is involved in the planning of the attack. State agents know where the respective terrorists are, and they are able to kill them. Several variants could be formulated that increase the necessity to act. The state knows the kind of attack, as well as the time at which it will take place, but not the location at which the attack will be carried out. If the time of attack is close enough, such information makes it less likely that state agents can prevent the attack at a different moment. One could alternatively add that terrorists are known to be on their way to carry out the attack, but the moment cannot be assessed as imminently prior to the harming act. In any of these cases, the state agents have good reason to believe that they will be able to prevent the attack only by killing certain terrorists.

Now, do such extreme circumstances justify the killing of a terrorist prior to the moment when the harming act is imminent? The opposing position is absolutism. Absolutists hold that acts cannot be justified at all if they cannot be justified in reference to rights and duties themselves. Regardless of the consequences, if an individual is wronged by being killed, and if the act is thus immoral, it cannot be justified. Accordingly, the threat to many individuals does not justify targeting one individual whose right to life would thereby be violated.[33]

Both the 'dirty hand' position and the absolutist position lack strong normative reasons for rejecting one another. While the absolutist argues that there cannot be any exception to the prohibition to kill on deontological grounds, the 'dirty hand' theorist argues that the demand of necessity gains primacy at a certain point. Moreover, these situations are highly divisive. They likely trigger more diverting intuitions in people than the question of whether consequences generally justify conduct. While some may be strongly convinced that certain severe consequences have the power to justify certain acts, others may feel that the moral prohibitions of killing retain prevailing normative power. Others still may hold a less extreme view. They may feel that it is wrong to violate someone's right to life. At the same time, they may assert the necessity of action that follows from the severity of the consequences of not acting. Those with these latter intuitions may describe the situation as a moral dilemma. Thomas Nagel's formulation with regard to giving up discrimination between combatants and the rest of the population seems to apply here. He holds:

> [W]hen an absolutist knows or believes that the utilitarian cost of refusing to adopt a prohibited course will be very high, he may hold to his refusal to adopt it, but he will find it

---

33 Coady (2002, 17–20), for example, formulates such an absolute position with regard to the prohibition of killing innocents to ward off a 'supreme emergency' (Walzer 1977, 251–268) during warfare.

difficult to feel that a moral dilemma has been satisfactorily resolved. The same may be true of someone who rejects an absolutist requirement and adopts instead the course yielding the most acceptable consequences. In either case it is possible to feel that one has acted for reasons insufficient to justify violation of the opposing principle.[34]

Despite the theoretically slightly complicated idea that doing what is unjust and morally wrong can be morally justified and thus morally right, I find myself torn between the different positions. It is difficult to come to a certain final position when confronted with some version of the hypothetical cases. The question with regard to these versions of the example is whether or not, in light of such extreme cases, one is prepared to answer that one may, or even ought to, disregard the moral prohibition at play. Positioning ultimately ends up being a decision. Nevertheless, some considerations can be helpful.

First of all, both positions – absolutism and the 'dirty hands' tradition – must cope with serious risks and burdens. In the face of a highly destructive terrorist attack, the absolutist position risks that the attack cannot be stopped at all. Provided the attack will be carried out, there may not be any further options to prevent it. In order to protect the terrorist's right to life, the absolutist, then, risks the death of a large number of innocent individuals. The 'dirty hands' position on the targeted killing accepts violating someone's right to life and thus a fundamental moral prohibition. Moreover, it does so in response to probabilities rather than facts. Supposing a state knows that terrorists plan a highly destructive attack, it still cannot predict with certainty whether the attack can be prevented by killing. Neither can it predict with certainty that the attack will actually take place. By killing the terrorist prior to the moment of imminence of the harming act, the agent, then, risks *unnecessarily* violating the terrorist's right to life.

To some, the burden faced by the absolutist position may, at first, appear to be less acceptable than the burden the 'dirty hands' position must shoulder. After all, the former position risks the life of a large number of citizens, while the latter risks immorally killing a limited number of individuals. Moreover, one may argue, the terrorist attack would injure and kill fully innocent individuals, while the killing of terrorists would affect individuals who, although not guilty in a manner that makes them liable to attack, are not innocent in the full sense. They have at least been involved in terrorism and brought about the situation.

Yet, this argument is misleading in several respects. First, as previously argued at several points, it is misleading, dangerous and false to suggest that ter-

---

34 Nagel 1979, 73.

rorists are in a relevant sense less innocent than other innocent individuals. Terrorists remain innocent with regard to killing until the point of imminent attack. Any other description would rupture the formulated account of defence rights, if not any limits to state action.

Secondly, some may deem the judgment of the example as formulated here relatively clear. The state knows that there will be a terrible attack, it knows who is involved, and it has strong reason to believe that there is no way of preventing the attack except by killing the terrorist. The attack may even be known to be very close, as in cases in which the state knows that the terrorist is on his or her way to carry out the attack. In reality, however, this level of certainty is impossible. States will, necessarily, act on the basis of intelligence. Intelligence, at best, may be relatively clear about the planning of an attack, and perhaps about some of the individuals involved. Certainty is surely less likely regarding the individuals who must be killed in order to prevent the attack. Moreover, certainty about the correct nature of intelligence is difficult to obtain. The state will, at best, be *relatively* sure that an attack will take place. It may similarly have *relatively* secure information about who is involved and when the attack will take place. In the case of the terrorists on their way to carry out an attack, the state will *hold* them to be on their way, yet can probably never be sure. Hence, a more realistic description, accounting for these uncertainties, shows that more is at stake than initially stated. The terrorists' right to life would be violated, perhaps unnecessarily, because there may have been other opportunities to prevent the attack, or because killing them could not prevent the attack. Moreover, a more realistic description also shows that the lives of individuals not engaged in the planning of the particular attack are at stake.

Fourth, when discussing possible conflicts of rights, I argued that in killing (in this respect) innocent individuals, states not only seriously wrong these individuals, but also sidestep their duty to protect individuals under their authority. They violate one of the most profound principles characterizing such protection, and that is that no one may be killed prior to the moment of imminence of the harming act.

As such, a more realistic description of the situation shows that more is at stake overall with the 'dirty hands' position than initially stated. It additionally highlights the crucial importance of the goods at risk. Still, one may be convinced by the tremendous consequences that one may not be able to prevent without an allowance for lethal action. Two additional concerns with regard to the 'dirty hands' position remain, however. The first concern regards formulating an exception from the deontological grounds on the basis of the scenarios I have outlined. The example necessarily invokes intuitions and, based on these, acceptance of certain state conduct. Given certain extreme (though, even with the changes I introduced, relatively unrealistic) examples,[35] the willingness to assume the risk of unnecessarily killing (in this respect) innocent individuals increases. After accepting the killing of terrorists for such examples, states run the risk of applying force to an extent that they would not have done if force applied under such unrealistic conditions enjoyed less approval. This danger stretches beyond the fight against terrorism. Other serious crimes, at some stage, may be held to pose such a serious threat that the offender must be killed rather than detained. Slippery slope arguments do not enjoy many friends in philosophical discussions. Moreover, they can always be countered by arguing that one has to formulate strict requirements in order to limit the risk of sliding down the slope, so to speak. Nevertheless, whatever preconditions are formulated, the acceptance of such serious rights violations in discussing even extreme circumstances changes the attitude towards instrumental rights violation as such.

This risk becomes even more worrisome in light of the vague nature of the preconditions involved, which prompts questions such as those explored above: how many individuals must be at risk in order to assume justification for killing a terrorist who, it is claimed, is involved in a predicted attack? On what basis can states decide that killing the terrorist is the least destructive means available? What characterizes such a moment? How sure must states be? In light of this vagueness, it is the lives of (in this respect) innocent individuals that are at stake in accepting the 'dirty hands' position. What is at stake as well, however, is the acceptance of clear limits to state force.

These arguments cannot nullify the force of the powerful images of the enormous consequences in the scenario where terrorists are not killed prior to the moment deontology allows. Nevertheless, the more realistic presentation should, I believe, have tipped the balance in favour of adhering to absolutism. This certainly applies to those cases of targeted killing that target terrorists not considered to be on their way to carrying out a terrorist attack. A moral prohibition as fundamental as the prohibition against killing cannot possibly be abandoned on the basis of mere probabilities. The situations in which the terrorist is held to be on the way to carry out a disastrous attack involve more uncertainty and must be more cautiously considered.

Even describing such an extreme situation and accepting it as realistic for the sake of argument should, at best, leave one torn between consequentialist

---

35 Frank Sauer (2007) gives an interesting overview of recent scholarly positions on the likelihood of terrorists being able to buy, steal or construct working nuclear and radiological weapons.

considerations and absolutism. It seems that consequentialist considerations develop sufficient force to diminish the normative force of an absolutist position. At the same time, the moral prohibition of killing prior to the moment of imminence seems to develop equally strong force to provoke doubt regarding the consequentialist calculation.

That said, I would like to formulate a stricter general conclusion with regard to the formulation of permissibility of killing in reference to the cases I examined. Given the risks incumbent in formulating conclusions in light of these hypothetical situations, an absolute position should be maintained regarding such extreme examples.[36]

This position may seem problematic in two respects. On the one hand, it may seem contradictory to argue that one should not positively reply to such examples and, at the same time, not give a clear answer as to whether or not, with regard to a certain individual, an extreme case could justify the targeting and killing of terrorists. On the other hand, the individuals involved and responsible for deciding are left to assess the given situations. This may sound unfair. Nevertheless, it is the only answer I can give at this point. It accounts for the fact that a conflict exists between hypothetical cases and reality, as well as between positions in existing situations and general statements as to justified conduct.

There is an additional consideration in not giving a positive answer to such extreme examples. If such cases can be justified at all, the decision to act needs to have been developed carefully. If the decision to act required merely considering the applicability of a certain formulated moral permission, the decision runs the danger of being made too easily. Any appropriate decision requires the burden of individual responsibility for such an act, which necessarily involves questioning one's conscience. In other words, only maximum deliberation could make the unjust act acceptable. This again may be held to be unfair. Nevertheless, it seems to be convincing in the light of the seriousness of the decision.

With respect to the 'dirty hands' position, I have hitherto ignored the fact that innocent third parties may be, and often are, harmed in the course of target-

---

36 Jeremy Waldron (2011, in particular 11–14) raises a stronger point, and argues against morally questioning certain fundamental rules, such as the prohibition of murder (or the absolute prohibition of killing innocents). His reasoning, however, points at a similar worry. He argues that 'a norm regarding homicide needs deeper underpinnings than simply acceptance of the balance of reason that supports it' (13), because the temptation to unjustifiably kill under certain circumstances, e.g. in the heat of battle or when there are many lives at stake, can be very high. Such norms should therefore not be questioned. I would probably not go so far. Certainly however, if one shares Waldron's point one should not question the fundamental norms at stake with regard to the targeted killing of terrorist in light of hypotheticals.

ed killings. Little more need be said with regard to this particular problem. That innocent third individuals die or are seriously harmed in the course of targeted killings increases the burden of the 'dirty hands' position. It strengthens the point I have made with regard to targeted killing based on the evaluation of the killing of the specific terrorist concerned.

Concluding remarks

The legal and the moral arguments about the justifiability of targeted killing of terrorists developed in this book do not address identical questions, and the assessments differ regarding individual aspects of the analysis. Specifically, discrepancies can be noted with regard to targeted killing of terrorists in armed conflicts. In international armed conflicts, for example, the moral analysis (not, in this respect, differentiating between international and non-international armed conflicts) theoretically considers certain terrorists as combatants, and, as such, liable to attack, while these individuals would be considered civilians by international humanitarian law. Moreover, international humanitarian law, for example, provides justification under certain circumstances for targeting terrorists who constitute civilians, which exceeds the justification provided by moral considerations for armed conflicts.

That said, the legal and moral analyses correspond and support each other with regard to the overall result, as well as with regard to the assessment of realistically relevant situations of targeted killing of terrorists. In the given examples of concrete discrepancies, this, first of all, is due to the fact that conflicts with terrorists do not typically trigger armed conflicts according to either legal or moral analysis. Possible discrepancies between the legal and moral assessments with regard to armed conflicts, therefore, are typically irrelevant for realistically relevant situations. With regard to the first example, morality then limits the justifiability of targeted killing to cases that largely match those recognized by international humanitarian law. It does so by rejecting justifiability if the targeted combatant cannot be distinguished from a non-combatant, or if the act causes disproportionate harm to non-combatants. With regard to the second example, international humanitarian law allows the targeting of civilians for the time they carry their weapons, and, hence, are able to harm the enemy. First, this does not typically correspond to the period during which actual targeted killings of alleged terrorists are carried out, and secondly, in many cases, this coincides with situations of an imminent harming act, i.e with situations that would be assessed positively by both a moral and a legal analysis, but no longer constituted targeted killings.

In other words, if the moral and legal assessments of the justifiability of targeted killing of terrorists developed in this book differ, this rarely concerns practically relevant cases, and the differences are limited to nuance. Overall, the two different assessments' conclusions strongly support each other. Both international law and morality provide justification for targeted killing of terrorists under certain corresponding circumstances. Applied to realistic situations and actually occurring circumstances, however, they typically do not.

This can be illustrated in some more detail. Targeted killings of terrorist are prohibited in peacetime situations, both morally and legally. Several arguments which have sometimes been presented to morally justify targeted killings of terrorists do not provide any such justification. The practice cannot be morally justified with reference to revenge or punishment, nor on the basis of considering the consequences, nor by arguing that (specific) terrorists, due to their conduct, lose rights protection which otherwise every singly individual possesses. Defence is the only theoretically sound basis for moral justification. But even on this basis, targeted killings of terrorists cannot be morally justified. This corresponds to the legal assessment. Both morally and legally, lethal acts of force by states can only be justified in defence of an imminent threat to someone's life or the equivalent. This reflects an internationally shared understanding of the right to life, as set out in the CCPR, as well as a plausible understanding of the moral limits to deprivation of life. Given that targeted killings, by definition, take place prior to such a moment, they cannot be justified. The prohibition against harming innocent third parties adds another factor excluding justifiability for targeted killings of terrorists that have such effects. In practice, morality during peacetime may possibly provide an exception to this conclusion for the case in which abstaining from an act of targeted killing would cause horrendous consequences. This case, however, is rather unrealistic in light of actual cases of targeted killing of alleged terrorists. Moreover, such justification should not be formulated on a theoretical level.

Both the legal and the moral arguments give great importance to this peacetime result regarding the general justifiability of targeted killing of terrorists, because they both typically ascribe conflicts that are described as conflicts with terrorists to peacetime as opposed to war – in legal terms, armed conflicts – and, in this manner, typically regard actual cases of targeted killing of terrorists to be unjustified.

With regard to situations of armed conflict, neither the legal nor the philosophical argument allows for a reply as straightforward as the result formulated with a view to peacetime. Still, neither international law nor morality justifies targeted killings to an extent that would justify the practice in conflicts with terrorists that are currently described as such.

In international armed conflicts, which may occur with regard to conflicts with terrorists when terrorist acts are attributable to a state, in times of an ongoing armed conflict during occupation, or if the targeted terrorist participates in an ongoing international armed conflict, international humanitarian law prohibits targeted killings except while the targeted person is actively involved in hostilities. In terms of the examined cases of targeted killing of terrorists, this realistically limits legally justifiable killing of terrorists to situations in which the terrorist is reliably on his or her way to carry out an attack (case 1) and to situations in which the attack is determinable (case 2), provided the targeted terrorist is actively engaged in this hostile act and carries arms, enabling him or her to harm others at any time, and provided convincing evidence can be established as to this activity. The only exception is the theoretical case in which the targeted person is incorporated into state armed forces but deemed to be a non-state terrorist, owing to his or her non-state terrorist activities. This makes him or her, as a combatant, a legitimate target at any time, provided he or she is not *hors de combat*. Given actual targeted killings of terrorists and the logic of the practice, this case is, however, highly improbable and unrealistic. In any case, targeted killing of terrorists can then only be justified if it is carried out on the territory of any of the states involved, and if it does not cause disproportionate harm to innocent third parties.

International humanitarian law theoretically also justifies certain targeted killings if a conflict with terrorists can be considered a non-international armed conflict. It theoretically also justifies targeted killings of terrorists who participate in a non-international armed conflict between a different non-state group and a state, provided the targeted person can be considered a member of the armed forces and is distinguishable from civilians. If the terrorists constitute civilians, they can only be targeted while they participate in the hostilities, limiting justified attacks to targeted killings of case 1 and some forms of case 2. As with international armed conflicts, none of these constellations, however, is typically reflected in actual conflicts with terrorists or, in fact, corresponds to actual cases of targeted killings of alleged terrorists. Conflicts with terrorists regularly fail to reach an extent – in terms of the extent and continuity of the violence applied as well as the organizational structure of, and connection between, terrorist groups – that would make them non-international armed conflicts. Terrorists participating in ongoing conflicts between other groups and a state do not typically constitute members of the armed forces. If they do, they are not typically attacked when sufficiently distinguishable from civilians. Moreover, actual targeted killings are, in the vast majority of cases, directed against individuals going about their daily business. This renders them illegal, regardless of whether the targeted individuals are civilians. Finally, the proportionality requirement sets limits which many actual targeted killings of alleged terrorists fail to meet.

The moral analysis of the justifiability of targeted killing of terrorists during warfare strongly corresponds in terms of its results. As with international humanitarian law, just war reasoning in principle justifies targeted killing of terrorists, if the targeted terrorist participates in a war as a combatant, provided his or her killing does not cause disproportionate harm to non-combatants. If these preconditions are fulfilled, the terrorists may be targeted regardless of whether they are involved in actual harming acts at the time of attack. If the terrorist must be considered a civilian, he or she may only be targeted directly prior to the execution of a harming act. Protection of non-combatants finally implies that individuals may in any case only be targeted if they can be distinguished from protected individuals, i.e. non-combatants or civilians not currently taking an active part in the hostilities.[1]

In light of this result of the moral and legal analyses in this book, I would like to end with a brief note regarding today's reality. I did not assess individual cases of targeted killing which have occurred throughout history or are being carried out today. However, even on the basis of the preconditions for a possible justification of targeted killing of terrorists developed in this book, it is obvious that international law and morality are currently at stake. It may be possible that single instances of the current practice of targeted killing could be justified. Yet, if at all, this applies only to very isolated cases. This result disqualifies general justifications offered to entire campaigns of targeted killings of alleged terrorists. And it is, of course, disturbing with regard to those states that have made and increasingly do make targeted killing a strategy in their fight against terrorism. As troubling, however, are the reactions of governments not currently engaged themselves in targeted killings as well as those of the general public. Current targeted killings do not receive fierce, let alone much, criticism except from certain small groups. The practice is instead accompanied by (increasing) acceptance and disinterest. This is unsettling with regard to current state killings, but equally so with regard to the prevailing general inclination to ignore law and morality in the face of danger.

---

1 With regard to international armed conflicts, the mentioned differences may apply. As addressed above, these differences, however, do not lead to substantial differences in the final assessment of the justifiability of targeted killing of terrorists, and even less so with regard to practically relevant cases.

References

Albrecht, Peter-Alexis (2005), '"Krieg gegen den Terror" – Konsequenzen für ein rechtsstaatliches Strafrecht', in *Zeitschrift für die gesamte Strafrechtswissenschaft* 117 (4), 852–864.

Aldrich, George H. (2002), 'The Taliban, Al Qaeda, and the Determination of Illegal Combatants', in *The American Journal of International Law* 96 (4), 891–898.

Alexander, Larry (2000), 'Deontology at the Threshold', in *San Diego Law Review* 37, 893–912.

Anderson, Chris A. (1992), 'Assassination, Lawful Homicide, and the Butcher of Baghdad', in *Hamline Journal of Public Law and Policy* 13, 291–310.

Anderson, Kenneth (2011), 'Targeted Killing and Drone Warfare: How We Came to Debate Whether There Is a "Legal Geography of War"', in Peter Berkowitz (ed.), *Future Challenges in National Security and Law* (Stanford, CA: Hoover Institution Press), 1–18. Available at: http://media.hoover.org/documents/FutureChallenges_Anderson.pdf, retrieved 22 March 2012.

Aponte, Alejandro (2004), *Krieg und Feindstrafrecht* (Baden-Baden: Nomos).

Baxter, Richard R. (1951), 'So-Called "Unprivileged Belligerency": Spies, Guerrillas, and Saboteurs', in *British Yearbook of International Law* 28, 323–345.

Beard, Jack M. (2002), 'America's New War on Terror: The Case for Self-Defense Under International Law', in *Harvard Journal of Law and Public Policy* 25 (2), 559–590.

Ben-Naftali, Orna/Michaeli, Keren R. (2003), '"We Must Not Make a Scarecrow of the Law": A Legal Analysis of the Israeli Policy of Targeted Killings', in *Cornell International Law Journal* 36, 233–292.

Benvenisti, Eyal (1993), *The International Law of Occupation* (Princeton/New Jersey: Princeton University Press).

Beres Louis R. (1991), 'The Permissibility of State-sponsored Assassination During Peace and War', in *International and Comparative Law Journal* 5, 231–249.

Bergen, Peter/Tiedemann Katherine (2010), *The Year of the Drone: An Analysis of U.S. Drone Strikes in Pakistan, 2004–2010*, available on http://counterterrorism.newamerica.net/drones, retrieved 22 March 2012.

Betts, Richard K. (2002), 'The Soft Underbelly of American Primacy: Tactical Advantages of Terror', in *Political Science Quarterly* 117 (1), 20–36.

Bielefeld, Heiner (2004), 'Das Folterverbot im Rechtsstaat', Policy Paper No. 4, Deutsches Institut für Menschenrechte.

Blank, Laurie R. (2010), 'Defining the Battlefield in Contemporary Conflict and Counterterrorism: Understanding the Parameters of the Zone of Combat', in *Georgia Journal of International and Comparative Law* 39 (1), 1–38.

Blum, Gabriella/Heymann, Philipp (2010), 'Law and Policy of Targeted Killing', in *Harvard National Security Journal* 1, 145–170.

Blumenwitz, Dieter (2002), 'Einsatzmöglichkeiten der Bundeswehr im Kampf gegen den Terrorismus', in *Zeitschrift für Rechtspolitik* 3, 102–106.

Bond, James E. (1974), *The Rules of Riot: Internal Conflict and the Law of War* (Princeton/New Jersey: Princeton University Press).

Boot, Max (2002), 'Retaliation for Me, But Not for Thee', in *The Weekly Standard* 8 (10), 18 November 2002 (online/no page numbers). Available at http://www.weeklystandard.com/Content/Public/Articles/000/000/001/883gplpc.asp?-page=2, retrieved 13 June 2012.

Bossuyt, Marc J. (1987), *Guide to the 'Travaux Préparatoires' of the International Covenant on Civil and Political Rights* (Dordrecht/Boston/Lancaster: Martin Nijhoff Publishers).

Bothe, Michael (2001), 'Friedenssicherung und Kriegsrecht', in Wolfgang Graf Vitzthum (ed.), *Völkerrecht* (Berlin/New York: Walter de Gruyter, 2nd ed.), 603–679.

Bothe, Michael (2003), 'Terrorism and the Legality of Pre-emptive Force', in *European Journal of International Law* 14 (2), 227–240.

Boyle, Kevin (1985), 'The Concept of Arbitrary Deprivation of Life', in Bertrand G. Ramcharan (ed.), *The Right to Life in International Law* (Dordrech/Boston/Lancaster: Martinus Nijhoff Publishers), 221–244.

Brockhaus (2006), Vol. 21 (Leipzig: F.A. Brockhaus GmbH, 21st ed.).

Brough, Michael W. (2003), 'The POW in a Time of Terrorism: An Investigation into Moral Status', Joint Services Conference on Professional Ethics 2003. Available at http://www.usafa.edu/isme/JSCOPE03/jscope03.html, retrieved 17 October 2008.

Brownlie, Ian (1958), 'International Law and the Activities of Armed Bands', in *International and Comparative Law Quarterly* 7, 712–785.

Bruha, Thomas (2002), 'Gewaltverbot und humanitäres Völkerrecht nach dem 11. September 2001', in *Archiv des Völkerrechts* 40, 383–421.

Bruha, Thomas/Bortfeld, Matthias (2001), 'Terrorismus und Selbstverteidigung: Voraussetzungen und Umfang erlaubter Selbstverteidigungsmaßnahmen nach den Anschlägen vom 11. September 2001', in *Vereinte Nationen* 5, 161–167.

Byers, Michael (2002), 'Terrorism, the Use of Force and International Law after 11 September', in *International and Comparative Law Quarterly* 51, 401–414.

Byers, Michael (2005), *War Law: International Law and Armed Conflict* (London: Atlantic Books).

Byman, Daniel (2006a), 'Targeted Killing, American-Style: Israel's Experience in Taking Out Terrorists Offers Lessons for the United States', in *The Los Angeles Times*, 20 January 2006, Part B, Pg. 13.

Byman, Daniel (2006b), 'Do Targeted Killings Work?', in *Foreign Affairs* 85 (2), 95–111.

Cancio Meliá, Manuel (2005), 'Feind"strafrecht"?', in *Zeitschrift für die gesamte Strafrechtswissenschaft* 117 (2), 267–289.

Cassese, Antonio (1981), 'The Status of Rebels under the 1977 Geneva Protocol on Non-International Armed Conflicts', in *The International and Comparative Law Quarterly* 30 (2), 416–493.

Cassese, Antonio (1989), 'The International Community's "Legal" Response to Terrorism', in *International and Comparative Law Quarterly* 38, 589–608.

Cassese, Antonio (2005), *International Law* (Oxford/New York: Oxford University Press, 2nd ed.)

Cassese, Antonio, 'Expert Opinion: On Whether Israel's Targeted Killings of Palestinian Terrorists is Consonant with International Humanitarian Law'. Written at the request of the Petitioners in *The Public Committee Against Torture et al. v. The Government of Israel et al.* (no date of writing available). Available at http://www.stoptorture.org.il/en/node/761, retrieved 6 October 2008. [Quoted as Cassese (Expert Opinion)].

Cerone, John (2002), 'Status of Detainees in International Armed Conflict, and their Protection in the Course of Criminal Proceedings', in *American Society of International Law*, January

2002 (online/no page numbers). Available at http://www.asil.org/insights/insigh81.htm, retrieved 25 May 2007.

Coady, C. A. J. (Tony) (1985), 'The Morality of Terrorism', in *Philosophy* 60, 47–69.

Coady, C. A. J. (Tony) (1993), 'Dirty Hands', in Robert E. Goodin/Philip Pettit (eds.), *A Companion to Contemporary Political Philosophy* (Oxford: Blackwell Publishers), 422–430.

Coady, C. A. J. (Tony) (2001), 'Dirty Hands', in Laurence Becker/Charlotte Becker (eds.), *The Encyclopedia of Ethics*, Vol. 1 (New York/London: Routledge, 2nd ed.), 407–441.

Coady, C. A. J. (Tony) (2002), 'Terrorism, Just War and Supreme Emergency', in C.A.J. (Tony) Coady/Michael P. O'Keefe (eds.), *Terrorism and Justice: Moral Argument in a Threatened World* (Melbourne: Melbourne University Press), 8–21.

Coady, C. A. J. (Tony) (2004), 'Defining Terrorism', in Igor Primoratz (ed.), *Terrorism: The Philosophical Issues* (Houndmills/New York: Palgrave Macmillan), 3–14.

Coady, C. A. J. (Tony) (2008), *Morality and Political Violence* (New York: Cambridge University Press).

Coll, Alberto R. (1987), 'The Legal and Moral Adequacy of Military Responses to Terrorism', in *Proceedings of the American Society of International Law*, 297–307.

Condorelli, Luigi (1989), 'The Imputability to States of Acts of International Terrorism', in *Israeli Yearbook on Human Rights* 19, 233–246.

Cottingham, John (1979), 'Varieties of Retribution', in *The Philosophical Quarterly* 29 (116), 238–246.

Daase, Christopher/Spencer, Alexander (2010), 'Terrorismus', in Carlo Masala/Frank Sauer/Andreas Wilhelm (eds.), *Handbuch der Internationalen Politik* (Wiesbaden: VS Verlag für Sozialwissenschaften), 403–425.

Darnstädt, Thomas/Hujer, Marc/Schmitz, Gregor P. (2012), 'Bushs Erbe', in *Der Spiegel* 11, 12 March 2012, 94–96.

David, Steven R. (2002a), 'Commentary: The Necessity of Targeted Assassination', in *The Los Angeles Times*, 25 July 2002, Part B, Pg. 13.

David, Steven R. (2002b), 'Fatal Choices: Israel's Policy of Targeted Killing', in *Mideast Security and Policy Studies* 51, 1–26.

David, Steven R. (2003a), 'Israel's Policy of Targeted Killing', in *Ethics and International Affairs* 17 (1), 111–126.

David, Steven R. (2003b), 'If Not Combatants, Certainly Not Civilians (Reply to Yael Stein)', in *Ethics and International Affairs* 17 (1), 138–140.

Detter (DeLupis), Ingrid (2000), *The Law of War* (Cambridge: Cambridge University Press, 2nd ed.).

Dinstein, Yoram (1981), 'The Right to Life, Physical Integrity, and Liberty', in Louis Henkin (ed.), *Covenant on Civil and Political Rights* (New York/Guildford: Columbia University Press), 114–137.

Dinstein, Yoram (1989), 'The Distinction Between Unlawful Combatants and War Criminals', in Yoram Dinstein (ed.), *International Law at a Time of Perplexity: Essays in Honour of Shabtai Rosenne* (Dordrecht: Martinus Nijhoff Publishers), 103–116.

Dinstein, Yoram (2002), 'Unlawful Combatancy', in *Israel Yearbook on Human Rights* 32, 247–270.

Dinstein, Yoram (2004), *The Conduct of Hostilities under the Laws of International Armed Conflict* (Cambridge: Cambridge University Press).

Dinstein, Yoram (2005), *War, Aggression and Self-Defence* (Cambridge/New York: Cambridge University Press, 4th ed.).

Dörmann, Knut (2003), 'The Legal Situation of "Unlawful/Unprivileged Combatants"', in *International Review of the Red Cross* 85 (849), 45 – 73.

Dörmann, Knut/Colassis, Laurent (2004), 'International Humanitarian Law in the Iraq Conflicts', in *German Yearbook of International Law* 47, 293 – 342.

Downes, Chris (2004), '"Targeted Killings" in an Age of Terror: The Legality of the Yemen Strike', in *Journal of Conflict and Security Law* 9, 277 – 294.

Draper, Gerald I. A. D. (1971), 'The Status of Combatant and the Question of Guerrilla Warfare', in *British Yearbook of International Law* 45, 173 – 218.

Dudkevitch, Margot/O'Sullivan, Arieh (2001), 'Terrorists Hit Gilo in First Mortar Attack: After IAF Gunships Kill Four Hamas Bombers in Bethlehem Air Strike', in *The Jerusalem Post*, 18 July 2001, Pg. 1.

Dworkin, Anthony, 'The Yemen Strike: The War on Terrorism Goes Global', *Crimes of War Project* (online/no page numbers/no date of writing available). Available at http://www.crimesofwar.org/onnews/news-yemen.html, retrieved 18 March 2007.

Eisenstadt, Michael (2001), '"Preemptive Targeted Killing" As a Counterterror Tool: An Assessment of Israel's Approach', in *PeaceWatch* 342, 28 August 2001 (online/no page numbers). Available at http://www.washingtoninstitute.org/policy-analysis/view/preemptive-targeted-killings-a-s-a-counterterror-tool-an-assessment-of-israe, retrieved 13 June 2012.

Ellis, Anthony (1992), 'Deontology, Incommensurability and the Arbitrary', in *Philosophy and Phenomenological Research* 52 (4), 855 – 875.

Engert, Florian (2005), *Einheitstäter oder getrennte Behandlung von Täter und Teilnehmer? Die Wege des österreichischen und deutschen Strafrechts* (Frankfurt a.M./Berlin/Bern: Peter Lang).

Feinstein, Barry (1976), 'Self-Defence and Israel in International Law: A Reappraisal', in 11 *Israel Law Review*, 516 – 562.

Fischer, Horst (2004), 'Friedenssicherung und friedliche Streitbeilegung (15. Kapitel)', in Knut Ipsen (ed.), *Völkerrecht* (Munich: C.H. Beck, 5th ed.), 1065 – 1194.

Fitzpatrick, Jean (2003), 'Speaking Law to Power: The War Against Terrorism and Human Rights', in *European Journal of International Law* 14, 241 – 264.

Foot, Philippa (2002), 'The Problem of Abortion and the Doctrine of Double Effect', in Philippa Foot, *Virtues and Vices and other Essays in Moral Philosophy* (Oxford: Clarendon Press), 19 – 32; reprinted from *Oxford Review* 5, 1967, 5 – 15.

Franck, Thomas M. (2001), 'Terrorism and the Right of Self-Defense', in *The American Journal of International Law* 95, 839 – 843.

Franck, Thomas M. (2002), *Recourse to Force: State Action Against Threats and Armed Attacks* (Cambridge: Cambridge University Press).

Fronhöfer, Dirk (1994), *Der internationale Menschenrechtsschutz bei inneren Konflikten* (Regensburg: S. Roderer Verlag).

Frostad, Magne (2005), *Jus in Bello After September 11, 2001* (Baden-Baden: Nomos).

Frowein, Jochen A. (1996), 'Article 2: Recht auf Leben', in Jochen A. Frowein/Wolfgang Peukert (eds.), *Europäische Menschenrechtskonvention. EMRK-Kommentar* (Kehl/Straßburg/Arlington: N.P. Engel Verlag, 2nd ed.), 28 – 39.

Frowein, Jochen A. (2002), 'Der Terrorismus als Herausforderung für das Völkerrecht', in *Zeitschrift für ausländisches und öffentliches Recht und Völkerrecht*, 879 – 905.

Gabriel, Larisa/Kälin, Walter (1994), 'Human Rights in Times of Occupation: An Introduction', in Walter Kälin (ed.), *Human Rights in Times of Occupations: The Case of Kuwait* (Berne: Stämpfli+Cie AG Berne), 1–67.

Gasser, Hans-Peter (1994), 'Schutz der Zivilbevölkerung', in Dieter Fleck (ed.), *Handbuch des humanitären Völkerrechts in bewaffneten Konflikten* (Munich: Beck'sche Verlagsbuchhandlung), 168–235.

Gellman, Barton (2002), 'Terrorism's Peril Undiminished: Nation Struggles on Offense and Defence, and Officials Still Expect New Attacks', in *The Washington Post*, 24 December 2002, Part A, Pg. 1.

Geraghty, Tony/Leigh, David (2002), 'The Name of the Game is Assassination', in *The Guardian*, 19 December 2002 (online/no page numbers). Available at www.guardian.co.uk/world/2002/dec/19/usa.comment, retrieved 22 October 2012.

Gewirth, Alan (1981), 'Are There Any Absolute Rights?', in *The Philosophical Quarterly* 31 (122), 1–16

Gill, Terry D. (1988), 'The Law of Armed Attack in the Context of the Nicaragua Case', in *Hague Yearbook of International Law* 1, 30–58.

Godfrey, Brenda L. (2003), 'Authorization to Kill Terrorist Leaders and Those who Harbor Them: An International Analysis of Defensive Assassination', in *San Diego International Law Journal* 4, 491–512.

Gow, David (2001), 'Bush Gives Green Light to CIA for Assassination of Named Terrorists', in *The Guardian*, 29 October 2001 (online/no page numbers). Available at www.guardian.co.uk/world/2001/oct/29/afghanistan.terrorism3, retrieved 22 October 2012.

Grabenwarter, Christoph (2005), *Europäische Menschenrechtskonvention* (Munich: C.H. Beck).

Gray, Christine (2006), 'The Bush Doctrine Revisisted: The 2006 National Security Strategy of the USA', in *Chinese Journal of International Law* 5 (3), 555–578.

Greenwood, Christopher (1991), 'Customary Law Status of the 1977 Geneva Protocols', in Astrid J.M. Delissen/Gerard J. Tanja (eds.), *Humanitarian Law of Armed Conflict: Challenges Ahead* (Dordrecht/Boston/London: Martinus Nijhoff Publishers), 93–114.

Greenwood, Christopher (1994), 'Anwendungsbereich des humanitären Völkerrechts', in Dieter Fleck (ed.), *Handbuch des humanitären Völkerrechts in bewaffneten Konflikten* (Munich: Beck'sche Verlagsbuchhandlung), 34–55.

Greenwood, Christopher (2002), 'International Law and the "War Against Terrorism"', in *International Affairs* 78 (2), 301–317.

Gross, Emanuel (2001), 'Thwarting Terrorist Acts by Attacking the Perpetrators or Their Commanders as an Act of Self-Defense: Human Rights Versus the State's Duty to Protect its Citizens', in *Temple International Comparative Law Journal* 15, 195–246.

Gross, Emanuel (2005), 'Thought is Self-Defence Against Terrorism – What Does it Mean?: The Israeli Perspective', in *Temple Political and Civil Rights Law Review* 14, 579–597.

Gross, Michael L. (2003), 'Fighting by Other Means in the Mideast: A Critical Analysis of Israel's Assassination Policy', in *Political Studies Association* 51, 350–368.

Gross, Michael L. (2006), 'Assassination and Targeted Killing: Law Enforcement, Execution or Self-Defence?', in *Journal of Applied Philosophy* 23 (3), 323–335.

Gross, Michael L. (2010), *Moral Dilemmas of Modern War: Torture, Assassination, and Blackmail in an Age of Asymmetric Conflict* (Cambridge: Cambridge University Press).

Harder, Tyler J. (2002), 'Time to Repeal the Assassination Ban of Executive Order 12,333: A Small Step in Clarifying Current Law', in *Military Law Review* 172, 1–39.

Hart, Herbert (1968), *Punishment and Responsibility* (Oxford: Clarendon Press).

Hassan, Parvez (1969), 'The Word "Arbitrary" as Used in the Universal Declaration of Human Rights: "Illegal" or "Unjust"', in *Harvard International Law Journal* 10, 225–262.

Heintschel v. Heinegg, Wolff/Gries, Tobias (2000), 'Der Einsatz der Deutschen Marine im Rahmen der Operation "Enduring Freedom"', in *Archiv des Völkerrechts* 40, 145–182.

Heintze, Hans-Joachim (2004), 'On the Relationship Between Human Rights Law Protection and International Humanitarian Law', in *International Review of the Red Cross* 86 (856), 789–814.

Hersh, Seymor (2002), 'Geheimdienste: Weltweite Jagd', in *Der Spiegel* 52, 21 December 2002, 105.

Ho, James C./Yoo, John C. (2003a), 'International Law and the War on Terrorism', 1–20. Available at http://www.law.berkeley.edu/files/yoonyucombatants.pdf, retrieved 13 June 2012.

Ho, James C./Yoo, John C. (2003b), 'The Status of Terrorists', in *UC Berkeley Public Law and Legal Theory Research Paper Series* 136, Research paper, 1–20.

Ipsen, Knut (1994), 'Kombattanten und Nichtkombattanten', in Dieter Fleck (ed.), *Handbuch des humanitären Völkerrechts in bewaffneten Konflikten* (Munich: Beck'sche Verlagsbuchhandlung), 56–88.

Jakobs, Günther (1985), 'Kriminalisierung im Vorfeld einer Rechtsgutsverletzung', in *Zeitschrift für die gesamte Strafrechtswissenschaft* 97 (4), 751–785.

Jakobs, Günther (2000), 'Das Selbstverständnis der Strafrechtswissenschaft vor den Herausforderungen der Gegenwart (Kommentar)', in Albin Eser/Winfried Hassemer/Björn Burkhardt (eds.), *Die Deutsche Strafrechtswissenschaft vor der Jahrtausendwende: Rückbesinnung und Ausblick* (Munich: C.H. Beck), 47–56.

Jakobs, Günther (2004), 'Bürgerstrafrecht und Feindstrafrecht', in *Onlinezeitschrift für Höchstrichterliche Rechtsprechung im Strafrecht* 5 (3), 88–95.

Jakobs, Günther (2005), 'Terroristen als Personen im Recht?', in *Zeitschrift für die gesamte Strafrechtswissenschaft* 117 (4), 839–851.

Jinks, Derek (2003a), 'State Responsibility for the Acts of Private Armed Groups', in *Chicago Journal of International Law*, 83–95.

Jinks, Derek (2003b), 'September 11 and the Laws of War', in *Yale Journal of International Law* 28 (1), 1–50.

Jinks, Derek (2004), 'The Declining Significance of POW Status', in *Harvard International Law Journal* 45 (2), 367–442.

Johnston, David/Sanger David E. (2002), 'Yemen Killing Based on Rules Set Out by Bush', in *The New York Times*, 6 November 2002 (online/no page numbers). Available at http://www.nytimes.com/2002/11/06/international/middleeast/06YEME.html?pagewanted=all, retrieved 13 June 2012.

Jonas, George (2005), *Vengeance: The True Story of an Israeli Counter-Terrorist Team* (New York/London/Toronto: Simon&Schuster Paperbacks).

Jones, Seth G./Libicki, Martin C. (2008), *How Terrorist Groups End: Lessons for Countering al Qa'ida* (Santa Monica: RAND Corporation). Available at http://www.rand.org/pubs/monographs/2008/RAND_MG741-1.pdf, retrieved 22 March 2012.

Joseph, Sarah/Schultz, Jenny/Castan, Melissa (2004), *The International Covenant on Civil and Political Rights: Cases, Materials, and Commentary* (Oxford: Oxford University Press, 2nd ed.).

Kaufman, Edy/Weiss Fagen, Patricia (1981), 'Extrajudicial Executions: An Insight into the Global Dimensions of a Human Rights Violation', in *Human Rights Quarterly* 3 (4), 81–100.

Kasher, Asa/Yadlin, Amos (2005), 'Military Ethics of Fighting Terror: An Israeli Perspective', in *Journal of Military Ethics* 4 (1), 3–32.

Kendall, J. Nicholas (2002), 'Israeli Counter-Terrorism: "Targeted Killings" Under International Law', in *North Carolina Law Review* 80, 1069–1088.

Kienapfel, Diethelm (1971), *Der Einheitstäter im Strafrecht* (Frankfurt a.M.: Vittorio Klostermann).

Kimminich, Otto (1979), *Schutz der Menschen in bewaffneten Konflikten: Zur Fortentwicklung des humanitären Völkerrechts* (Müchen/Mainz: Kaiser/Matthias-Grünewald-Verlag).

Kirgis, Frederic L. (2001), 'Addendum: Security Council Adopts Resolution on Combating International Terrorism', in *American Society of International Law Insight*, 1 October 2001 (online/no page numbers). Available at http://www.asil.org/insights/insigh77.htm#addendum7, retrieved 27 April 2002.

Klein, Aaron J. (2005), *Striking Back: The 1972 Munich Olympics Massacre and Israel's Deadly Response* (New York: Random House Trade Paperbacks).

Kober, Avi (2007), 'Targeted Killing during the Second Intifada: The Quest for Effectiveness', in *Journal of Conflict Studies* 27 (1) (online/no page numbers). Available at http://journals.hil.unb.ca/index.php/JCS/article/view/8292/9353, retrieved 22 March 2012.

Krajewski, Markus (2002), 'Selbstverteidigung gegen bewaffnete Angriffe nicht-staatlicher Organisationen – Der 11. September und seine Folgen', in *Archiv des Völkerrechts* 40 (2), 183–214.

Kreß, Claus (1995), *Gewaltverbot und Selbstverteidigungsrecht nach der Satzung der Vereinten Nationen bei staatlicher Verwicklung in Gewaltakte Privater* (Berlin: Duncker und Humblot).

Kretzmer, David (2005), 'Targeted Killing of Suspected Terrorists: Extra-Judicial Executions or Legitimate Means of Defence?', in *European Journal of International Law* 16, 171–212.

Kunz, Josef L. (1947), 'Individual and Collective Self-Defense in Article 51 of the Charter of the United Nations', in *The American Journal of International Law* 41 (4), 872–879.

Lauterpacht, Elihu (1968), 'The Legal Irrelevance of the "State of War"', in *Proceedings of the American Society of International Law*, 58–68.

Lawrence, Bruce (ed.) (2005), *Messages to the World: The Statements of Osama bin Laden* (London/New York: Verso).

Luft, Gal (2003), 'The Logic of Israel's Targeted Killing', in *Middle East Quarterly* 10 (1), 3–7.

Mallison, Thomas W./Mallison, Sally V. (1977), 'The Juridical Status of Irregular Combatants under the International Humanitarian Law of Armed Conflict', in *Case Western Reserve Journal of International Law* 9, 39–78.

Marcoux, Laurent Jr. (1982), 'Protection from Arbitrary Arrest and Detention Under International Law', in *Boston College International and Comparative Law Review* 5, 345–376.

Margolick, David (2003), 'Israel's Payback Principle', in *Vanity Fair* 509, 1 January 2003, Pg. 40.

Matheson, Michael J. (2002), 'U.S. Military Commissions: One of Several Options', in *American Journal of International Law* 96, 354–358.

Mayer, Jane (2009), 'The Predator War', in *The New Yorker*, 26 October 2009 (online/no page numbers). Available at http://www.newyorker.com/reporting/2009/10/26/091026fa_fact_mayer, retrieved 13 June 2012.

Mayntz, Renate (2003), 'Organisational Forms of Terrorism: Hierarchy, Network, or a Type sui generis?', Max-Planck-Institut für Gesellschaftsforschung (MPIfG), 4 (4) Discussion Paper, 1–22.

Mazzetti, Mark/Schmitt, Eric/Worth, Robert F. (2011), 'Two-Year Manhunt Led to Killing of Awlaki in Yemen', in *The New York Times*, 30 September 2011 (online/no page numbers). Available at http://www.nytimes.com/2011/10/01/world/middleeast/anwar-al-awlaki-is-killed-in-ye-men.html?pagewanted=all, retrieved 13 June 2012.

McDougal, Myres S. (1963), 'The Soviet-Cuban Quarantine and Self-Defense', in *American Journal of International Law* 57 (3), 597–604.

McMahan, Jeff (2004), 'The Ethics of Killing in War', in *Ethics* 114, 693–733.

McMahan, Jeff (2006b), 'The Ethics of Killing in War', in *Philosophia* 34 (1), 23–41.

McMahan, Jeff (2006c), 'Killing in War: A Reply to Walzer', in *Philosophia* 34 (1), 47–51.

McMahan, Jeff (2008), 'Debate: Justification and Liability in War', in *The Journal of Political Philosophy* 16 (2), 227–244.

McManus, Doyle (2003), 'A U.S. License to Kill', in *The Los Angeles Times*, 11 January 2003, Part A, Pg.1.

Meisels, Tamar (2004), 'Targeting Terror', in *Social Theory and Practice* 30 (3), 297–326, with minor changes reprinted as chapter 5, in Meisels, Tamar (2008), The Trouble with Terror: Liberty, Security, and the Response to Terrorism (Cambridge: Cambridge University Press)

Melzer, Nils (2008), *Targeted Killing in International Law* (Oxford: Oxford University Press).

Menke, Christoph/Pollmann, Arnd (2007), *Philosophie der Menschenrechte* (Hamburg: Junius).

Meron, Theodor (1995), 'Extraterritoriality of Human Rights Treaties', in *American Journal of International Law* 89, 78–82.

Meron, Theodor (2000), 'The Humanization of Humanitarian Law', in *American Journal of International Law* 94, 239–278.

Meyer, Josh (2006), 'CIA Expands Use of Drones in Terror War', in *The Los Angeles Times*, 29 January 2006, Part A, Pg. 1.

Meyrowitz, Henri (1972), 'Le Droit de la Guerre et les Droits de L'Homme', in *Revue du droit public et de la science politique en France et a l'étranger* 5, 1059–1105.

Miller, Seumas (2009), *Terrorism and Counter-Terrorism: Ethics and Liberal Democracy* (Malden/Oxford/Melbourne: Blackwell Publishing).

Moir, Lindsey (2002), *The Law of Internal Armed Conflict* (Cambridge: Cambridge University Press).

Moore, Michael (1997), *Placing Blame: A General Theory of the Criminal Law* (Oxford: Clarendon Press).

Moore, Molly (2003), 'Israel's Lethal Weapon of Choice', in *The Washington Post*, 29 June 2003, Part A, Pg. 1.

Murphy, Richard/Radsan, Afsheen J., 'Due Process and Targeted Killings of Terrorists', in *Cardozo Law Review* 31 (2), 405–450.

Mushkat, Marion (1978), 'The Development of International Humanitarian Law and the Law of Human Rights', in *German Yearbook of International Law* 21, 150–168.

Nagel, Thomas (1979), 'War and Massacre', in Nagel, Thomas, *Mortal Questions* (Cambridge/New York/Melbourne: Cambridge University Press), 53–74; with small changes reprinted from *Philosophy and Public Affairs* 1 (2), 1972, 123–144.

Neumann, Gerald L. (2003), 'Humanitarian Law and Counterterrorist Force', in *European Journal of International Law* 14 (2), 283–298.

Nolte, Georg (1999), *Eingreifen auf Einladung: Zur völkerrechtlichen Zulässigkeit des Einsatzes fremder Truppen im internen Konflikt auf Einladung der Regierung* (Berlin/Heidelberg/New York: Springer).

Nolte, Georg (2004), 'Preventive Use of Force and Preventive Killings: Moves into a Different Legal Order', in *Theoretical Inquiries in Law* 5 (1), 111–129.

Nowak, Manfred (2005), *U.N. Covenant on Civil and Political Rights, CCPR Commentary* (Kehl: Norbert Paul Engel Verlag, 2nd ed.).

Nozick, Robert (1974), *Anarchy, State and Utopia* (Oxford: Blackwell).

Nozick, Robert (1981), *Philosophical Explanations* (Oxford: Oxford University Press/Clarendon Press).

Nsereko, Daniel D. (1985), 'Arbitrary Deprivation of Life: Controls on Permissible Deprivation', in Bertrand G. Ramcharan (ed.), *The Right to Life in International Law* (Dordrech/Boston/Lancaster: Martinus Nijhoff Publishers), 245–283.

O'Connell, Mary E. (2005), 'When Is a War Not a War? The Myth of the Global War on Terror', in *ILSA Journal of International and Comparative Law* 2 (2), 535–539.

O'Connell, Mary E. (2009), 'Combatants and the Combat Zone', in *University Richmond Law Review* 43, 845–864.

O'Connell, Mary E. (2010), 'Unlawful Killing with Combat Drones: A Case Study of Pakistan 2004–2009', *Notre Dame Law School Legal Studies Research Paper No. 09–43*, 1–26. Available at http://ssrn.com/abstract=1501144, retrieved 22 March 2012.

Oeter, Stefan (1994), 'Kampfmittel und Kampfmethoden', in Dieter Fleck (ed.), *Handbuch des humanitären Völkerrechts in bewaffneten Konflikten* (Munich: Beck'sche Verlagsbuchhandlung), 89–167.

Ostrovsky, Victor/Hoy, Claire (1991), *By Way of Deception: The Making and Unmaking of a Mossad Officer* (New York: St. Martin's Paperbacks).

O'Sullivan, Arieh (2000) (contribution by Etgar Lefkovits), 'IDF slays Islamic Jihad Master Bomber', in *The Jerusalem Post*, 12 December 2000, Pg. 4.

Parks, W. Hays (1990), 'Air War and the Law of War', in *Air Force Law Review* 32, 1–226.

Partsch, Karl J.(1965), 'Human Rights and Humanitarian Law', in Rudolf Bernhardt (ed.), *Encyclopedia of Public International Law*, Vol. 2 (Amsterdam/Lausanne/New York: Elsevier), 910–912.

Partsch, Karl J. (1982), 'Protocol II, Parts I and II', in Michael Bothe/Karl Josef Partsch/Waldemar Solf (eds.), *New Rules for Victims of Armed Conflicts: Commentary on the Two 1977 Protocols Additional to the Geneva Conventions of 1949* (The Hague/Boston/London: Martinus Nijhoff Publishers), 622–654.

Paulus, Andreas/Vashakmadze, Mindia (2009), 'A symmetrical War and the Notion of Armed Conflict: A Tentative Conceptualization', in *International Review of the Red Cross* 91 (873), 95–125

Paust, Jordan J. (2001/2002), 'Use of Armed Force against Terrorists in Afghanistan, Iraq, and Beyond', in *Cornell International Law Journal* 35, 533–557.

Paust, Jordan J. (2004), 'Post 9/11 Overreaction and Fallacies Regarding War and Defense, Guantanamo, the Status of Persons, Treatment, Judicial Review of Detention, and Due Process in Military Commissions', in *Notre Dame Law Review* 79, 1335–1364.

Paust, Jordan J. (2010), 'Self-Defense Targetings of Non-State Actors and Permissibility of U.S. Use of Drones in Pakistan', in *Journal of Transnational Law and Policy* 19 (2), 237–280.

Pincus, Walter (2003), 'Missile Strike Carried Out With Yemeni Cooperation: Official Says Operation Authorized Under Bush Finding', in *Journal of Military Ethics* 2 (3), 2003, 227–229; reprinted from *The Washington Post*, 6 November 2002, Part A, Pg. 10.

Plaw, Avery (2009), 'The Legality of Targeted Killing as an Instrument of War: The Case of the US Targeting of Qaed Salim Sinan al-Harethi', in Nolen Gertz (ed.), *War Fronts: Interdisciplinary Perspectives on War* (Oxford: Inter-Disciplinary Press), 67–79.

Primoratz, Igor (1987), 'The Middle Way in the Philosophy of Punishment', in Ruth Gavison (ed.), *Issues in Contemporary Legal Philosophy: The Influence of H.L.A. Hart* (Oxford: Clarendon Press), 193–220.

Primoratz, Igor (1989), *Justifying Legal Punishment* (New York: Humanity Books).

Primoratz, Igor (2004), 'What is Terrorism?', in Igor Primoratz (ed.), *Terrorism: The Philosophical Issues* (Houndmills/New York: Palgrave Macmillan), 15–27.

Primoratz, Igor (2007), 'A Philosopher Looks at Contemporary Terrorism', in *Cardozo Law Review* 29 (1), 33–51.

Prittwitz, Cornelius (2005), 'Feindstrafrecht', in Arno Pilgram/Cornelius Prittwitz (eds.), *Kriminologie: Akteurin und Kritikerin gesellschaftlicher Entwicklung* (Baden-Baden: Nomos), 215–228.

Ramcharan, Bertrand G. (1985a), 'The Concept and Dimensions of the Right to Life', in Bertrand G. Ramcharan (ed.), *The Right to Life in International Law* (Dordrech/Boston/Lancaster: Martinus Nijhoff Publishers), 1–32.

Ramcharan, Bertrand G. (1985b), 'The Drafting History of Article 6 of the International Covenant on Civil and Political Rights', in Bertrand G. Ramcharan (ed.), *The Right to Life in International Law* (Dordrech/Boston/Lancaster: Martinus Nijhoff Publishers), 42–56.

Randelzhofer, Albrecht (2002), 'Article 51', in Bruno Simma (ed.), *The Charter of the United Nations* (Oxford: Oxford University Press, 2nd ed.).

Ratner, Steven R. (2007), 'Predator and Prey: Seizing and Killing Suspected Terrorists Abroad', in *The Journal of Political Philosophy* 15 (3), 251–275.

Ravi, Daniel/Melman, Yossi (1990), *Every Spy a Prince: The Complete History of Israel's Intelligence Community* (Boston: Houghton Mifflin Company).

Raz, Joseph (1984), 'On the Nature of Rights', in *Mind* 93 (370), 194–214.

Reismann, Michael W. (1999), 'International Legal Responses to International Terrorism', in *Houston Journal of International Law* 22 (1), 3–61.

Roberts, Adam (1990), 'Prolonged Military Occupation: Israeli-Occupied Territories Since 1967', in *The American Journal of International Law* 84 (1), 44–103.

Robertson, Arthur H. (1968/1969), 'The United Nations Covenant on Civil and Political Rights and the European Convention on Human Rights', in *British Yearbook of International Law* 43, 21–48.

Rodin, David (2002), *War and Self-Defense* (Oxford: Oxford University Press).

Rodin, David (2004), 'Terrorism without Intention', in *Ethics* 114 (4), 772–791.

Rogers, Anthony P.V./McGoldrick, Dominic (2011), 'Assassination and Targeted Killing: The Killing of Osama Bin Laden', in *International and Comparative Law Quarterly* 60, 778–788.

Rosas, Allan (1976), *The Legal Status of Prisoners of War* (Helsinki: Suomalainen Tiedeakatemia).

Rowles, James P. (1987), 'Military Responses to Terrorism: Substantive and Procedural Constraints in International Law', in *Proceedings of the American Society of International Law*, 307–317.

Roxin, Claus (2003), *Strafrecht, Allgemeiner Teil, Vol. 2* (Munich: C.H. Beck, 3rd ed.).

Roxin, Claus (2006), *Strafrecht, Allgemeiner Teil, Vol. 1* (Munich: C.H. Beck, 4th ed.).

Saliger, Frank (2006), 'Feindstrafrecht: Kritisches oder totalitäres Strafrechtskonzept?', in *JuristenZeitung* 61 (15/16), 756–762.

Sassòli, Marco (2004), 'Use and Abuse of the Laws of War in the "War on Terrorism"', in *Law and Inequality: A Journal of Theory and Practice* 22 (2), 195–221.

Sauer, Dirk (2005), 'Das Strafrecht und die Feinde der offenen Gesellschaft', in *Neue Juristische Wochenschrift* 24, 1703–1705.

Sauer, Frank (2007), 'Nuklearterrorismus: Akute Bedrohung oder politisches Schreckgespenst?', HSFK-Report (Hessische Stiftung Friedens- und Konfliktforschung) 2/2007.

Schachter, Oscar (1989), 'The Lawful Use of Force by a State Against Terrorists in Another Country', in *Israeli Yearbook on Human Rights* 19, 209–231.

Schindler, Dietrich (1979), 'Kriegsrecht und Menschenrechte', in Ulrich Häfelin/Walter Haller/Dietrich Schindler (eds.), *Menschenrechte, Föderalismus, Demokratie: Festschrift zum 70. Geburtstag von Werner Kägi* (Zürich: Schulthess Polygraphischer Verlag).

Schmid, Alex P. (1983), *Political Terrorism: A Research Guide to Concepts, Theories, Data Bases, and Literature* (Amsterdam: North-Holland Publishing Compagny).

Schmitt, Michael N. (1992), 'State-Sponsored Assassination in International and Domestic Law', in *Yale Journal of International Law* 17, 609–685.

Schmitt, Michael N. (2004), '"Direct Participation in Hostilities" and 21st Century Armed Conflict', in Horst Fischer/Ulrike Froissart/Wolff Heintschel von Heinegg/Christian Rapp (eds.), *Krisensicherung und Humanitärer Schutz – Crisis Management and Humanitarian Protection: Festschrift für Dieter Fleck* (Berlin: Berliner Wissenschafts-Verlag).

Schmitt, Michael N. (2010), 'Drone Attack Under the *Jus as Bellum* And *Jus in Bello*: Clearing the "For of Law"', in Michael N. Schmitt/Louise Arimatsu (eds.), *Yearbook of International Humanitarian Law* 13 (The Hague: T.M.C. Asser Press), 311–326.

Schmitz-Elvenich, Heiko (2008), *Targeted Killing: Die völkerrechtliche Zulässigkeit der gezielten Tötung von Terroristen im Ausland* (Frankfurt a.M./Berlin/Bern: Peter Lang).

Schneckener, Ulrich (2006), *Transnationaler Terrorismus: Charakter und Hintergründe des 'neuen' Terrorismus* (Frankfurt a.M.: Surkamp).

Sharkey, Noel (2010), 'Saying "No!" to Lethal Autonomous Targeting', in *Journal of Military Ethics* 9 (4), 369–383.

Singer, Peter W. (2009), *Wired for War: The Robotics Revolution and Conflict in the 21st Century* (New York: Penguin Press).

Sofaer, Abraham D. (1989), 'The Sixth Annual Waldemar A. Solf Lecture in International Law: Terrorism, the Law, and the National Defense', in *Military Law Review* 126, 89–123.

Solf, Waldemar (1982), 'Protocol I, Parts III and IV (Section I Chapter I-V), Protocol II, Part IV', in Michael Bothe/Karl Josef Partsch/Waldemar Solf (eds.), *New Rules for Victims of Armed Conflicts: Commentary on the Two 1977 Protocols Additional to the Geneva Conventions of 1949* (The Hague/Boston/London: Martinus Nijhoff Publishers), 183–388 and 667–692.

Stahl, Adam (2010), 'The Evolution of Israeli Targeted Operations: Consequences of the Thabet Thabet Operation', in *Studies in Conflict and Terrorism* 33, 111–133.

Stahn, Carsten, 'Security Council Resolutions 1368 (2001) and 1373 (2001): What they Say and What They Do Not Say', in *European Journal of International Law Discussion Forum: The Attack on the World Trade Center – Legal Responses*. Available at http://www.ejil.org/forum_WTC/ny-stahn.pdf, retrieved 19 April 2002.

Stahn, Carsten (2004), '"Nicaragua is dead, long live Nicaragua" – the Right to Self-defence Under Art. 51 UN-Charter and International Terrorism', in Christian Walter/Silja Vöneky/Volker Röben/Frank Schorkopf (eds.), *Terrorism as a Challenge for National and International Law: Security versus Liberty?* (Heidelberg/New York: Springer-Verlag Berlin), 827–877.

Statman, Daniel (2003), 'The Morality of Assassination: A Response to Gross', in *Political Studies* 51, 775–779.

Statman, Daniel (2004), 'Targeted Killing', in *Theoretical Inquiries in Law* 5 (1), 179–198.

Stein, Yael (2001), *B'Tselem Position Paper – Israel's Assassination Policy: Extrajudicial Executions* (translated by Maya Jhonston), 1–14.

Strawser, Bradley J. (2010), 'Moral Predators: The Duty to Employ Uninhabited Aerial Vehicles', in *Journal of Military Ethics* 9 (4), 342–368.

Stuesser, Lee (1987), 'Active Defense: State Military Response to International Terrorism', in *California Western International Law Journal* 17 (1), 1–42.

Tams, Christian J. (2009), 'The Use of Force against Terrorists', in *European Journal of International Law* 20 (2), 359–397.

Teichman, Jenny (1989), 'How to Define Terrorism', in *Philosophy* 64 (250), 505–517.

Thomas, Ward (2005), 'The New Age of Terrorism', in *School of Advanced International Studies Review of International Affairs* 25 (1), 27–39.

Thomson, Judith J. (1986a), 'Self-Defence and Rights', in Judith J. Thomson, *Rights, Restitution and Risk: Essays in Moral Theory*, edited by William Parent (Cambridge, Massachusetts/London: Harvard University Press), 33–48.

Thomson, Judith J. (1986b), 'Killing, Letting Die, and the Trolley Problem', in Judith J. Thomson, *Rights, Restitution and Risk: Essays in Moral Theory*, edited by William Parent (Cambridge, Massachusetts/London: Harvard University Press), 78–93; reprinted from *The Monist* 59 (2), 1976, 204–217.

Thomson, Judith J. (1986c), 'The Trolley Problem' in: Judith J. Thomson, *Rights, Restitution and Risk: Essays in Moral Theory*, edited by William Parent (Cambridge, Massachusetts/London: Harvard University Press), 94–116; reprinted from *The Yale Law Journal* 94 (6), 1985, 1395–1415.

Thomson, Judith J. (1991), 'Self-Defense', in *Philosophy and Public Affairs* 20 (4), 281–310.

Tinnin, David B. (1977), in collaboration with Christinsen, Dag, *Vegeltungskomando: Israels Geheimdienst jagt die Attentäter von Munich* (Frankfurt a.M.: S. Fischer Verlag).

Tomuschat, Christian (2001), 'Der 11. September und seine rechtlichen Konsequenzen', in *Europäische Grundrechte Zeitung* 28 (21–23), 535–545.

Tomuschat, Christian (2003), *Human Rights: Between Idealism and Realism* (Oxford: Oxford University Press).

Uniacke, Suzanne (1994), *Permissible Killing: The Self-Defence Justification of Homicide* (Cambridge: Cambridge University Press).

Uniacke, Suzanne (2000), 'Why Is Revenge Wrong?,' in *The Journal of Value Inquiry* 34, 61–69.

Vöneky, Silja (2001), *Die Fortgeltung des Umweltvölkerrechts in internationalen bewaffneten Konflikten* (Berlin/Heidelberg/New York: Springer).

Vöneky, Silja (2004), 'Die Anwendbarkeit des humanitären Völkerrechts auf terroristische Akte und ihre Bekämpfung', in Dieter Fleck (ed.), *Rechtsfragen der Terrorismusbekämpfung durch Streitkräfte* (Baden-Baden: Nomos), 147–166.

Wachtel, Howard A. (2005), 'Targeting Osama Bin Laden: Examining the Legality of Assassination as a Tool of U.S. Foreign Policy', in *Duke Law Journal* 55, 677–710.

Waldron, Jeremy (2003), 'Security and Liberty: The Image of Balance', in *Journal of Political Philosophy* 11 (2), 191–210.

Waldron, Jeremy (2011), 'Can Targeted Killing Work as a Neutral Principle?', *New York University School of Law, Public Law Research Paper No. 11–20*, 1–14. Available at http://ssrn.com/abstract=1788226, retrieved 14 October 2011.

Walker, Nigel (1999), 'Even More Varieties of Retribution', in *Philosophy* 74 (290), 595–605.

Walter, Christian (2004), 'Zwischen Selbstverteidigung und Völkerstrafrecht: Bausteine für ein internationales Recht der "päventiven Terrorismus-Bekämpfung"', in Dieter Fleck (ed.), *Rechtsfragen der Terrorismusbekämpfung durch Streitkräfte* (Baden-Baden: Nomos), 23–42.

Walzer, Michael (1977), *Just and Unjust Wars: A Moral Argument with Historical Illustrations* (New York: Basic Books, 3rd ed.).

Walzer, Michael (2004), 'After 9/11: Five Questions About Terrorism', in Michael Walzer, *Arguing About War* (New Haven/London: Yale University Press), 130–142.

Walzer, Michael (2006a), 'Terrorism and Just War', in *Philosophia* 34 (1), 3–12.

Walzer, Michael (2006b), 'Response to Jeff McMahan', in *Philosophia* 34 (1), 19–21.

Walzer, Michael (2006c), 'Response to McMahan's Paper', in *Philosophia* 34 (1), 43–45.

Watkin, Kenneth W. (2004), 'Controlling the Use of Force: A Role for Human Rights Norms in Contemporary Armed Conflict', in *American Journal of International Law* 98 (1), 1–34.

Watkin, Kenneth W. (2005), 'Warriors Without Rights? Combatants, Unprivileged Belligerents, and the Struggle Over Legitimacy', Harvard Program on Humanitarian Policy and Conflict Research Occasional Paper Series (2), 1–75.

Wedgwood, Ruth (2002), 'Al Qaeda, Terrorism, And Military Commissions', in *American Journal of International Law* 96, 328–337.

Wellman, Carl (1979), 'On Terrorism Itself', in *Journal of Value Inquiry* 13 (4), 250–258.

Wijze de, Stephen (2009), 'Targeted Killing: A "Dirty Hands" Analysis', in *Contemporary Politics* 15 (3), 305–320.

Wilner, Alex S. (2010), 'Targeted Killings in Afghanistan: Measuring Coercion and Deterrence in Counterterrorism and Counterinsurgency', in *Studies in Conflict and Terrorism* 33 (4), 307–329.

Wolfrum, Rüdiger/Philipp, Christiane E. (2002), 'The Status of the Taliban: Their Obligation and Rights under International Law', in *Max Planck Yearbook of United Nations Law* 6, 559–601.

Woodworth, Paddy (2001), *Dirty War, Clean Hands: ETA, the GAL and Spanish Democracy* (Cork: Cork University Press).

Zaibert, Leo (2006), 'Punishment and Revenge', in *Law and Philosophy* 25, 81–118.

Zussman, Asaf/Zussman Noam (2005), 'Targeted Killings: Evaluating the Effectiveness of a Counterterrorism Policy', Discussion Paper No. 2005.02, Research Department of the Bank of Israel, 1–45. Available at http://www.bankisrael.gov.il/deptdata/mehkar/papers/dp0502e.htm, retrieved 16 January 2007.

Index

www.ingramcontent.com/pod-product-compliance
Lightning Source LLC
Chambersburg PA
CBHW052120270326
41930CB00012B/2692